F O R U M

FAVORITE RECIPES

FROM

FRIENDS OF THE FORUM SCHOOL

compiled and edited by

THE FORUM QUORUM

Mrs. Joseph L. Baker
Mrs. Harry N. Ives
Mrs. Frederick J. Kaiser, Jr.
Mrs. William T. Knight, III
Mrs. Richard W. Poor
Mrs. Richard R. Ryen
Mrs. Joseph Sage
Mrs. Earl A. Samson, Jr.
Mrs. A. Steffee Smith
Mrs. Kenneth S. Talbot
Mrs. Alonzo L. Van Wart
Mrs. Reginald F. Wardley
Mrs. Arthur S. Whittemore, Jr.

1968

Cover and illustrations by Anne S. Samson

First Printing (5,000)	October 1968
Second Printing (5,000)	March 1969
Third Printing (5,000)	October 1969
Fourth Printing (5,000)	March 1970
Fifth Printing (5,000)	November 1970
Sixth Printing (5,000)	June 1971
Seventh Printing (10,000)	December 1971
Eighth Printing (10,000)	November 1972
Ninth Printing (10,000)	June 1973
Tenth Printing (10,000)	October 1973
Eleventh Printing (10,000)	September 1974
Twelfth Printing (10,000)	December 1974
Thirteenth Printing (25,000)	October 1975
Fourteenth Printing (25,000)	December 1976
Fifteenth Printing (25,000)	December 1977
Sixteenth Printing (25,000)	December 1978
Seventeenth Printing (25,000)	June 1980
Eighteenth Printing (25,000)	July 1981
Nineteenth Printing (25,000)	December 1982

Profit from the sale of this book
will be contributed to
The Forum School, Waldwick, N. J.

Printed in the United States of America
by
De Vries Brothers
Saddle Brook, New Jersey

PATRONS

Mrs. Charles W. Allen

Mrs. Raymond E. Banta

Mrs. Fredric S. Bayles

Mrs. David C. Beasley

Mrs. Eric H. Berg

Mrs. John C. Conklin, Jr.

Mrs. John P. Connelly, Jr.

Mrs. Paul R. Davis

Mrs. Charles P. De Yoe

Mrs. F. A. A. Dick

Mrs. Fairleigh Dickinson, Jr.

Mrs. Edward D. Doherty

Mrs. Henry B. Douglas

Mrs. Joseph L. Downs

Mrs. Richard N. Doyle

Mrs. Barbara B. Eaton

Mrs. John H. Eide

Mrs. W. Richard Goat

Mrs. George M. Griffith

Mrs. Richard A. Grimley

Mrs. Warren D. Haggerty, Jr.

Mrs. Irving R. Hayman

Mrs. W. Fletcher Hock, Jr.

Mrs. H. Dean Hopper

Mrs. Frederick J. Kaiser, Jr.

Mrs. William T. Knight, III

Mrs. Ian B. MacCallum

Mrs. Charles D. MacMakin

Mrs. Milton C. Maloney

Mrs. W. Claggett Martin

Mrs. Edward F. Merrey, Jr.

Mrs. Pressly M. Millen, Jr.

Mrs. Morris Mlotok

Mrs. O. George Philipp

Mrs. Richard W. Poor

Mrs. Charles G. Rodman

Mrs. Robert B. Ross

Mrs. Joseph Sage

Mrs. Lyman K. Shepard

Mrs. John W. Simmons

Mrs. Trygve B. Sletteland

Mrs. A. Steffee Smith

Mrs. Michael A. Stott

Mrs. Robert M. Stroker

Mrs. Kenneth S. Talbot

Mrs. Robert E. Taylor

Mrs. L. Russell Thacher

Mrs. Willard K. Thayer

Mrs. A. L. Van Wart

Mrs. Jack R. von Maur

Mrs. Reginald F. Wardley

Mrs. Arthur S. Whittemore, Jr.

Mrs. Albert Winterhalder, Jr.

Mrs. Dickens J. Wright

Mrs. Archer Young

Mrs. Joseph Zamer

THE FORUM SCHOOL

Within these pages you will find the culinary secrets of literally scores of Northern New Jersey homemakers and their friends who have shared their kitchen skills in order to help The Forum School.

When they gave their recipes--and when you bought this cookbook--more was being accomplished than spreading the food word for hungry epicures. The funds raised will give tangible help to a unique educational project, first of its kind to be established in New Jersey to meet the needs of emotionally disturbed children.

A state approved, non-profit, cooperative institution, The Forum School was established to provide day care for children suffering from severe emotional disturbances, allowing them to be treated and schooled while living at home, where loving care offers the optimum hope for a return to normal happy life. Children between the ages of 5 and 12 make up the student body. Of course such an educational project is costly; there must be a teacher for every three or four children, and the staff includes a psychiatrist, psychologist, psychiatric social worker and speech pathologist. A corps of dedicated volunteers assists.

It has often been a struggle during the years since The Forum School was founded in 1954, when classes met in two borrowed rooms in the VFW building in Carlstadt. Later the school occupied quarters in Paterson, and then moved to the Old Paramus Reformed Church in Ridgewood. "Angels" have helped to keep its doors open, largely through The Forum School Foundation, establishment of which was spearheaded by Mrs. Richard W. Poor of Ridgewood.

The Junior League of Englewood-Ridgewood, Inc., The Woman's Club of Ridgewood, the parents' group of The Forum School children, church groups and others have aided substantially. One of the projects has been to provide uniform hot lunches for the children--therapy for mind and soul as well as nourishment for the tummy. It was from this culinary interest that a group of volunteers conceived the idea for our cookbook. We called ourselves The Forum Quorum.

Today The Forum School is in its own building in Waldwick, New Jersey, which is specifically designed to meet the unique needs of the students. The new school with its added facilities was dedicated in November of 1970 and the enrollment was able to be increased considerably. Equipping the kitchen of the new building was accomplished with the first printing of this book. Proceeds have been used since then to help erase the mortgage. Recently, we aided the foundation in purchasing a house adjacent to our property in order to start a pre-vocational program. In early 1975, a four room addition to the main building will be completed. This will give us much needed office and classroom space.

FOREWORD

FORUM FEASTS is the best cookbook of its kind I have ever seen. I ought to know because I have been collecting church, club, Junior League and such cookbooks for years! I wish everyone who is lucky enough to own a copy as much joy as I have had myself in trying its clear and well-written recipes. When you add to that the knowledge that it is sold for such a unique and important cause, owning FORUM FEASTS is an unbeatable experience I should like to share with every-one. May its editors have the well-deserved success which begins to show in the fact that, in a very short time indeed, they are publishing a second edition - this one.

Charlotte Adams
Cookbook Author and Editor

"I know that many of you, like me, are collectors of special cookbooks and I should like to say at once that FORUM FEASTS is remarkable of its kind. First, it has been carefully and well edited (unique in this field). Second, it has not just one or two, but many truly original recipes between its handsome green and white covers. . . . The recipes come from all over this country and several foreign countries as well."

From Amy Vanderbilt's NEWSLETTER

To all of the busy, warm-hearted men and women who took time to share their favorite recipes with us, go our sincere thanks and gratitude. Our special thanks go to the Patrons who so generously enabled us to get a financial start with our first printing. We are especially grateful to the late Mrs. Donald B. Read and Mr. William W. W. Knight formerly of Ridgewood for their editorial help and advice, and to all those friends who have helped with this project in such ways as editing, proofreading and typing. To those who have tested recipes and given us their prized kitchen secrets and to the husbands who have lent their moral support, patience and encouragement, as well as advice and labor, we wish to express our heartfelt thanks.

We hope you will enjoy using this book as much as we have enjoyed putting it together. We have tried to indicate helpful information for you such as whether the dish can be frozen or prepared ahead of time; whether it is easy or complicated to prepare; and about how long it will take to make from start to finish and seasonings are to their personal tastes. Most of these directions have been suggested by our contributor-cooks. Happy cooking, even happier eating, and happiest of all the satisfaction of knowing you have helped The Forum School.

We wish we could mention each and every person who helped make this book such a success from its conception through this reprinting. We would particularly like to give credit to: Mrs. Bruce F. Banta, Mrs. John J. Baughan, Mrs. Stephen M. Bolster, Mrs. Thomas C. De Patie, Mrs. Richard A. Grimley, Mrs. Robert F. Hill, Mrs. Charles D. MacMakin, Mrs. James T. Rogers and Mrs. John A. Snyder.

With the fourth edition, The Forum Quorum became a part of the Parents Groups of The Forum School and we are most grateful for the help and enthusiasm of this dedicated organization. We are especially indebted to Mrs. John C. Meier, who has handled our shipping and accounting, and Mrs. Charles R. Buckley, Mrs. William L. Bradford and Mrs. Frank Sanclementi who have helped deliver books for us. We wish we could mention each parent and friend who has continually aided us in so many ways as our project has grown. We could not have handled the continued production of the book without every one of them and their great loyalty, interest and enthusiasm which we know will continue.

The Forum Quorum

Table of Contents

Table of Hints

All starred items (*) are recipes appearing in the Index.

Appetizers

EASY CHEESE BALL

Serves: 6-8

Easy   Do ahead

Preparing: 5 min.
Chilling: 30 min.

8 oz. cream cheese, softened
  (I use Philadelphia)
1 jar pimento cheese
1 jar soft blue cheese
  (I use Roka)
chopped pecans

Mix cheeses together and roll into a ball.
Then roll ball in chopped pecans. Chill.
Serve as a spread.

Miss Susan L. Hinman, Suffern, N. Y.

BRANDY CHEESE BALL

Yield: 2-1/2 cups

"A nice combination of cheese tastes!"

Easy   Do ahead

Preparing: 15 min.
Chilling: 2 hrs.

12 oz. club cheese
  (I use Wispride)
8 oz. cream cheese
4 oz. bleu cheese
1-3/4 oz. brandy
pistachio nuts

Blend together softened cheeses. Add and
blend the brandy. Refrigerate until cool.
Make into a large ball or 2 smaller ones,
and roll each ball in the pistachio nuts.
Wrap in foil to refrigerate.

Mrs. Kenneth S. Talbot, Ridgewood

CHEESE BALL

Serves: 12-20

"A great Christmas hors d'oeuvre."

Easy   Do ahead

Preparing: 15 min.

8 oz. cream cheese
8 oz. Cheddar cheese slices
  (I use Kraft Olde English)
4 oz. blue cheese
2 green onions, chopped
dash Worcestershire sauce
lemon juice to taste
chopped parsley
optional - slivered almonds
       pimento
       stuffed olives

Soften cheese. Blend all ingredients. Roll
into ball. Roll in parsley (and slivered
almonds). Or, shape into form of a Christmas
tree. Slice pimento and stuffed olives and
decorate tree.

Mrs. John C. Bennett, Ridgewood

11

CHUTNEY CHEESE CANAPE

Serves: 12

"This recipe is requested each time it is served. So festive looking!"

Easy   Do ahead   Preparing: 10 min.
                                                     Chilling: 4 hrs.

8 oz. cream cheese
1/4 c. chutney
1/4 tsp. dry mustard
1 tsp. curry powder
toasted almonds
optional - pineapple half

Blend all the ingredients well. Chill for at least 4 hours. Scoop out a pineapple half and fill with mixture. Top with toasted al-monds. Serve with crackers. This is a quick recipe and may be made the day before using.

Mrs. Ralph E. Hansmann, Ridgewood

CURRY-CHUTNEY CHEESE BALL

Serves: 12

"Very simple, delicious hors d'oeuvres. Attractive to look at."

Easy   Do ahead   Preparing: 5 min.
                                                     Chilling: 2 hrs.

8 oz. cream cheese
1 tsp. curry
1/2 9-oz. jar chutney
 (I use Major Grey's)
optional - 1/2 c. almond bits,
           chopped fine

Mix curry well into softened cream cheese. Form into ball and refrigerate. Cut big pieces in the chutney in half. When ready to serve place curry-cheese ball on a plate. Pour chutney over it. Space crackers or melba rounds around it for spreading. Ball may also be rolled in finely ground almonds, if desired.

Mrs. Albert J. Morrison
Maichingen, W. Germany

MEXICAN DIP

Serves: 12-16

"A spicy Mexican-type dip that is great for a big party."

Easy   Do ahead   Preparing: 15 min.
                                                     Chilling: 1 hr.

1 can black bean soup
1 can bean with bacon soup
scant 1/4 soup can water
1 tsp. dry mustard
1/2 tsp. cayenne
1/2 tsp. chili powder
2 cloves garlic, pressed
4-5 drops Tabasco sauce
1 tbsp. vinegar
1/2 c. sour cream

Place undiluted soups and all ingredients, except the sour cream, in a saucepan and heat, stirring constantly. Add sour cream and simmer, stirring often, for 10 min. Cool, then chill for about 1 hr. Serve with corn chips or tortillas.

Mrs. Arthur Espy, II, Ho-Ho-Kus

VEGETABLE DIP

Yield: 2 cups

"Delicious, refreshing hors d'oeuvre. Vegetables are low calorie!"

Easy   Do ahead   Preparing: 10 min.
                                                    Chilling: 3 hrs. or more

1 c. mayonnaise
1/2 tbsp. lemon juice
1/2 c. chopped parsley
1 tbsp. grated onion
2 tbsp. chopped chives
1/2 c. heavy cream, whipped
1/4 tsp. salt
1/4 tsp. paprika
1/8 tsp. curry powder
1 minced garlic clove
vegetables for dipping

Mix all ingredients together and chill in refrigerator for several hours or overnight. Serve with carrot, green pepper and celery strips, cauliflowerets, or any other desired vegetables such as cherry tomatoes, radishes, zucchini or cucumber. Chill vegetables. Arrange on large platter around the dipping sauce. Especially nice in the hot weather.

Mrs. Thomas G. Parris, Jr., Ridgewood

RAW VEGETABLE DIP

Yield: 1 cup

"Delicious dip for the cocktail hour."

Easy   Do ahead   Preparing: 10 min.
                                                    Chilling: 1 hr.

1 c. sour cream
4 small garlic cloves,
   crushed
1 tsp. curry powder
1 tsp. chopped parsley
dash Worcestershire sauce
dash Tabasco sauce

Crush the garlic cloves. Mix garlic with sour cream and add the curry powder and chopped parsley. Blend well. Add remaining spices. Again blend and chill the mixture until ready to serve, or al least for 4 hours. Serve as a dip with attractively fixed vegetables such as mushrooms, cauliflower, cherry tomatoes or broccoli.

Mrs. Louis C. Goetting, III, Ridgewood

VEGETABLE SAUCE FOR DIPPING

Yield: 1-1/2 cups

"Great to keep on hand for quick parties! Keeps for weeks."

Easy   Do ahead   Preparing: 10 min.
                                                    Chilling: 1 hr.

1 c. mayonnaise
1-1/2 c. chili sauce
1 small onion, grated
2 heaping tbsp. horseradish
2 tsp. mustard seeds
Tabasco sauce to taste

Blended together, this dip is delicious for shrimp or raw vegetables such as cauliflower and cucumber.

Mrs. James D. Patton, Saddle River

13

SHRIMP DIP

Yield: 2 cups

"Everytime I serve this someone asks for the recipe."

Easy   Do ahead   Preparing: 15 min.
                                Chilling: 2 hrs.

15 large shrimp, fresh or
   frozen
1/2 c. mayonnaise
5 drops Tabasco sauce
2 tsp. onions, grated
salt
pepper
2 tbsp. dry sherry
light cream

Mince shrimp with sharp knife. Add other ingredients, except cream. Adjust seasonings. Gradually add enough cream to make mixture easy to spread. Serve with crackers or "Bugles." Chill.

Mrs. Samuel D. Koonce, Ridgewood

SEAFOOD DIP

Yield: 2 cups

Easy   Do ahead   Preparing: 10 min.
                                Chilling: 2 hrs.

1 4-1/2 oz. can lobster,
   shrimp or crabmeat
8 oz. cream cheese
2 tsp. chili sauce
2 tsp. horseradish
1/3 c. mayonnaise
1 tsp. lemon juice
salt to taste

Cut lobster into small pieces (or clean other shellfish), and add to softened cream cheese. Add all ingredients and mix well. Chill. Serve with potato chips or crackers.

Mrs. Morton Evans, Canton, Mass.

CLAM DIP

Serves: 6-8

"This is very popular - especially if you don't mention 'clam' until it's tasted."

Easy   Do ahead   Preparing: 10 min.

2 8-oz. pkgs. cream cheese
dash seasoned salt
2 tsp. Worcestershire sauce
1 can minced clams

Put softened cream cheese in large bowl. Cream. Add salt. Add clams and juice 1 tbsp. at a time and cream. Add Worcestershire sauce. Continue until consistency of heavy cream. Taste for seasoning, adding more if desired. If stored overnight in refrigerator, be sure to remove in time for it to soften up. If a small group of 6-8, I serve this in fish shells with bowl of potato chips to each one.

Miss Jean Gillmor, Ridgewood

EASY DIP

Yield: 1/2 cup

Very easy   Do ahead   Preparing: 5 min.

1 can deviled ham
1 chopped onion, med. size
mayonnaise

Mix and use as a dip for practically anything.

Mrs. Elliot Snow, Ridgewood

14

DEVILED HAM DIP OR SPREAD

Yield: 2 cups

"Flavorful dip and a good spread for sandwiches."

Easy   Do ahead   Preparing: 10 min.
                                                    Chilling: 1 hr.

2 4-1/2 oz. cans deviled ham   Combine all the ingredients and mix well.
8 oz. cream cheese, softened   Chill. Serve with crackers or melba toast
1 tbsp. catsup   rounds. May be made a day or two ahead of
2 tsp. finely chopped onion   time.
3 tbsp. chopped stuffed
  green olives   *Mrs. Harry N. Ives, Ridgewood*

CURRY DIP

Yield: 1 pint

"A delicious dip for shrimp or any raw vegetables."

Easy   Do ahead   Preparing: 10 min.

1 pt. mayonnaise   Mix all ingredients together and chill.
3 tbsp. chili sauce   Keeps indefinitely in the refrigerator.
3 tsp. curry powder   Especially good on raw vegetables such as
1/4 tsp. salt   carrots, asparagus tips, cauliflowerets,
1/4 tsp. pepper   celery, etc.
1 tbsp. garlic powder
1 tbsp. grated onion with
  juice
1 tbsp. Worcestershire sauce   *Mrs. James T. Rogers, Ridgewood*

RED CAVIAR DIP

Serves: 12

Easy   Do ahead   Preparing: 10 min.
                                                    Chilling: 1 hr.

1/4 lb. cream cheese   Beat together the cream cheese and sour
1 c. sour cream   cream. Fold in the onion and red caviar.
1/2 lb. red caviar   Chill.
  (2 small jars)
3 tbsp. grated onion   *Mrs. A. Steffee Smith, Ridgewood*

HOT CRABMEAT COCKTAIL DIP

Yield: 3 pints
      (Serves 30)

"This is such a delicious dip!"

Easy   Freeze   Preparing: 15 min.
                                                    Cooking: 15 min.

3 8-oz. pkgs. cream cheese   Cream cheese, mayonnaise, wine, then all the
1/2 c. mayonnaise   seasonings. Pick over crabmeat. Fold into
2/3 c. dry white wine   mayonnaise mixture by hand (Do not use a
garlic salt   beater.) Heat in double boiler and serve hot
2 scant tsp. prepared mustard   in a chafing dish. Use crackers and rounds of
2 tsp. confectioners' sugar   toasted party rye. If to be halved, use 2 cans
1 tsp. onion juice   crab.
dash seasoned salt
3 10-3/4 oz. cans crabmeat   *Mrs. Charles R. Moog, Ridgewood*

COCKTAIL CHEESE BALLS (Meatballs)

Yield: 25 balls

"A different tasting meatball."

Easy   Do ahead   Preparing: 15 min.
                                                    Browning: 10 min.

1 lb. ground lean chuck or
  round steak
1/2 c. fresh bread crumbs
1/3 c. crumbled Roquefort
  cheese
2 tsp. finely chopped onion
3/4 tsp. salt
1/4 tsp. ground black pepper
1 egg
3 tbsp. milk or stock
butter

Combine all ingredients except butter.
Shape into balls about 3/4" in diameter. Do
ahead to this point. Just before serving,
brown balls on all sides in hot butter.
Serve hot on toothpicks.

Mrs. Richard C. Baxter, Ridgewood

SOPHISTICATED MEATBALLS

Serves: 20 or
        4-6 as maindish

"Meatballs in the gourmet class! This won first prize in a newspaper contest."

Easy   Do ahead   Preparing: 30 min.
                                                    Cooking: 15 min.

1 lb. ground beef
1/3 c. dry bread crumbs
1/3 c. milk
1 egg
2 tbsp. chopped onion
1/2 tsp. salt
pepper to taste
2 tbsp. oil
1 can mushroom soup
8 oz. cream cheese
1/2 c. water
salad oil for browning

Combine beef, bread crumbs, milk, beaten
egg, onions, salt and pepper and shape into
balls (small for hors d'oeuvres, otherwise
large ones). Brown balls in oil in a frying
pan. Cover and cook 15 min. Remove balls,
pour off drippings and stir in mushroom soup,
cream cheese and water. May be served from
chafing dish or if as a main dish, serve
over noodles.

Mrs. Charles L. Van Inwagen, Ridgewood

GLAZED MEATBALLS

Yield: About 50 small balls

"A really different cocktail meatball. No browning necessary."

Average   Do ahead   Preparing: 20 min.
                                                    Cooking: 25 min.

1-1/2 lbs. ground chuck
1-1/2 slices white bread
1 egg
2 tbsp. minced green onion
2 tbsp. minced parsley
1/2 tsp. ground cinnamon
1 tsp. salt
1/2 tsp. pepper
1 12-oz. jar crabapple jelly
1/2 c. catsup
1/3 c. seedless raisins

Soak bread in a little cold water until
soft. Squeeze dry and mash well. Add to
meat together with egg, onion, parsley,
cinnamon, salt and pepper. Blend thoroughly
and form into one-inch balls. In a large
skillet combine jelly, catsup and raisins.
Slowly bring this mixture to a boil. Stir to
blend. Add meatballs. Simmer slowly for
25 min. or until cooked. Turn meatballs carefully after 10-15 min. Serve in a chafing
dish.

Mrs. Thomas G. Parris, Jr., Ridgewood

COCKTAIL HOT DOGS

Serves: 12-16

"Great in a chafing dish."

Easy   Do ahead   Preparing: 5 min.

1 or 2 pkgs. small cocktail
  hot dogs
1 bottle pure currant jelly
prepared mustard to taste

Melt jelly in saucepan and add mustard. Simmer 1 min. and pour over cooked hot dogs. Serve hot, on toothpicks.

Mrs. H. B. Millican, Jr., Saddle River

JELLIED PATE DE FOIE GRAS

Serves: 10

"This recipe came from Manoir Richelieu in Canada."

Easy   Do ahead   Preparing: 15 min.
                                                    Chilling: 4-5 hrs.

1 can consomme
  (I use Campbell's)
dash Worcestershire sauce
1 env. unflavored gelatin
  (I use Knox)
1/4 c. water
dash salt and pepper
2 cans pate de foie gras
  (Imported if possible;
  if not, use 1 can of
  liver paste)

Heat the consomme. Add salt, pepper and Worcestershire sauce. Dissolve gelatin in cold water. Add consomme to the gelatin mixture and pour a small amount into the bottom of a well oiled 1-qt. mold. In a mixing bowl mash the pate with a fork. If necessary, reheat the remaining consomme and pour piping hot over the pate, stirring until mixture is smooth. Pour into the mold and chill for 4 or 5 hours before serving. Turn out on a platter about 30 min. before serving. Serve with melba toast or any unsweetened cracker.

Mrs. Frank J. Davies, Franklin Lakes

BRAUNSCHWEIGER CANAPE

Serves: 20-30

"Delicious and can easily be cut in half."

Easy   Do ahead   Preparing: 6 min.
                                                    Chilling: 2 hrs.

2 cans beef consomme
2 env. unflavored gelatin
  (I use Knox)
1 lb. liverwurst
8 oz. cream cheese
a bit of grated onion
4 drops Worcestershire sauce
2-3 dashes garlic salt
sliced olives

Heat the consomme and dissolve gelatin in it. Oil a mold (approx. 1 qt. or 2 ice cube trays). After slicing the olives, arrange them on the bottom of the mold. Pour a thin layer of the heated consomme on the olives and put into freezer for 5 min. (until consomme hardens). Mix the liverwurst and cheese together and pour remainder of the consomme into it. Add the rest of the seasonings and beat with mixer until smooth. Pour over the hardened olive mixture. This recipe will keep refrigerated for 3 weeks. Before serving, unmold. Serve with crackers.

Mrs. W. G. Massey, Ridgewood

ONIONS FIRST

Yield: 2 cups

"Particularly nice for outdoor parties or onion lovers!"

Easy   Do ahead

Preparing: 15 min.
Chilling: 8 hrs.

3 large red onions, sliced
   paper thin
1 lemon, sliced paper thin
1/2 salad or olive oil
1/4 c. vinegar
2 tbsp. lemon juice
1 tsp. savory
1/2 tsp. salt

Layer onion and lemon slices in a bowl,
ending with a few lemon slices. Combine
the remaining ingredients and pour over all.
Chill for 8 hours, or overnight, basting
frequently with the dressing. Drain and
serve as a relish or hors d'oeuvre. While
this cannot be frozen, it can be made several
hours ahead or up to 2 days ahead of time.
Serve on cocktail rye bread.

Mrs. Philip M. Johnson, Ridgewood

MARINATED MUSHROOMS

Serves: 8

Easy   Do ahead

Preparing: 10 min.
Marinating: 24 hrs.

2 4-oz. cans mushroom caps
1/2 c. tarragon vinegar
1/2 c. dark brown sugar
1/2 tsp. black peppercorns
1 bay leaf
1 clove garlic, sliced

Drain mushrooms, reserving juice. Measure
mushroom juice, adding water if necessary to
make 1 c. Pour into a pan and add vinegar,
sugar and seasonings. Boil and pour over
mushrooms. Cover tightly and refrigerate
at least 24 hrs.

Mrs. Arthur S. Whittemore, Jr., Ridgewood

HOT MUSHROOM HORS D'OEUVRES

Yield: 1 pt.

"A different, elegant appetizer. Always a hit!"

Easy   Freeze

Preparing: 20 min.
Heating: 10 min.

1 lb. fresh mushrooms
3 tbsp. butter
2 c. water
3 tbsp. flour
dash Kitchen Bouquet
2 medium onions

Wash mushrooms and cut off stems. Take
half of the stems and boil with 2 c. of
water to make a broth. Slice the onions
fine and saute in butter. When partially
cooked add sliced mushroom caps and remaining stems, sliced. Saute until done. When
cooked make a gravy by adding flour and
1-1/2 c. liquid broth to mixture. Add
Kitchen Bouquet. Freeze, if necessary.
When ready to serve spread on toast
fingers (1" by 2") and heat in oven.

Mrs. M. Parker Butts, Weston, Mass.

STUFFED MUSHROOMS

Serves: 8

"Low calorie, non-filling and good before a hearty dinner."

Average   Do ahead   Preparing: 20 min.
Chilling: 3 hrs.

1 lb. mushrooms
2 3-oz. pkgs. cream cheese
1 10-1/2 oz. can minced clams
1 tbsp. diced pimento
2 tbsp. minced scallions
1/4 tsp. garlic salt
1/4 tsp. Worcestershire sauce
1/2 tsp. salt
dash of pepper
optional - pistachio nuts
          black olives

Pick your mushrooms, choosing those the size of a quarter. Remove stems, peel caps or scrub them well under cold water. With fork, mix cheese until smooth and creamy. Add remaining ingredients and mix well. Fill caps with stuffing, heaping it a bit. Decorate each with a sprig of parsley. Cover with Saran wrap and chill until serving time - at least 3 hours. Filling and caps may be done the day before and chilled separately. Combine shortly before use. Pistachio nuts or black olives may also be used for decoration.

Mrs. W. Dean Ferres, Ramsey

MUSHROOM HORS D'OEUVRE TURNOVERS

Yield: 6-8 doz.

"Sensational and so versatile; can be stuffed with so many things!"

Complicated -   Freeze   Preparing: 20 min.
  worth it   Chilling: 4 hrs.
                                      Assembling: 1 hr.
                                      Baking: 30 min.

8 oz. cream cheese
1/2 lb. butter
2-1/4 c. flour
1 tsp. salt

1 egg

Mushroom Filling:
3 tbsp. butter
1 large onion,
  finely chopped
1/2 lb. fresh mushrooms
1/4 tsp. thyme
1/2 tsp. salt
freshly ground pepper
2 tbsp. flour
1/4 c. sweet or sour cream

Knead cream cheese, butter, flour and salt into a dough and roll in a ball. Wrap in wax paper and chill for 4 hrs. Roll out on a floured board to 1/8" thick and cut with a 2-1/2" round cutter. Place 1 small tsp. filling on half of each, fold over to make a half circle and seal edges with water, pressing together with a fork. Poke a small hole in the top of each. Place on a cookie sheet and freeze. When frozen, transfer to a plastic bag for storage. When ready to serve, brush lightly with a lightly beaten whole egg and bake at 325° for 30 min. or until brown.

Mushroom Filling: Heat butter in skillet and brown onion. Add mushrooms and cook 3 min. Add thyme, salt and pepper and sprinkle with flour. Stir in cream until thickened. Can also be filled with chopped liver, liver pate, crab, shrimp, lobster, chicken or anything you wish.

Mrs. David Liebeskind, Fair Lawn

STUFFED GOUDA OR EDAM CHEESE

Serves: A crowd

"Easy to do, but looks as if it took hours."

Easy   Do ahead   Preparing: 15 min.

Gouda or Edam cheese
mayonnaise
Worcestershire sauce
Tabasco sauce
chopped walnuts
thin crackers

Hollow cut cheese leaving shell 1/8" thick. Grate cheese and mix with enough mayonnaise to moisten. Season with Tabasco and Worcestershire. Add chopped walnuts. Mix well and pile back into shell. Chill. Let stand 20 min. at room temperature before serving. Serve with thin crackers.

Mr. Edwin F. Bernhardt, Cheese Shop Ridgewood

CHEESE-ONION PENNIES

Yield: 5-6 doz.

"Crisp, delicious hot or cold hors d'oeuvre. A snap!"

Easy   Freeze   Preparing: 10 min.
                                                  Browning: 10 min.

1 stick butter or marg.
1/2 lb. sharp cheese,
   grated fine
1 c. flour
1/2 pkg. onion soup mix
dash red pepper

Have cheese and butter at room temperature. Mix all ingredients together until well blended, using fingers if necessary. Form in rolls about 1-1/2" in diameter. Wrap in waxed paper then seal and freeze. While still cold slice thin and bake at 375° for about 10 min. until brown at edges. Serve hot or cold. Can be frozen again after cooking. These keep well for months.

The Forum Quorum

ZIPPY CHEESE PUFFS

Yield: 5 doz.

Easy   Part do ahead   Preparing: 5 min.
                                                         Broiling: 4 min.

1 c. mayonnaise
1/3 c. grated Parmesan cheese
2 tsp. Worcestershire sauce
1 tbsp. sherry
crisp crackers

In small mixer bowl combine first four ingredients. Beat until thoroughly mixed. Drop by teaspoonfuls onto your favorite cracker. Broil 4" from heat for 3 or 4 min. or until puffed and lightly browned.

Mrs. Robert F. Treat, Ridgewood

CELERY CANAPES

Serves: 10-12

Easy   Do ahead   Preparing: 5 min.
                                                    Chilling: 1 hr.

8 oz. cream cheese
1/4 c. chutney
1 tbsp. curry
1 bunch celery

Wash and separate celery pieces. Mince chutney and mix in with curry and cream cheese. Stuff each celery piece with cheese mixture and chill. Slice diagonally just before serving.

Mrs. Allen D. Patterson, Saddle River

CHEESE PUFFS

Yield: 6 doz.

"Delicious and light; serves a large party."

Easy   Freeze   Preparing: 30 min.
                                                  Cooking: 20 min.

1 loaf unsliced bread
1 stick butter
3 oz. cream cheese
2 egg whites
1/4 lb. sharp cheese

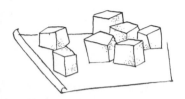

Melt the cheese and butter in a double boiler. Beat the egg whites until stiff. Cut the bread into 1-inch cubes. Fold egg whites into cheese and dip the bread cubes into mixture until they are covered. Chill on a cookie sheet. Bake at 400° about 20 min. or until brown. These may be frozen on a cookie sheet and stored in plastic bags indefinitely. For a different taste add a little scraped onion, or bacon crumbs, or top with paprika.

Mrs. Frank J. Davies, Franklin Lakes

SHERRY AND CHEESE DROPS

Yield: 4 doz.

"Delicious appetizer that can be easily stored."

Average   Freeze   Preparing: 10 min.
                                                  Baking: 10 min.

2 c. flour
1/2 c. softened butter
1 c. grated American or
    process cheese
1/2 c. sherry
1/2 tsp. salt
1/2 tsp. onion salt
1/2 tsp. garlic salt
1/4 tsp. paprika
1/4 tsp. Worcestershire sauce

Mix all ingredients until blended. Form into balls the size of large marbles. Place on ungreased baking sheet and flatten slightly. Bake at 450° for 10 min. These can be cooked, then frozen and reheated. They may also be used right away.

Mrs. Richard D. Major, Allendale

BACON CHEESE PUFFS

Yield: 2 doz.

"These may be frozen unbaked. Bake when needed."

Average   Freeze   Preparing: 30 min.
                                                  Baking: 20 min.

6 pieces bread, sliced thin
12 slices bacon
1 c. grated Swiss cheese

Trim crusts and cut each slice of bread into four squares. Butter lightly, if you wish. Cut bacon slices in two (each piece 3" long). Lay one piece of bread in the center of each piece of bacon, sprinkle amply with grated cheese, and roll up. Secure with toothpick and place on rack in shallow pan. Scatter remaining cheese on top. Bake in 400° oven for 20 min. until lightly browned. Serve immediately.

Mrs. Bruce K. Byers, Ridgewood

CHEESE WHIZZERS

Yield: 3-4 doz.

"Hot, delicious and so simple."

Easy   Do ahead

Preparing: 15 min.
Baking: 15-20 min.

1 med. jar soft cheese spread
   (I use Cheez Whiz)
1 lb. bacon
1 loaf sliced white bread

Cut slices of bread and bacon into thirds.
Spread bread with Cheese Whiz. Roll up, wrap
around with bacon, and spear shut with toothpick. Place on broiling rack and bake at 350°
for 15-20 min.

Mrs. William C. Bartlett, Jr., Ridgewood

HOT OLIVE-CHEESE PUFFS

Yield: 2 dozen

Easy   Freeze

Preparing: 10 min.
Baking: 10-15 min.

1 c. grated sharp cheese
3 tbsp. soft butter
1/2 c. flour
1/4 tsp. salt
1/2 tsp. paprika
24 stuffed olives

Blend cheese with soft butter. Stir in
flour, salt and paprika. Mix well. Wrap
1 tsp. of dough around each olive, covering
completely. Bake at 400° for 10-15 min. or
until lightly browned.

Mrs. A. Edward Conti, Ridgewood

OYSTER PUFFS

Serves: 4

"A great treat for oyster lovers."

Easy   Part do ahead

Preparing: 10 min.
Broiling: 5 min.

4 slices white toast
2 tbsp. soft butter
3/4 tsp. prepared mustard
8 oz. can oysters, drained
1/4 c. grated process cheese

Remove crusts from toast and cut each piece
into four squares or rounds. Cream together
butter and mustard. Spread on toast pieces.
Place one oyster on each piece of toast and
top with cheese. Place on a cookie sheet
and broil 5 min. or until browned and hot.
Serve immediately.

Mrs. Arthur Espy, II, Ho-Ho-Kus

WINE SPREAD

Serves: 4-6

"This is a good mixture to keep on hand and use when unexpected guests arrive."

Easy   Do ahead

Preparing: 5 min.

3 oz. Roquefort cheese
3 tbsp. sherry or red wine
1-1/2 oz. butter (3 tbsp.)

Blend all ingredients well with a wooden
spoon and place in refrigerator until wanted.

Mr. Edwin F. Bernhardt, Cheese Shop, Ridgewood

ROQUEFORT CREAM SPREAD

Serves: 4-6

Easy   Do ahead   Preparing: 10 min.

3 oz. cream cheese
1/4 c. crumbled Roquefort
1/2 tsp. grated onion
few drops lemon juice
few drops Worcestershire

Blend all ingredients well and serve on crisp crackers.

Mr. Edwin F. Bernhardt, Cheese Shop, Ridgewood

FRENCH BRIE BRILLIANT

Yield: 36 canapes

"Good used hot or cold."

Easy   Do ahead   Preparing: 15 min.
                                                    Chilling: 1 hr.
                                                    Standing: 1 hr.

1/2 lb. French Brie cheese
1/4 c. sour cream
10 French black olives
1 tbsp. chopped chives or
  scallions

Use cheese at room temperature. Blend with sour cream. Pit olives and mince. Add olives and chives to cheese. Chill until ready to serve. Remove from refrigerator 1 hr. before serving to bring cheese to spreading consistency. Spread on toast points and broil 2-3 min. until cheese is bubbly. Serve hot. Also good served cold as a spread for crackers.

Mr. Edwin F. Bernhardt, Cheese Shop, Ridgewood

PATÉ CAKE SPREAD

Serves: 12

"An elegant-appearing, but easy, appetizer."

Easy   Do ahead   Preparing: 10 min.
                                                    Chilling: 2 hrs.

2 4-1/2 oz. cans deviled ham
1 tbsp. minced onion
8 oz. cream cheese
1/4 c. sour cream
2-1/2 tsp. sharp mustard
truffles, pickles, pimentos,
  etc., for garnishing

Mix deviled ham with minced onion. Form into a patty-like cake and refrigerate until firm. Meanwhile, blend remaining ingredients together. Frost the ham cake with the cheese mixture and garnish with truffles, pickles, pimentos, etc. Chill 1-2 hrs. before serving with crackers.

Mrs. James W. Allred, Ridgewood

BOLOGNA PIES

Yield: 2 dozen

Easy   Do ahead   Preparing: 10 min.
                                                    Chilling: 2 hrs.

1/4 lb. cream cheese
1/2 tsp. dry mustard
12 slices bologna
3 tbsp. finely chopped
  pickles

Soften cream cheese and blend in mustard. Spread 9 slices of bologna with cream cheese in stacks of threes. Cover each stack with a slice of bologna. Roll the stacks in the pickle. Wrap in wax paper. Chill 2 hrs. Cut into pie-shaped wedges.

Mrs. A. Steffee Smith, Ridgewood

SPICED PECANS

Yield: 2 cups

"Excellent hors d'oeuvres."

Easy   Do ahead   Preparing: 10 min.
Baking: 20-30 min.

1/4 c. butter
1/2 tsp. Tabasco sauce
1 tsp. Worcestershire sauce
1 tbsp. garlic salt
2 c. large pecan halves

Melt butter and add spices. Coat the nuts in this mixture and toast them at 375° until brown (20 or 30 min.). Shake the nuts occasionally as they toast. Drain on brown paper.

Mrs. Franklin A. A. Dick, Princeton, N. J.

PEANUT FINGER CANAPES

Serves: 4-8

"An unusual and very simple canape that everyone loves. Easily doubled."

Easy   Do ahead   Preparing: 10 min.

6 slices thinly sliced bread
1/2 c. peanut butter
1/2 c. butter
bread crumbs

Remove crusts from bread and cut into 1/2" thin fingers. Place in a slow 250° oven and toast until brown. Shake them occasionally to toast evenly. In a double boiler melt butter with peanut butter. When done, shake crumbs from fingers and dip in peanut butter mixture. Put on a piece of wax paper until cool. Shake in bread crumbs. Serve or store in refrigerator tightly sealed.

Mrs. F. Marsena Butts, Lincoln, Mass.

APPETIZER HAM PIE

Serves: 4-6

"How to impress guests with a real easy one."

Easy   Do ahead   Preparing: 15 min.
Baking: 10 min.

1 single pie crust pastry
1 can (3 oz.) deviled ham
3 tbsp. bottled sweet
  pickle relish

Roll out pastry to a circle 1/8" thick on lightly floured board. Place on cookie sheet, fold edge up slightly and flute; or, put in a cut-down aluminum pie pan. Mix deviled ham with pickle relish and spread evenly over pastry. Bake in hot over (450°) 10 min. or until top is golden. Remove to serving plate; cut in small wedges.

Mrs. Richard C. Baxter, Ridgewood

SCALLOPS WITH GREEN SAUCE

Serves: 8

"This is unusual served as an hors d'oeuvre or as a salad."

Easy   Do ahead   Preparing: 15 min.
                                                    Cooking: 5 min.
                                                    Chilling: overnight

1-1/2 lbs. sea scallops
1 bay leaf
1 onion, chopped
salt and pepper to taste
1/2 tsp. dried dill
15 oz. bottle dry vermouth

Green Sauce:
1 c. mayonnaise
1/4 c. minced parsley
1/4 c. minced chives or
   green onion tops
1/2 c. minced spinach
1/2 tsp. dried dillweed
   (more, if desired)

Cut scallops into bite-size pieces. Heat vermouth with seasonings. Cook until white and tender, about 5 min. Drain, saving liquid, and cool both separately. Combine and refrigerate overnight.

Sauce: Mix all ingredients together and refrigerate overnight. Serve so scallops can be dipped.

Mrs. Warren C. Lane, Jr., Worcester, Mass.

BAKED STUFFED CLAMS

Yield: 24 stuffed clams

Average   Freeze   Preparing: 30 min.
                                                     Baking: 15 min.

fresh bread crumbs
1-1/2 doz hard-shelled, med.,
   fresh clams (littleneck,
   cherrystone)
1/4 lb. butter
1/2 onion, chopped
2/3 c. flour
2 c. milk
1/2 c. clam juice
1/2 tsp. nutmeg
2 tbsp. parsley, chopped
dash red pepper
2 tbsp. melted butter

Make bread crumbs in blender using about 3 pieces of bread. Set aside. Cook clams in a little water saving a bit of juice and shells. Chop clams, a few at a time, by just clicking the blender on and off. Use a bit of juice if necessary. Make a thick roux of melted butter and flour with the onion mixed in the butter. Add milk to make a cream sauce. Add the chopped clams and nutmeg, parsley and red pepper. Freeze at this point, if desired. If to be served the same day, chill, as stuffing is more easily done when cold. Stuff scrubbed clam shells with mixture and top with bread crumbs which have been tossed in 2 tbsp. butter. Bake at 375° until brown.

Mrs. John W. Foster, Jr., Montvale

SARDINE-ONION SURPRISE

Serves: 4

Easy   Do ahead   Preparing: 10 min.

1 3-1/2 oz. can sardines
1 medium onion
1 tbsp. mayonnaise

Finely chop onion and mix with the other two ingredients. Serve on crackers.

Mr. Leonard Van Arsdale, Allendale

SALMON HORS D'OEUVRES

Serves: 18-20

"Looks so great and fun to decorate."

Easy   Do ahead   Preparing: 20 min.
Chilling: 1 hr.

1 lb. can red salmon
3 sticks celery
onion powder
juice of 1/2 lemon
1/2 tsp. celery seed
mayonnaise
salt
pepper
1 green olive
2 ripe olives
slices of lemon, thin
paprika
parsley
crackers

Mix salmon, celery which has been finely chopped, onion powder and celery seed with enough mayonnaise to moisten. Season with salt and pepper. Pat into the shape of a fish on a serving tray. Decorate with green olive for the eye, thin strips of ripe olive for scales, and a sprinkling of paprika. Encircle with parsley. Half cut through thin lemon slices and twist to make decorative trimmings. Chill. Serve with crackers.

Mrs. Richard D. Major, Allendale

SHRIMP AND ARTICHOKE APPETIZER

Yield: 12-16

Easy   Do ahead   Preparing: 15 min.
Marinating: 2 hrs.

2 pkgs. frozen artichoke
  hearts
48 medium shrimp
2 egg yolks
1 c. olive oil
1/2 c. peanut oil
1/2 c. wine vinegar
4 tbsp. Dijon mustard
4 tbsp. minced parsley
4 tbsp. chopped chives
2 tbsp. minced shallots

Cook artichokes, drain and chill. Cook and chill shrimp. Place egg yolks, oils, vinegar and mustard in a mixing bowl. Beat well. Add remaining ingredients, then shrimp and artichokes. Marinate in the refrigerator at least 2 hrs., turning artichokes and shrimp occasionally.

Mrs. Irving R. Hayman, Ridgewood

SHRIMP MARINADE

Serves: 12-16

Easy   Do ahead   Preparing: 15 min.
Marinating: 24 hrs.

2 lbs. shrimp, shelled
3/4 c. olive oil
1/2 c. chopped onions
2 cloves garlic, minced
2 tsp. salt
1/4 tsp. pepper
1 tsp. paprika
1/2 c. cider vinegar
1/4 tsp. dry mustard
1/8 tsp. dried, ground
  red peppers
1 onion, thinly sliced

Wash and dry shrimp. Heat 1/4 c. oil in skillet. Saute onions and garlic 5 min. Add shrimp, 1 tsp. salt, pepper and paprika. Saute 5 min. Cool 20 min. Mix together remaining oil, salt, vinegar, mustard and red peppers. Arrange layers of shrimp and sliced onions in a bowl or jar and pour marinade over it all. Cover. Marinate in refrigerator for 24 hrs. When serving, remove shrimp from marinade and put on toothpicks.

Mrs. Herman Van Nouhuys, Ho-Ho-Kus

CRABMEAT CANAPE

Yield: 48 canapes

"Easily prepared and a sure-fire hit!"

Average   Freeze   Preparing: 30 min.
                                             Cooking: 10 min.

1 can crabmeat or
  frozen king crab
2 eggs, hard cooked
1 tbsp. chopped onion
1 tbsp. flour, rounded
2 tbsp. butter
1/2 c. milk
dash cayenne pepper
1 loaf firm white bread
  (day-old)
butter or marg. for browning

Make a thick cream sauce from the butter, flour and milk and bring to a gentle boil. Saute the onion and add to the sauce. Cut up hard cooked eggs and add the eggs and crabmeat to the sauce. Remove from heat and add dash of cayenne. Refrigerate until chilled. Remove crusts from bread and spread the sauce mixture between two pieces of bread as you would a sandwich. Wrap in heavy-duty foil and either freeze at this point or refrigerate. Should be prepared early in the day for an evening party or frozen ahead. If frozen, remove a few hours before serving as it will cut better. Cut sandwiches in half and each half into thirds, making six. Fry on both sides in butter or margarine. Should be crisp. Enjoy!

Mrs. Taubert Stein, Ridgewood

SPLASHED SHRIMP

Serves: 6-8

"A good, hot appetizer with a ginger zip!"

Easy   Do ahead   Preparing: 15-30 min.
                                            Cooking: 7 min.

2 lbs. fresh shrimp or
  1-1/2 lbs. frozen
2 tbsp. oil
2 tbsp. soy sauce
1-1/2 tbsp. sugar
2-1/2 tbsp. sherry
2 or 3 large scallions
2 tbsp. powdered ginger
salt to taste

Cook shrimp in boiling water, then wash, shell and clean. Pat dry. Heat oil in skillet until hot. Sift the ginger over shrimp until it is lightly coated on both sides. Add shrimp to the skillet and fry for 6 min., stirring off and on. Chop up scallions (including green ends) into fine pieces. Add sugar, soy sauce, salt and sherry. Let them cook together a minute. Stir in scallions and coat with the mixture. Remove from skillet and serve. May be made early in the day, refrigerated, and then reheated before serving.

Mrs. Thomas C. De Patie, Ridgewood

SHRIMP RELISH HORS D'OEUVRES

Serves: 8

"A delicious way to serve cold shrimp."

Easy   Do ahead   Preparing: 10 min.
                                         Marinating: 1 hr. or more

1 lb. cooked shrimp
1 c. minced onion
1/2 c. parsley, chopped
2/3 c. oil
1/3 c. vinegar
1 clove garlic
1-1/2 tsp. salt
pepper
2 cans Italian mushrooms

Combine shrimp, onion, parsley and mushrooms (oil and all) in a bowl. Mix remaining ingredients and beat well. Pour over shrimp mixture and chill at least one hour.

Mrs. Richard A. Grimley, Ridgewood

HOT CRAB SPREAD

Serves: 14

"Especially good if blender made, but not absolutely necessary."

Easy   Do ahead   Preparing: 20 min.
                                         Heating: 15 min.

8 oz. cream cheese
1 tbsp. milk
1 6-1/2 oz. can flaked crab
2 tbsp. finely chopped
  onion
1/2 tsp. horseradish, cream
  style
1/4 tsp. salt
dash of pepper
1/3 c. or more sliced almonds

Combine and blend softened cream cheese and the milk. Add crabmeat which has been picked over and cleaned, onion, horseradish, salt and pepper. Blend well or blend in the blender, and spoon into an ovenproof dish. Sprinkle with the sliced almonds and bake at 375° for 15 min.
Serve hot with crackers or party rye bread. This may be made a day ahead and heated before serving.

Mrs. Pressly M. Millen, Jr., Ho-Ho-Kus

CHINESE CHEATERS

Yield: 20 hors d'oeuvres

"So called because the Chinese make their own dough."

Average   Do ahead   Preparing: 30 min.
                                         Baking: 10 min.

2 tbsp. minced onion
2 tbsp. green pepper
2 tbsp. celery
4 water chestnuts, chopped
3 tsp. soy sauce
2 dashes M.S.G.
1 can tiny shrimp
2 tbsp. butter
2 pkgs. frozen biscuits
  (10 per pkg.)
  (I use Pillsbury's)

Saute onion, green pepper and celery briefly in butter. Add water chestnuts which have been chopped, soy sauce and shrimp. Flatten biscuits. Put one tsp. of filling into each biscuit and pinch together to close. Put in greased baking pan and bake in 475° oven about 10 min. or until brown. Serve hot.

Mrs. John E. Clark, Ridgewood

ASPARAGUS CANAPES

Yield: 5-1 2 doz.

"Always well received by 'boys and girls' alike!"

Average

Freeze

Preparing: 30 min.
Baking: 15 min.

1 can Mary Washington-style
  asparagus (I use Del Monte)
1 regular loaf bread
8 oz. Roquefort cheese
8 oz. cream cheese
1 tbsp. mayonnaise
1 egg, beaten
butter, melted

Cut all crusts off the bread. Roll bread out flat. Spread with the mixture of cheeses, mayonnaise and egg. Top with one stalk of asparagus per slice of bread. Roll up and cut in three pieces. Dip each piece in melted butter. Place on ungreased cookie sheet. This may be made the day before or frozen ahead before baking. When ready to bake, cook at 350° for about 15 min. or until well browned. There is enough cheese mixture for 2 cans of asparagus and 2 loaves of bread.

Mrs. Ralph B. Metzger, Ridgewood

BAKED CHICKEN WINGS

Serves: 30

"Canape for an outdoor party."

Easy

Do ahead

Preparing: 15 min.
Baking: 1 hr.

4 lbs. chicken wings
1/2 c. butter or margarine
1 c. grated Parmesan cheese
2 tbsp. chopped parsley
1 tbsp. oregano
2 tsp. paprika
1 tsp. salt
1/2 tsp. pepper

Cut tips from chicken wings and discard. Cut wings in half at joint, making 2 pieces. Melt butter. Mix remaining ingredients. Dip wings in butter, then in cheese mixture. Arrange in shallow baking dish on foil. Drizzle with remaining butter and bake in 350° oven about 1 hour. This may be prepared the night before and reheated.

Dr. Oswald B. Deiter, Ridgewood

ESCARGOTS

Serves: 4

"So elegant, but really not as difficult as they may seem."

Easy

Do ahead

Preparing: 10 min.
Cooking: 10 min.

24 snails, canned
1 tbsp. parsley
1 tbsp. garlic, chopped fine
1 tbsp. chopped shallots
1 tbsp. dry white wine
1 tbsp. snail juice
pinch salt
dash pepper
1/4 lb. butter

Mix all ingredients, except snails, very well. Take the snails from shells. Place a dab of the butter mixture in each shell, a snail, then cover with butter mixture. Arrange on plates; place in 350° oven. When butter starts to bubble (about 10 min.) they are ready to serve. French bread helps.

Mr. Edwin F. Bernhardt, Cheese Shop, Ridgewood

Appetizer Additions

Use a canape tray instead of first course for a formal dinner.

* Pumpkin seeds are great with drinks! When making Jack-O-Lanterns, remove
    membrane from seeds; place in a shallow pan with butter and salt. Toast
    seeds in a slow oven, stirring often, for about 1 hour.

* Snappy dips may be made by adding one half of a 7-oz package of salad
    dressing mix to 1/2 pt. sour cream. (Good Seasons Cheese Garlic
    Dressing is especially delicious.)

* A very nice spread is made by mixing 1-3/4 c. grated Holland Leyden cheese
    with 1/4 c. mayonnaise, 1 tbsp. grated onion, and a small can of
    deviled ham. Serve on crackers or pumpernickel bread.
    Sent by Mr. Edwin F. Bernhardt, Cheese Shop, Ridgewood

* For a Cheddar-curry spread place in your blender 1 c. shredded Cheddar cheese
    with 6 oz. cream cheese, 1/4 c. chutney, a dash of Tabasco, 1 tbsp.
    chopped green onion, 2 tbsp. sherry, 1/2 tsp. curry powder and a bit of
    salt. Blend for a few seconds and serve on crackers or with fruit.
    Sent by Mrs. Oswald B. Deiter, Ridgewood

* Quick Gouda Appetizers

    Place a small wedge of Gouda between wedges of apple on skewers.

    Place a cube of cheese between 2 cubes of ham on a toothpick.

    Place a cube of cheese between 2 cubes of pineapple on a toothpick.

    Slice small Vienna franks into small rounds. Make small cheese balls
        and roll in parsley. Place cheese between two frank slices.

    Take a large apple, grapefruit or cabbage and cut one side or bottom
        off slightly. Put on serving plate and stick skewers of stuffed
        or ripe olives and cubes of cheese into it.
        Sent by Mr. Edwin F. Bernhardt, Cheese Shop, Ridgewood

Beverages

THE BEST COFFEE ON THE EASTERN SEABOARD

Make as much of this as you desire.

Easy   Serve immediately   Preparing: 10 min.

water
coffee

Boil desired amount of water in a saucepan. Remove from flame and wait 10 sec. Then dump in desired amount of coffee. Stir. Wait 2 min. Stir again. Pour one cup cold water over the surface. Wait 5 min. Decant through strainer and enjoy. NEVER BOIL.

Mr. Leonard Van Arsdale, Allendale

FRESH ICED TEA   Serves: 8

"A weight watcher's beverage."

Easy   Do ahead   Preparing: 10 min.

6 tea bags
juice of 2 lemons, unstrained
  (remove seeds)
2 tbsp. liquid sweetener
  (I use Sucaryl)
1 9-cup Pyrex pot or steel pan
  (not aluminum)

Put tied tea bags into 6 c. boiling water. Let boil one minute. Remove from heat and let tea bags steep for 10 min. Squeeze and remove tea bags. Add cold water to 9-cup level. Remove seeds only from juice - do not strain. Add lemon juice and segments and sweetener. Serve in tall glass with ice. Add sprig of mint and cherry, if desired. Can be done one day ahead.

Mrs. Frank Sanclementi, Jr., Haskell, N. J.

SPICED TEA (or spiked)   Serves: 10

"Nice change from straight tea or coffee."

Easy   Do ahead   Preparing: 5 min.
                                                 Setting: 25 min.

2 oranges, squeezed
1 lemon, squeezed
2 sticks cinnamon
1 tsp. whole cloves
1 c. sugar (less if desired)
2 tbsp. tea
optional -
  1 tsp. rum per cup

Pour 2 qts. boiling water over juice of oranges, lemon, the rinds, cinnamon, cloves and sugar. Let stand 20 min. Add tea and let steep 5 min. Will keep until needed in refrigerator. A teaspoon of white rum per cup and this really warms the cockles of my heart!

Mrs. William.K. Gregg, Ho-Ho-Kus

INSTANT RUSSIAN TEA   Yield: 90 cups

Easy   Do ahead   Preparing: 10 min.

1 large jar "Tang" (2-1/2 c.)
1 c. instant tea with lemon
  and sugar
1-1/2 c. sugar
2 tsp. cinnamon
1 tsp. ground allspice
1 tsp. ground cloves

Mix all ingredients together. Use 1 tbsp. of mix per cup. Store in jar in refrigerator.

Mrs. Edith Koen, Arlington, Va.

TOMATO JUICE COCKTAIL

Yield: 1 quart

"Marvelous to have handy at a cocktail party for those who 'would rather not

Easy   Do ahead   Preparing: 5 min.
                                                   Chilling: 1 hr.

14 oz. tomato juice
1/2 tsp. grated onion
1 tsp. finely chopped celery
2 tbsp. lemon juice
1/4 tsp. Worcestershire sauce
1/2 tsp. sugar
1/2 tsp. salt
1/2 tsp. horseradish

Combine all ingredients. Chill for 1 hr., strain and serve.

Mrs. Reginald F. Wardley, Ridgewood

CRANBERRY SPARKLE PUNCH

Yield: 5 qts.

Easy   Do ahead   Preparing: 5 min.
                                                   Chilling: 1 hr.

2 qts. cranberry juice
   cocktail
2 12-oz. cans pineapple-
   orange juice
1 qt. ginger ale
2 tsp. lime juice
1/2 c. confectioners' sugar

Chill and combine all but ginger ale. Add ice; garnish with fruit. Add chilled ginger ale just before serving.

Mrs. Everett M. Johnson, Ridgewood

FRUIT PUNCH

Yield: 1-1/2 qts.

"Very appealing to children, teetotalers, and fugitives from cocktail partie

Easy   Serve immediately   Preparing: 5 min.

1 small can frozen orange or
   tangerine juice
1 can frozen pineapple juice
1 can frozen lemonade
1 qt. ginger ale

Defrost juices, combine with ginger ale and pour over ice block or ice cubes.

Mrs. David F. Cook, Passaic

MULLED WINE

Yield: 1 qt.

"Wonderful for a cold fall night - and it smells so good!"

Easy   Do ahead   Preparing: 10 min.
                                                   Heating: 10 min.

1 lemon
2/3 c. sugar
2 c. water
1/2 tsp. allspice
1 tsp. whole cloves
2 cinnamon sticks (3")
1 bottle (4/5 qt.) Burgundy
   (or other good dinner wine)

Slice lemon (do not peel) and combine with sugar, water and spices. Heat to boiling and boil gently for 10 min. Turn heat low, add wine and heat very hot. (Do not boil.)

Mrs. Charles R. Herman, Ridgewood

pretty and festive."

y   Do ahead   Preparing: 10 min.

r 4 c. sugar   Dissolve 3 c. sugar in lemon juice.
. lemon juice   Dredge cubed, fresh pineapple in I c. sugar.
ineapple, cubed   (If canned pineapple is used, do not dredge
or 4 c. canned cubes) in sugar.) Combine these in a chilled punch
/2 qts. ice water   bowl. Add a block of ice, water and sauterne
ottle (4/5 qt.) chilled or Rhine wine. Just before serving, add
auterne or Rhine wine strawberries which have been lightly sugared.
t. strawberries   Add champagne. Whee!
arge bottles chilled
hampagne   *Mrs. Everett M. Johnson, Ridgewood*

PUNCH   Yield: 3 qts.
                                              (24 punch cups)

is can easily be multiplied. So great!"

y   Do ahead   Preparing: 10 min.

t. rum   Mix all ingredients, except soda, in a
t. lemon juice   gallon jug. Put the batch in a cool place
I use Realemon)   for one or two days. When ready to serve,
t. strong tea   pour batch over a block of ice and add soda.
 lb. granulated sugar
t. soda   *Mrs. Richard L. Prescott, Ridgewood*

PUNCH FOR A CROWD   Yield: 12 qts.

ure 8 servings per quart.

y   Do ahead   Preparing: 6 min.
                                              Chilling: 1 hr.

bs. loaf sugar   Dissolve sugar in just enough water to
er   make a thick syrup. Add remaining ingredi-
t. orange juice   ents. Chill and dive in!
t. lemon juice
ottles rum
ottles sparkling water
ottle Cointreau   *Mrs. Everett M. Johnson, Ridgewood*

EAPPLE DAIQUIRI (Strawberry or Banana)   Yield: 1 drink
                                              (multiply as needed)

is is a favorite in the Virgin Islands."

y   Serve immediately   Preparing: 2 min.

 c. canned pineapple   Put all ingredients into a blender and
or 2 slices)   run until smooth. Serve immediately in
z. pineapple juice   frosted old-fashioned glasses with a short
h lime juice   straw.
/2 oz. light rum
shed ice   Ed. Note: This can also be done with
                       frozen strawberries or fresh bananas.

                       Mrs. Arthur S. Whittemore, Jr., Ridgewood

PEACH DAIQUIRIS

Serves: 4

"A light and delicious start for a ladies' luncheon."

Easy Do ahead Preparing: 10 min.

1 pkg. frozen peaches
6 oz. light rum
  (dark can be used)
juice of 1-1/2 lemons or
  3 tbsp. Realemon
crushed ice

Combine partially frozen peaches, juice and all, rum and lemon juice in blender and blend at high speed until very well mixed. Just before serving, add crushed ice and blend again. Can be done one hour before serving.

Mrs. David F. Bolger, Ridgewood

FORESTER FROST

Serves: 1

Easy Serve immediately Preparing: 2 min.

In tall glass mix:
1 tsp. sugar
splash water
juice of 1/2 lemon
crushed ice
1-1/2 oz. Old Forester
1 tsp. creme de menthe
cherry and lemon peel garnish

Muddle sugar and water in chilled glass. Add lemon juice and pack with crushed ice. Pour the "Old Forester" over this. Pour in creme de menthe and stir well. Garnish with cherry and lemon peel.

Mrs. Thomas H. Boyd, Clifton

SANGRIA (Spanish wine punch)

Yield: 1-1/2 qts.

"A delightful summer drink for luncheon or cookout. Light and delicate."

Easy Serve immediately Preparing: 5 min.

1 bottle wine (white,
  red or champagne)
1/2 bottle club soda
sugar
1 small glass cognac

Mix all ingredients together. Serve in pitcher with orange and lemon slices and lots of ice.

Mrs. Allan Benz, Ridgewood

CHRISTMAS ICE RING

Yield: 1 ring

"This is beautiful for a Christmas punch bowl."

Easy Do ahead Preparing: 20 min.

water to fill mold
a few spiced crabapples
a few preserved kumquats
a few red maraschino cherries
a few green maraschino
  cherries
a few holly leaves

Fill a ring mold (with a large center that is big enough for your ladle to fit through) with water up to one inch of the top. Place in freezer until it is solid. On top of ice arrange fruit (with stems) and leaves in groups to make a pretty wreath. Pour on 1/4 inch more water. Return to freezer until fruit is frozen in solid. When frozen, remove by running under hot water. Store in plastic bag. When ready to use, place in punch bowl fruit side up. It will float on top of punch.

Mrs. Robert F. Treat, Ridgewood

EASY WHISKEY SOURS

Serves: as many as you want

"Easily made in whatever quantity you desire."

Easy — No need to do ahead — Preparing: 2 min.

1 can lemonade
1 lemonade can liquor
  (bourbon, rye, or scotch)
1/2 lemonade can water
large ice chunk
maraschino cherries
thin lemon slices

Mix undiluted lemonade and equal amount of liquor. Then add half a can of water (or no water if you want your guests on their ears quicker). Pour over a large ice chunk or ice ring in a punch bowl. Decorate with lemon slices and cherries. Serve over ice cubes in old fashioned glasses. (One small can of lemonade will give you 4 ample drinks.)

Mrs. Henry B. Douglas, Saddle River

CHRISTMAS EGG NOG

Serves: 20

"Sure to add to a festive occasion."

Easy — Serve immediately — Preparing: 15 min.

6 eggs, separated
3/4 c. sugar
1 qt. milk or 1 pt. milk
  and 1 pt. cream
1 pt. whiskey
1 oz. rum
optional -
  block of vanilla ice cream

Beat egg whites until stiff. Add 1/4 c. sugar to whites when stiff. Beat yolks and add 1/2 c. sugar while beating. Mix whites with yolks. Stir in milk, whiskey and rum very slowly. Serve plain in bowl or over vanilla ice cream to be even better and also to keep it chilled. Serve with Christmas cookies. Perfect!

Mrs. John E. Button, Saddle River

SWEDISH GLOGG

Serves: 20 (punch cups)

"Delicious. Guaranteed to knock out a cold!"

Average — Do ahead — Preparing: 30 min.

1 fifth claret
1 fifth port wine
1 pint brandy or aquavit
1 c. blanched almonds
1 c. raisins
1 stick cinnamon
10 whole cardamon seeds
  (pod cracked slightly)
5 cloves
1 c. sugar
1 piece ginger root

Put spices in small cloth bag. Add to wine with raisins and almonds and simmer for a few minutes. Do not boil. Add sugar slowly, stirring. Add brandy or aquavit. Remove cloth bag of spices. Keep hot over low heat and serve in heated mugs with a few raisins and almonds in each cup. It is advisable to remove the bag of spices immediately after it is made, as otherwise it may be too spicy or seasoned.

Glogg may be kept in well corked or sealed bottles or jars with the raisins and almonds. Then just heat, without boiling, before serving. Some suggest using 12 lumps of sugar in a strainer and pouring the brandy or aquavit slowly over it.. As sugar absorbs liquor, set fire to it and continue pouring. Put out flames as sugar melts and add sugar that remains to wine mixture. It is not necessary to burn the brandy, as that only burns the expensive liquor. Skol!

Mrs. Eric H. Berg, Ridgewood

37

Beverage Briefs

To avoid "skin" forming on top of cocoa, beat until frothy with a whisk or rotary beater as soon as cocoa is made.

Use white facial tissue to line the coffee basket when perking coffee – you'll have clear coffee and an easy-to-clean basket.

* Try a few pieces of chocolate bits in demitasse for a mocha flavor.

Leftover coffee and tea make nice ice cubes that don't dilute your drink.

* To make iced tea that does not cloud, fill a large glass bottle with cold water and add tea (2 tsp. to I qt. of water). Set in the sun for 2 hours and strain immediately. Store in refrigerator. Or, just add 4 tsp. to a qt. of. cold water and let stand overnight, then strain an refrigerate.

Iced tea requires only half as much sugar if sweetened hot rather than co

* For lemonade and other summer drinks, use a spiced sugar syrup. Cook in the water which will be used to make the syrup I stick cinnamon, 3-4 whole cloves, 3-4 allspice berries. For a thin syrup use I part sugar to 2 parts water. *Sent by Mrs. James Rogers, Ridgewood*

* For an easy, delicious champagne punch mix 2 qts. sauterne, I qt. dry champagne, and I qt. ginger ale. Decorate with whatever fruit desire *Sent by Mrs. Everett M. Johnson, Ridgewood*

* To make lots of Old Fashioneds (13 or more), with a muddler mash the peel one lemon with 7 tsp. sugar, 10 dashes of bitters and 1/2 c. boiling water. Place in a large screw-top jar and add a bottle of whiskey. not refrigerate. The longer it sets the better. Serve in old fashio glasses over shaved ice, garnished with orange slices and cherries.

* Two and one-half parts Scotch with one part honey makes a "near Drambuie" guaranteed to fool your friends.

Freeze berries (almost any type) or cherries in ice cubes for pretty drin Leaves such as mint, lemon verbena, thyme, oregano, marjoram are als nice. A bit of cucumber, stuffed olive or lemon twist are great for martini on the rocks. Try a mandarin orange slice or other citrus f in ice cubes. When releasing, do not use the handle; run briefly un hot water.

Color ice cubes with liqueurs like creme de menthe or cherry herring for different twist in sours, collins, etc. Use 3 tbsp. per qt. liquid. Or, add a few drops of bitters for rosy ice cubes.

To make crystalline-clear ice, use boiled water that has been well chille then freeze. Or, use bottled, distilled water.

To crush ice easily, fill a plastic milk or juice carton with water. Fre When ready for crushed ice, slam it hard on a heavy cement walk unti thuds. You'll have crushed ice that can be restored in the freezer.

To frost glasses for chilled fruit juices, dip rim of the glass into frui juice, then into granulated sugar. Chill until ready to serve.

Breads

NANCY'S DILLY CASSEROLE BREAD

Serves: 10-12

"'Dilly' is the word! Great for beginners, no kneading, only the mixer."

Easy   Freeze

Preparing: 10 min.
Raising: 1 hr. 30 min.
Baking: 50 min.

1 pkg. dry yeast
1/4 c. warm water
1 c. creamed cottage cheese
2 tbsp. sugar
1 tbsp. instant minced onion
1 tbsp. butter
2 tsp. dill seed
1 tsp. salt
1/4 tsp. soda
1 egg, unbeaten
2-1/2 c. all-purpose flour
  (or a bit less)
melted butter

Heat cottage cheese to lukewarm. Soften
yeast in water. Combine in mixing bowl
cottage cheese, sugar, onion, butter, dill
seed, salt, soda, egg and softened yeast.
Add flour to form a stiff dough, beating well
after each addition. (If using the mixer,
start at low speed.) Cover. Let rise in a
warm place (85°-90°) until light and doubled
in size, 50-60 min. Stir down dough. Turn
into well greased 8 inch round (1-1/2 qt.)
casserole. Let rise in warm place until light
30-40 min. Bake at 350° for 40-50 min. until
golden brown. Brush with soft butter and
sprinkle with salt. This can be made the day
before. If so, slice almost through after
cooling and wrap in foil. Warm in the oven
before serving.

Mrs. Theodore M. Grell, Ridgewood

HOMEMADE BREAD

Yield: 1 loaf

"Smells so good in the kitchen!"

Average   Freeze

Preparing: 15 min.
Rising: 2 hrs.
Baking: 45 min.

1 pkg. dry yeast
1 c. warm water
4 tbsp. sugar
1 tsp. salt
2 tbsp. shortening
4 c. instant flour
melted butter

Mix yeast with warm water and 3 tbsp. sugar.
Let it dissolve for about 1/2 hr. until foam
is formed. In a separate bowl mix salt, shortening, 1 tbsp. sugar and flour. Knead for
10 min. The mixture should be sticky. Stir
both mixtures together. Put into a greased bowl
in the form of a ball and let rise for 2 hrs.
With your fist punch down dough. Flatten the
dough out on a counter to the same width as
a 1-1/2 qt. loaf pan and twice the length.
Roll the dough up and place in the well greased
pan so both sides of the dough are touching
the pan sides. Let rise for 1 hr. in a warm
spot (top of the stove is good). Brush top
with butter and bake in a preheated 375° oven
for 45 min.

Mrs. Eric A. Berg, Pomona, N.Y.

EASY CRUSTY FRENCH BREAD

Serves: 8-10

"Easy and delicious with a heavenly baking aroma. Wonderful toasted."

Easy   Freeze   Preparing: 5 min.
                                                  Rising: 2 hrs.
                                                  Baking: 1 hr.

1 pkg. dry yeast
2 c. warm water
4 c. instant mixing flour
1 tbsp. sugar (optional)
2 tsp. salt
melted butter

Dissolve yeast in 1 c. warm water. Measure flour, sugar and salt together in a large bowl and stir in dissolved yeast. Add enough of the second cup of water to hold dough together. Mix until soft and sticky and cover with cloth. Set in a warm spot (top of the stove is good) and let rise to double in bulk about 1 hr. When dough is high and spongy, beat down with hands and divide into two parts. Put into two greased, 6 inch loaf Pyrex baking dishes. Cover again and let rise to top of dish. Brush tops with melted butter. Bake at 400° for 1 hr. Heat before serving.

Mrs. L. Russell Thacher, Jr., Ridgewood

GOUGÉRE BREAD

Serves: 8

"Sensational, easy cheese bread."

Average   Freeze   Preparing: 10 min.
                                                  Baking: 45 min.

1 c. water
8 tbsp. butter
1 tsp. salt
1/8 tsp. pepper
1 c. flour
4 eggs
1 c. finely diced sharp
cheese

Place water, butter, salt and pepper in a pot and heat until butter is melted and mixture is boiling rapidly. Add flour to mixture all at once and continue cooking and stirring until mixture forms a ball and leaves sides of pan clean. Remove from heat. Beat in eggs, one at a time, incorporating each thoroughly before adding next egg. Stir in all but 2 tbsp. of cheese. Place rounded tablespoons of dough on a lightly greased baking sheet in a ring 8 or 9 inches in diameter, leaving center space 2-1/2 inches in diameter. Sprinkle dough with remaining cheese. Bake at 425° for 45 min. or until well puffed and golden brown.

Variation: Make hors d'oeuvre puffs by placing rounded separate tablespoons of dough on a cookie sheet and cook for a shorter time. Fill with creamed mixture of leftover meats or fowl.

Mrs. John M. Handley, Ridgewood

42

WHOLE WHEAT BREAD

Yield: 1 loaf

"It's so good with a cup of tea! Marvelous slightly toasted in the oven."

Easy   Freeze   Preparing: 10 min.
Baking: 1 hr. 30 min.

1 c. white flour
2 c. whole wheat flour
1/2 c. sugar
1 tsp. salt
1 tsp. soda
1-1/2 c. milk
1/2 c. molasses

Sift dry ingredients together. Combine liquid ingredients and blend with the dry ingredients. Mix with the electric mixer until well blended. Bake in a greased, 9x5 inch loaf pan at 325° for 1-1/2 hrs. Wrap in foil and store in the refrigerator so you may slice off pieces as needed.

Mrs. Pressly M. Millen, Jr., Ho-Ho-Kus

DATE AND NUT BREAD

Yield: 1 loaf

"A dark, moist, rich bread."

Easy   Freeze   Preparing: 30 min.
Baking: 1 hr. 10 min.

3/4 c. chopped walnuts
1 c. dates, cut up
1-1/2 tsp. baking soda
1/2 tsp. salt
3 tbsp. shortening
3/4 c. boiling water
2 eggs
1 tsp. vanilla
1 c. sugar
1-1/2 c. flour

Mix nuts, dates, soda and salt with a fork. Add shortening and water and let stand for about 20 min. Beat eggs with a fork and add vanilla, sugar and flour. Mix with date mixture until just blended. Pour into a greased 9x5 inch loaf pan and bake at 350° for 1 hr. to 1 hr. and 10 min., or until done. Cool in pan at least 10 min. before removing. Cool overnight before slicing.

Mrs. Arthur S. Whittemore, Jr., Ridgewood

NUT BREAD

Yield: 3 small loaves
or 2 large loaves

"A touch of almond gives this a distinctive flavor."

Easy   Freeze   Preparing: 10 min.
Baking: 45 min.

3 c. flour
1 tsp. salt
3 tsp. baking powder
1/2 c. sugar
1/4 c. shortening
1 tsp. almond flavoring
1 egg
1-1/4 c. milk
1 c. chopped walnuts

Sift together flour, salt and baking powder. Cream sugar, shortening and almond flavoring; then beat in egg. Add milk alternately with dry ingredients. Stir in nuts. Grease three 3x7 inch pans (or two larger ones). Bake at 325° for 45 min. Bread is done when golden brown on top and top cracks slightly.

Mrs. Joseph Sage, Ramsey

BROWN BREAD

Yield: 2 loaves

"A real Maine recipe."

Easy   Freeze   Preparing: 10 min.
                                                  Cooking: 1 hr. 15 min.

1 c. flour
1 c. All-Bran
1 c. quick rolled oats
1/2 c. molasses
1-1/2 c. buttermilk
2 tsp. soda
1 tbsp. sugar
dash of salt
optional -
    1/2 c. chopped walnuts
    1 c. raisins

Combine all ingredients and place in two well greased #303 cans (stewed tomato cans) or one 1 qt. mold. Fill to 1/4 inch of top. Cover with double thickness of wax paper and tie on with string. Put in the pressure cooker with 4 c. water around it. Steam for 20 min. without the indicator on. Then cook for 40 min. with the pressure set at 15 lbs. Cool at once. (This may be done by placing cans on a trivet in a heavy kettle with 1 inch water. Cover. Use high heat, then when steam escapes use low heat and steam for 1-1/2 to 2 hrs.)

Mrs. Charles J. Miller, Ramsey

BANANA BREAD

Yield: 1 2-lb. loaf or
       2 small loaves

"A great treat made from 'tired Chiquitas.'"

Easy   Freeze   Preparing: 15 min.
                                                  Baking: 1 hr.

3 large ripe bananas
1 egg, well beaten
1 c. sugar
3 tbsp. butter, melted
2 c. flour
1 tsp. soda
1 tsp. baking powder
1/2 tsp. salt

Mash bananas well and mix with beaten egg. Add sugar and mix thoroughly. Melt butter and add to the banana mixture. Sift together remaining dry ingredients and add to banana mixture. Bake in a greased 5x9 inch pan (2 lb loaf pan) or two smaller pans. Bake at 350° for 1 hr. If using smaller pans, bake for 40 min.

Mrs. Stanley R. Johnson, Ridgewood

CRANBERRY BREAD

Yield: 1 small loaf

"Great plain or spread with cream cheese."

Easy   Freeze   Preparing: 20 min.
                                                  Baking: 1 hr.

2 c. flour
1/2 tsp. salt
1/2 tsp. soda
1-1/2 tsp. baking powder
2 tbsp. butter
1 c. sugar
1 egg, beaten slightly
juice of 1 orange
grated rind of 1 orange
boiling water
1 c. whole cranberries
1/2 c. chopped walnuts

Sift all dry ingredients together. Dust cranberries and nuts with flour. Place juice rind of orange in a measuring cup and add boiling water to make 3/4 c. Blend butter and sugar until creamy, add slightly beaten egg, then orange juice mixture. Blend this with nuts and cranberries into dry ingredients. Place in a greased, small loaf pan and bake at 325° for 1 hr.

Mrs. Seymour Canter, Paterson

44

AUNT ADELE'S LEMON BREAD

Yield: 1 loaf

"As quick as a wink and you've made the best fruit-flavored tea bread!"

Easy   Freeze   Preparing: 15 min.
                                                  Baking: 1 hr.

1 c. sugar
5 tbsp. butter
2 eggs
grated rind of 1 lemon
1/2 c. milk
1/2 tsp. salt
1-1/2 c. flour
1 tsp. baking powder
optional -
  1/2 c. nuts, chopped fine

Glaze:
juice of 1 lemon
1/2 c. sugar

Blend butter and sugar until creamy. Beat in eggs. Add milk and mix well. Sift dry ingredients together, add to batter and beat until smooth. Add lemon rind and nuts. Place in a greased bread pan about 4x8 inches and bake at 350° for 1 hr. While bread is baking, mix the lemon juice and sugar for glaze until sugar is dissolved. Spoon glaze over <u>hot</u> bread before removing from pan. Continue to do so until bread has absorbed all of the glaze. This is especially good served with fruit salad.

Mrs. Graham B. Conklin, Ridgewood

ORANGE BREAD (Cake)

Yield: 1 loaf

"A pleasant change from dinner rolls, and so easy."

Easy   Freeze   Preparing: 10 min.
                                                  Baking: 45 min.

2 tbsp. butter
3/4 c. sugar
2 c. flour
2 tsp. baking powder
1 egg, beaten
juice of 1 orange
grated rind of 1 orange
milk (about 1/2 c.)

Cream butter and sugar. Sift flour and baking powder together. Put orange juice and rind into a measuring cup and add enough milk to make 3/4 c. total. Blend with all other ingredients. Place in a well greased loaf pan and bake at 375° for 45 min.

Variation: Add 1/2 c. fresh cranberries that have been cut in half. Especially nice at Christmastime.

This makes a delicious dessert served warm or cold with orange sauce or whipped cream.

Mrs. William J. F. Dailey, Jr., Ridgewood

CHEESE STICKS

Yield: 2 doz.

"These are a bit unusual as they start from the lowly hot dog bun."

Easy   Do ahead   Preparing: 15 min.
                                                  Baking: 6-8 min.

1/4 lb. butter or margarine
1/2 tsp. seasoned salt
  (I use Lawry's)
1/2 tsp. seasoned pepper
  (I use Lawry's)
1 c. grated Parmesan cheese
6 hot dog buns

Split buns in half and halve again. Soften butter and add salt, pepper and cheese. Spread this mixture on 2 sides of the rolls. Bake at 425° for 6-8 min. Excellent with salads.

Mrs. B. F. Martin, Grosse Pointe, Mich.

45

ICEBOX CINNAMON MUFFINS

Yield: 20 med. muffins

"Delicious as a hot bread with ham dinners or with coffee."

Easy   Do ahead   Preparing: 10 min.
                                              Baking: 25 min.

2 c. flour
2 tbsp. cinnamon
pinch of salt
4 tsp. baking powder
1 c. sugar
1 c. milk
1/2 c. butter, melted
2 eggs, beaten
1/2 c. nuts

Sift flour twice, then sift with cinnamon, salt and baking powder. Then add remaining ingredients and mix. Store in refrigerator or put in greased muffin pans and bake at 350° for 20-25 min. This may be stored in the refrigerator for a few days and the batter used cold from the refrigerator and baked immediately.

Mrs. Robert P. Viarengo, Ridgewood

BLUEBERRY MUFFINS DELUXE

Yield: 12

Easy   Do ahead   Preparing: 10 min.
                                              Baking: 20 min.

2 c. biscuit mix
1/4 c. sugar
1 egg, slightly beaten
1 c. milk
2 tbsp. salad oil
1/2 tsp. vanilla
1/2 c. wheat germ
1 c. blueberries (if frozen,
   defrost and drain)

Combine biscuit mix with wheat germ and sugar. Mix egg, milk, oil and vanilla. Add to dry ingredients and blend well. Fold in blueberries. Fill greased muffin pans 2/3 full. Bake at 400° for about 20 min.

Mrs. Joseph L. Baker, Ridgewood

EASY BREAKFAST MUFFINS

Yield: 8 muffins

"A snap to make and so special on a Sunday morning."

Easy   Freeze   Preparing: 10 min.
                                              Baking: 20 min.

1 c. flour
1/3 c. sugar
pinch of salt
1 tsp. baking powder
1 egg
1/2 c. milk
2 tbsp. butter

Melt butter and add to beaten egg and milk. Mix or sift dry ingredients together and add to egg-milk mixture. Stir and mix well. Pour into well greased or teflon muffin pans. Bake at 400° for 20 min. Dates, blueberries, nuts may be added for a change.

Mrs. F. Marsena Butts, Lincoln, Massachusetts

UNFAILING POPOVERS

Yield: 1 doz.

"Perfect for the quick and easy Sunday breakfast."

Easy   Do not freeze   Preparing: 5 min.
                                               Baking: 30 min.

1 c. flour
1 c. cold milk
2 eggs
1/2 tsp. salt

Mix flour and salt and sift over beaten eggs. Add milk all at once. Beat with a rotary beater until batter is without lumps. Fill greased gem pans or Pyrex cups (not necessary to grease the Pyrex) to 2/3 full. Place in cold oven. Bake at 450° for about 30 min. or until popovers are light brown.

Mrs. Martin Doviak, Glen Rock

SOUR CREAM COFFEE CAKE

Serves: 16

"Delicious! Sometimes called 'heaven food.'"

Easy   Freeze   Preparing: 15 min.
                                               Baking: 45 min.

1/4 lb. butter
1 c. sugar
2 eggs
1 c. sour cream
1 tsp. baking soda
1-1/2 c. flour
1-1/2 tsp. baking powder
1 tsp. vanilla

Topping:
1/4 c. sugar
2 tbsp. chopped nuts
  (filberts, almonds or walnuts)
1 tbsp. cinnamon

Cream butter and sugar. Add eggs, then sour cream which has been mixed with soda. Blend well. Add flour and baking powder. Blend in vanilla. Pour one half of mixture into a greased, 9 inch square or tube pan. Sprinkle one half of topping over it. Pour in rest of mixture and sprinkle with remaining topping. Bake at 350° for 45 min. Serve warm for tea or Sunday breakfast. (The topping can also be made with brown sugar.)

Mrs. Michael Zuber, Wayne

HAYES CRUMB CAKE

Serves: 10-12

"Quick and easy one-bowl cooking!"

Easy   Freeze   Preparing: 5-10 min.
                                               Baking: 30 min.

2 c. flour
2 c. brown sugar
1/2 c. margarine
1 egg
1 c. sour milk
1 tsp. vanilla
1 tsp. baking soda
1/2 tsp. baking powder
1/2 tsp. salt
1/4 c. nuts
optional - raisins

Sift flour and brown sugar together. Cut in cold margarine with two knives until it is like coarse corn meal (like mixing biscuits). Keep 1/2 c. of mixture aside. Make a well in the remaining mixture and add remaining ingredients. Blend together and add raisins if desired. Pour into an 11x13 inch greased pan. Cover with reserved crumb mixture and nuts. Bake at 375° for 30 min. Best served warm.

Mrs. Richard D. Major, Allendale

COFFEE PASTRY

Yield: 2 coffee rings

"A delicious cake variation of cream puff pastry. Simple and fast."

Easy   Freeze   Preparing: 10 min.
                                          Baking: 35 min.

1/2 c. shortening
1/8 tsp. salt
1/2 c. boiling water
1 c. flour
4 eggs

Glaze:
1 c. confectioners' sugar
small amount of water

Add shortening and salt to boiling water. Bring to a boil again.. Reduce heat; add flour all at once and stir vigorously until ball forms around the spoon, leaving the pan clean. Remove from heat; add eggs, one at a time, beating thoroughly after each addition. Continue beating until mixture is thick and shiny and breaks from spoon. Shape into a horseshoe, circle or figure-eight cake by dropping by spoonfuls onto an ungreased cookie sheet. Make two rings. Bake at 450° for 15 min. Reduce heat to 350° and bake 20 min. more. When cool, brush lightly with glaze of confectioners' sugar and water.

Mrs. Robert C. Nienaber, Ridgewood

MOCK STRUDEL

Yield: 4 doz.

"Delicious with coffee or tea."

Complicated   Freeze   Preparing: 15 min.
                                          Rising: overnight
                                          Baking: 55 min.

1/4 lb. butter
1/4 lb. margarine
2 c. unsifted flour
1/2 pt. sour cream

Jelly Mixture:
1/2 jar pineapple preserves
1/2 jar apricot preserves
1/2 jar orange marmalade
  (or other flavors)

Dry Mixture:
3/4 c. bread crumbs
juice of 1/2 lemon
1/2 c. sugar
1 c. chopped nuts
cinnamon

confectioners' sugar

Mix butter, margarine, flour and sour cream well with hands. It will be very sticky. Divide into four pieces and wrap in wax paper and refrigerate overnight. Next day roll each piece out thin on a floured board. Spread with jellies that have been mixed together. Mix the remaining ingredients together and sprinkle over the jelly mixture. Roll up like a jelly roll and slice almost through in pieces sliced about one inch apart. Bake on a greased cookie sheet at 375° for 45 min. Sprinkle with confectioners' sugar 5-10 min. after removing from oven. Separate pieces and serve. If this is to be frozen, do so prior to baking.

Mrs. Charles Chotiner, Fair Lawn

BUTTERSCOTCH CURLS

Yield: 1 to 1-1/2 doz.

"Delicious for afternoon tea or for breakfast."

Easy   Freeze   Preparing: 15 min.
                                                  Baking: 25 min.

2 c. flour
1/4 c. sugar
1/2 tsp. salt
2-1/2 tsp. baking powder
3 tbsp. shortening
1/3 c. milk
1/4 lb. margarine
1-1/2 c. dark brown sugar
cinnamon

Mix flour, sugar, salt and baking powder. Cut in shortening and add milk (a bit more may be necessary). Make a tight dough. Roll dough out to 1/4 inch thick and pour margarine, which has been melted and cooled, over the dough. Cover with brown sugar and sprinkle with cinnamon. Roll up like a jelly roll and cut into 12 pieces (18 if making tea cakes) and put into cup cake tins. Bake at 375° for 20-25 min. or until brown. Turn out onto cooling rack. These will stay fresh for several days if kept in a plastic bag.

Mrs. Jake Schornagel, Paterson

APRICOT SQUARES

Yield: 2 doz.

"Elegant, sweet fruit bars. So good for a fancy coffee."

Average   Freeze   Preparing: 20 min.
                                                  Baking: 55 min.

1/2 c. butter
1/4 c. sugar
1 c. sifted flour

1/3 c. sifted flour
1/2 tsp. baking powder
1/4 tsp. salt
1 c. light brown sugar
2 eggs, beaten
1/2 tsp. vanilla
1/2 c. chopped nuts
1/2 c. dry apricots
confectioners' sugar

Snip apricots into small pieces with scissors into a saucepan with a little water. Steam for a short time until soft but not sloppy. Mix first three ingredients until crumbly. Pack into a greased, 8 inch square pan and bake at 350° for 25 min. Beat brown sugar and eggs. Add remaining dry ingredients and mix well. Blend in vanilla, nuts and apricots. Spread over the baked layer. Bake again for 30 min. Cool. Cut into small bars, dipping the knife in ice water as you do so. Roll in confectioners' sugar.

Mrs. Carl D. Nelke, Ridgewood

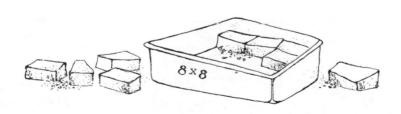

RAISIN HARVEST COFFEE CAKE

Serves: 16

"Great for a brunch or when the girls are coming for coffee."

Easy   Freeze

Preparing: 15 min.
Baking: 1 hr.

1-1/2 c. sifted flour
3-3/4 tsp. baking powder
1/2 tsp. salt
3/4 c. sugar
3/4 c. butter
2 c. peeled cooking apples,
  chopped fine
1-1/2 c. dark seedless raisins
2 large eggs
1 tbsp. milk
sugar for topping

Resift flour with baking powder, salt and sugar into a mixing bowl. Add butter and mix until mixture is like fine bread crumbs. Stir in apples and raisins and add well bea- eggs and milk. Beat thoroughly. Batter wi be stiff. Spread in a well greased, 9 inch square pan and sprinkle <u>generously</u> with suga Bake at 350° for 55-60 min. Allow to cool slightly before cutting and serve warm.

Mrs. R. J. Van Gytenbeek, Saddle River

WAFFLES

Serves: 4-6

"Ideal breakfast, lunch or dessert fare."

Easy   Freeze

Preparing: 10 min.
Cooking: 5 min.

1-3/4 c. sifted flour
  (all purpose)
3 tsp. baking powder
1 tsp. salt
2 eggs, separated
1-1/4 c. milk
1/2 c. oil or melted
  shortening
optional - 1 c. blueberries

Beat egg whites stiff and set aside. Sift together dry ingredients. Combine beaten egg yolks and milk. Stir into dry ingredients. Stir in oil or shortening. Fold in egg white Do not overmix. Bake in a waffle iron. If using berries, fold in at the very end. Serv with maple syrup, confectioners' sugar or hon and butter.

<u>For dessert</u>: Top with fresh strawberries and ice cream or whipped cream.

<u>For lunch</u>: Serve with creamed chicken or chipped beef on top.

Mrs. A. Steffee Smith, Ridgewood

50

ANCAKES (Blueberry or Apple)

Serves: 4

asy   Part do ahead   Preparing: 5 min.
Cooking: 5 min.

-1/2 c. flour
-1/2 tsp. baking powder
 tbsp. sugar
/4 tsp. salt
 eggs
-1/4 c. milk
 tbsp. melted shortening
ptional -
 1 can blueberries
   (or 1 c. fresh) or
 1 c. grated apples

Mix ingredients in order and cook in a
hot frying pan which has been well greased.
To add blueberries, drain juice from can and
add to batter. This mixture of dry ingredients may be premixed and stored in a glass
jar. Add eggs, milk and shortening when
ready to serve.

Mrs. Robert E. Taylor, Ridgewood

RMAN EGG PANCAKES

Serves: 4-6

"Delicious and much easier and faster than they sound."

sy   Serve immediately   Preparing: 10 min.
Cooking: 10 min.

c. flour
4 c. milk
 egg
sh of salt
tional -
diced ham or
precooked bacon

pping:
can sliced peaches

Mix all ingredients together to form a
batter of pancake consistency, adding more
milk if necessary. Pour batter into a large
9 or 10 inch greased and hot skillet so as
to cover the entire bottom of the pan to a
depth of about 1/8 inch. Fry until brown on
the bottom and edges curl. You may want to
make slits in the bottom to let the uncooked
batter reach the pan. Turn over using two
spatulas and cook on the other side. Remove
from the pan to a plate and keep warm in the
oven while cooking more pancakes. This
recipe will make 2 or 3 large cakes. Stack
the pancakes 2 or 3 high and serve by cutting
pie-fashion. Serve with canned sliced peaches
and syrup over them.

Mrs. Robert C. Nienaber, Ridgewood

Bread Bonanzas

To make bread crusty, brush top and sides with an egg white diluted with
   1 tbsp. water 5 min. before end of baking. Cool loaves in a draft or
   before an open window.

Press large rounds of fresh bread into muffin tins and brown in the oven
   for nice bread cups.

* For nice bread fingers, slice hot dog rolls in half crosswise, then in
   quarters lengthwise. Butter with herb butter, garlic butter, etc.,
   and brown in the oven.

* For delicious breakfast rolls, take refrigerator crescent rolls and roll
   with a preserve or jam or small fruit such as prune, cherry, or
   apricot. Bake as directed on the package.

If you heat bakery rolls at 175° for 20-30 min. instead of a faster oven,
   they can be reheated again without becoming hard.

Knead pastry with the heel of the hand, always - it is the coolest part of
   the hand.

To make lighter muffins, put greased pans into the oven for a few moments
   before pouring in batter.

A bit of sugar in the batter of pancakes or waffles will make them brown
   more quickly.

Combine maple syrup and butter and heat for pancakes and waffles.

To keep raisins from sinking to the bottom when baking, put them into your
   flour sifter; sift the flour and they'll remain, well coated.

Raisins that have become too dry can be puffed again by washing and placing
   in a covered dish in a 350° oven until they puff out.

* To zip up French bread, combine 1/4 lb. soft butter with 1 pkg. onion soup
   mix. Mix well and spread on bread.

* Try melting 1 stick of butter and adding 1/4 tsp. thyme, 1/4 tsp. oregano,
   1/4 tsp. basil and a minced garlic bud. Simmer for 20-30 min. and cover
   two loaves of French bread. Everyone loves it!

When using frozen berries in breads and pancakes, etc., only partially defrost.
   They will not bleed in cooking. You may need to cook a bit longer.

Cheese and Eggs

Y RAREBIT   Serves: 4

delicious, easy luncheon dish."

y   Do ahead   Preparing: 10 min.

b. sharp cheese   Grate cheese and add salt, mustard and
tsp. salt to taste   Worcestershire. Place over medium heat and
sp. dry mustard   slowly add evaporated milk while stirring.
sp. Worcestershire sauce   (Add more milk if you want a thinner rarebit.)
arge can evaporated milk   Place a slice of ham on each toast square then
lices cooked ham   pour rarebit over this. Top with paprika and
lices toast   a slice of tomato. Thicken with flour if
lices tomato   desired.
rika
ional - flour   *Mrs. Robert A. Don, Ridgewood*

EBIT   Serves: 4

is can easily be reheated."

y   Do ahead   Preparing: 25 min.

bsp. butter   In top of double boiler melt butter and
bsp. flour   blend in flour. Cook 5 min. Gradually
. milk   add milk. Dissolve bouillon in water and
. hot water   add. Then add mustard, Worcestershire
ouillon cube   and grated cheese. Stir and cook until
sp. dry mustard   thickened (15-20 min.). Keep hot in covered
sp. Worcestershire sauce   double boiler or reheat. Do not freeze.
 lb. sharp Cheddar cheese
                             Mrs. Warren D. Haggerty, Jr., Ridgewood

CHE LORRAINE   Serves: 6

opping on floor is the only danger. Absolutely infallible otherwise."

y   Freeze   Preparing: 30 min.
                                                   Baking: 45 min.

pie shell, uncooked   Bake pie shell at 400° for 10 min. Fry bacon
lices bacon   until crisp and drain. Saute onions. Overlap
thin slices Swiss cheese   bacon and cheese to cover bottom of the crust.
ggs, lightly beaten   Add onion. In a separate bowl combine eggs,
. heavy cream   cream, milk, flour with a pinch of nutmeg, a few
. whole milk   grains of cayenne and black pepper. If preparing
bsp. flour   ahead, but not freezing, stop here and let shell and
und nutmeg   custard mixture stand at room temperature. Do not
enne pepper   refrigerate. Immediately before cooking, pour
ck pepper   custard mixture over bacon and cheese. Bake at 400°
bsp. diced onion   for 15 min. and at 325° for 30 min. If freezing,
                            prepare fully and bake before freezing. Reheat,
                            frozen, at 350° for 30 min.

                                 Ed. Note: Mr. Edwin F. Berhardt suggests
                            as alternate, using 5 eggs and 1/4 c. Roquefort
                            cheese in place of Swiss cheese.

                             Mrs. Ernest R. L. Zellweger, Saddle River

ONION CHEESE PIE

Serves: 6-8

Average   Mostly do ahead   Preparing: 15 min.
                                          Baking: 40-45 min.

2 9" unbaked pie shells
  (frozen are fine)
1 c. sliced onions
2 tbsp. butter
3 eggs
1-1/2 c. milk
1 tsp. salt
pepper
1/2 tsp. basil
2 c. grated Cheddar cheese

Saute onion in butter. Beat eggs and add milk, salt, pepper, basil and onions. Divide cheese in half and spread evenly in bottom of each pie crust. Pour milk mixture over cheese in both pies. Bake at 400° for 40-45 min. Allow to set 5 min. before serving.

Mrs. Samuel A. Everitt, Mahwah

NEVER-FAIL SOUFFLE

Serves: 4-6

"A light, easy and nourishing luncheon main dish."

Easy   Part do ahead   Preparing: 20 min.
                                     Baking: 50-60 min.

1/4 c. prepared biscuit mix
  (I use Bisquick)
1/2 tsp. dry mustard
1 c. milk
1 c. grated cheese
  (American or Cheddar)
3 eggs, separated
1/4 tsp. cream of tartar

Preheat oven to 350°. Mix biscuit mix and mustard in saucepan. Add a small amount of milk to make a paste, then add remaining milk gradually. Bring to a boil and boil 1 min., stirring constantly. Add cheese and remove from heat. Do ahead to this point, if desired. Stir into slightly beaten egg yolks. Beat whites with cream of tartar until stiff enough to hold soft peaks, then fold into cheese mixture. Bake in an ungreased 1-1/2 qt. baking dish set in a pan of hot water. Bake for 50-60 min. until a silver knife inserted near the center comes out clean.

Mrs. Joseph Sage, Ramsey

MOCK CHEESE SOUFFLE

Serves: 4-6

"If you get flustered getting a souffle to the table, try this one."

Easy   Do ahead   Preparing: 30 min.
                                Refrigerating: overnight
                                Baking: 45 min.

6 slices bread, cubed
1/2 lb. sharp Cheddar cheese,
  grated
6 eggs
2 c. milk
1 tsp. dry mustard
1/2 tsp. salt
2 tbsp. melted butter

Bake bread cubes in a 250° oven for 20 min. Meanwhile, grease a 2 qt. casserole. Arrange bread and cheese in layers. Beat eggs and add milk, mustard and salt; pour mixture over bread and cheese. Drizzle melted butter over all. Refrigerate, covered, overnight. Uncover and bake at 400° for 45 min. or until done. Be sure to bake in a pan of hot water.

Mrs. Walter J. Hood, Ridgewood

SWISS FONDUE

Serves: 1

Multiply as needed.

Average   Part do ahead   Preparing: 10 min.

6-7 oz. Swiss cheese, grated
  (Ideally half Emmental,
  half Gruyere)
6-8 oz. white bread, cubed
1/3 c. dry white wine
1 tsp. lemon juice

Per fondue:
1 clove garlic
2 tsp. corn flour
  (I use Argo)
1-2 oz. kirsch
  (See No. 4 below)
spices per taste -
  pepper
  paprika
  nutmeg

Rub inside of heavy iron pot or "caguelon" with garlic. Pour in wine mixed with lemon juice. Put on high heat on stove. As soon as mixture is hot add cheese, stirring constantly. When this starts to cook add corn flour diluted with kirsch. Let cook 2-3 min. Fondue is now ready. Transfer to a chafing dish and place on table or bring caguelon to the table. Season as desired.

Fondue Gruyere: Use Swiss Gruyere in place of Swiss - a slightly sharper fondue.

Appenzeller Fondue: Try half Appenzeller and half Swiss.

Mr. Edwin F. Bernhardt, Cheese Shop, Ridgewood

TIPS ON FONDUE

1. Use well aged cheese. If you use an immature cheese result will be stringy and gummy.

2. No special pots are needed, but start on the stove and transfer to a preheated chafing dish.

3. Serve with tossed salad with a tart or sweet dressing.

4. If you do not have kirsch, you may use a light rum, cognac, applejack or a dry white wine.

TIME SAVING TIPS

1. Shred cheese ahead and store in Saran wrap in refrigerator.

2. Cut bread cubes ahead. Wrap and keep fresh.

3. Add cheese by handfuls, stirring constantly with a wooden spoon.

FONDUE CUSTOMS

If bread falls off the fork into fondue, ladies must pay with a kiss to the nearest man; men must pay for the next round of wine.

Mr. Edwin F. Bernhardt, Cheese Shop, Ridgewood

CHEESE FONDUE JANIE

Serves: 8

Easy   Do ahead

Preparing: 15 min.
Chilling: overnight
Baking: 1 hr.

8 slices stale bread
1-1/2 lbs. sharp Cheddar
  cheese, grated
6 eggs beaten slightly
2-1/2 c. half and half
1 rounded tsp. brown sugar
1/4 tsp. paprika
1 onion, finely minced
1/2 tsp. dry mustard
1/2 tsp. seasoning salt
  (I use Beau Monde)
1/2 tsp. salt
1/8 tsp. pepper
1/2 tsp. Worcestershire sauce
1/6 tsp. cayenne

Slice bread medium thick; cut off crusts. Butter bread generously and dice about 1/4 inch square. Butter large, flat casserole. Arrange diced bread on the bottom, put in generous layer of grated cheese over bread, then another layer of bread squares. Put remaining cheese on top of second layer of bread. Beat eggs, add dry ingredients, milk and cream. Pour over cheese and bread. Let set overnight in refrigerator. Take out two hours before serving time. Let stand 1/2 hr. Set in shallow pan in which a flat bag has been placed. Cover with 1/2 inch cold water. Bake at 300° for about 1 hr. Let stand 20 min. before serving.

Mrs. Charles R. Herman, Ridgewood

EGGS MORNAY

Serves: 6

"This is great with hot biscuits and bacon or ham."

Easy   Serve immediately

Preparing: 15 min.
Baking: 30 min.

8 hard cooked eggs, halved
4 tbsp. butter
4 tbsp. flour
1-1/2 c. milk
1/2 c. heavy cream
salt
fresh ground black pepper
nutmeg
3/4 c. grated Gruyere cheese
1/3 c. grated Parmesan cheese

Preheat oven to 450°. Arrange eggs, cut side down, in a buttered baking dish. Melt butter; blend in flour, then milk, using a wire whisk. Add cream and seasonings. Add Gruyere cheese and pour sauce over eggs. Sprinkle with Parmesan cheese. Bake until brown on the top (20-30 min.).

Mrs. William T. Knight, III, Saddle River

EGGS OH-LA-LA

Serves: 4

"Scrambled eggs with a different flavor."

Easy   Serve immediately

Preparing: 5 min.
Cooking: 5 min.

4 eggs, separated
1/4 c. milk
1 tbsp. fresh chives
dash seasoned salt
1/2 tsp. salt
1/8 tsp. pepper
1/2 can mushroom soup

Beat egg yolks slightly and mix with other ingredients, except the whites. Beat whites stiff and fold into first mixture. Cook over low heat, stirring until firm.

Mrs. Joseph L. Baker, Ridgewood

SWISS EGGS

Serves: 6

"Good supper or luncheon dish."

Average   Serve immediately   Preparing: 10 min.
Baking: 30 min.

1/4 lb. Swiss cheese
2 tbsp. butter
1/2 c. cream
1/4 tsp. salt
dash pepper
1 tsp. mustard or curry
6 eggs, beaten slightly

Sliver cheese and spread over bottom of a buttered 2 qt. casserole. Dot with butter. Mix cream with seasonings and mustard (or curry). Pour half over the cheese. Add slightly beaten eggs. Add remaining half of cream mixture. Bake at 325° for 30 min. or until eggs are set.

Mrs. Theodore R. Wolf, Ridgewood

EGGS DIVAN

Serves: 4-5

"The perfect brunch dish."

Easy   Part do ahead   Preparing: 20 min.
Baking: 25 min.

1 pkg. frozen broccoli spears
6 hard cooked eggs
1 small can deviled ham
1/4 tsp. Worcestershire sauce
1/2 tsp. grated onion
1/2 tsp. salt
1/2 tsp. dry mustard
1 tbsp. milk

Sauce:
2 tbsp. flour
1-1/2 tbsp. butter, melted
1/2 tsp. dry mustard
1/2 tsp. salt
1 c. milk
1 c. grated sharp cheese
buttered bread crumbs

Cook broccoli as directed on package. Slice eggs lengthwise and remove yolks. Mash yolks and add deviled ham, Worcestershire sauce, onion, salt, mustard and milk. Mix well and fill egg whites. Place broccoli in a buttered 8x8 inch dish. Place eggs on top.

Sauce: Blend flour, butter and seasonings; add milk and cheese. Heat until thick and smooth, stirring constantly. Pour over eggs and top with bread crumbs. Bake at 350° for 25 min.

Mrs. Harry N. Ives, Ridgewood

Cheese and Egg Enlightenments

Add 1 tsp. of salt to water to keep egg white from escaping a cracked shell when being boiled.

A little vinegar in the water prevents the white of a poached egg from spreading.

Grease teflon pan with Crisco before putting water into pan to poach eggs – eggs will not stick.

Freeze leftover egg whites in the ice cube tray, one per cube, and keep stored in a plastic bag in the freezer.

For perfect hard-cooked eggs, have eggs at room temperature or place under warm running water for a few minutes. Carefully place in barely simmering, salted water and simmer slowly for exactly 12 minutes. Constantly roll the eggs for the first 1 to 1-1/2 min. to center the yolks. Never boil violently. Immediately submerge in cold water. To peel, crack the large end (air pocket is usually there) and peel with wet hands or under running water. Yolks will be clear yellow. Dark edges come from overcooking and not cooling eggs immediately.

For hard cooked eggs the easy way, place eggs in cold water to cover, bring to a boil, cover tightly, turn off heat and leave eggs at least 15 min., all day if you like.

To tell a hard-cooked egg from an uncooked one, spin the eggs on their sides. The hard-cooked egg will spin like a top while the uncooked one will wobble and not spin.

Use an electric hand beater at 45° angle when beating egg whites or yolks. This will give you much greater volume.

Egg is considered beaten when no lumps fall from the fork yet it is not frothy. This takes about 20 strokes with a fork.

When beating egg yolks and sugar, blend until mixture falls from the beater in a ribbon which does not re-incorporate into the mixture in a few seconds.

* Serve scrambled eggs on fried tomato slices with hot canned mushroom soup as a sauce.

* For a delicious variety to scrambled eggs, cut fresh 1/2 inch cubes of bread and fry in lots of butter until brown, add eggs and scramble all together.

* A good way to use up those colored Easter eggs is to make creamed eggs. Put sliced eggs into a cream sauce and serve over toast which has been topped with deviled ham with a bit of grated onion added. A delicious supper dish.

When grating cheese, place measuring cup over a sheet of wax paper; any scraps can easily be picked up and placed in the cup.

To slice mozzarella cheese easily, cut with a knife you keep putting under very hot running water.

Meats

ROAST BEEF A LA MODE

Serves: 8

"Beef and potatoes all in one with an unusual, delicious sauce."

Average   Part do ahead   Preparing: 15 min.
                                            Simmering: 15 min.
                                            Roasting: 1-1/2 to 2 hrs.

4 lb. center-cut roast beef
  (oven type)
3 9-oz. pkgs. frozen French
  fried potatoes

Sauce:
3 tbsp. salad oil
1/2 c. chopped onion
1 clove garlic, chopped
8 oz. can tomato sauce
1-1/4 tsp. salt
1/4 c. catsup
2 tbsp. red vinegar
1/4 c. Burgundy wine
1 tbsp. Worcestershire sauce
1 tsp. chili powder
1/2 tsp. dry mustard
2 tbsp. water

Roast beef in 325° oven according to your favorite method. Meanwhile, make the sauce.

Sauce: In a small saucepan saute onion and garlic in oil until quite tender, about 5 min. Add tomato sauce, 1/2 tsp. salt and remaining sauce ingredients. Mix well. Bring to a boil and simmer, uncovered, about 15 min. About 45 min. before roast is done, add potatoes to the roasting pan and sprinkle potatoes with 3/4 tsp. salt. Drizzle 3/4 c. sauce over potatoes and toss to coat them. Brush remaining sauce over the roast and baste frequently with sauce until meat is done.

Mrs. James W. Allred, Ridgewood

63

ROAST BEEF RARE

Serves: 8

"Very easy and very good."

Easy   Do ahead   Preparing: 10 min.
Baking: 2-3/4 hrs. plus
1/2 hr. heating

3 rib roast beef

Bring rib roast to room temperature. Preheat oven to 450°. Place beef in an uncovered pan without water or salt. Cook 45 min. without opening door. Turn off heat and leave beef in oven with door closed for 2 hrs. Serve immediately if desired; or, retain meat at room temperature. To serve, place in a preheated 350° oven for 1/2 hr. Season before or after warming period.

Mrs. Austin Boyd, Jr., Ridgewood

BEEF FONDUE

Serves: 4-6

"Great on a cold, snowy night or after a day of skiing."

Easy   Do ahead   Preparing: 1 hr.

salad oil
1-1/2 lbs. beef tenderloin

Garlic Butter Sauce:
1/2 c. butter
1 clove garlic

Anchovy Butter Sauce:
2 tbsp. olive oil
1/2 tsp. paprika
1/8 tsp. pepper
1 2-oz. can anchovy fillets
1/2 c. butter

Caper Sauce:
1/4 c. drained sour pickles,
  chopped
2 tbsp. capers, chopped and
  drained
1 c. mayonnaise
1-1/2 tsp. prepared mustard
1-1/2 tsp. parsley, snipped

Tomato Sauce:
1 8-oz. can tomato sauce
1/3 c. bottled steak sauce
2 tbsp. brown sugar
2 tbsp. salad oil

Horseradish Cream:
1 c. sour cream
3 tbsp. drained horseradish
dash paprika
1/4 tsp. salt

Have meat trimmed and cut in 3/4 inch cubes. Pour salad oil (or half butter and half oil) into a fondue cooker or deep chafing dish to depth of 1-1/2 inches. Place on range and bring to 425°. Take to table. Place over alcohol burner or sterno. Set out bowls of several sauces. Each guest spears and dips own meat until desired doneness; then into sauces.

Garlic Butter: Whip butter with crushed garlic clove until fluffy.

Anchovy Butter: Drain anchovies. Mix all ingredients until smooth.

Caper Sauce: Mix all ingredients.

Tomato Sauce: Mix all ingredients and bring to a boil. Serve hot.

Horseradish Cream: Mix all ingredients together and chill.

Mrs. Peter H. Zecher, Ho-Ho-Kus

64

POT ROAST

Serves: 8-10

"My family's favorite. It improves with freezing."

Easy   Freeze   Preparing: 30 min.
                                                  Cooking: 2 hrs.

4-5 lb. brisket of beef
6 onions, sliced
4 bay leaves
1/2 c. catsup
1 tbsp. Worcestershire sauce
1 clove garlic
seasoned salt
  (I use Lawry's)
black pepper

Rub brisket thoroughly with garlic and season generously with seasoned salt and freshly ground pepper. Meanwhile, preheat heavy pot (Dutch oven). When drop of water bubbles, place meat in pot and sear until very brown. Turn often. When meat is brown (about 15-20 min.) add sliced onion, bay leaves, catsup and Worcestershire. Cover tightly and cook on low heat for 2 hrs. or until meat is tender. Remove meat from gravy. If desired, put all liquid, onion and bay leaves in the blender at high speed for a rich, thick, non-fattening onion gravy. Slice meat on serving platter, cover with gravy and serve. To reheat, place in a shallow baking dish, cover with foil and bake at 350° for 15 min.

Mrs. David Rukin, Saddle River

FOIL BRISKET

Serves: 8

"An easy, delicious meal dish - and no roaster to clean!"

Easy   Do ahead   Preparing: 15 min.
                                                  Baking: 3 hrs.

3 lb. fresh brisket of beef,
  straight cut
2 tbsp. butter
1 pkg. onion soup mix
  (I use Lipton)
1/2 lb. fresh mushrooms
  (or frozen)

On a large sheet of heavy aluminum foil dab half the butter. Sprinkle half the dry soup mix. Trim fat from meat and place meat on mix. Dab top of brisket with remaining butter and sprinkle with the rest of the mix. Surround meat with sliced mushrooms. Wrap foil around meat so it is closed in snuggly and subsequent juices will not escape. Place in shallow pan in 350° oven and cook for 3 hrs. Open carefully; there will be lots of gravy!

For variation: About 1-1/2 hrs. before end of cooking time, add peeled potatoes, carrots cut into large pieces, and onions. Add more water and soup mix if more gravy is desired. Reseal. The whole dinner is done at once with vegetables cooked in a delicious gravy.

Mrs. Paul L. Hensel, Ridgewood

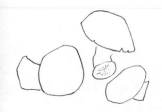

SAUERBRATEN

"Wonderful served with potato pancakes and red cabbage or a salad."

Long, but worth it   Do ahead   Preparing: 1 hr., plus
                                               Marinating: 3 days
                                               Cooking: 3-1/2 hrs.

1-5 lb. pot roast

Marinade:
1 qt. water
1 qt. cider vinegar
1 onion, sliced
3 bay leaves
1 tsp. peppercorns
1/4 c. sugar

Sauce:
1/4 c. sugar
1/4 c. white vinegar
4-6 gingersnaps
1 c. sour cream

Bring water and cider vinegar to a boil. Add onion, bay leaves, peppercorns and sugar. Add meat. Let this cool and put into refrigerator, covered, for three days so it is well marinated.

To cook: Put meat in a Dutch oven and place in a preheated 450° oven for 20 min. Add 1 c. marinade and cover the meat. Bake at 300° for 3 hrs. Add more marinade if necessary. Turn meat occasionally.

Sauce: Caramelize sugar by putting into a saucepan with white vinegar and cooking slowly. The vinegar will dissipate and the sugar will slowly caramelize. Stir constantly Crush ginger snaps. In a large skillet put caramelized sugar and add about one cup of marinade gradually. Then add gingersnaps and blend in. Cook until thick and smooth. Add sour cream. When hot, serve on meat. Add more marinade if the sauce is too thick.

Mrs. Robert R. Deutsch, Mahwah

STUFFED BEEF TENDERLOIN

Serves: 6-8

"For the special dinner! Worth the extra time it takes."

Average   Do ahead   Preparing: 45 min.
                                                Baking: 1 hr.

1/4 c. butter
1 medium onion, chopped
1/2 c. diced celery
1 4-oz. can sliced mushrooms,
  drained well
2 c. soft bread crumbs
1 tsp. salt
1/8 tsp. black pepper
1/2 tsp. basil leaves
1/8 tsp. parsley flakes
3 lbs. beef tenderloin,
  trimmed
4 slices bacon

Melt butter in a small skillet over low heat. Add onion, celery and mushrooms and saute until onion is soft and transparent - about 10 min. Place bread crumbs in a 1 qt. bowl. Add salt, pepper, basil leaves and parsley flakes, melted butter and onion mixture. Lightly mix until well blended. Make a lengthwise cut three-quarters of the way through the tenderloin. Place the stuffing lightly in the pocket formed by the cut. Close the pocket by fastening meat together with wooden toothpicks. Place bacon strips diagonally across the top, covering the picks and the pocket. Place stuffed meat in a 3 qt oblong glass dish or pan. Bake, uncovered, i a 350° oven for one hour (medium rare). Serv with broiled tomatoes and broccoli.

Mrs. Charles W. Allen, Ridgewood

BEEF FILETS IN RED WINE SAUCE

Serves: 4

"Perfect when you want to prepare a last-minute gourmet dish."

Easy   Serve immediately   Preparing: 5 min.
                                          Cooking: 10 min.

4 small individual steaks,
  1" thick*
4 tbsp. butter
1 med. onion, chopped fine
3/4 c. red wine

Put 2 tbsp. butter into each of two heavy skillets large enough to hold all steaks in a single layer. Heat butter to the bubbly stage and saute steaks for 3-4 min. Turn the steaks and saute the other side for 3-4 min. longer (for medium rare; longer for more well done). Remove steaks to a warm platter. Saute onion in the same pan juices until tender (about 1 min.). Pour in the wine and boil it down quickly, scraping the juices from the bottom of the pan. Cook until sauce is quite thick. Pour over steak and serve immediately.

*Use club, small sirloin, rib or any lean, tender steaks.

Mrs. Henry Pildner, Jr., Greenwich, Conn.

BAKED STEAK

Serves: 4

"A different way of cooking steak."

Easy   No need to do ahead   Preparing: 10 min.
                                           Baking: 45 min. minimum

1 4-lb. sirloin or porter-
  house steak 2" thick
1 large lemon
catsup
2 tbsp. Worcestershire sauce
1 medium onion, sliced

Place steak in an uncovered baking pan. Salt and pepper both sides. Cut lemon into 1/4 inch slices and spread over the top. Squeeze the juice of the lemon ends over the top. Spoon catsup over the steak. Sprinkle Worcestershire over steak. Slice onion and place on steak. Bake at 350° for 45 min. for rare steak - longer for well done - and baste. Slice vertically.

Mrs. Peter H. Zecher, Ho-Ho-Kus

MARINATED FLANK STEAK

Serves: 4

"Completely delicious and so easy!"

Easy   Do ahead   Preparing: 5 min.
                                Marinating: 4 hrs.
                                Cooking: 8 min.

1 flank steak, 1-1/2 to 2 lbs.
1/2 bottle soy sauce
  (5-6 oz. bottle)
2 tbsp. brown sugar
1/2 tsp. ground ginger
1/2 tsp. dry mustard
pinch onion powder

Mix ingredients; pour over flank steak and marinate about 4 hrs. Take from marinade and broil 4 min. on each side. Slice diagonally into thin slices. Marinade may be stored in refrigerator for future use.

Mrs. T. W. Bartram, Ramsey

MARINATED LONDON BROIL

Serves: 8

"Wonderful for a summer party. Men love to cook and eat it!"

Easy   Do not do ahead   Marinating: 30 min.
                                                 Cooking: 20-30 min.

1 4-lb. beef round,
   London broil cut
1 pkg. bleu cheese salad
   dressing mix
   (I use Good Seasons)
3 tbsp. olive or salad oil
3 tbsp. red wine

     Combine salad mix, olive oil and wine. Spread mixture over both sides of meat; marinate 30 min. Barbecue outdoors (or broil indoors) until done to desired degree. Slice diagonally, thin. Good served with baked potato with sour cream, asparagus vinaigrette, rolls and light dessert.

Mrs. Richard A. Grimley, Ridgewood

LONDON BROIL WITH OLIVE SAUCE

Serves: 4

"The sauce is great and can be used on leftover steak."

Easy   Preparing: 20 min.

1 flank steak, 1-1/2 to 2 lbs.
1/2 c. butter
1/2 tsp. chopped garlic
1/4 c. chopped, stuffed green
   olives
1 tsp. lemon juice
1 tsp. chopped chives or
   green onion tops
pepper to taste
optional - 1 tsp. basil

     Broil steak 2 to 3 inches from heat 8 min. on each side. Cut thin slices across grain. Melt butter; add garlic. Cook until butter is slightly browned. Add remaining ingredients. Heat. Serve over steak.

Mrs. Carlton H. Butcher, Ridgewood

SWISS STEAK MONTEREY

Serves: 6

"Quite economical; terrific for sour cream fans!"

Average   Do ahead   Preparing: 20-30 min.
                                             Cooking: 2 - 2-1/2 hrs.

2 to 2-1/2 lbs. round or
   chuck steak
1/3 c. flour
1 tsp. salt
1/2 tsp. garlic salt
1/4 tsp. pepper
3 tbsp. cooking fat
2 8-oz. cans tomato sauce
1 pkg. onion soup mix
1 c. (1/2 pt.) sour cream

     Cut meat into serving-size pieces. Combine flour, salt, garlic salt and pepper. Rub or pound into all sides of meat. Heat fat in heavy skillet or Dutch oven; brown meat on all sides. Add tomato sauce and onion soup mix; cover. Simmer 2 to 2-1/2 hrs. or until meat is tender. Can be done ahead to this point. Remove meat; keep warm. Skim off gravy. Stir sour cream slowly into gravy. Reheat just until hot, do not boil. Return meat to pan.

Mrs. Robert C. Burnet, Glen Ridge

CUBED STEAK SUPREME

Serves: 5

"Delicious with a salad, baked potatoes and sour cream, and rose wine."

Easy   Part do ahead   Preparing: 5 min.
                                                  Marinating: 1 hr.
                                                  Broiling: 10 min.

5 cubed steaks
salt
pepper
2 bay leaves
1 small clove garlic, sliced
1/2 tsp. fresh chives,
  if available
2/3 c. French dressing

Season meat to taste with salt and pepper. Place on a platter. Put bay leaves, garlic and chives on meat and cover with dressing. Cover with plastic wrap and place a plate on top. Let stand for 1 hr. At end of hour spoon dressing on other side, then remove all the dressing you can from the meat. Broil a few minutes on each side.

Mrs. Joseph L. Baker, Ridgewood

PRESSURE COOKER ROULADES

Serves: 6

"I always make this when I have guests for dinner because it's different."

Average   Do ahead   Preparing: 40 min.
                                                  Cooking: 1 hr.

12 thin sliced steaks for
  rolling (called roulades)
1 12-oz. bag frozen chopped
  onion (2 c.)
1 lb. bacon
salt
pepper
1/2 c. water

Allow two roulades per person. Thaw frozen onions and pour off water. Allow 2 slices bacon for each roulade. Dice bacon and cook slowly; drain, reserving fat. Add equal amount of thawed onion to diced bacon (about 2 tbsp. onion to 2 slices bacon). Mix together and add few shakes of salt and pepper. Divide this mixture among the slices of roulades (about 3 heaping tbsp. on each), placing it on the center of each slice. Roll each one up and fasten with round toothpick. Heat fat saved from bacon and brown roulades on all sides in pressure cooker. Add 1/2 c. water, set lid on #10 pressure and cook for one hour. Makes a good deal of gravy. Serve with mashed potatoes and favorite vegetable.

Mrs. William L. Bradford, Wyckoff

BEEF STEW

Serves: 4

"One of the best stews I've ever tasted and the easiest to prepare."

Easy   Do ahead   Preparing: 10 min.
                                                  Baking: 5 hrs.

1-1/2 lbs. stew beef
1 c. sliced carrots
1 c. sliced onions
1 8 oz. can tomato sauce
salt
pepper
1 can white potatoes
flour for thickening

Combine all ingredients, except potatoes and flour, in a Dutch oven (iron if possible) and bake, covered, at 250° for 5 hrs. Add canned potatoes and thicken with flour just before serving.

Mrs. John D. Dorsey, Ridgewood

IKE'S BEEF STEW

Serves: 12

"Great when a football game has your husband stuck in front of the TV."

Average   Freeze   Preparing: 1/2 hr.
                                 Simmering: 3 hrs.

4 lbs. sirloin or top round
1/3 c. shortening or butter
3 cans (10-1/2 oz.) condensed
  bouillon
3 cans water
4 peppercorns
2 bay leaves
6 whole cloves
1 tsp. thyme
pinch cayenne
2 med. cloves garlic, halved
12 small Irish potatoes,
  halved
12 small onions
1 bunch carrots
4 med. tomatoes
flour

Have beef cut into 1-1/2" cubes. Cut carrots into 1 inch pieces. Peel tomatoes and cut into eighths. Brown beef in shortening. Add bouillon and water. Simmer, covered, until meat is tender, about 1-1/2 to 2 hrs. Add bouquet garni (peppercorns, bay leaves, cloves, thyme, cayenne and garlic tied loosely in cheesecloth or clean, thin white cloth) and vegetables. Cover and simmer until vegetables are tender, 30-45 min. Remove bouquet garni bag. Drain off liquid and thicken with a beef roux made by combining 2 tablespoons each of flour, water and stew stock for each cup of liquid. Blend and add to liquid. Cook, stirring constantly, until thickened. Pour liquid back over stew and simmer a few minutes longer. If freezing, omit potatoes until ready to serve and add precooked potatoes.

Mrs. Albert F. Lilley, Allendale

FLEMISH BEEF STEW

Serves: 6

"I have made this for 30 people. It freezes beautifully."

Average   Freeze   Preparing: 45 min.
                 Best made ahead   Cooking: 45 min. to 1-1/2 hrs.

2 lbs. bottom round
salt
pepper
4 slices bacon
2 medium onions, sliced
1-1/2 tbsp. flour
2 c. ale or beer
1 small bay leaf
pinch thyme
1 clove garlic
1 tbsp. sugar
1 tsp. vinegar

Cut beef into 1-1/2" cubes. Cook bacon until crisp in a heavy skillet. Break up and put into a heavy earthenware pot. Saute onions lightly in bacon fat and add to pot. In remaining fat, brown beef cubes well, adding more bacon fat if necessary. Sprinkle flour over browned meat, stir until it is absorbed. Remove skillet from fire and add beer gradually, stirring constantly until well blended. Add to pot with bay leaf, thyme, garlic stuck on a toothpick, sugar and vinegar. Stir well, bring to a boil, cover closely and simmer about 45 min. or until meat is tender. Check to be sure liquid has not cooked away (it won't if it is covered tightly). Add more beer if necessary. This can also be oven baked at 325° for 1-1/2 hrs.

Mrs. Jay W. Jackson, Ridgewood

70

BOEUF BOURGUIGNON

Serves: 4

"Very good flavor. Nothing to do the day it's served!"

Average   Freeze

Preparing: 45 min.
Cooking: 2-1/2 hrs.

1-1/2 lbs. rump beef, cubed
2 onions, sliced
24 tiny whole onions (fresh)
1/2 c. sliced mushrooms
1/2 c. diced bacon
4 tbsp. butter
1 tbsp. flour
2 cloves garlic, crushed
bouquet garni
  (bay leaves, thyme, parsley)
red wine (Beaujolais best)
salt
pepper
chopped parsley

Brown beef and onions quickly in 3 tbsp. butter in a stew pan. Add flour and mix together for 1-2 min. over medium heat. Add garlic and pour in sufficient wine to cover. Brown bacon in one tbsp. butter and add to stew pan with bouquet garni, salt and pepper. Cover and cook gently for 2 hrs. Remove meat and pass sauce through a fine sieve lined with cheesecloth to catch fat. Return sauce and meat to pan. Add baby onions and cook 15 min.; then add raw mushrooms. Cook gently for another 15 min. Sprinkle with chopped parsley before serving.

Mrs. Robert P. Viarengo, Ridgewood

BEEF BURGUNDY

Serves: 4

"Very good for entertaining as it can be reheated in the oven."

Average   Freeze

Preparing: 30 min.
Baking: 2 - 2-1/2 hrs.

2-1/2 lbs. stew meat
5 tbsp. butter or margarine
1/4 lb. salt pork
flour
1 bunch scallions
2 medium onions
1/2 carrot
1 tbsp. chives
1 clove garlic
8 peppercorns
1 bay leaf
pinch marjoram
pinch thyme
pinch tarragon
Burgundy wine
tarragon vinegar

Chop the scallions, onions and carrot and set aside. Dice the piece of salt pork. Dredge the meat with flour. Heat 3 tbsp. butter or margarine in skillet, add pork and brown. Add stew meat and brown well on all sides. Remove these to a Dutch oven and add 2 tbsp. more of butter to skillet. Lightly brown onions, scallions, carrot and add 1 tbsp. chives and crushed garlic. Pour tarragon vinegar over these and simmer one min. Wrap bay leaf, thyme, and tarragon in a piece of cheesecloth to make a bouquet garni. Add this to the meat along with the onion mixture. Crush peppercorns and add these, plus a generous pinch of marjoram. Pour Burgundy over the whole thing and put into a 350° oven for about 2 to 2-1/2 hrs., being careful things don't stick to the pan bottom. Add more wine if needed. Serve with noodles and a green salad.

Mrs. Robert R. Deutsch, Mahwah

BRAISED BEEF CASSEROLE

Serves: 4

Easy   Do ahead   Preparing: 20 min.
                                         Baking: 1-1/2 hrs.

1 box frozen peas, cooked
1-1/2 lbs. round steak,
   1/2" thick
1/4 c. flour
1 tsp. salt
2 tbsp. shortening
1/2 c. chopped onion
1 clove garlic, sliced thin
1/2 c. hot water
1/2 c. liquid from peas
1 tbsp. lemon juice
1/8 tsp. ground cloves
1/4 tsp. marjoram
2 tbsp. catsup
3 stalks celery
1 can mushrooms

Cut meat into 1/2 inch strips. Sprinkle with flour and salt (or shake in a paper bag). Brown in hot fat. Put into a 2 qt. casserole. Cut celery into 1 inch pieces and add to casserole along with remaining ingredients. Cover and bake at 325° for 1-1/2 hrs. Serve plain or with buttered noodles.

Mrs. Robert E. Taylor, Ridgewood

HUNGARIAN GOULASH

Serves: 6

"The real thing from a member of the 1960 U. S. Culinary Olympic team."

Average   Do ahead   Preparing: 30 min.
                                         Simmering: 2-1/2 hrs.

4 lbs. lean shin (beef)
1 lb. onions, chopped
1 medium bay leaf
2 tsp. sweet paprika
1 clove garlic
2 tsp. salt
3 cans tomato paste
2 tbsp. shortening
peel of 1 lemon
   (yellow only)
1/8 tsp. caraway seeds

Cut beef shin into long strips, about 3 inches thick, then across grain not thicker than 3/4 inch. Stew onions in shortening in heavy bottom pot and bring to a golden color. Slice meat in a hot frying pan until it takes color, not more than one layer at a time. Add meat to onions. Stir in paprika. Add tomato paste, bay leaf and salt. Cover with water and simmer about 2-1/2 hrs. When done, grate lemon peel, chop caraway seeds fine and add. Serve with noodles and applesauce.

Mr. William W. Schmitz, Ho-Ho-Kus

SOUR CREAM GOULASH

Serves: 4

Easy   Freeze   Preparing: 20 min.
                                         Cooking: 1-3/4 hrs.

1/2 lb. mushrooms
1-1/2 tbsp. butter
2 lbs. stewing beef
2 large onions, sliced
1 tbsp. curry powder
1 c. consomme
1 c. dry red wine
1-1/2 tbsp. flour
1 tbsp. prepared horseradish
2 c. sour cream
salt to taste

In a large, ovenproof skillet saute mushrooms in butter. Add beef, onions, curry powder, consomme and red wine. Bring to a boil. Cover and bake at 325° for 1-1/2 hrs. or until meat is tender. Remove to range surface. Combine flour and small amount of water to make paste. Stir into hot mixture. (If you want to do ahead, chill at this point; then reheat and continue.) Add horseradish, sour cream and salt. Reheat, but do not boil, stirring. Serve over cooked rice.

Mrs. John D. Dorsey, Ridgewood

BEEF STROGANOFF

Serves: 4

Average   Do ahead

Preparing: 20 min.
Cooking: 10 min.

1 tbsp. flour
1/2 tsp. salt
1 lb. beef tenderloin,
   cut in 1/4" wide strips
2 tbsp. butter
1 c. thinly sliced mushrooms
1/2 c. chopped onions
1 clove garlic, minced
2 tbsp. butter
3 tbsp. flour
1 tbsp. tomato paste
1-1/4 c. beef stock or
   1 can beef broth
1 c. sour cream
2 tbsp. cooking sherry

Starting at top of list of ingredients, combine flour and salt, and dredge meat. Heat skillet, add butter and meat; brown quickly. Add mushroom slices, onion and garlic. Cook 3-4 min. or until onion is barely tender. Remove all from skillet. Add butter and blend in flour; add tomato paste. Slowly stir in meat stock. Stir constantly until mixture thickens. Return meat mixture to skillet. Add sour cream and sherry. Heat briefly. Serve over rice or noodles.

Mrs. Carlton H. Butcher, Ridgewood

EASY BAKED STROGANOFF

Serves: 6-8

"An easy way to a company meal."

Easy   Do ahead

Preparing: 10 min.
Baking: 3 hrs.

1 can cream mushroom soup
1 can cream celery soup
1 pkg. dry onion soup mix
   (I use Lipton's)
2/3 c. red wine
2 lbs. lean beef cubes, 1-1/2"
   (chuck, rump or round)
1 tsp. M.S.G.
optional -
   1/4 lb. mushrooms
   1 can onions

Blend soups, mix and wine together in a 2 qt. casserole. Season. Add beef cubes and cover. Bake at 275° for 3 hrs. Stir two or three times during cooking. If mushrooms are desired, add last 45 min. If you wish this browned well, uncover for the last 45 min. Add onions before serving if desired.

Mrs. Burton F. Bowman, Franklin Lakes

"SECOND NIGHTER" BEEF STROGANOFF

Serves: 4-6

"A tasty dish prepared from leftover beef. Quick to prepare."

Easy   Freeze

Preparing: 20 min.
Baking: 25 min.

1 large or 2 med. onions
2 tbsp. butter or margarine
2 c. diced, leftover roast
   beef
1 c. leftover or canned
   beef gravy
1 tbsp. tomato paste or
   catsup
mashed potatoes
1/2 pt. sour cream

Saute onions, sliced, in butter or margarine. (Or, add 2 tbsp. instant minced onion to the gravy.) Add meat, gravy and tomato paste. Simmer 10 min.; stir in sour cream. Transfer to a 2 qt. casserole. Can be frozen at this point. Bake, covered, at 350° for 20-25 min.; longer if frozen. Remove cover. Arrange mashed potatoes around edge, or serve potatoes separately. Can be frozen as a leftover, also.

Mrs. G. Albert Haas, Wyckoff

HAMBURGER STROGANOFF   Serves: 4-6

"An excellent variation of a favorite dish."

Easy   Do ahead   Preparing: 10 min.
                                                     Simmering: 10 min.

1/2 c. minced onion   Saute onion in butter until golden. Stir
1/4 c. butter   in beef, garlic, flour, M.S.G., salt, pepper,
1 lb. ground beef   paprika and mushrooms; saute 5 min. Add
1 clove garlic, minced   undiluted soup; simmer 10 min. Stir in sour
2 tbsp. flour   cream; sprinkle with parsley or chives.
1/4 tsp. M.S.G.
2 tsp. salt
1/4 tsp. pepper
1/4 tsp. paprika
1 lb. mushrooms, sliced
1 can cream chicken soup
1 c. sour cream
snipped chives or parsley   *Mrs. Robert E. Taylor, Ridgewood*

CHOPPED STEAK PORT-SALUT   Serves: 2

Easy   No need to do ahead   Preparing: 5 min.
                                                     Cooking: 5 min.

1 lb. chopped beef   Make beef into four 4-oz. patties. Divide
4 oz. Port-Salut cheese   each patty in half and in centers of four
butter   halves place a slice of Port-Salut cheese.
salt   Cover with remaining patty halves. Seal meat
pepper   edges and sprinkle with seasonings. Brown
                           patties in hot buttered skillet for 3-5 min.
                           on each side. Serve hot.

                               Mr. Edwin F. Bernhardt, Cheese Shop, Ridgewood

BARBECUED BEEF   Serves: 4

"This is a wonderful way to use leftover, cold roast beef."

Easy   Do ahead   Preparing: 10 min.
                                                     Cooking: 20 min.

1-1/2 - 2 c. cooked roast beef   Combine sugar, vinegar, mustard, lemon
2 tbsp. sugar   juice, salt, paprika, pepper, cold water,
2 tbsp. vinegar   butter, onion slices and green pepper which
2 tsp. prepared mustard   has been cut into strips. Simmer, uncovered,
2 tsp. lemon juice   for 20 min. Add catsup, M.S.G. and beef
1 tsp. salt   which has been cut into strips. Refrigerate.
1 tsp. paprika   To serve, heat and top with chopped parsley
1/4 tsp. pepper   and celery leaves. Serve with noodles,
3/4 c. cold water   mashed potatoes or toasted hamburger buns.
4 tbsp. butter
1 med. onion, sliced thin
1/4 green pepper
1/2 c. catsup
1 tsp. M.S.G.
parsley
celery leaves   *Mrs. John J. Baughan, Ridgewood*

CRUNCHY-TOPPED MEAT LOAF   Serves: 6

"Children love it; easy to prepare, too."

Easy   Freeze   Preparing: 15 min.
                                                  Baking: 1 hr.

1 lb. ground chuck   Grease a shallow baking pan or flat
1/4-1/2 c. dry oatmeal   casserole dish. Mix ingredients (except
3 pieces bread, broken into   bacon and saltines) thoroughly and mound
  pieces   in pan. Spread cracker crumbs over meat
3/4 c. chili sauce   and place strips of bacon on top. Bake
1 egg   at 350° for one hour.
1 med. onion, chopped
1 tsp. Worcestershire sauce
1 tsp. salt
1/4 tsp. pepper
4 slices bacon
3 saltines, crumbled   *Mrs. Harold R. Hiser, Jr., London, England*

SWEET AND SOUR MEAT LOAF   Serves: 4

"Especially good on a cold winter's night."

Average   Do ahead   Preparing: 15 min.
                                                  Baking: 1 hr.

1-1/2 lbs. chopped chuck   Mix all ingredients and form into a loaf.
1/2 c. bread crumbs   Brown lightly under the broiler. Mix together
1 onion, grated   the sauce ingredients and pour over the meat
1/2 8-oz. can tomato sauce   loaf. Bake at 350° for one hour, basting
salt   often with sauce. Serve with mashed potatoes
pepper   as the sauce is especially good.

Sauce:
1/2 8-oz. can tomato sauce
1 c. water
2 tbsp. vinegar
2 tbsp. prepared mustard
2 tbsp. brown sugar   *Mrs. H. B. Millican, Jr., Saddle River*

MEAT LOAF   Serves: 6

"We enjoy this; it is light textured and juicy."

Easy   Do ahead   Preparing: 10 min.
                                                  Baking: 1 hr.

2 lbs. ground chuck   Preheat oven to 375°. In large bowl mix
2 c. corn flakes   all ingredients in order listed. Mix lightly
1 can tomato soup   with fork. When well blended, put into meat
1 c. milk   loaf pan. Do not pack down. Bake for 1 hr.
1 egg   Good with baked potatoes put in to bake before
2 tsp. oregano   preparing meat loaf.
1 tsp. salt
1/2 tsp. pepper   *Mrs. Donald W. Coyle, Ridgewood*

LIZANN'S ROUND MEAT LOAF

Serves: 6

"A little different and attractive way to serve meat loaf."

Easy   Freeze   Preparing: 10 min.
                                                  Baking: 1 hr.

1 egg
1-1/2 lbs. ground beef
3 slices soft bread,
  torn into pieces
1 c. milk
1/4 c. minced onion
1 tbsp. Worcestershire sauce
1/4 tsp. salt

Heat oven to 350°. In a bowl beat egg slightly. Add remaining ingredients and mix well. Shape meat loaf mixture into a round layer pan, 9x1-1/2 inches. Press a hole in the center (to hold excess fat). Pat top of meat loaf to make smooth. Bake for one hour.

To serve: Cut meat loaf into 6 pie-shaped wedges. Place each wedge on a plate and top with a scoop of mashed potatoes.

Miss Lizann Wardley, Ridgewood

BEEF AND RICE EN CROÛTE

Serves: 8

"An original of mine. Either an elegant meat loaf or a poor man's coulibriac."

Complicated   Do ahead   Preparing: 20 min.
                                                  Setting: overnight
                                                  Baking: 10 min.

1 tbsp. butter
2 tbsp. chopped onion
1 sliced carrot
1/2 c. Bulgar wheat pilaf*
1 c. cold water
2/3 c. cooked rice (minute)
2 tbsp. butter
1 tbsp. oil
2 tbsp. chopped onion
2 tbsp. chopped green pepper
1/2 lb. ground veal
2 lbs. ground beef
4 tbsp. chili sauce
salt
pepper
1 tsp. chopped parsley
1/2 tsp. dried oregano
2 pkgs. refrigerator biscuits
2 eggs, slightly beaten
flour

In a large frying pan, melt butter over medium heat. Add onion and carrot and saute 3 min. Add Bulgar wheat and saute 3 min. more until golden and crisp. Add water and bring to a boil. Reduce heat and simmer 15 min. Put this into a large mixing bowl and add the cooked rice. Put pan back on medium heat and melt butter and oil. Add onion and pepper and cook until golden. Add veal and beef. Cook 2 min. - no longer. Meat should still be pink-red. Put meat mixture in with rice mixture, add chili sauce, salt, pepper and herbs. Mix in the eggs to hold, and shape into 2 large loaves (or individual loaves). Place on an ovenproof platter. Roll out refrigerator rolls on a floured board and cover the loaves all around. Wrap in plastic wrap and put into refrigerator overnight. Unwrap plastic wrap and bake in 400° oven for 8-10 min.

*Available in gourmet shops;
e.g., Cheese Shop, Ridgewood

Mrs. Allen D. Patterson, Saddle River

SWEET MEATBALLS

Serves: 6

"A 'made-up' recipe that's a children's favorite. Great for hors d'oeuvres."

Average   Freeze   Preparing: 45 min.
                                 Baking: 45 min.

2 lbs. ground chuck
4 eggs
1/2 c. flavored bread crumbs
1 tsp. oregano
1 tsp. chopped parsley
1 tsp. basil
1/4 c. water
1/2 small jar currant jelly
1/2 bottle chili sauce
1 tsp. mustard
  (I use Dusseldorf or
  Dijon)
1/4 c. water

Combine first seven ingredients and form meatballs. Broil on 2 sides. Drain off fat and place browned meatballs in casserole. Combine in saucepan currant jelly, chili sauce, mustard and water. Simmer until jelly melts. (Add more water if necessary to thin sauce.) Pour over meatballs in casserole and bake at 350°, covered, for 1/2 hr. Uncover and bake, basting, for 15 min. Serve with Noodle-Sour Cream Casserole on page 176. (If using for hors d'oeuvre, make small meatballs.)

Mrs. James M. Shavick, Ridgewood

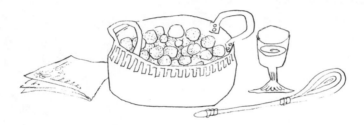

RUSSIAN MEATBALLS

Serves: 8

"An inexpensive 'Beef Stroganoff' - delicious!"

Average   Freeze   Preparing: 20 min.
                                 Standing: 1 hr.
                                 Cooking: 25 min.

2-1/2 lbs. beef or veal,
  ground
1/2 lb. lean pork, ground
2-1/4 c. corn flakes,
  rolled fine
1 c. milk
2 eggs
1 tsp. salt
1/4 tsp. pepper
1/2 tsp. grated lemon rind
1/4 tsp. nutmeg
3 c. sliced onions
1 c. sour cream
1 can consomme
2 tbsp. flour
1/4 c. dry vermouth

Mix meat, corn flakes, milk and slightly beaten eggs. Add seasonings. Mix well and let stand one hour. Shape into small balls and brown in fat. Add sliced onions and cook 20 min. Remove from pan to casserole. Freeze at this point, if desired. Add sour cream to drippings in pan. Thicken with flour mixed with consomme. Cook until blended (do not boil). Pour over meatballs. Before serving, add vermouth. Delicious served with new potatoes and buttered beets or string beans.

Mrs. Floyd Fortuin, Wyckoff

MEATBALLS WITH SOUR CREAM

Serves: 4

"Great in the electric fry pan."

Average   Do ahead   Preparing: 1-1/2 hrs.

4 slices white bread
1 lb. ground beef
1 med. onion, finely minced
1 tbsp. butter or margarine
1-1/2 tsp. salt
1/8 tsp. pepper
2 tbsp. chopped parsley
fine dry bread crumbs
3 tbsp. shortening
1 c. sour cream

Cut crusts off bread, soak in water until saturated, then squeeze dry and add to ground beef. Add onions, which have been cooked in butter or margarine until soft and yellow. Add seasonings and parsley. Shape into meatballs the size of golf balls. Roll in bread crumbs and brown on all sides in shortening. Place meatballs in top of double boiler or electric skillet. Freeze at this point, if desired. Before serving, heat and add sour cream to top of meatballs. Simmer only until sour cream is hot.

Mrs. Paul J. McCrohan, Clifton

BEEF AND NOODLE CASSEROLE

Serves: 25

"Children love this sans onions; adults, too, with them."

Easy   Freeze   Preparing: 20 min.
                                        Baking: 30 min.

4 lbs. ground beef
3 12-oz. pkgs. fine noodles
4 cans mushroom soup
1/2 c. chopped onion
salt (or seasoned salt)
1/2 lb. butter or margarine

Brown beef and onion in about one tbsp. butter, then simmer slowly until meat is well done. Add cooked noodles, mix with a fork and add mushroom soup and melted butter. Bake at 350° for 30 min.

Mrs. Warren S. Malhiot, Ho-Ho-Kus

JOHNNY MAZETTE

Serves: 12

"Wonderful to have on hand, frozen, for a hungry crowd."

Average   Freeze   Preparing: 30 min.
                                        Baking: 35 min.

2 c. chopped green pepper
1 c. chopped celery
2 c. chopped onions
1 lb. ground beef
1 lb. ground pork
1 c. margarine or butter
2 tsp. salt
1/2 c. chopped, stuffed olives
1 can sliced mushrooms
1 can tomato soup
1 can meatless tomato-
  mushroom sauce
1 lb. broad noodles
2 c. grated American cheese

In large skillet saute pepper, celery, onions and meats in hot margarine or butter. Add salt. Reduce heat; cook 5 min. Stir in olives, mushrooms and juice, soup, and tomato-mushroom sauce. Cook 5 min. more. Cook noodles and drain. Turn noodles into a 14x10x2-1/2 inch pan. Add sauce gradually, stirring well. Sprinkle cheese on top. Bake at 350° for 35 min.

Mrs. Edward H. Decker, Ridgewood

HUNTER'S LUNCH

Serves: 12

"Can be frozen or made the day before. Good for a crowd."

Average   Freeze   Preparing: 1-1/4 hrs.
                                      Baking: 30 min.

3 lbs. ground round
1 #2 can tomatoes
1 lb. fresh mushrooms
4-6 onions, chopped
1/2 lb. spaghetti
1 box frozen peas, cooked
1 can pimentos, chopped
1/2 lb. American cheese,
  grated

Simmer ground round, tomatoes, mushrooms, and onions in large, uncovered pot for 1 hr. Meanwhile, cook peas and cook and drain spaghetti. Add peas, spaghetti and pimentos to meat mixture. Stir half of the cheese into the mixture. Pour into large 3 qt. casserole and sprinkle remaining cheese on top. Brown in 300° oven about 30 min. Good served with garlic bread and tossed salad.

Mrs. E. E. Hinman, Suffern, New York

DINNER-IN-A-DISH

Serves: 2-3

Easy   Do ahead   Preparing: 20 min.
                                        Baking: 45 min.

2 tbsp. shortening
1 small onion, chopped
1 green pepper, sliced
1/2 lb. hamburger
1/2 tsp. salt
1/8 tsp. pepper
1 egg
1 c. whole kernel corn
2 tomatoes, sliced
1/2 c. bread crumbs

Saute pepper and onion in oil for 3 min. Add meat and seasoning and remove from heat. Stir in egg. Put 1/2 c. corn into a baking dish, then half the meat mixture. Next add a layer of sliced tomatoes. Repeat layers. Cover last layer of tomatoes with crumbs and dot with butter. Bake at 375° for 45 min.

Mrs. Harry D. Adamy, Ridgewood

HAMBURGER PIE (a casserole)

Serves: 6

"A good family dish, but festive enough for company."

Easy   Do ahead   Preparing: 15 min.
                                        Baking: 30 min.

1 c. biscuit mix
1/3 c. milk
1 tbsp. salad oil
2 onions, sliced
1 lb. ground beef
1 tsp. salt
1/4 tsp. pepper
3 tbsp. catsup
2 tbsp. biscuit mix
2 eggs, slightly beaten
1 c. cottage cheese
paprika

Combine 1 c. biscuit mix and milk. Knead gently ten times. Roll out to fit into a 9 inch pie pan. Crimp edge. Saute onion in oil. Add ground beef and cook until slightly browned. Stir in salt, pepper, catsup and the 2 tbsp. biscuit mix. Spread in dough-lined pan. Blend eggs with cottage cheese and pour over meat. Sprinkle with paprika. Bake at 350° for 30 min. Cut into wedges and serve. Good with a tossed green salad.

Mrs. William S. Enchelmeyer, Glen Rock

SKILLET BEEF AND NOODLES

Serves: 4

"A good, very quick supper."

Easy   Do ahead   Preparing: 15 min.
Cooking: 20 min.

1 lb. ground beef
2 tbsp. salad oil
1 pkg. onion soup mix
20-oz. can tomatoes
1-1/2 c. thin noodles,
  uncooked
1 tbsp. prepared mustard
1/2 tsp. salt
1/2 tsp. sugar
1/4 tsp. oregano
1 c. water
pepper
1 c. whole kernel corn

Brown beef in oil in skillet for about
10 min. Add remaining ingredients and
simmer, covered, about 20 min. Stir
occasionally.

Mrs. Kenneth E. Leslie, Ramsey

QUICK AND EASY FAMILY BEEF CASSEROLE

Serves: 4-6

"Very easy, one-dish cooking."

Easy   Do ahead   Preparing and
Cooking: 20 min.

1 lb. ground chuck
2 tbsp. butter or margarine
1-2 onions, sliced
1-3 tsp. celery salt to taste
salt
pepper
8 oz. uncooked noodles
3 c. tomato juice
1 c. sour cream

Cook onions in butter or margarine until
transparent. Add chuck and brown. Add
celery salt, salt, pepper, uncooked noodles
and tomato juice. Simmer until noodles are
tender. Do ahead to this point, if desired.
Just before serving, stir in sour cream.
Serve with green salad and hot breads.

Mrs. John J. Baughan, Ridgewood

QUICK GROUND CHUCK AND MACARONI CASSEROLE

Serves: 4-6

"Have an easy dinner with this casserole, green salad, French bread and fruit."

Easy   Freeze   Preparing: 15-20 min.
Baking: 30 min.

1 onion, diced
1 tbsp. oil
1/2 green pepper, diced
1 lb. chopped chuck
1 8-oz. can Spanish-type
  tomato sauce
2 cans macaroni with cheese
  sauce (I use Franco-
  American)
bread crumbs
1/2 c. grated cheese

Saute onion and green pepper in oil until
onion is golden. Add chopped chuck and brown.
Add tomato sauce and macaroni with cheese
sauce. Top with crumbs and grated cheese.
Serve directly from top of stove or put into
a 1-1/2 qt. casserole and heat in 350° oven
for 30 min.

Mrs. Robert C. Mackenzie, Jr., Ridgewood

HAMBURGER-CORN CASSEROLE

Serves: 24-30

"An easy casserole which can be prepared in advance and frozen."

Easy   Freeze   Preparing: 15 min.
                                      Baking: 45 min.

4 lbs. ground beef
oil
3 med. onions, chopped
  (3 cups)
3 12-oz. cans whole kernel
  corn
3 cans cream chicken soup
3 cans cream mushroom soup
3 c. sour cream
3/4 c. chopped pimentos
2 tsp. salt
1-1/4 tsp. M.S.G.
3/4 tsp. pepper
9 c. medium noodles
bread crumbs
butter
paprika

Brown meat in oil. Add onions; cook until tender but not brown. Add drained corn and next 7 ingredients. Mix well. Cook noodles, drain and add. Pour into three 13x9x2-5/8 inch Pyrex dishes. Cover top with bread crumbs. Dot with butter and sprinkle with paprika. Bake at 350° for 45 min. or until bubbly. Serve with tossed green salad and French bread.

Mrs. William W. Weleck, Jr., Ridgewood

COMPANY BEEF CASSEROLE

Serves: 6

"For company or family; it is easy and delicious."

Average   Do ahead   Preparing: 30 min.
                                      Baking: 30 min.

1 lb. chopped meat
2 tbsp. butter or margarine
1 onion, chopped
1 pepper, chopped
2 8-oz. cans tomato sauce
8 oz. wide noodles
1 c. cottage cheese
8 oz. cream cheese
1/2 c. sour cream

Brown onion and pepper in butter or margarine. Add meat and brown. Add tomato sauce. Cook noodles and drain. In another bowl combine cheeses and sour cream. Put half of noodles in a buttered, 2-qt. casserole. Spread cheese mixture over this. Top with remaining noodles and cover this with meat mixture. Bake at 350° for 30 min.

Mrs. Barbara B. Eaton, Ridgewood

BAKED NOODLES AND BEEF

Serves: 12-16

"Great for a crowd."

Easy   Freeze   Preparing: 30 min.
                                      Baking: 1 hr.

1 large pkg. wide noodles
1 green pepper
2 large onions, chopped fine
butter
salt
pepper
3 lbs. ground round
1 lb. Cheddar cheese
2 cans tomato soup
2 cans tomato sauce

Brown pepper and onion in butter with salt and pepper. Cook beef with the above for 20 min. Cut cheese finely and add to meat. When melted, mix in tomato soup and tomato sauce. Mix all of this with noodles which have been cooked. Place in a covered 3 qt. casserole and bake at 400° for 30 min. Turn oven down to 325° and cook 30 min. longer.

Miss Susan Hinman, Suffern, New York

BEAN-BURGER MEAT CASSEROLE

Serves: 4-6

"Men seem to enjoy this hearty dish. Inexpensive, delicious and different."

Easy   Do ahead   Preparing: 10 min.
                                             Baking: 30-40 min.

1 lb. ground round
1 tsp. salt
1/4 tsp. pepper
1 tbsp. butter
1 med.-large can baked beans
  (I always use B & M)
1 med. onion, sliced thin
2/3 c. catsup
1/2 c. brown sugar
2-3 slices bacon

Place meat, salt and pepper in skillet and saute in butter until brown. In a flat casserole make two layers of meat, beans, onions, catsup and brown sugar. Top with bacon strips. Bake in 350° oven for 30-40 min. Can be made in the morning, covered with Saran wrap and refrigerated until time to bake.

Mrs. Henry J. Hostrup, Ramsey

GOURMET CASSEROLE

Serves: 10-15

"This is great for an informal dinner; salad and hot bread make a meal."

Easy   Freeze   Preparing: 30 min.
                                             Cooking: 1 hr.

1 8-oz. pkg. thin noodles
3/4 c. stuffed olives, sliced
1 can mushroom soup
1-1/4 c. milk
1/2 c. chopped onion
2 tbsp. butter
2 lbs. ground beef
1/2 lb. Cheddar cheese,
  grated
2 tbsp. chopped parsley
1/2 lb. slivered almonds
1 c. chow mein noodles
salt & pepper to taste

Cook noodles, drain. Mix soup and milk together. Add soup and milk, olives and parsley to noodles. Mix well. Saute onions in butter, add meat and brown together. Stir in grated cheese. Bake in a greased, 4 qt. casserole dish at 350° for 30 min. Remove from oven, add nuts and chow mein noodles over top and bake 20 min. more.

Mrs. Henry B. Douglas, Saddle River

SPANISH RICE CASSEROLE

Serves: 5-6

"Children love this and it's a great success with adults. So-o-o easy!"

Easy   Do ahead   Preparing: 20 min.
                                             Cooking: 20 min.

1-1/2 lbs. ground beef
1 small can whole kernel corn
2 cans Spanish rice dinner
  (I use Menner's)
1 can tomato sauce
  (I use Hunt's)
1/2 c. water
dash catsup
onion salt
pepper
Italian flavored bread crumbs

Brown beef in pan, breaking up with a spoon. Drain off excess fat and sprinkle meat liberall with onion salt and pepper. Meanwhile, in a 2 qt. casserole, mix Spanish rice, whole kernel corn, tomato sauce and catsup. Add the beef an sufficient water to moisten (at least 1/2 c.). Mix thoroughly and top with a good amount of bread crumbs. Brown at 400° for about 20 min. This can be expanded almost indefinitely.

Mrs. William Davis Jones, Ridgewood

CORNISH PASTIES

Serves: 6

"These are native New Zealand dishes and are great!"

Average   Do ahead   Preparing: 1 hr.
Cooking: 2-1/2 hrs.

Pastry:
2 c. flour
1/2 lb. margarine
1 tsp. salt
7 tbsp. cold water
  (1/2 c. less 1 tbsp.)

Pastry: Cut margarine into flour and salt with pastry blender. Add water all at once. Stir lightly with spoon and then use fingers to gather the dough into a ball. Roll out on a floured board. Cut into rounds 4 inches in diameter.

Filling:
2 lbs. chuck steak
1 large onion
1 tsp. salt
1 tsp. M.S.G.
1 beef bouillon cube
flour to thicken
pepper

Filling: Chop onion and brown in a little hot fat. Remove from pan. Cut meat into small cubes, flour, and brown in hot fat. Pour off excess fat. Add water to barely cover the meat. Add salt, pepper, M.S.G. and bouillon cube. Simmer gently for 2 hrs. and thicken with flour. Allow to cool. Place in spoonfuls on uncooked pastry rounds. Moisten the edges and join pastry edges at center top and pinch together. Bake at 450° for 15 min.

Mrs. Ernest Duncan, East Brunswick

GROUND MEAT PASTIES

Serves: 4

"A quicker version of the Cornish Pasties."

Easy   Do ahead   Preparing: 15 min.
Baking: 15 min.

1 lb. ground round
1 tsp. salt
1/2 tsp. M.S.G.
1 beef bouillon cube
1 c. soft bread crumbs
1 onion
1 egg
pinch poultry seasoning

Dissolve bouillon in 1/4 c. boiling water and add to bread crumbs in a bowl to soften. Add ground meat, salt, chopped onion, M.S.G. and egg. Mix well. Place uncooked mixture on uncooked pastry rounds about 4 inches in diameter. Fold pastry like a turnover. Pinch edges. Bake at 450° for 15 min.

Mrs. Ernest Duncan, East Brunswick

CHILI

Serves: 4

"Great for teenagers. They can do this themselves."

Easy   Do ahead   Preparing: 15 min.
Cooking: 1-1/2 hrs.

1 lb. chopped meat
2 onions, diced
1 med. size bottle catsup
1 1-lb. can red kidney beans
salt to taste
pepper to taste
1/4 tsp. chili powder or
  to taste

Brown onions and meat. Add remaining ingredients and simmer for about 1-1/2 hrs., stirring occasionally. Good with tossed salad and garlic bread.

Mrs. James R. Toombs, Ridgewood

CHILI FOR A GANG

Serves: 10-12

"Add more chili powder and Tabasco if you are looking for a hot dish."

Easy   Do ahead   Preparing: 15 min.
                                                    Cooking: 1 hr.

1/2 - 1 c. chopped onions
1 tbsp. salad oil
3 lbs. ground chuck
1/2 c. chopped celery
1 tsp. celery seed
2 cans red chili beans
2 cans tomatoes
2 tsp. salt
1 tbsp. chili powder
1/2 tsp. Tabasco sauce

Brown onions in oil in heavy skillet.
Add chuck, celery and celery seed; brown.
Add remaining ingredients and cook slowly
for one hour.

Mrs. Richard D. Jones, Mercer Island, Wash.

QUICK AND EASY STUFFED PEPPERS

Serves: 4

"One of my husband's favorites."

Easy   Do ahead   Preparing: 15 min.
                                                    Baking: 30 min.

2 large green peppers
1 lb. ground chuck
1/4 tsp. garlic powder
1/2 tsp. pepper
1/2 tsp. salt
2 tbsp. butter
1 tsp. oregano
1 1-lb. can Spanish rice
4 slices sharp Cheddar cheese

Halve green peppers lengthwise and remove
core and seeds. Place peppers in a pot and
cover with boiling water. Simmer 5 min.
During this time season beef with garlic
powder, pepper and salt. Shape meat into a
flat cake and saute in butter until browned
on outside, but still quite rare inside.
Remove peppers from water, drain and place
in a shallow baking dish. Stir oregano into
Spanish rice. Break up meat and toss with
rice. Stuff peppers with mixture and top
each with a slice of cheese. Bake at 350°
until heated through and cheese is melted
(20-30 min.). Can be done up to 2 days ahead.

Mrs. John E. Button, Saddle River

STUFFED PEPPERS

Serves: 4

"Simply the best you have ever!"

Easy   Do ahead   Preparing: 10 min.
                                                    Simmering: 2 hrs.

4 large green peppers
1 lb. beef, ground
1/2 lb. pork, ground
1 egg
salt
pepper
stalk of celery, chopped
parsley
thyme
1/2 c. rice
3 cans tomato soup
3 cans water

Wash peppers and cut off tops; remove
centers. Mix together soup and water, and
set aside. Combine remaining ingredients
and stuff into peppers. Place peppers in
soup mixture and simmer 2 hrs., covered.
Can be done one day ahead.

Mrs. Gordon W. Laird, Maplewood

QUICK CHIPPED BEEF

Serves: 4

"A very quick and easy supper dish."

Easy   Do ahead   Preparing: 5 min.

1 can frozen potato soup
1/2 can milk (soup can)
5-oz. jar dried beef
toast

Defrost potato soup. Combine with milk and heat. Add dried beef which has been cut into small pieces. Serve on toast points.

Mrs. Harry D. Adamy, Ridgewood

HOT CORNED BEEF BAR-B-QUES

Serves: 8

"Good for a late evening meal at an informal party."

Average   Freeze   Preparing: 15 min.
                                                     Cooking: 20 min.

1 tsp. chili powder
2 tbsp. cider vinegar
2 tbsp. Worcestershire sauce
1/8-1/4 tsp. cayenne
3/4 c. catsup
3/4 c. water
2 12-oz. cans corned beef
8 hamburger buns
8 whole sweet pickles

Put first 6 ingredients into a skillet and mix well. Add corned beef, breaking it up. Cook, uncovered, over medium heat, stirring occasionally, about 20 min. or until most of liquid has evaporated and mixture is thick. Broil split hamburger buns about 2 min. or until lightly toasted. Spoon mixture onto bottom of buns, put on tops and garnish with a sweet pickle on a toothpick. Can be made early in the day or frozen and reheated.

Mrs. David F. Bolger, Ridgewood

SOUTHERN BURGERS

Serves: 4

"This is a nice change from Sloppy Joes for teenagers (or anyone)!"

Easy   Do ahead   Preparing: 10 min.
                                                         Simmering: 15 min.

1 lb. ground beef
1 medium onion, diced
1 tbsp. catsup
1 tbsp. prepared mustard
1 can chicken gumbo soup

Brown beef and onion in hot fat. Stir In catsup, mustard and soup. Simmer until thickened a bit (about 15 min.). Spoon over toasted, split buns.

Mrs. J. A. McIlhatten, Ridgewood

SLOPPY JOES

Serves: 6-8

"Always a hit. Most people end up eating it with a spoon instead of on buns!"

Easy
                    Do ahead   Preparing: 15 min.
                                                         Cooking: 1 hr.

1 lb. chopped meat
2 small onions or 1 med.
med. size bottle chili sauce
salt to taste
pepper to taste
1/2 green pepper, diced
optional -
   garlic clove, minced

Brown chopped meat, onion and green pepper. Add chili sauce and other ingredients. Simmer one hour. Serve on hamburger buns.

Mrs. James R. Toombs, Ridgewood

FORUM SCHOOL SLOPPY JOES

Serves: 20 children

"Favorite with any small fry! Popular with the Forum School children."

Easy   Do ahead   Preparing: 20 min.
                                                    Simmering: 30 min.

5-6 lbs. chopped chuck
1 large onion, chopped
1 stalk celery, chopped fine
1/2 c. chopped green pepper
1 c. catsup
3 8-oz. cans tomato sauce
salt
pepper
Worcestershire sauce

Brown onion, celery and green pepper in a large skillet (or 2 smaller ones). Add chopped beef, and brown. Add catsup, tomato sauce, and seasonings to taste. Simmer for 30 min. (or longer for more flavor). Spoon off excess fat. Serve on split hamburger buns. Older children prefer spicier Sloppy Joes - substitute barbecue sauce for catsup and/or tomato sauce. More sauce can be added for sloppier Joes.

Mrs. Joseph Sage, Ramsey

MILLION DOLLAR SPAGHETTI (Casserole)

Serves: 6

"This recipe won a trip to Italy for a friend who passed it on to me."

Average   Do ahead   Preparing: 30 min.
                                                    Baking: 45 min.

1 7-oz. pkg. thin spaghetti
1 tbsp. butter
1-1/2 lbs. ground beef
salt
pepper
2 8-oz. cans tomato sauce
8 oz. cream cheese
1/4 c. sour cream
1/2 lb. cottage cheese
1/3 c. scallions
1 tbsp. minced green pepper
2 tbsp. melted butter

Cook spaghetti and drain. Saute beef in butter until brown. Add tomato sauce, salt and pepper. Remove from heat. Combine cottage cheese, cream cheese, sour cream, scallions and green pepper. In a square 2 qt. casserole spread cne half the spaghetti and cover with cheese mixture. Add remainder of spaghetti and pour melted butter over spaghetti. Spread tomato-meat sauce over top. Chill. Remove from refrigerator 20 min. before baking. Bake at 350° for 45 min. or until hot and bubbly. Especially good served with green salad and French bread.

Mrs. F. Irving Walsh, Ho-Ho-Kus

SPAGHETTI DINNER

Serves: 4-6

"A very good, easy to fix, and inexpensive dinner."

Easy   Freeze

Preparing: 25 min.
Cooking: 20 min.

1 - 1-1/2 lbs. chopped beef
1 clove garlic
1 large Bermuda onion
1 green pepper
2 cans tomato soup
3 tbsp. butter
1 lb. mushrooms
1 small jar stuffed olives
1 lb. sharp Cheddar cheese
1 lb. spaghetti

Chop onion and pepper; saute in butter with meat and crushed garlic. Add soup and cook 5 min. Saute mushrooms separately and add to the sauce. When ready to serve, pour sauce over the hot, cooked, drained spaghetti. Slice olives and grate cheese; add right before serving. The hot spaghetti and sauce will melt the cheese. Good with mixed green salad and fruit or a very light dessert.

Mrs. Warren W. Otis, Ridgewood

SWEET AND HOT SPAGHETTI SAUCE

Serves: 12-14

"Marvelous spaghetti sauce!"

Average   Freeze

Preparing: 30 min.
Cooking: 1 hr. plus

3 onions, chopped
3 cloves garlic, crushed
6 tbsp. olive oil
1-1/2 - 2 lbs. ground chuck
1-1/2 lbs. sweet sausage
3/4 lb. hot sausage
3 large cans tomatoes
6 cans tomato paste
10 tsp. salt (3 tbsp. + 1 tsp.)
4-1/2 tsp. sugar
3/4 tsp. crushed red pepper
1-1/2 tsp. basil
3 lbs. spaghetti

Cut sausage into small pieces. Cook onions in oil. Add beef and stir until no longer pink. Add all other ingredients except basil and spaghetti. Simmer at least one hour. Add basil. Cook spaghetti. Serve over spaghetti.

Mrs. Irving R. Hayman, Ridgewood

TEENAGE MULLIGAN STEW

Serves: 12

Average   Do ahead

Preparing: 10 min.
Cooking: 15 min.

2 lbs. frankfurters
1-1/2 lbs. bacon
2 cans (1 lb. 5 oz.) butter beans
2 cans (1 lb. 5 oz.) lima beans
2 cans (12 oz.) corn
3 cans (8 oz.) tomato sauce
2 tbsp. chili powder
2/3 lb. diced American cheese
2 cans French fried onions

Cut franks into 1/2 inch slices and cook 5 min. in boiling water. Drain and keep hot. Fry bacon until crisp, and crumble. Put aside. Drain all the canned vegetables; add to franks. Add tomato sauce and heat until boiling. Stir in chili powder and cheese; cook and blend until cheese melts. Serve in large bowls with toasted rolls and top with the bacon and French fried onions. Coleslaw and an ice cream sundae bar make for a great party.

Mrs. A. Steffee Smith, Ridgewood

FRANKFURTER-APRICOT CURRY

Serves: 6

"A different, delightful way to serve franks."

Easy   Do ahead   Preparing: 30 min.

1 1-lb. can apricot halves
2 tbsp. cornstarch
1 tsp. curry powder
1 tsp. salt
1 12-oz. can apricot nectar
1 lb. frankfurters,
  cut in diagonal chunks
1 c. rice
parsley garnish

Drain apricots, reserving 1/2 c. syrup. In saucepan mix cornstarch and seasonings. Add reserved syrup and nectar. Cook, stirring until clear and thick. Cook rice according to package directions. Add franks and apricots to syrup mixture and heat gently Serve on hot rice and garnish with parsley.

Mrs. Oswald B. Dieter, Ridgewood

SUE'S MEXICAN ENCHILLADAS

Serves: 4

"Not only different, but tantalizingly good. Worth the effort!"

Average   Freeze   Preparing: 40 min.
                                                     Cooking: 1 hr.

1 doz. tortillas*
1 onion, diced
1 lb. ground chuck (lean)
1 can mild enchilada sauce
  (I use El Paso brand)
1 lb. Cheddar cheese, grated
salt & pepper to taste
2 tbsp. chili powder
1 large can pitted ripe
  olives, chopped

*Canned tortillas may be used, but freshly baked ones are available at Mexican grocery stores in New York; e.g., Casa Moneo, 218 West 14th St.

Fry meat and onion seasoned with chili powder, salt and pepper. Pour off grease and add meat to olives and 3/4 of cheese. Fry tortillas in small amount of shortening until it pops (takes only a second). Remove and dip in pan of hot enchilada sauce which has been diluted with half water. For dipping process suggest using corn tongs. Place tortillas on flat surface. Put approximately 1 full tbsp. meat mixture in each, and roll. Line rolled tortillas in large bake pan. Freeze at this point. Cover with remaining cheese and pour some hot sauce over. Bake in 350° oven for about 1 hr. Serve with refried beans (heated in a double boiler), corn chips, red wine and tossed salad.

Mrs. Graham B. Conklin, Ridgewood

ROAST LEG OF LAMB

Serves: 8-10

"A delicious way to serve roast lamb."

Easy   Do ahead   Preparing: 10 min.
Roasting: 3-4 hrs.

1 leg of lamb, 6-7 lbs.
4 med. onions, sliced
4 med. carrots, sliced
6 stalks celery, diced
3 bay leaves
1 c. water
salt & pepper to taste

Place vegetables, bay leaves and water in bottom of roasting pan. Place meat on top with skin side up. Roast in hot oven (450° to 475°) about 25 min. or until meat has browned. Turn meat so that fat side is up. Lower temperature to moderate (350° to 375°). Roast until done. Roasting time is usually 30 min. per pound. Remove roast and vegetables to heated platter and place in warm oven. Strain liquid from roasting pan and skim off excess fat. Serve with Sour Cream-Red Wine Sauce on page 106.

Mrs. Morton Evans, Canton, Mass.

STUFFED LEG OF LAMB

Serves: 8

"A good company dish! Make gravy to serve with it."

Complicated (worth it)   Do ahead   Preparing: 20 min.
Roasting: 4 - 4-1/2 hrs.

7 or 8 lb. leg of lamb, boned
1 medium onion, chopped
2 tbsp. butter
4 c. bread crumbs
1 6-oz. can whole mushrooms
1 4-1/2 oz. jar stuffed
  olives, sliced
3/4 c. chopped parsley
1 tsp. salt
2 tsp. poultry seasoning
pepper

Stuff leg of lamb with all ingredients which have been mixed well together. Fasten with skewers. Roast at 325° for 40 min. per lb.

Mrs. John E. Button, Saddle River

89

ROAST HERBED LEG OF LAMB

Serves: 8-10

"This gets raves whenever it's served."

Average   Do ahead

Preparing: 20 min.
Marinating: overnight
Roasting: 2 - 2-1/2 hrs.

1 c. white wine
1/2 c. water
1 c. olive oil
1 tbsp. lemon juice
1 med. onion, chopped
2 cloves garlic
1-1/2 tsp. salt
1 tsp. tarragon vinegar
1 tsp. crushed marjoram
1 tsp. crushed rosemary
8 whole peppercorns, crushed
4-6 lb. leg of lamb
2 tbsp. flour

Combine wine, water, oil, lemon juice and onion. Mash garlic with salt. Add to above. Stir in vinegar and herbs. Lay lamb with the fell (skin) pulled off in a roasting pan. Pour wine mixture over it; let marinate overnight, turning occasionally in liquid. About 3 hrs. before serving, pour off the marinade into a bowl. Place meat on rack in roasting pan and set it in preheated 325° oven. Baste with marinade occasionally until thermometer reads 170° to 180° (2 to 2-1/2 hrs.). Remove meat to hot platter. Let stand 10-15 min. Serve with gravy made from drippings in pan.

Mrs. Bruce K. Byers, Ridgewood

SHISH KABOB (Lamb)

Yield: 12 skewers

"This can also be done with beef."

Easy   Part do ahead

Preparing: 10 min.
Marinating: 2 hrs.
Barbecuing: 30 min.

5-7 lb. leg of lamb, boned
6 green peppers
6 large yellow onions
48 cherry tomatoes
optional -
  48 med., fresh mushrooms

Marinade:
3/4 c. hot water
1/3 c. soy sauce
1/4 c. honey
2 tbsp. oil
2 tbsp. lemon juice
2 cloves garlic, crushed

6 or 12 long skewers

Cut lamb into 1-1/2 inch cubes. Combine al marinade ingredients and place in a large bow Marinate 48 cubes of meat for 2 hrs. or overnight in refrigerator, turning a few times. Cut peppers into quarters and then in half, giving 8 large pieces each. Cut onions into quarters and split into 8 pieces per onion. Before serving skewer in this order: piece o green pepper, piece of onion, cube of meat, tomato; repeat so as to have 4 pieces of meat on each skewer, ending with an extra piece of green pepper. (Put mushrooms on as well, if using.) Grill 5 inches from heat for 15 min.; turn and cook about 15 min. longer. Freeze any leftover, unmarinated meat in plastic bags, 4 or 8 to a bag, for later use.

Mrs. Richard W. Poor, Ridgewood

SPECIAL SHOULDER LAMB CHOPS   Serves: 4

"A delicious variation on this more economical cut of lamb."

Easy   No need to do ahead   Preparing: 5 min.
                                                    Baking: 45 min.

4 shoulder lamb chops   Salt and pepper the chops and lay them in
1 large onion   a shallow baking dish. Cover each with a
1 large tomato   slice of onion, then on top of that a slice
fresh dill, chopped   of tomato. Sprinkle fresh dill generously
                            over all. Add cold water until chops are
                            about half submerged. Bake at 375° for
                            45 min. Serve with noodles or rice.

                                Mrs. Lucien R. Tharaud, New York City

DOLMATHES (Stuffed Grape Leaves)   Serves: 4-6

"I once had this at the best Greek restaurant in New York. This is as good."

Average   Do ahead   Preparing: 30 min.
                                                    Cooking: 45 min.

1 lb. ground lamb, lean   Mix lamb with egg. Add onion, rice,
   (or beef)   parsley, mint, olive oil and 1/4 c. water.
1 egg, beaten   Season to taste. Rinse grape leaves and
1 med. onion, finely chopped place a spoonful of meat mixture on the dull
1/2 c. raw rice   side of each leaf. Roll, folding ends in as
1/4 c. chopped parsley   you go to seal in mixture. Place folded side
1 tsp. fresh mint leaves,   down in a saucepan, making more than one
   chopped (or 1/2 tsp.   layer if necessary. Add bouillon and remain-
   dried mint)   ing water. Cover and simmer for 45 min. Cook
2 tbsp. olive oil   ahead if desired, but be sure to reserve broth
1-3/4 c. water   for sauce. Serve with Avgolomono Sauce (below)
salt   Delicious served with a Greek table wine (if
pepper   you can find one) or any nice white wine.
1/2 jar grape leaves*   Very rich. Serve with a salad using "Feta"
1-1/2 c. undiluted beef   cheese.*
   bouillon

*Grape leaves are available at specialty food shops. The Cheese Shop locally
carries them. They also have Feta, a marvelous Greek cheese.

AVGOLEMONO SAUCE (Egg-Lemon Sauce)   Serves: 4-6

Use over Dolmathes (Stuffed Grape Leaves)

2 eggs   Beat eggs and add lemon juice. Slowly add
juice of 1 lemon   some of the hot broth reserved from the Grape
                            Leaves to eggs while continuing to beat. Stir
                            egg mixture into remaining broth. Remove from
                            heat. Cover and let stand for 5 min. to
                            thicken (it will). Serve at once. Do not
                            reheat.

                                Mrs. B. M. Brown, Ridgewood

JAEGERSCHNITZEL (German pork filets)

Serves: 4

Easy   Do ahead

Preparing: 10 min.
Cooking: 40 min.

4 pork filets
  (or thin pork chops)
salt
pepper
2 onions, sliced
3 tbsp. flour
butter
small can mushrooms
1 heaping tsp. instant beef
  bouillon (I use Maggi's)

Salt and pepper the filets, then turn in flour until well coated. Fry slowly in butter along with onions and mushrooms. When done (about 15 min. each side), remove from pan and keep warm. Pour one cup warm water into the pan and loosen the juices. Then add bouillon and more flour if you want a thicker gravy; simmer for one min. Place filets on serving platter and cover with gravy. Serve with noodles and tossed salad.

Mrs. John B. Winter, Paramus

PORK CHOP MARINADE

Serves: 4

"A delicious, unusual flavor especially when charcoal broiled."

Easy   Do ahead

Preparing: 10 min.
Marinating: 3 days
Broiling: 20 min.

4 pork chops, 1" thick
olive oil   ) equal parts
wine vinegar)
1 clove garlic
bay leaf
2 peppercorns
salt to taste
pepper to taste
optional - pinch dry mustard

Combine all marinade ingredients. Pour over chops and marinate several days, turning occasionally. When ready to serve, broil until done.

Mrs. John D. Dorsey, Ridgewood

PORK CHOPS IN WHITE WINE

Serves: 4

"Elegant enough for company; easy enough for family."

Easy   Do ahead   Preparing: 10 min.
Baking: 1-1/2 hrs.

4 large pork chops, 1" thick
2 large onions
flour
salt
pepper
1/2 c. white wine
1 tsp. soy sauce

Saute onions in butter or margarine until brown. Use a frying pan which is ovenproof. Add pork chops and brown well on both sides. Sprinkle with flour, salt and pepper. Over this pour wine which has been mixed with the soy sauce. Cover and cook in the oven at 350° for about 1-1/2 hrs. Serve with rice.

Mrs. Joseph L. Baker, Ridgewood

PORK CHOPS IN GRAVY

Serves: 6

"A real easy one that makes its own gravy."

Easy   Do ahead   Preparing: 10 min.
Baking: 1 - 1-1/2 hrs.

6 large pork chops
1 can cream vegetable soup

Brown chops well in a frying pan and transfer to a large, flat casserole. Cover them with the undiluted soup. Bake, covered, at 350° for 1 - 1-1/2 hrs.

Mrs. Harry F. Jones, III, Westfield

PORK CHOP CASSEROLE

Serves: 6

Average   Do ahead   Preparing: 20 min.
Cooking: 1-1/2 hrs.

6 large pork chops,
   center cut
salt to taste
pepper to taste
1 tbsp. onion soup mix
rosemary to taste
1 1-lb. jar applesauce
1 c. cranberries
1/4 c. dry vermouth

Brown chops in frying pan with salt, pepper, onion soup mix and rosemary. Put applesauce and cranberries into a 2 qt. casserole. Add chops and sauce to casserole. Add vermouth. Cover and bake in 325° oven 1-1/2 hrs.

Mrs. Oswald B. Deiter, Ridgewood

HAM LOAF WITH HORSERADISH SAUCE

Serves: 10

"Buffet fare. Cozy up to your butcher; some are testy about meat grinding."

Average   Do ahead   Preparing: 30 min.
Baking: 1-1/4 hrs.

1 lb. smoked cottage ham
1 lb. fresh pork
1 c. soft bread crumbs
1/2 c. milk
1 egg, beaten
2 tbsp. lemon juice

Sauce:
4 tbsp. horseradish
1 tbsp. sugar
1/2 tsp. salt
2 tsp. prepared mustard
1 tsp. vinegar
paprika to taste
1/2 pt. heavy cream, whipped

Have butcher grind meat together. Mix well the meat, bread crumbs, milk, egg and lemon juice. Put into loaf pan and bake in 350° oven for 1-1/4 hrs. Pour off grease when baked.

Sauce: Mix all ingredients together and whip some more!

Serve with scalloped potatoes and tossed salad.

Mrs. A. L. Van Wart, Ridgewood

HAM AND VEAL LOAF

Serves: 10-12

"This is a nice change and excellent as a leftover."

Average   Do ahead   Preparing: 15 min.
Baking: 2 hrs.

1-1/2 lbs. lean veal
1 lb. pork shoulder
3/4 lb. ham
3 eggs
1/2 large green pepper
medium onion
1 small can tomatoes
1-1/4 c. catsup
1/4 lb. soda crackers,
  mashed
few drops water
few strips bacon for garnish

Have meats ground together. Combine with the remaining ingredients, except bacon. Mound firmly in a roasting pan or pat loosely in a meat loaf pan (9x4x3) and lay strips of bacon across the top. Bake at 350° for 2 hrs. or until done.

Mrs. Michael O. Albl, Midland Park

HOT HAM MOUSSE

Serves: 4

"This recipe turns leftover ham into a most delicately-flavored dish."

Easy   No need to do ahead   Preparing: 15 min.
Baking: 35 min.

2 c. cooked ham,
  ground very fine
2 eggs, separated
  (3 if they are small)
pepper
dash of cayenne
pinch marjoram
pinch sweet basil
1 c. heavy cream or
  1 c. med. cream sauce
2 tbsp. sherry or Madeira

Add well beaten egg yolks, seasonings, cream and wine to the ham and mix well. Fold in stiffly beaten egg whites and turn into a greased 5 cup casserole. Bake in 325° oven until firm, about 35 min. Serve with riced potatoes and buttered string beans.

Mrs. Jay W. Jackson, Ridgewood

CHEESE-BROCCOLI-HAM STRATA

Serves: 12

"Wonderful for a luncheon or Sunday night supper."

Easy   Do ahead

Preparing: 25 min.
Regrigerating: 6 hrs. -
                overnight
Cooking: 55 min.

12 slices white bread
3/4 lb. sharp Cheddar cheese,
  sliced
1 10-oz. pkg. frozen chopped
  broccoli
2 c. diced cooked ham
6 eggs, slightly beaten
3-1/2 c. milk
2 tbsp. instant minced onion
1/2 tsp. salt
1/4 tsp. dry mustard

Cook and drain broccoli. With a doughnut cutter or with large and smaller size glasses cut 12 "doughnuts" and "holes" from the bread. (Bread that has been frozen and then defrosted cuts easiest.) Remove the crusts from the bread scraps and fit them into the bottom of a 13x9x2 inch baking pan. Layer in the cheese, broccoli and ham. Arrange the bread "doughnuts" and "holes" over the top. Combine the remaining ingredients and pour over the top. Refrigerate overnight or at least 6 hrs. Bake, uncovered, in a 325° oven for 55 min.

Mrs. Jack A James, Ridgewood

HAM ROLLS FOR LUNCHEON

Serves: 4

"Delicious, different luncheon dish."

Easy   Do ahead

Preparing: 10 min.
Chilling: 4 hrs.

6 oz. cream cheese, softened
1 c. celery cut very fine
1 tsp. lemon juice
1 c. crushed pineapple,
  drained
1 lb. sliced boiled ham
  cut double thick

Mix cream cheese, celery and lemon juice and spread over ham slices. Put I tsp. pineapple on end of each ham slice and roll up as a jelly roll. (If regular thickness, use two slices of ham.) Chill for about 4 hrs. Serve as individual rolls giving two per serving.

Mrs. Willard Harrer, Glenside, Pa.

HAM LOAF

Serves: 4-6

"This is delicious and a cinch to make!"

Easy   Do ahead

Preparing: 15 min.
Baking: 1-1/2 hrs.

1 lb. fresh ham or pork
1 lb. smoked ham
1 c. milk
1 c. fine bread crumbs
2 eggs, beaten
1 small can pineapple slices
maraschino cherries

Have butcher grind meats together. Mix meat, milk, bread crumbs and eggs together. Place in 9x5x4 inch loaf pan. Decorate top with pineapple slices and cherries. Bake at 350° for I-I/2 hrs. Good with horseradish sauce made by mixing horseradish with sour cream.

Horseradish sauce:
1 tbsp. horseradish
1 c. sour cream

Mrs. David H. Hinchcliff, Wyckoff

95

CURRANT-GLAZED APPLE-FILLED HAM SLICES

Serves: 4-6

"Delicious, different treat with ham."

Easy   Do ahead   Preparing: 30 min.
Baking: 1 hr.

1 can (1 lb. 6 oz.) apple
  pie filling
1/3 c. seedless raisins
1/4 c. chopped pecans
2 center cut ham slices,
  smoked, 1/2" thick

Glaze:
1 10-oz. jar currant jelly
1/4 c. light corn syrup
2-3 tbsp. prepared horse-
  radish
3/4 tsp. dry mustard

Combine pie filling, raisins and pecans.
Mix. Place one ham slice in a lightly greased,
shallow baking pan. Spread filling over slice
and cover with second slice. Cover. Bake at
350° for 1/2 hr. After ham has been cooking
for 1/2 hr., baste with following glaze.

Glaze: Combine jelly, syrup, horseradish
and mustard. Stir together and bring to a
boil. Baste ham every 10 min. for the last
1/2 hr. of cooking. Bake one hour in all,
no more. Delicious served with sweet potato
balls. (See page 178)

Mrs. George M. Griffith, Franklin Lakes

GLAZED SUGAR-CURED HAM STEAK

Serves: 2

This recipe won the 1960 Gold Medal of the Culinary Olympics.
The donor was the originator and a member of the U. S. team.

Easy   No need to do ahead   Preparing: none
Cooking: 5 min.

1 3/4-1b. slice pre-cooked ham
2 heaping tsp. sugar
1-1/2 oz. Burgundy or claret
optional - raisins

Put sugar into a heavy pan which has been
heated over very high heat. When sugar starts
to melt, place ham steak in pan and fry to a
mahogany brown. Turn. Pour wine over ham.
Take off heat. Cover pan and let stand for
3 min. Serve immediately. If raisins are
desired, pour boiling water over them the
night before and cover immediately. Add
raisins to sauce when serving.

Mr. William W. Schmitz, Ho-Ho-Kus

HAM SCALLOP CASSEROLE

Serves: 4-6

"This is a quick and easy family dinner."

Easy   Do ahead   Preparing: 10 min.
Baking: 1 hr.

2 ham steaks, 1/2" thick
1 or 2 boxes scalloped
  potato mix (depends on
  your family's appetite)

Put one ham steak on bottom of casserole
to fit ham. Put in potatoes and mix according to package directions. Place second ham
steak on top. Cover and bake at 350° for
one hour.

Mrs. Maurice Muser, Jr., Ridgewood

SWEET AND SOUR PORK

Serves: 4-6

"A great party meal served in a chafing dish. Easily multiplied."

Average   Freeze

Preparing: 30 min.
Cooking: 1-1/2 hrs.

2 tbsp. bacon fat
1-1/2 lbs. lean pork strips
1 #2 can pineapple chunks
1/2 c. water
1/3 c. vinegar
1/4 c. brown sugar
2 tbsp. cornstarch
1/2 tsp. salt
1 tbsp. soy sauce
3/4 c. thinly sliced
   green pepper
1/2 c. thinly sliced onions

Day or more before: Cook pork in bacon fat in large skillet until it is golden on all sides. Drain pineapple and reserve juice. Combine water, vinegar, brown sugar, cornstarch, soy sauce, salt and 3/4 to I c. pineapple syrup. Cook until clear and slightly thickened (about 2 min.). Add meat and cook, covered, over low heat one hour or until meat is done. Refrigerate or freeze at this point.

Before serving: Defrost, if frozen, then 30 min. before serving heat mixture over low heat until steaming hot. Add vegetables and pineapple. Cook about 2 min. Serve in a chafing dish with rice as a side dish.

Mrs. Richard W. Poor, Ridgewood

MINCEMEAT GLAZE SPARERIBS

Serves: 4-6

"Nice to serve alfresco with other goodies!"

Easy   Do ahead

Preparing: 10 min.
Baking: 2 hrs.

1 lb. spareribs
1 13-oz. can consomme
   madrilene
1-1/2 c. mincemeat
3 tbsp. vinegar
2 tbsp. soy sauce

Arrange spareribs in shallow baking pan. Bake in 500° oven for 30 min. Pour off fat. Bake at 300° for 30 min. Again pour off fat. Combine consomme madrilene, mincemeat, vinegar and soy sauce. Mix well. Pour over ribs. Bake at 300° for one hour. Baste with sauce while cooking. Great as appetizer or main course.

Mrs. William W. Weleck, Jr., Ridgewood

BARBECUED HAM

Serves: 6

"Excellent for informal gatherings."

Easy   Freeze

Preparing: 10 min.
Cooking: 1-1/2 hrs.

1 c. catsup
1 c. chili sauce
2 c. water
1/2 c. brown sugar
2 tbsp. vinegar
1 tsp. dry mustard
1 lb. boiled ham,
   sliced very thin

Mix all ingredients, except ham. Simmer slowly for one hour. Add ham and continue to simmer for I/2 hr. Serve on heated round buns with either potato salad or coleslaw. Sauce can easily be frozen or done ahead.

Mrs. Raymond N. Gorcyca, Allendale

ITALIAN PORK AND RICE CASSEROLE

Serves: 6-8

"Especially good for a buffet supper dish. A hardy casserole men love."

Average   Do ahead   Preparing: 45 min.
                                                       Baking: 1-1/2 hrs.

Sauce:
2 med. onions, sliced
1 clove garlic, minced
2 tbsp. salad oil
10-3/4 oz. can beef gravy
3 8-oz. cans tomato sauce
optional -
   3 oz. can whole mushrooms,
   undrained
   2 tbsp. minced parsley

3 lbs. loin of pork,
   cut from bone
salt
pepper
2 tbsp. salad oil
2 c. raw regular rice
3-4 med. onions, sliced
3 large green peppers
1/2 tsp. salt

Sauce: Make sauce first. Saute onions and garlic in oil until golden. Add gravy, tomato sauce, mushrooms and parsley. Simmer, uncovered, for 30 min.

Cut pork into 1/4 inch slices. Cut peppers into eighths. Sprinkle pork with salt and pepper. Saute pork (a few pieces at a time) in oil until brown. When all are brown, remove last from pan. Add a little of the sauce to the pan drippings, stir well and return all to the sauce. In a 3 qt. casserole arrange one half of the pork slices. Top with all the rice, which has been mixed with one half of the sauce. Layer one half of the onions, then layer one half of the peppers. Add remaining pork, remaining onions and peppers. Sprinkle with salt. Pour on remaining sauce and bake at 350° for 1-1/2 hrs.

Mrs. Timothy M. Tamblyn, Saddle River

PORK CHOP AND SAUERKRAUT CASSEROLE

Serves: 4

"A good winter casserole."

Easy   Do ahead   Preparing: 15 min.
                                                       Baking: 40 min.

8 pork chops
4 strips bacon
1 can sauerkraut
2 tbsp. dark brown sugar

Cook bacon strips in skillet; remove and drain. Crumble and set aside. Brown chops well and fast in bacon fat. Remove chops and drain off some of the fat. Place chops in casserole. Drain sauerkraut and rinse. Toss in pan with remaining fat. Add brown sugar and crumbled bacon. Toss together. Pour over chops and bake, covered, at 350° for 30 min. Remove cover and bake about 10 min. longer. Serve with glazed squash rings or glazed fried apples.

Mrs. Edward C. Kaiser, Ridgewood

CREPES LASAGNE (Also a basic crepes recipe)   Serves: 8

"Great dish for 'after the cocktail party' or for teenagers."

Average

Part do ahead
Part freeze

Preparing: 30 min.
Cooking: 30 min.
Baking: 45 min.

Crepes:
1-1/2 c. milk
1 whole egg
1 egg white
1 tbsp. melted butter
dash salt
1 c. + 2 tbsp. sifted flour

Filling:
1 lb. Italian sausage
  (sweet, spiced or mixed)
1 c. ricotta cheese
1 c. grated mozzarella cheese
  (or slices)

Topping:
8 oz. tomato sauce
approximately 20 oz. spaghetti
  sauce with meat
3/4 tsp. oregano
1/2 tsp. M.S.G.
1/8 tsp. seasoned pepper
1/4 tsp. basil, crushed
1 c. grated Parmesan cheese
black olives for garnish

Crepes: Combine all ingredients and beat smooth. Heat a lightly greased skillet until a drop of water sizzles and disappears immediately. Pour 1/3 c. batter into skillet and tilt quickly in all directions to cover bottom evenly with a thin film of batter. Cook over medium heat until light brown. Turn (using two spatulas is the easiest way). Cook other side. Remove from pan and stack between wax paper layers while cooking remaining crepes. If freezing, wrap stack in foil or place in plastic bag.

Filling: Cook sausage and slice thinly. Spread crepes with ricotta cheese and sprinkle with sausage slices. Top with mozzarella and roll up. Place in a large, flat Pyrex baking dish with the crepes seam down.

Topping: Combine all ingredients, except Parmesan cheese, in a saucepan. Bring to a boil and simmer, uncovered, for 30 min. Pour over the crepes to just cover; reserve any remaining to use when serving. Cover dish with foil and bake at 350° for 30 min. Remove foil. Sprinkle with Parmesan and bake, uncovered, for 15 min. more. Serve from pan. Garnish with black olives.

Ed. Note: This is a basic crepes recipe and can be used filled as a main dish with almost any desired filling (creamed chicken, shellfish, asparagus, etc.). It is great topped with hollandaise sauce and lightly broiled. For dessert crepes they may be filled or stacked with jams, jellies, fresh fruit, etc., and served with or without a flaming brandy sauce.

Mrs. Richard C. Baxter, Ridgewood

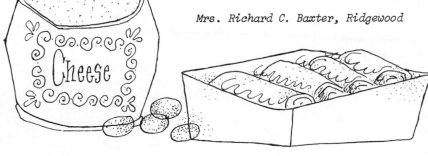

Veal

VEAL AMANDINE

Easy

Do ahead

Serves: 3-4

Preparing: 20 min.
Cooking: 1 hr.

1 lb. veal steak
flour
1 tbsp. salad oil
salt
pepper
1/2 c. sour cream
1/4 c. roasted, slivered
  almonds

Cut veal into 1-1/2 inch squares and dip into flour. Brown in hot oil. Salt and pepper to taste. Add enough hot water to barely cover the meat. Cover and cook slowly 30-40 min. or until the meat is tender. Remove lid and continue cooking until almost all of the liquid has evaporated. Can be done ahead to this point. Stir in sour cream and cook slowly for 5 min. Stir in half of the almonds. Serve over cooked rice or noodles and sprinkle remaining almonds over the top.

Miss Susan L. Hinman, Suffern, New York

VEAL MARENGO

Serves: 8

"Great for buffets served in casserole or chafing dish."

Average

Do ahead

Preparing: 20 min.
Cooking: 1 hr. 5 min.

6 tbsp. oil
3 lbs. lean veal,
  cut into 1-1/2" cubes
2 small onions, chopped fine
9 tomatoes or 1 large can
5-1/2 tsp. salt
1/4 tsp. pepper
generous dash paprika
5 tsp. flour
3-1/2 c. chicken broth
1 c. dry white wine
12-14 small whole carrots
8 whole white onions, peeled
18-20 whole button-size
  mushrooms
10-oz. pkg. frozen peas
chopped parsley

Brown veal rapidly in hot oil in large heavy kettle over high heat. Add chopped onions, tomatoes which have been peeled, seeded, and coarsely chopped, salt, pepper and paprika. Stir in flour, chicken broth and wine. Cover and simmer 30 min. Add carrots and white onions; simmer another 30 min. when meat should be fork tender. Five minutes before serving add peas, being careful not to overcook peas. Sprinkle with chopped parsley and serve with garlic bread and green salad. Best made a day ahead, still adding peas just before serving.

Mrs. John L. Dwyer, Franklin Lakes

VEAL MARSALA

Serves: 6

"The secret is to pound veal slices before you begin - the thinner the better."

Average   Do ahead   Preparing: 30 min.
Baking: 30 min.

12 large slices scaloppine
  of veal
flour
salad oil
2-3 tbsp. butter
1/2 lb. sliced fresh mushrooms
2 tbsp. chopped chives
2 tbsp. chopped parsley
1-1/2 c. beef broth
  (or bouillon)
1/2 c. Marsala wine
paprika
salt
pepper

Dust veal slices lightly in flour. Heat 3-4 tbsp. salad oil in skillet. Saute quickly 3 or 4 slices of veal at a time over high heat until browned. Transfer slices to a serving dish or casserole and sprinkle each slice with paprika. Add more oil if necessary and repeat process for remaining slices of veal. Melt butter in skillet. Add mushrooms and saute about 5 min. Add chives, parsley, salt and pepper to taste, beef broth and wine. Simmer 5 min. Pour the above over veal slices in the casserole. Place casserole in 350° oven for 1/2 hr. Serve with hot buttered noodles or Noodle Casserole on page 176.

Mrs. S. Robert Herring, Ridgewood

VEAL SCALOPPINE

Serves: 6-8

"Simple - but for the gourmet palate."

Average   Do ahead   Preparing: 1 hr.

3 lbs. veal cut into
  thin slices
flour for dredging
2 shallots, chopped
1 tsp. M.S.G.
1/2 c. white wine
1/8 tsp. pepper
1/4 c. butter
2 tsp. beef stock base
2 c. water
1 3-oz. can sliced mushrooms
  or 1/2 lb. fresh
salt to taste

Pound veal until thin. Dredge with flour. Heat butter in skillet and add veal. Brown on all sides. Remove from pan. Add mushrooms and shallots; saute. Add water, beef stock, M.S.G. and pepper. Bring to boil and simmer one or two min. Add veal to mixture, then wine. Simmer 15 to 20 min. until done. If sauce needs thickening, do so with flour. Can be done the day before and reheated. Delicious and colorful with grilled tomatoes and green noodles.

Mrs. Robert R. Gulick, Ramsey

VEAL SCALOPPINE CASSEROLE

Serves: 6

"This can be multiplied to any number with more veal."

Average   Freeze   Preparing: 20 min.
Baking: 45 min.

6 veal scaloppine,
  pounded thin
1 egg, beaten
bread crumbs
butter or margarine
1 can mushroom soup
1 small can chopped mushrooms
1/2 c. white wine

Dip veal in egg, then in bread crumbs. Brown lightly in butter or margarine and place in buttered casserole. Add mushroom soup, chopped mushrooms and wine. Heat at 325° for 45 min. Serve with noodles or rice.

Mrs. George M. Himadi, Ft. Lauderdale, Fla.

VEAL IN CAPER SAUCE

Serves: 4

"I became a 'neetsy-keen' mother-in-law with this one!"

Average   Do ahead   Preparing: 30 min.
                                                  Baking: 1 hr. 15 min.

8 scaloppine of veal
2 eggs
1/4 c. milk
salt to taste
1 c. fine bread crumbs
4 tbsp. oil
  (I use Wesson)
2/3 c. dry sauterne

Sauce:
stick of butter
1 large lemon
1/2 bottle capers, drained
dash salt

Beat eggs and milk together. Add salt. Dip veal into egg mixture and then into crumbs. Repeat to coat each piece twice. Saute in oil until golden brown, a few scaloppine at a time. Transfer to a Pyrex 9x14 inch baking pan. Do not stack the veal, but it can overlap a bit if necessary. Pour wine over all and cover tightly with foil. Bake at 325° for about 1 hr. 15 min. or until wine is evaporated.

Sauce: In a pipkin or small saucepan melt butter, then add the juice of the fresh lemon, capers, and a dash of salt. Heat, but do not boil. Transfer veal to a warm platter and spoon caper sauce over all. Serve with fettuccine (page 176) or risotto (page 174) and a tossed salad with a light vinegar and oil dressing. Pouilly-Fuisse wine is great with this.

Mrs. Robert F. Hill, Wyckoff

VEAL BIRDS

Serves: 4

"A little complicated, but worth it."

Complicated   Do ahead   Preparing: 30 min.
                                                  Cooking: 1 hr.

8-12 Italian-style veal
  cutlets

Stuffing:
2 medium onions
6 slices bread, crumbed
salt
pepper
basil
1 clove garlic, crushed
1 c. celery, finely chopped
1/4 c. butter or margarine

Gravy:
1/2 lb. fresh mushrooms
  (or 4-oz. can)
1 medium onion, chopped
1/4 c. butter or margarine
2 chicken bouillon cubes
2 c. water
1/4 c. sherry
flour

Chop onions and brown in butter or margarine. Add bread crumbs made by rubbing bread over grater. Salt and pepper. Add basil and crushed garlic. Add finely chopped celery and make a stuffing, adding more butter if necessary. Pound the cutlets out very thin, stuff and roll. Hold together with a skewer or with fine string. Brown well in butter or cooking oil. Remove from pan and brown chopped onion and mushrooms. Put in bouillon cubes and 1/4 c. sherry. Thicken a bit with flour. Put veal back into pan and cook slowly for 1 hr. or until done. Or, place in a casserole, covering halfway with gravy, and cook at 325° in oven for 1 hr. Serve over hot rice.

Mrs. Gerald F. Corcoran, Ramsey

VEAL A LA SUISSE CASSEROLE

Serves: 6

"A delicious blend of flavors. Nice company dinner with only a salad to add."

Average Do ahead

Preparing: 30 min.
Refrigerating: overnight
Baking: 1-1/2 hrs.

1-1/2 lbs. thin veal cutlets
1/2 lb. thin Swiss cheese
3 tbsp. flour
1-1/2 tsp. paprika
3 tbsp. butter
4 oz. broad noodles
1/2 lb. cooked ham (not thin)
1 can beef gravy
1/2 c. light cream
1/2 c. white wine
1 pkg. frozen cut green beans

Have butcher flatten veal to 1/4 inch; cut into serving-size pieces. The day before serving, place a slice of cheese on half of the veal pieces; top each with a second piece of veal. Combine flour and paprika and coat veal. In hot butter in a heavy skillet, brown veal very well, adding more butter as needed; remove veal. Meanwhile, start cooking noodles as package directs. Cut ham into 12 chunks. Brown ham slightly in same skillet. Remove. In same skillet stir gravy into cream. Simmer, stirring, about 10 min. or until smooth and thickened. Stir in wine. Using a 2 qt. casserole place half noodles on bottom, then layer of gravy, veal and then ham; repeat layers. Refrigerate, covered, overnight. About 1-3/4 hrs. before serving, remove from refrigerator. Bake, covered, at 375° for 1-1/2 hrs. Cook green beans and sprinkle over top of dish to serve.

Mrs. Kenneth C. Beltramini, Ho-Ho-Kus

VEAL CASSEROLE

Serves: 4

"Unusual, smooth (like beef stroganoff) and economical!"

Average Do ahead

Preparing: 25 min.
Cooking: 1 hr.

1-1/2 lbs. boneless veal,
  cubed
1-1/2 - 2 tbsp. butter
1 med. onion, sliced
1/2 lb. sliced mushrooms
1 tbsp. chopped parsley
1 tbsp. flour
3 tbsp. water
1/4 c. white wine
3/4 c. sour cream
1/2 tsp. salt
1/8 tsp. freshly ground pepper

Brown veal in butter in skillet. Remove meat to ovenproof dish. Add onion and mushrooms to skillet, stir and saute lightly. Remove skillet from heat and slowly stir in the remaining ingredients. Pour sauce over meat in baking dish. Cover and bake at 250° for one hour or until done. Serve with noodles.

Mrs. Robert B. Fast, Ridgewood

TWENTY MINUTE CASUAL DISH

Serves: 6-8

"An excellent luncheon dish."

Easy   Do ahead   Preparing: 20 min.
                                                    Cooking: 1 hr.

1 lb. veal
1 lb. pork
1/2 lb. pkg. fine noodles
salt
1 small pkg. process cheese
1 green pepper
1 small jar pimentos
1 med. can creamed white corn
1 small onion
1 c. chopped celery
1/2 - 3/4 c. grated cheese
1/2 c. corn flakes
1/4 c. melted butter

Cut veal and lean pork into bite-size pieces. Cover with water and simmer 20 min. Add uncooked noodles and salt. Cut pepper, onion and celery into small pieces and add to meat. Simmer another 20 min. Drain and add process cheese which has been cut into small bits, then add pimento. When the cheese has melted place in a flat 9x13 inch baking dish. Freeze or prepare ahead to this point. Thaw, if necessary, then 1/2 hr. before serving cover with corn and top with corn flakes which have been mixed with melted butter. Top with grated cheese and bake at 350° for 20 min. or until bubbly.

Mrs. Edward D. Doherty, Ridgewood

THIN VEAL FORESTER

Serves: 4

"A quick dish with a different flavor."

Easy   Serve immediately   Preparing: 10 min.
                                                    Cooking: 20 min.

1-1/2 lbs. veal cutlets,
   thinly cut
1 clove garlic
1/2 c. flour
1/2 c. butter or margarine
1/2 lb. fresh mushrooms,
   thinly sliced
salt
pepper
1/3 c. dry vermouth
1 tsp. lemon juice
3 tsp. chopped parsley

Pound veal so it is very thin. Rub well with garlic clove and dredge in flour. Melt butter or margarine in a large skillet with a cover. Add veal and saute until golden on both sides. Heap mushrooms on veal and season with salt and pepper. Pour vermouth over and cover skillet. Cook over low heat for 20 min. being sure veal is moist at all times. Add 1 tsp. of water at a time if it seems to get dry. When serving sprinkle with lemon juice and chopped parsley.

Mrs. A. Steffee Smith, Ridgewood

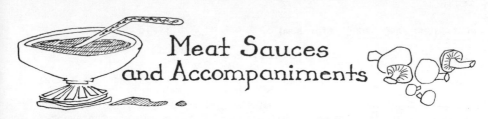

Meat Sauces and Accompaniments

OUR FAVORITE BARBECUE SAUCE

Yield: 2 cups

"This is our favorite; excellent on hamburgers, chicken and spare ribs."

Easy   Do ahead   Preparing: 5 min.
                                Simmering: 10 min.

1/2 can beer
1/2 c. molasses
1/2 c. chili sauce
1/4 c. prepared mustard
1 small onion, chopped
dash Worcestershire sauce
salt
pepper

Blend all ingredients together in a saucepan and bring to a boil. Simmer for 10 min.
If it gets too thick, just add more beer.
What you don't use right away may be stored
in the refrigerator for a couple of weeks.

Mrs. John L. Dwyer, Franklin Lakes

LAW SCHOOL BARBECUE SAUCE

Yield: 2 cups

"A marvelous way to spruce up inexpensive cuts of meat."

Easy   Do ahead   Preparing: 10 min.
                                Simmering: 15 min.

1 c. vinegar
1 clove garlic (or garlic
   powder)
1 tbsp. olive oil
   (or vegetable oil)
2-1/2 tbsp. Worcestershire
1/2 c. sugar
1/2 c. catsup
1 tsp. dry mustard
1 tbsp. salt
dash paprika
dash Tabasco sauce

Put vinegar into heavy skillet and add all
other ingredients. Bring to a slow boil,
reduce heat and simmer for 15 min. Use on
spareribs, painting it on when they are on
the grill or just add the ribs to the
sauce and cook on top of the stove in a
skillet. Good, too, on chicken and steak -
on everything!

Mrs. Albert F. Lilley, Allendale

GREATEST CUMBERLAND SAUCE

Yield: 3/4 cup

"Tangy - that just-perfect complement for one roast duck."

Easy   Do ahead   Preparing: 10 min.

3 tbsp. red currant jelly
2 tbsp. port wine
2 tbsp. orange juice
1 tbsp. lemon juice
1 tsp. prepared mustard
1 tsp. paprika
1/2 tsp. ground ginger
3 tbsp. grated orange rind

Melt jelly until it is liquid. Cool. Add
wine, juices and spices. Cover rind with cold
water and bring to a boil. Drain. Add rind
to the first mixture and serve individually
over each portion OR cover duck with sauce
before carving.

Mrs. William B. Atwood, Mahwah

105

GREATEST MUSTARD SAUCE (for ham)   Yield: 2 cups

"Easy, easy, easy. Great for a party ham!"

Easy   Do ahead   Preparing: 15 min.

1 c. granulated sugar   Mix sugar and mustard together. Add
1 rounded tbsp. dry mustard   vinegar and water slowly to the sugar.
3/4 c. cider vinegar   Add eggs last and cook, stirring con-
1/4 c. water   stantly until it thickens (10-15 min.).
3 eggs, beaten   This can be served hot or cold. Will
                                   store in refrigerator for one month.

Mrs. Willaim B. Atwood, Mahwah

ORANGE SAUCE   Yield: 1-1/2 cups

"Adds a real party flavor to sliced ham."

Easy   Do ahead   Preparing: 10 min.
                                                     Cooking: 10 min.

8 tbsp. sugar   Combine all ingredients except marmalade
3 tsp. corn starch   and orange slices. Cook and stir until
1/2 tsp. salt   thickened and clear. Add marmalade and
1/2 tsp. cinnamon   orange slices.
18 cloves
4 tsp. grated orange rind
1 c. orange juice
2 tsp. lemon juice
1/3 c. orange marmalade
5 orange slices, halved   *Mrs. W. Bruce Boyle, Ft. Lauderdale, Fla.*

QUICK SAUCE FOR SLICED STEAKS   Yield: 1 cup

"Great on all steaks and chopped meats. Marvelous for barbecues."

Easy   Do ahead   Preparing: 10 min.

1/2 c. catsup   Warm catsup in a double boiler. In a
1/2 c. butter   separate pan warm the butter and add to
Worcestershire sauce   catsup. Stir. Add Worcestershire to
                                   taste. Pour over sliced steak.

Mr. William W. Schmitz, Ho-Ho-Kus

SOUR CREAM-RED WINE SAUCE FOR ROAST LAMB   Serves: 10-14

"Marvelous on stuffed roast lamb or chops." (See page 89)

Easy   Do ahead   Preparing: 15 min.

1/3 c. butter   Melt butter in top of double boiler. Add
1-1/2 c. red currant jelly   jelly and one cup of wine. Add liquid from
1-1/2 c. dry red wine   roasting pan. Stir in flour. When thickened
1/2 c. flour   add rest of wine. When ready to serve, stir
1-1/2 pts. sour cream   in sour cream and reheat. Save leftover sauc
                                   for lamb chops!

Mrs. Morton Evans, Canton, Mass.

COLBERT SAUCE

Serves: 4-6

"A great, different sauce for fish, chops or steaks."

Easy   Do ahead   Preparing: 5 min.

1/2 c. butter, melted
1/2 tsp. beef extract
  (I use Bovril)
2 tbsp. chopped parsley
2 tbsp. chopped chives
2 tbsp. lemon juice

Stir beef extract into warm butter until smooth. Add remaining ingredients. Serve over baked or fried fish or over chops or steaks. May be reheated.

Mrs. John A. Snyder, Ridgewood

YORKSHIRE PUDDING

Serves: 6

"Perfect with Roast Beef."

Easy   Serve immediately   Preparing: 10 min.
                                                  Baking: 35 min.

7/8 c. flour
1/2 tsp. salt
1/2 c. milk
2 eggs, beaten
1/2 c. water

Have all ingredients at room temperature. Sift dry ingredients together. Add milk gradually, stirring all the time. When smooth, add well beaten eggs. Continue beating and add water. Beat vigorously or use blender for 15 sec. Preheat oven to 400°. Make the batter at least one hour before baking. Beat again just before pouring into 1/4 inch of smoking, hot beef drippings in a 9x10 inch pan. Bake 20 min. at 400° then reduce heat to 350° and bake for 15 min. more.

Mrs. S. William Walstrum, Ridgewood

YORKSHIRE PUDDING (Muffins)

Serves: 6

"Serve with roast beef."

Easy   Do ahead   Preparing: 10 min.
                                                  Refrigerating: overnight
                                                  Baking: 20 min.

1 c. milk
1 c. flour
1/4 tsp. salt
2 eggs, beaten
1 tbsp. dry onion soup mix

Slowly add milk to flour and salt. Then add eggs and onion soup mix. Beat 2-3 min. Let stand overnight or a few hours in the refrigerator. Pour one-half inch deep in muffin pans (preferably cast iron) which have been greased and heated. (Use beef drippings for the greasing if desired.) Bake at 450° for about 20 min. or until puffed and brown. Serve hot.

Dr. Oswald B. Deiter, Ridgewood

Meat Magnifications

When gravy or cream sauce is lumpy, whip briskly with a wire whisk or egg
beater. If condition is really bad, pour through a strainer.

Freeze leftover gravy in an ice cube tray. When frozen, transfer to a
plastic bag. Use as much as you want.

Instant potato makes a great thickening for stews and gravies - will not lump.

* When planning to serve bacon to a crowd, fry the bacon the day before and
lay it out on a cookie sheet on paper towels, cover with one of our
many "wraps" and store it in the refrigerator or freezer. When needed,
reheat it in a 300-325° oven for a short time (just long enough to
heat through). *Sent by Mrs. James T. Emery, Ridgewood*

Broil bacon after dipping into beaten egg and then crushed cracker crumbs for
a different taste.

Baste meat with an artist's trick - use a paint brush kept for this purpose.
This is a good trick for the outdoor barbecues, too.

Shape ground meat into patties before freezing - a block of ground meat is
hard to thaw for use. Place a double layer of wax paper or foil between
layers - you only need to take out the desired number of patties and
they thaw quite quickly.

Add a grated, raw potato to each pound of ground meat for juicy hamburgers.

Dipping your fingers in water when making meatballs will prevent sticking.

Put a strip of bacon on the bottom of your meat loaf pan to keep it from
sticking.

For quick meat loaf, put it into individual muffin pans - takes about half the
time of a large loaf.

Place a piece or two of dry bread under the broiler pan - it soaks up the fat
drippings and reduces smoking and fires.

If freezing stews, omit the potatoes. Add these, partially cooked, when reheating. Potatoes do not freeze very well.

Most meats may be cooked frozen, without thawing; however, they will be a
little tougher than if cooked while at room temperature.

It is best to thaw meats in the refrigerator or you will lose the lovely
juices. After thawing, bring them to room temperature for perfect
cooking.

Allow about twice the cooking time when cooking frozen meats.

Tenderize meat with a few drops of vinegar - no change in taste. It will
start the cooking faster, too.

* Garnish meats with chutneyed peach halves. Butter peaches, bake at 350° for
10 min., fill with chutney and heat 5 min. more.

Poultry

OVEN BARBECUED CHICKEN

Serves: 8

"This is best done the day before and reheated in sauce before serving."

Easy   Do ahead   Preparing: 15 min.
                                                    Baking: 1-1/2 hrs.

8 chicken breasts
2 bay leaves
6 garlic cloves, cut
1 large onion, sliced
paprika

Sauce:
3 c. tomato juice
3 tsp. salt
1/2 tsp. pepper
1/2 tsp. dry mustard
2 tsp. sugar
3 tbsp. Worcestershire sauce
1-1/2 c. vinegar
1/2 tsp. red pepper
        or
dash Tabasco sauce
1/2 stick margarine

Put chicken breasts skin side up in broiler pan or other shallow pan. Tuck slices of onion under each piece. Dust with paprika.

Sauce: Mix remaining ingredients and pour over chicken. Should be 1/4 to 1/2 inch deep. Bake 1-1/2 hrs. at 300° or until done, basting occasionally. Leftover sauce may be stored in the refrigerator for future use.

Mrs. Pressly M. Millen, Jr., Ho-Ho-Kus

CHICKEN CONTINENTAL

Serves: 4-6

"Easy enough for everyday; tasty enough for company."

Easy   Do ahead   Preparing: 20 min.
                                                    Cooking: 20 min.

1 fryer, cut up
butter or margarine

Sauce:
1 can cream chicken soup
2-1/2 tbsp. grated onion
1 tsp. salt
dash pepper
1 tbsp. minced parsley
1/2 tsp. celery flakes
dash thyme
1-1/3 c. water
1-1/3 c. uncooked instant
  rice
paprika

Fry or bake chicken in the usual manner with a little butter until brown.

Sauce: Combine soup, onion, salt, pepper, parsley, celery flakes and thyme in a saucepan. Mix well. Add water and mix well again. Bring to a boil, stirring constantly. Pour instant rice into a shallow 1-1/2 qt. casserole. Stir 1 c. of the soup mixture over rice to moisten well. Place chicken over rice and cover chicken with remaining soup mixture (1/3 c.). Cover and bake at 375° for 20 min. Sprinkle with paprika.

Mrs. Harry N. Ives, Ridgewood

CHICKEN GUMBO

Serves: 8-10

Complicated   Freeze

Preparing: 40 min.
Simmering: 3 hrs.

4 lb. dressed hen
1 c. chopped onions
1 c. chopped celery
3 tbsp. flour
2 gal. warm water
gumbo file*
  (sassafras and thyme)
1 c. oil
4 cloves garlic, minced
green onion tops
parsley, chopped
salt
pepper
red pepper

Roux:
1-1/2 c. oil
1-1/2 c. flour

*File available on spice
rack in grocery store.
(McCormick's gourmet)

Cut up hen and season generously with salt and peppers. Fry in oil in heavy pot over medium heat until golden brown. Pour excess oil from pot and save for roux. Add chopped onions and celery to chicken and cook slowly uncovered until onions wilt. Make a roux by putting 1-1/2 c. oil (including the oil saved from the chicken) in a heavy iron pot over high heat. When hot gradually stir in 1-1/2 c. flour. Stir constantly. After flour and oil are combined, turn fire down very low and cook until golden brown. Stir constantly. Put in a separate container immediately to keep from getting too dark. Pour excess oil off top. After roux is made, dissolve it in 2 gal. warm water. Add garlic, then add roux mixture to chicken. Simmer the combined mixture slowly in uncovered pot until chicken is tender. Serve in soup plates. Before serving, sprinkle chopped green onion tops and parsley and a dash of file in each plate. Serve with rice and a green salad.

Mrs. Sheridan P. Wait, Paramus

HOT CHICKEN SALAD CASSEROLE

Serves: 8

"Suggest not serving this to visitors from Pittsburgh - everybody there uses it for buffet dinners."

Average   Do ahead

Preparing: 20 min.
Marinating: overnight
Baking: 1/2 - 1 hr.

8 chicken breasts
French dressing (I use Wish-
  bone's French with garlic)
1 c. chopped celery
1 c. mayonnaise
1 lb. jar soft cheese spread
  (I use Cheez Whiz)
1 can French fried onions
optional - 1 c. almonds or
             pecans

Day before boil chicken breasts, cool, remove meat from bones and cut into bite-size pieces. Toss in French dressing and marinate overnight. Next day add celery and mayonnaise to taste (be generous with the mayonnaise) to make a chicken salad. Nuts may also be added, if desired. Place salad evenly in a baking dish and spread jar of cheese spread on top. Cook at 350° for 1/2 hr. (or a little longer if not starting from room temperature). Put can of French fried onions on top and put back in the oven for 5 min. longer.

Mrs. J. A. McIlhatten, Ridgewood

BAKED CHICKEN AND RICE   Serves: 4

"This is tasty the second time around as a leftover."

Easy   No need to do ahead   Preparing: 10 min.
                                                    Baking: 2 hrs.

4 chicken legs with thighs   In a greased roaster, mix rice, onion soup
1 c. uncooked rice   mix and water. Place chicken on top and
1 pkg. onion soup mix   bake at 350° covered for 1 hr. Uncover and
3 c. water   cook a second hour. Chicken breasts may also
                              be used, but watch out for the small bones.

Mrs. Robert W. Peterson, Ramsey

COQ AU VIN   Serves: 4-6

"I like this for serving crowds as it serves well after making ahead."

Average   Do ahead   Preparing: 20 min.
                                                    Cooking: 1 hr.

2 fryers, cut up   Brown chicken in butter or margarine. Place
2-3 strips bacon   in a 2 qt. Pyroceram casserole or large frying
1/2 tsp. salt   pan. Cook bacon and reserve. Season chicken
1/8 tsp. pepper   with salt and pepper. Add onions, drained,
1 can small onions   and mushrooms (fresh can be used, if desired)
1 pkg. frozen mushrooms Cook slowly for about 10 min. Combine wine,
3 c. red wine   consomme, tomato paste, crushed garlic (if
1 c. chicken consomme   desired), thyme, bay leaf and bacon. Add to
        or   chicken and simmer for about 30 min. or until
1 c. chicken bouillon   chicken is done. Remove chicken and thicken
1/2 tbsp. tomato paste   sauce in casserole by combining flour and
garlic clove   melted butter and adding slowly to hot liquid,
1/4 tsp. thyme   blending with a wire whip. Return chicken to
1 bay leaf   casserole and baste with sauce. If using fry-
1/4 c. flour   ing pan, transfer to casserole. May be
1/2 stick butter   reheated over low heat in oven or in a chafing
                         dish. Serve with rice and a tossed salad.

Mrs. Maurice Muser, Jr., Ridgewood

COMPANY CHICKEN   Serves: 6

"Great for garlic lovers."

Average   Do ahead   Preparing: 15 min.
                                                    Baking: 1 hr.

2 c. bread crumbs   Mix crumbs, cheese, garlic, salt and pepper
3/4 c. Parmesan cheese   in bowl. Wash chicken and pat dry. Dip in
1 clove garlic, crushed melted butter and coat with mixture. Arrange
2 tbsp. salt   in a roasting pan; do not let the chicken
1/8 tsp. pepper   pieces overlap. Dot with butter and bake at
2 frying chickens, cut up 350° for 1 hr. Do not turn.
1/4 lb. melted butter or
   margarine
2 tbsp. butter   *Mrs. Russell B. Grant, Ridgewood*

CHICKEN BURGUNDY   Serves: 4-6

"Very easy, but real company fare."

Easy   Best not done ahead   Preparing: 20 min.
                                                   Cooking: 1-1/4 hrs.

2 fryers, cut up   Coat chicken with flour, salt and pepper
flour   mixture. Brown in butter or margarine.
salt   Transfer to a large kettle and cover chicken
pepper   with red wine. Cover and simmer slowly for
4 c. red wine   about l hr. Saute mushrooms and pour into
1-1/2 lbs. fresh mushrooms chicken. Cook 15 min. more. Add drained
1 can small onions   onions. Serve with saffron rice or wild rice.

                        Mrs. John D. Dorsey, Ridgewood

CHICKEN IN THE POT   Serves: 6

"Marvelous company fare with little time spent in preparation."

Easy   Do ahead   Preparing: 10 min.
                                             Baking: 1-1/2 - 2 hrs.

6 chicken breasts, boned   Place l stick butter and onion in bottom of
1 medium onion, sliced   a bean pot or heavy covered casserole. Alterna
1 small bag poultry stuffing layers of chicken breasts and poultry stuffing.
  (I use Bell's)   Sprinkle with salt and pepper occasionally. To
salt   with a second stick of butter and cover tightly
pepper   so pot is air tight. Bake at 350° for l-1/2 to
2 sticks butter or margarine 2 hrs. or until done. You now have chicken,
                             gravy and stuffing all ready to eat.

                        Mrs. Clark H. Hower, Wyckoff

CHICKEN STEW   Serves: 4

"Tastes so much better than its name!"

Easy   Freeze   Preparing: 30 min.
                                               Cooking: 1-1/4 hrs.

6 chicken legs with thighs   Fry chicken in garlic and oil. Add onions,
2 tbsp. salad oil   tomatoes, mushrooms, bouillon cubes and
1 clove garlic   seasonings. If using fresh mushrooms, saute
1 8-oz. can onions   them in butter before adding. Simmer mixture
1 lb. can stewed tomatoes   for l hr. Mix flour with wine and add chicken
1 4-oz can mushrooms   mixture. Simmer for 5 more minutes. Remove
  (or 1/4 lb. fresh mushrooms) bay leaf. Serve sprinkled with chopped parsley
2 chicken bouillon cubes   on rice, either white or wild, or the wild rice
parsley   mixture. Can be done the day ahead and slowly
salt   reheated.
pepper
thyme
1 bay leaf
3 tbsp. flour
1/3 c. white wine   *Mrs. Arthur H. Kiendl, Jr., Mount Hermon, Mass.*

BRUNSWICK STEW

Serves: 6

"A truly southern dish."

Average   Freeze

Preparing: 15 min.
Simmering: 3-4 hrs.

1 large hen or 2 frying
  chickens (4-1/2 - 5 lbs.)
2 qts. water
1 tbsp. salt
1 pkg. whole frozen corn
4 med. onions, chopped
1 pkg. frozen okra (or canned)
2 large green peppers, chopped
3 ripe tomatoes, quartered
  (or #2-1/2 can)
1 pkg. frozen lima beans
1/2 tsp. black pepper
2 dashes Tabasco sauce
1 bay leaf

Disjoint chicken and put into the pot with salt. Cover with water and bring to a boil. Simmer gently until meat parts company from the bones (1 to 1-1/2 hrs.). Add vegetables (a formidable-looking array, but they simmer down). Add salt to taste, black pepper, Tabasco and bay leaf. Simmer the stew, letting it get thick. If vegetables are holding their shape, add more water. Stir frequently so vegetables will not scorch. The stew will cook in about 2 to 2-1/2 hrs. When thick remove all skin and bones. Ladle generously into bowls or serve over rice. Corn bread or hush puppies are boon companions. When freezing, omit okra and add only at the last.

Mrs. Eric H. Berg, Ridgewood

COMPANY CHICKEN CASSEROLE

Serves: 6

"My favorite chicken dish."

Average   Do ahead

Preparing: 30 min.
Baking: 1-1/2 - 2 hrs.

6 chicken breasts,
  boned and split
salt
pepper
1/4 c. butter or margarine
2 No. 2 cans tiny potatoes
1 c. cooked ham, diced
1/2 lb. mushrooms, sliced
5 tbsp. butter or margarine
6 tbsp. flour
3 c. cream
1-1/2 c. dry white wine
1/2 lb. green seedless grapes

Season chicken with salt and pepper and brown in butter or margarine. Transfer to large casserole. Drain potatoes. Brown potatoes in the same pan in which the chicken was browned. Place them on top of the chicken. Add ham pieces and mushrooms. Make a cream sauce by melting the 5 tbsp. butter in a large saucepan. Blend in flour and then slowly add cream and wine, stirring constantly until smooth and thickened. Add more seasoning if you wish. Pour over the casserole. Cover. Chill, if done ahead. Bake at 350° for 1 to 1-1/2 hrs. or until chicken is tender. Add the grapes and bake 10 min. more. (Drained canned grapes may be used if necessary. If so, cook only 5 min. longer.) Serve with green vegetables and salad.

Mrs. John L. Dwyer, Franklin Lakes

CHICKEN WITH CURRANT JELLY SAUCE

Serves: 4

Easy   Do ahead

Preparing: 10 min.
Baking: 1 hr. 10 min.

1 chicken, cut up
4 tbsp. butter
1 tbsp. dry mustard
1 tbsp. dry tarragon

Sauce:
1/2 c. red currant jelly
1/2 c. sherry
1 tbsp. lemon juice
salt
1 tbsp. butter
1 tbsp. cornstarch
3 cloves

Spread first three ingredients on chicken. Cook for 20 min. in foil-lined roasting pan at 450°. Reduce heat to 325° and cook for an additional 1/2 to 3/4 hr.

Sauce: Dissolve cornstarch in sherry and combine remaining ingredients. Cook until sauce is the consistency you prefer. Serve separately at the table.

Mrs. John J. Baughan, Ridgewood

CHICKEN!

Serves: 6

"Everyone who eats this always wants the recipe."

Easy   Do ahead

Preparing: 20 min.
Baking: 40 min.

2 broilers, cut up
6 tbsp. butter
1 large onion
8 slices bacon, diced fine
2 tbsp. flour
1 tbsp. curry
1 c. condensed beef broth
1/4 c. orange marmalade
2 tbsp. catsup
2 tbsp. lemon juice

Melt butter in large frying pan. Dip and cover pieces of chicken with butter. Remove to baking dish. In another pan brown bacon and onions; gradually add flour, stirring until smooth. Add remaining ingredients. Simmer 15 min. Put half of this sauce on the chicken and allow to bake at 400° for 20 min. Add remaining sauce and bake another 20 min.

Mrs. Charles R. Moog, Ridgewood

BUNNY'S CHICKEN SURPRISE

Serves: 6

"Never gets stringy or dry. Reheats very well."

Easy   Freeze

Preparing: 5 min.
Baking: 1-3/4 hrs.

6 double chicken breasts or
  2 broilers, cut up
1 can cream mushroom soup
3/4 can dry vermouth
1 can pitted ripe olives,
  drained
garlic salt
salt
pepper
2 tbsp. salad oil

Put oil in bottom of roasting pan. Season chicken with garlic salt, salt and pepper. Put chicken in roasting pan in oven at 500° for 10 min. to seal juices. Remove chicken from oven and add drained ripe olives. Add undiluted mushroom soup mixed with vermouth. Return to 350° oven for 1-1/2 hrs. Turn chicken three times during baking time.

Mrs. Stewart F. Alexander, Park Ridge

CHICKEN DIVAN

Serves: 6-8

"Real party fare! Worth the extra effort to prepare."

Complicated   Do day or two ahead   Preparing: 2-1/2 hrs.
                                                   Refrigerating: overnight
                                                   Baking: 30 min.

3 or 4 full chicken breasts
2 tsp. poultry seasoning
  (I use Bell's)
salt
1 small onion
piece of celery
1 bunch broccoli

Sauce:
4 tbsp. chicken fat
4 tbsp. flour
salt
2 c. chicken broth
1 c. heavy cream, whipped
1 c. salad dressing
  (I use Miracle Whip)
2 tbsp. sherry
1 tbsp. Worcestershire sauce
1 c. grated Parmesan cheese

Wash chicken breasts; cover with water. Add poultry seasoning, salt, onion and celery. Simmer about 2 hrs. or until chicken is soft to the knife. Cool chicken in its own broth; take meat off bone and slice thin. Cook one bunch of broccoli until barely tender. Line a shallow 2 qt. Pyrex dish with broccoli. Lay chicken over it. Cover with sauce.

Sauce: Skim chicken fat; add flour and salt and 2 c. of the chicken broth. Bring to a boil as if making white sauce. Fold in whipped cream, salad dressing, sherry and Worcestershire sauce. Cover with Parmesan cheese. Refrigerate overnight. Bake at 350° for 30 min. or until thoroughly heated.

Mrs. William H. Floyd, Ridgewood

CHICKEN NOEL (Casserole)

Serves: 8

"This is simple to prepare and especially good for buffets."

Easy   Do ahead   Preparing: 15 min.
                                Baking: 1 hr.

4 large whole chicken breasts
  boned and cut in half
1 can mushroom soup
1 small can mushroom caps
1 c. sour cream
1 c. sherry
2 pkgs. frozen broccoli
  spears
1/2 lemon
paprika

Cook broccoli in usual manner. Place in a buttered flat casserole. Squeeze lemon over broccoli. Place chicken breasts skin side up on broccoli. Combine soup, mushroom caps, sour cream, and sherry and pour over chicken. Sprinkle with paprika generously. Bake at 350° for 1 hr. Delicious with wild rice and tossed salad.

Mrs. Reynolds Somers, Saddle River

CHICKEN LIVERS

Serves: 6

"Delicious, easy way to cook chicken livers with its own luscious gravy."

Easy   Eat right away   Cooking: 15 min.

1 lb. chicken livers
1 tsp. salt
1/8 tsp. pepper
1/4 c. flour
3 tbsp. butter
3 tbsp. oil
2 tbsp. onions, chopped
2 c. fresh mushrooms, sliced
    or
1 large can mushrooms
1 tsp. cornstarch
1/4 c. water
1/2 c. dry vermouth
1 c. chicken broth

Remove fat and tissue from livers, separate them. Place flour, salt and pepper in a plastic bag. Shake chicken livers a few at a time in the bag to coat well. Saute them in 2 tbsp. butter and 2 tbsp. oil in a frying pan until brown. In a second pan add I tbsp. butter and I tbsp. oil and saute sliced mushrooms and onions. Combine the two. Dissolve cornstarch in water. In the second pan, make a gravy by thickening the liquid with cornstarch mixture. Add vermouth and I c. chicken broth. Pour over livers and bring to a boil. Serve on rice.

Mrs. Charles J. Miller, Ramsey

BROILED CHICKEN

Serves: 6

"Wonderful; great cold the next day."

Easy   No need to freeze   Preparing: 10 min.
                                                    Broiling: 30-40 min.

2 quartered broilers
  (or as many as needed)
garlic salt
cracked pepper
sauterne
butter

Do not remove any fat from chicken. Clean thoroughly and cut off wing tips and remove breast bones. Butter the bottom of the broiler pan and arrange chicken, skin side down. Do not use the broiler grill; chicken must cook in its own juices. Salt and pepper chicken to taste and dot liberally with butter Place on bottom shelf of broiler and leave door open a crack. Broil about 15 min. Add sauterne to taste about 1/4 c. at a time. Broil 15 min. more, basting a couple of times. Turn, butter and salt again and continue broiling. Add more wine and cook until chicken is golden, basting frequently. For dark skin, let it cook longer. Remove to heated platter and garnish with parsley. Serve with juices which have been put in a heated pitcher. The gravy is marvelous on mashed potatoes. This will keep for as long as 3 hours if kept in 170° oven.

Mrs. Charles D. MacMakin, Ridgewood

CHICKEN BREASTS IN SOUR CREAM

Serves: 4

"This is very elegant and so easy."

Easy   Do ahead   Preparing: 15 min.
                                                    Baking: 1-1/2 hrs.

4 chicken breasts
1 3-oz. can mushrooms,
  sliced
1 can cream mushroom soup
1/2 soup can sherry
1 c. sour cream
paprika

Arrange chicken in a shallow baking dish so that pieces do not overlap. Cover with mushrooms (do not use juice). Combine mushroom soup, sherry and sour cream. Stir until well blended. Pour over chicken, completely covering it. Dust with paprika. Bake at 350° for 1-1/2 hrs.

Mrs. Arthur J. Partrick, Ridgewood

ELEGANT CHICKEN

Serves: 6-8

"An easy do ahead that is a gourmet's delight."

Easy   Do ahead   Preparing: 15 min.
                                                    Baking: 3 hrs.

4 whole boned chicken breasts
8 bacon slices
4 oz. chipped beef
1 can mushroom soup
1/2 pt. sour cream
paprika

Halve chicken breasts and wrap each half in bacon. Cover the bottom of a greased 8x12 in. baking dish with chipped beef. Arrange chicken on top of this. Blend soup and sour cream and pour over chicken breasts. Sprinkle with paprika. Refrigerate at this point, if desired. Bake uncovered at 275° for 3 hrs.

Mrs. David F. Dolger, Ridgewood

BAKED MARINATED CHICKEN

Serves: 4

"This is easy. You can do as much chicken as your pan will hold."

Easy   Freeze   Preparing: 10 min.
                                                    Marinating: 24 hrs.
                                                    Baking: 45 min.

4 whole chicken breasts,
  boned, skinned and split
1 c. Italian dressing
1/2 c. white wine (or rose)
salt
pepper
paprika
1 stick butter, melted

Wash chicken and marinate in Italian dressing, to which you have added white wine, for 24 hrs. in refrigerator. Turn a few times. An hour or two before cooking, salt each piece of chicken and place on a jelly-roll pan or cookie sheet with sides. Do not have pieces touching. Drizzle with melted butter, then sprinkle with pepper and paprika. Bake uncovered at 350° for about 45 min. Freeze and reheat, if desired. Garnish with watercress or parsley and serve on wild rice or half wild-half white rice mixture. Spoon juices over chicken.

Mrs. James D. Patton, Saddle River

119

BAKED CHICKEN SOUFFLE

Serves: 8

"A do-ahead bridge club goodie. Takes a little time, but well worth it."

Average   Do ahead   Preparing: 20 min.
Chilling: overnight
Baking: 1-3/4 hrs.

4 c. diced cooked chicken
8 slices white bread
1/2 lb. fresh mushrooms,
  sliced
1/4 c. butter
1 can water chestnuts,
  sliced
1/2 c. mayonnaise
8 slices sharp cheese
4 eggs, well beaten
2 c. milk
1 tsp. salt
1 can mushroom soup
1 can celery soup
1 jar (2 oz.) pimento,
  cut fine
2 c. buttered bread crumbs
  (coarse)

Line a large flat buttered pan with bread. Top with chicken. Cook mushrooms in butter for 5 min. Pour over chicken. Add water chestnuts and dot with mayonnaise. Cover with cheese. Combine eggs, milk and salt. Pour over all. Mix soups and pimento and spoon over mixture. Cover with foil and refrigerate overnight. Bake at 350° for 1-1/2 hrs. then uncover and sprinkle with crumbs and bake 15 min. more.

Mrs. Charles W. Allen, Ridgewood

SOUR CREAM CHICKEN MOUSSE

Serves: 8

"A simple, delicious luncheon dish always warmly received."

Easy   Do ahead   Preparing: 20 min.
Setting: 40 min.
Chilling: 2-4 hrs.

2 env. unflavored gelatin
1/2 c. cold water
2 c. boiling water
4 chicken bouillon cubes
      or
2 c. chicken broth
3 tbsp. lemon juice
1 tsp. dry mustard
2-1/2 tsp. curry powder
1 tsp. onion salt
2 c. sour cream
3 c. diced chicken breasts
1 c. finely chopped celery
1/4 c. finely chopped
  green pepper
1/4 c. roasted diced almonds

In a large bowl sprinkle gelatin over cold water. Let stand 5 min. Pour boiling water over bouillon (or use broth). Add lemon juice, mustard, curry and onion salt. Pour bouillon mixture over gelatin and stir until gelatin is dissolved. Cool 5 min. Stir in sour cream, mixing well. Refrigerate until this is the consistency of unbeaten egg white (about 40 min.). Fold in chicken, celery, green pepper and almonds. Mix well. Turn into a 1-1/2 qt. mold or 8 individual molds. Refrigerate, covered, until firm (4 hrs. for large mold; 2 hrs. for individuals). Serve with watercress or lettuce with tomato wedges. This can be made several days in advance.

Mrs. Paul R. Davis, Saddle River

CHICKEN-CHEESE MOUSSE (Mornay Sauce)   Serves: 6-8

"Marvelously different luncheon dish."

Moderately difficult   Do ahead   Preparing: 35 min.
                                                       Chilling: 3 hrs.

Mornay Sauce:
 triangles Gruyere cheese
 tbsp. freshly grated
 Parmesan cheese
 tbsp. butter or margarine
 tbsp. diced onion
/4 tsp. garlic salt
 tbsp. flour
/2 c. chicken broth
/2 c. heavy cream
/2 tsp. salt
pepper

 env. gelatin
/2 c. cold water
 tsp. lemon juice
/4 c. mayonnaise
/4 c. whipped cream
 c. bite-size chicken
-8 asparagus spears
sour cream or whipped cream
mayonnaise

Mornay Sauce: Grate cheese and have ready.
Melt butter in heavy saucepan over medium heat.
Add onion and cook 3 min. Add garlic salt and
flour and blend. Add chicken broth and heavy
cream. Stir until smooth. Add cheeses and
blend well. Season with salt and pepper.

Sprinkle gelatin on cold water to soften.
Sprinkle lemon juice over the gelatin mixture.
Add to Mornay Sauce and stir. Fold in mayonnaise
and whipped cream. Place asparagus spears in
mold in a decorative fashion. Add chicken to
sauce and slowly pour this into mold so as not to
disturb asparagus. Chill until set. Serve on
crisp lettuce with sour cream or whipped cream
folded into mayonnaise.

Mrs. Allen D. Patterson, Saddle River

CHICKEN CACCIATORE GENOA   Serves: 4

Average   Do ahead   Preparing: 20 min.
                                           Cooking: 40 min.

 broilers, 2-1/2 lbs. each
/4 lb. butter
/4 c. sliced green peppers
/4 c. sliced onions
 large mushrooms
 large tomatoes
 c. claret wine
 drops Tabasco sauce
 garlic clove
/2 tsp. oregano
 tsp. thyme
 c. beef broth
 tbsp. cornstarch
salt
pepper

Have butcher remove breast, rib and hip
bones from chicken. Saute in butter until
golden brown. Add garlic, salt, pepper,
beef broth, Tabasco and 2 c. claret. Cover
and simmer for 20 min. In another pot saute
sliced green peppers, mushrooms and onion
until they take color. Peel tomatoes and
cut into large cubes. Add to above vegetables.
Add oregano and thyme. Pour vegetables over
chicken and cook 10 min., then thicken with
cornstarch and remaining claret wine. Serve
immediately.

Mr. William W. Schmitz, Ho-Ho-Kus

CHICKEN EN PAPILLOTE
(Chicken with White Wine Sauce in Paper)

Serves: 4

"A most unusual way to serve chicken."

Average   Do ahead

Preparing: 15 min.
Cooking: 40-60 min. total
Heating: 10 min.

3 lb. frying chicken
1 tsp. salt
1/4 tsp. pepper
1/2 c. butter
1 tbsp. chopped shallots
4 tbsp. chopped mushrooms
1/2 c. dry white wine
1/4 c. dry vermouth
1/2 c. brown stock
2 tbsp. finely sliced,
  cooked ham
1 tbsp. chopped tarragon
1 tbsp. flour
1 tbsp. butter

Preheat oven to 400°. Cut chicken into quarters. Wipe parts with a damp cloth; salt and pepper. Saute in 1/2 c. butter over low heat until lightly browned on both sides. Remove chicken parts and keep warm. Add shallots to pan and cook for 1 min. Add mushrooms and cook for 5 min. Add wine and vermouth and cook until wine is reduced by half. Add brown stock and replace chicken parts. Cover and cook for 20 min. Remove chicken and keep warm.

Sauce: Add ham and tarragon to pan. Stir in, bit by bit, flour mixed to a smooth paste with butter. Cook, stirring, until sauce is smooth and has thickened.

Before serving: Cut parchment or heavy brown, unglazed paper large enough to envelop a piece of chicken. Rub on both sides with soft butter. Fold paper in the center and place a piece of chicken on one side. Cover with 3 or 4 tbsp. of the sauce. Bring edges of paper together, fold over in a double fold and crimp to seal tightly. Bake in the hot oven for 10 min. Serve the chicken in its paper wrapping, and let each guest unwrap his own portion at the table.

Mrs. Sheridan P. Wait, Paramus

CHICKEN OR TUNA CASSEROLE

Serves: 8

"The easy way with ingredients from the shelf."

Easy   Freeze

Preparing: 10 min.
Baking: 30 min.

2 tbsp. butter
1 small onion, chopped
1 small can mushrooms
2 small cans tuna or chicken
1-1/2 cans mushroom soup
1/2 soup can white wine
1 pkg. poultry dressing

Brown onion and mushrooms in melted butter. Reserve mushroom juice. Grease a large, flat baking dish (approximately 11x15 inches) and mix tuna or chicken with wine, soup, onion and mushrooms. Place in bottom of dish. Prepare dressing as package directs, using mushroom juice as part of the liquid. Place dressing over the meat mixture. Bake, uncovered, at 350° for 30 min.

Mrs. John H. Cline, St. Thomas, Virgin Is.

CZECHOSLOVAKIAN CHICKEN DINNER WITH DUMPLINGS   Serves: 4

Average   Freeze   Preparing: 30 min.
                                                   Simmering: 45 min.

2-1/2 lb. chicken, cut up   Disjoint chicken into serving pieces;
2-3 tbsp. shortening   brown in shortening. Add salt and enough
1 tsp. salt   water to let simmer. Cook until done.
1-2 c. water   In the meantime make the dumplings.

Dumplings: Dumplings: Mix saltines and almonds with
35-40 saltines, rolled fine   butter, egg and milk. Make into walnut-
1/4 c. finely chopped   size balls and drop into boiling water.
  blanched almonds   Cook 15 min.
1 egg
2 tbsp. butter, melted   Remove chicken, thicken gravy with flour
1/2 c. milk   and add sour cream and paprika. Add dump-
                              lings. This can be frozen and reheated.
2-3 tbsp. flour
1/2 pt. sour cream   *Mrs. Joseph Stehlik, Redding, Conn.*
paprika

VOLAILLE AU GRATIN   Serves: 4

"Chicken in a rice casserole, uncommonly rich and subtly blended."

Average   Do ahead   Preparing: 30-45 min.
                                                   Baking: 15 min.

1/2 stick butter   Melt half of the butter in a saucepan. Add
1 c. shredded onion   the onions and saute over medium heat until
1 c. rice, raw   the onion is soft, but not browned. Add
2-1/4 c. chicken stock   chicken stock (or canned broth), thyme, bay
1/4 tsp. thyme   leaf and parsley. Stir well. Cover and
1 large bay leaf   cook over low heat until the rice is tender
1 tbsp. chopped parsley   and the liquid has been absorbed (about
3 c. cooked chicken, diced   20 min.). Take out bay leaf and discard.
2 tbsp. flour   Butter a round baking dish or casserole.
2 c. medium cream   Pack rice around the sides of the casserole.
1 tsp. salt   Leave center vacant. Fill center with cubed
1/2 tsp. white pepper   chicken. Melt rest of butter in saucepan.
1/2 c. Gruyere cheese,   Stir in flour and blend well. Gradually add
  grated   cream as you stir. Keep stirring until mix-
                              ture reaches boiling point. Remove from heat.
                              Add salt, white pepper, and half of cheese.
                              Return to very low heat and cook and stir for
                              about 5 min. Pour this mixture over chicken
                              and rice in casserole. Sprinkle remaining
                              cheese over top. Bake at 400° for 10-15 min.
                              or until top is delicately browned.

Mrs. Bruce K. Byers, Ridgewood

CHICKEN IN WINE

Serves: 4

"A gourmet's delight."

Average   Do ahead   Preparing: 30 min.
Baking: 50 min.

3 whole chicken breasts,
  boned
1/4 c. butter
1 can cream chicken soup
3/4 c. sauterne
#5 can water chestnuts
3-oz. can mushrooms
2 tbsp. chopped green pepper
1/4 tsp. thyme

Lightly season chicken with salt and pepper. Brown in butter in frying pan. Transfer to a shallow baking dish. Add soup to drippings in frying pan and slowly add wine. Stir until smooth. Heat to boiling and pour over chicken. Slice water chestnuts and green peppers over chicken, add mushrooms and thyme. Cover with foil. Bake at 350° for 25 min. Remove foil and bake 20-30 min. longer. Serve with rice.

Mrs. Andrew J. Olejer, Ridgewood

CHICKEN DIABLE (Honey Chicken)

Serves: 6

"Call this 'Honey Chicken' for the children. Quick, easy and always a hit."

Easy   Freeze   Preparing: 10 min.
Baking: 1 hr.

3 lbs. chicken, cut up
  (or legs and thighs)
4 tbsp. butter
1/2 c. honey
1/4 c. prepared mustard
1 tsp. salt
1 tsp. curry powder

Wash, dry and skin chicken. Melt butter and add remaining ingredients. Roll chicken in mixture to coat both sides. Arrange meaty side up in a single layer with sauce over it. Bake at 375° for 1 hr. or until chicken is tender and glazed. (This amount of sauce will serve at least 10.) Serve with rice, peas and green salad with mandarin oranges.

Mrs. Robert R. Risch, Ridgewood

MEXICAN ORANGE CHICKEN

Serves: 4

"Easy to make, and a favorite with the whole family."

Easy   Do day ahead   Preparing: 20 min.
Cooking: 45 min.
Chilling: Overnight

1 fryer cut in pieces
1/2 tsp. salt
1/4 c. butter
2 tbsp. flour
2 tbsp. sugar
1/2 tsp. cinnamon
1/8 tsp. ginger
1/2 c. raisins
1/2 c. coconut
3 oz. frozen orange juice
water

Salt chicken, brown in butter, and remove from pan. Add flour and spices to drippings and stir to a smooth paste. Gradually add orange juice, which has been added to enough water to make 1-1/2 c. Stir until mixture comes to a boil. Add chicken and raisins. Simmer 45 min. Cool. Place in refrigerator overnight to mellow. Reheat following day. Sprinkle with coconut. Serve with buttered rice.

Mrs. J. David Justice, Ridgewood

CHICKEN CURRY CASSEROLE

Serves: 8

"Good to serve with rice for luncheon, supper or at a brunch."

Average   Do ahead   Preparing: 20 min.
                                             Cooking: 1 hr.

5 lbs. chicken breasts
2 tsp. salt
1/4 tsp. pepper
1/2 c. butter
1 tsp. curry powder
1/2 c. flour
1 tsp. salt
1/4 tsp. pepper
2 6-oz. cans mushrooms
1 pkg. frozen peas
2 c. crumbled potato chips
pimento

Wash chicken and place in a large kettle, adding salt and pepper. Add water to cover and cook gently until tender, about 40-50 min. Or, cook in a pressure cooker at 15 lbs. pressure for 20 min. Let chicken cool, bone, remove skin and cut in large cubes. Reserve chicken broth. Blend curry, flour, 1 tsp. salt, 1/4 tsp. pepper and about 1/2 c. broth. Cook 2 min. Slowly add 3-1/2 c. more broth and cook until thickened and bubbly. Combine with the chicken, mushrooms and peas which have been thawed. Pour into a shallow 3 qt. casserole and bake at 350° for 30-35 min. Sprinkle with potato chips and garnish with pimento. Serve with rice.

Mrs. S. William Walstrum, Ridgewood

CHICKEN KUNDOU

Serves: 10-14

"Rich and delicately flavored. A good party dish."

A little complicated,   Do ahead   Preparing: 2 hrs.
but not difficult   (Do a day ahead)

8 double chicken breasts
1/3 c. butter
1 c. chopped onion
1 clove garlic, chopped
2 tsp. salt
1 tbsp. powdered ginger
1/4 tsp. chili powder
1/2 c. canned tomatoes,
  drained
1 c. clear chicken broth
1/2 c. cashew nuts,
  finely chopped
1/2 c. flaked coconut
2 tbsp. cornstarch
1 c. heavy cream

Bone and skin chicken. Cut each breast in 4 pieces. Melt half the butter in a Dutch oven or deep iron skillet. Brown chicken lightly, about 8 pieces at a time. Remove. Add remaining butter as needed. When chicken is browned, saute onion and garlic in butter 5 min. or until golden. Return chicken to skillet. Add salt, ginger, chili, tomatoes, broth. Blend lightly then cover and cook over medium heat 15 min. Add nuts and coconut. Cover, cook over low heat 10 min. longer until chicken is tender. To cornstarch, slowly add cream then stir into cooking liquid. Stir constantly until sauce returns to boil. Simmer over low heat another 5 min. Cool. Refrigerate in cooking pot, overnight if desired. Near serving time, bring to room temperature; reheat over very low heat. Serve with noodles.

Mrs. J. David Justice, Ridgewood

125

CHICKEN CORDON BLEU

Serves: 8

"A marvelous party dish. So elegant!"

Average   Do ahead   Preparing: 20 min.
                   Baking: 40 min.

4 whole chicken breasts
8 3" square slices boiled ham
8 2x2" pieces (1 oz. each)
 Gruyere cheese
 (I use Swiss Knight)
1 stick butter or margarine
1 c. fresh bread crumbs
1 tsp. salt
1/4 tsp. paprika

Have the butcher halve, bone and skin the chicken breasts. Pull each half breast open in the middle to form a pocket. Fold ham around cheese and tuck into pocket. Melt butter in pie pan. Make fresh bread crumbs in blender if possible. Mix with salt and paprika in a second pie pan. Roll stuffed chicken breast in melted butter, then in the crumb mixture. Coat well. Place in a buttered baking dish and bake at 400° for 40 min. or until brown.

Mrs. Jay B. Goerk, Ridgewood

CHICKEN-GREEN BEAN CASSEROLE

Serves: 8

"An easy, self-seasoning recipe. Reheats well."

Easy   Do ahead   Preparing: 25 min.
                 Baking: 55 min.

4 whole chicken breasts
1 can cream mushroom soup
1/2 c. milk
1 tsp. salt
1-1/2 c. shredded Cheddar
 cheese or
1 can cheese soup, undiluted
2 pkgs. frozen French-style
 green beans, thawed
1 can (14-1/2 oz.) chop suey
 vegetables, drained
1/3 c. chopped onions
1 can (3-1/2 oz.) French
 fried onions

Cook chicken breasts 15 min. in pressure cooker or until done. Skin and cut into bite-size pieces. Combine mushroom soup, (cheese soup if used), milk and salt and stir until well blended. Fold in remaining ingredients, except French fried onions. Include shredded cheese if soup is not used. Spoon into 13x9x2 inch baking dish. Bake at 350° for 45 min. or until beans are tender. Top with French fried onions and bake for 10 min. more. You may want to use fewer green beans. If you double the recipe, do not use more than 3 pkgs. of beans.

Mrs. W. Dean Ferres, Ramsey

TURKEY STUFFING

Yield: Enough for a
   12 lb. bird

"A big favorite with us."

Easy   Do ahead   Preparing: 15 min.

1 loaf stale bread
4 stalks celery
2 onions
1 tbsp. poultry seasoning
1 tsp. thyme
3/4 stick margarine
3/4 c. water
2 chicken bouillon cubes
salt
pepper

Cut bread in cubes 1/2 in. square. Saute celery, which has been cut fine, in margarine until it is soft and yellow. Grate or cut onions fine. Add seasonings, celery and onion to bread. Add bouillon cubes to hot water. Add mixture to bread. Mix well. Chop through with a knife to make pieces smaller. Stuff bird just before cooking. Can be cooled and used later in cooled bird.

Mrs. William L. Bradford, Wyckoff

CHICKEN HAWAIIAN

Serves: 8

"So easy, attractive, and delicious!"

Easy   Do ahead

Preparing: 20 min.
Marinating: overnight
Baking: 45 min.

2 fryers, cut up
2/3 c. oil
1/3 c. vinegar

Marinate chicken overnight in enough oil and vinegar to cover.

Sauce:
3 tbsp. cornstarch
3/4 c. vinegar
1 c. sugar
dash Tabasco sauce
1 tbsp. Worcestershire sauce
1 tbsp. prepared mustard
2 green peppers
1 red pepper
1 #2-1/2 can pineapple chunks

Sauce: Cut peppers in strips. Combine cornstarch, vinegar and sugar. Cook until clear. Add everything except pineapple and cook until sauce is somewhat thickened. Add pineapple and mix through. Drain chicken. Broil on both sides until brown. Arrange in a casserole, pour sauce over it and bake at 350° for about 45 min.

Mrs. Irving R. Hayman, Ridgewood

CHICKEN TETRAZZINI

Serves: 12-16

"Mama Mia! It's good."

Average   Freeze

Preparing: 1 hr.
Chilling: 24 hrs.
Baking: 30 min.

1 5-lb. chicken
1 lb. bacon
7 or 8 med. onions
1 qt. canned tomatoes
2 large cans mushrooms
1 large jar stuffed olives
16 oz. spaghetti
cayenne pepper
salt
Parmesan cheese

Cook chicken until tender in plenty of water. Remove meat from bones and cut into bite-size pieces. Save broth. Cut bacon into small pieces; saute until crisp. Fry onions in bacon fat until tender. Add liquid from tomatoes and mushrooms to chicken broth. Add half of liquid from jar of olives to broth. Cook spaghetti in broth and liquids until tender. Let spaghetti absorb as much broth as possible. Add all other ingredients to spaghetti. Season with cayenne pepper and salt to taste. Mix well and place in casseroles. Cover and refrigerate at least 24 hrs. Sprinkle with Parmesan cheese. Bake at 350° for about 30 min. or until thoroughly heated.

Mr. Fred W. Vinroot, Ridgewood

CHICKEN AND NOODLES PARTY STYLE

Serves: 8-10

Easy   Do ahead   Preparing: 20 min.
                                         Baking: 30 min.

8 oz. med. noodles
1 can mushroom soup
2/3 c. milk
1/2 tsp. salt
1/2 tsp. poultry seasoning
6 oz. cream cheese
1 c. cottage cheese
1/4 c. chopped parsley
1/3 c. chopped onion
1/3 c. chopped green pepper
3 c. diced chicken, cooked
1-1/2 c. buttered bread crumbs

Cook noodles and drain. Mix soup, milk, salt and poultry seasoning; heat. Beat cheeses together and stir in parsley, onion and green pepper. Place half the noodles in a 3-1/2 to 4 qt. casserole and spread with half the cheese mixture, half the chicken, then half the soup. Repeat the layers. Top with bread crumbs. Bake at 375° for 30 min.

Mrs. John B. Ford, Ridgewood

CHICKEN AND PINEAPPLE

Serves: 4

"This looks good, tastes good and is easy to make."

Easy   Do ahead   Preparing: 20 min.
                                         Baking: 1 hr.

4 whole chicken breasts, split
  (boned, if desired)
oil or butter
1 c. orange juice
1 c. white wine
1/4 tsp. cinnamon
1/4 tsp. clove
1/2 c. raisins
1 small can pineapple chunks
2 tbsp. sugar

Brown chicken breasts in oil or butter. Mix all other ingredients together and pour over browned chicken in baking dish. Cover dish with foil or lid and bake at 325° for 1 hr. This is especially good if prepared a day ahead and reheated prior to serving.

Mrs. Thomas G. Parris, Jr., Ridgewood

Poultry Pluses

Do not stuff poultry or other meats before freezing.

Poultry may be stuffed the night before roasting as long as both the bird and the stuffing are well chilled before stuffing.

* If you have extra stuffing, form it into balls about the size of a tennis ball and place in greased muffin pans. Cook with the bird until brown. These make delicious leftovers.

Leftover, cooked stuffing is great when used as a stuffing for large mushroom caps.

A 3-1/2 lb. chicken will give you about 3 c. diced cooked chicken. Two whole chicken breasts (10 oz. each) will yield 1-1/2 to 2 c. cooked chicken or 12 thin slices white meat. Slice while well chilled.

Allow 1 lb. of chicken per person.

Soak fresh or frozen chicken (to defrost) in cold, heavily salted water. Meat will be pure white as it draws out the blood.

Seafood

SWORDFISH DELUXE

Serves: 4

"Delicious, and so quick to prepare."

Easy   Serve immediately   Preparing: 5 min.
Cooking: 15 min.

1 2" swordfish steak
2 tsp. rosemary
6 tbsp. butter
salt
1/4 c. white wine
oil

Dredge fish with flour and press rose-mary into the fish. Brush with oil. Place 5 tbsp. butter in a large skillet and add fish. Cook, turning once, until fish is flaky (about 15 min.). Sprinkle with salt and remove to a hot platter. Add wine and remaining butter to skillet and heat. Pour over fish. Serve.

Mrs. John H. Cline, St. Thomas, Virgin Is.

BAKED SOLE

Serves: 6

"Everyone who tastes this loves it."

Easy   Part do ahead   Preparing: 15 min.
Baking: 20 min.

1 tsp. salt
1/2 tsp. pepper
1/8 tsp. mace
1/8 tsp. thyme
2 lbs. fillet of sole
1/2 c. dry vermouth
2 tbsp. lemon juice
1/4 stick butter, melted
3 tbsp. onion, minced
1/4 lb. fresh mushrooms,
   sliced
2-3 tbsp. butter
6 lemon wedges
parsley

Mix together salt, pepper, mace and thyme. Dust both sides of fish with this. Arrange in a shallow baking dish that has been lightly greased. Mix together ver-mouth, lemon juice and melted butter. Pour over fish. Saute the sliced mushrooms in 2-3 tbsp. butter for about 5 min. Sprinkle the fish with minced onion and arrange mush-rooms around them. Bake at 350° for about 20 min. or until fish is done. Serve from baking dish or transfer to a warm platter. Garnish with mushrooms cooked with fish and with parsley and lemon wedges.

Mrs. Donald B. Read, Ridgewood

FILLET OF SOLE

Serves: 4

Average   Part do ahead   Preparing: 20 min.
Baking: 20 min.

6 fillets of sole
1 scallion, tops and
   bottoms chopped
salt
pepper
1 tsp. curry powder
3/4 c. dry sauterne or sherry
2 tbsp. butter
2 tbsp. flour
1/2 c. milk
2 tomatoes, quartered
1/4 lb. fresh mushrooms,
   quartered (or small can)
2 or 3 ripe olives

Put fillets and onion in a buttered skillet. Season with salt, pepper and curry powder. Add 1/2 c. wine and cook slowly until white (about 10 min.). Remove fillets to casserole. In skillet melt butter; blend flour. Stirring, add milk and remainder of wine. Cook until thick. Pour over fish in casserole and garnish with tomato, mushrooms and slices of olives. Dot with butter. Bake at 350° for 20 min.

Mrs. Morton Evans, Canton, Mass.

FLOUNDER PARMESAN

Serves: 4

Average   Do ahead   Preparing: 20 min.
                                                        Waiting: 15 min.
                                                        Cooking: 15 min.

4 flounder fillets   Wash and wipe fillets. Season with salt
salt   and pepper. Dust with flour and dip in egg.
pepper   Mix crumbs, cheese and seasonings. Dip fish
flour   in crumbs and coat well. Let stand for
2 eggs, beaten   15 min. (or refrigerate). Brown well in
fine bread crumbs   melted, frothy oil (or butter) on both sides.
1/2 c. grated Parmesan cheese Sprinkle with chopped parsley and oregano.
paprika   Serve with hot Tomato Sauce on page 148.
salt
cayenne
1 tbsp. chopped parsley
1/2 tsp. oregano
3 tbsp. butter or oil   *Mrs. George M. Griffith, Franklin Lakes*

BAKED SALMON

Serves: 8-10

"I know of nothing so popular and easy."

Easy   No need to do ahead   Preparing: 5 min.
                                                    Baking: 1 hr.

5-6 lb. piece salmon.   Lay fish on piece of foil in flat baking
1 tbsp. butter   pan. Sprinkle inside with salt and lemon
juice of 1/2 lemon   juice. Dot with butter. Bake at 325° for
1/2 tsp. salt   1 hr. Remove skin (it will slide off easily)
lemon wedges   and lay on hot platter. Garnish with lemon
parsley   wedges and parsley. Serve with tartar sauce
                            and cucumbers.

                             Mrs. Edward H. Page, Ridgewood

SALMON DIABLE

Serves: 4-6

Easy   Do ahead   Preparing: 10 min.
                                                    Baking: 45 min.

3/4 c. sour cream   Mix sour cream, sherry, lemon juice,
1/4 c. sherry   Worcestershire sauce, mustard and eggs.
1 tbsp. lemon juice   Stir in salmon, crumbs, parsley and onion.
1 tsp. Worcestershire sauce Add salt and pepper. Place in greased bak-
1/2 tsp. dry mustard   ing shells or individual casseroles and
2 eggs, slightly beaten   bake at 350° for 45 min. or until crispy
1 lb. can drained salmon   on top.
1/3 c. cracker crumbs
1/4 c. minced parsley
1/4 c. chopped onion
1 tbsp. (or less) salt
1/8 tsp. pepper   *Mrs. Morton Evans, Canton, Mass.*

SALMON AND CHEESE LOAF

Serves: 6

"Good served hot or cold!"

Easy   Do ahead   Preparing: 10 min.
                                                    Baking: 40 min.

2 c. salmon
1-1/2 c. grated sharp
   Cheddar cheese
1 egg, well beaten
3 tbsp. milk
1 tbsp. melted butter
1/2 tsp. salt
pinch pepper
cracker or bread crumbs

Flake salmon - keep juice. Combine all ingredients, using enough crumbs to make a stiff mixture. Grease pan. Shape into a loaf or use bread pan. Cover top with buttered crumbs. Bake at 375 for 35-40 min. or until crumbs are golden brown.

Mrs. James T. Emery, Ridgewood

SEAFOOD SUPREME

Serves: 4

"Marvelous company fare, even for those who don't usually care for fish."

Average   Part do ahead   Preparing: 30 min.
                                                    Broiling: 15 min.

4 codfish steaks or
   8 sole fillets
1/2 lb. cape scallops
1/2 lb. cooked shrimp
1 tbsp. sliced onion
2 slices carrot
dash thyme
dash parsley
1/2 c. water
1/2 c. dry white wine
paprika
parsley for garnish

If using sole, roll up into timbales. Poach cod or sole in water and wine to which onion, carrot, dash of thyme, and a dash of parsley have been added. (This makes a court bouillon.) Reserve liquid, then poach scallops in same liquid. Reserve. Have shrimp cooked separately. Cook the fish liquid down to 2/3 c. of fish bouillon. Remove fish to an ovenproof serving platter and scatter scallops and shrimp over steaks or around sole timbales. Pour sauce over all and sprinkle with paprika. Broil until golden. Garnish with parsley.

Sauce:
3 tbsp. butter
3 tbsp. flour
1/3 c. dry white wine
1 c. half-and-half cream,
   warmed
2/3 c. fish liquor
salt
cayenne
M.S.G.
1 can crab
   (I always use Geisha)
optional -
   1/2 c. grated sharp cheese

Sauce: Make a cream sauce with butter and flour, using wine, half-and half, and the fish liquor (which has been strained) as your liquid. Add salt, cayenne, M.S.G. and crab. Add grated cheese, if desired. Heat until smooth and pour over fish. Serve with parsley-buttered spring potatoes and half a tomato broiled with tarragon. A Batard Montrachet wine is excellent served with this.

Mrs. Robert F. Hill, Wyckoff

CAPE COD CASSEROLE (Scallops Casserole)

Serves: 8

Average   Freeze   Preparing: 30 min.
Baking: 45 min.

12 oz. thin noodles
2 lbs. scallops, quartered
1 c. butter
6 tbsp. flour
1/8 tsp. pepper
1/2 tsp. salt
4 c. milk
3/4 lb. fresh mushrooms
    or
8 oz. can sliced mushrooms
1/2 - 2/3 c. sherry
1/2 lb. sharp American cheese
paprika
optional -
  onion flakes
  1/2 c. chopped green pepper

Preheat oven to 350°. Cook noodles and drain. Saute scallops in 4 tbsp. butter. Pour noodles into a 4 qt. casserole. Melt 6 tbsp. butter and blend in flour, salt and pepper. Cook until smooth. Slowly add milk and cook until sauce thickens, stirring constantly. Add sherry. In the remaining 6 tbsp. butter, saute thinly sliced mushrooms over medium heat until tender. Drain. Add sauteed scallops, mushrooms and sherry sauce to noodles and mix. Top with grated cheese. Cover and bake at 350° for 45 min. Sprinkle with paprika and place under the broiler for 3 min. or until top is brown and bubbly. If freezing, omit sherry until you are about to bake dish. Allow 25 min. more in baking. Onion flakes and green pepper can also be added.

Mrs. Morton Evans, Canton, Mass.

DEVILED STUFFED LOBSTER TAILS

Serves: 6

Average   Do ahead   Preparing: 30 min.
Baking: 15 min.

1 pkg. (1-1/2 lbs.) South
  African lobster tails
2 tbsp. butter
1/4 c. minced onion
1 3-oz. can sliced mushrooms
1/4 c. minced green pepper
2 tbsp. flour
1/4 tsp. salt
1/8 tsp. pepper
1/2 tsp. dry mustard
1 tbsp. Worcestershire sauce
few drops Tabasco sauce
1 c. milk or cream
1 c. clam broth
2 egg yolks
1 c. Spanish sherry

Cook lobster tails according to package directions. Remove the lobster meat; cut into chunks. Reserve the lobster tail shells. In a heavy skillet melt the butter; add onion, mushrooms and green pepper. Saute until onions are straw colored. Stir in the flour, salt, pepper, mustard, Worcestershire and Tabasco sauce. Gradually stir in the milk and clam broth; cook until slightly thickened. Stir some of the sauce into the egg yolks; then add to the sauce in the skillet. Add the lobster meat and sherry. Spoon the mixture into the lobster tails. Bake in a 400° oven until the top is golden (15 min. - WATCH). Serve with lemon wedges.

Mrs. George M. Griffith, Franklin Lakes

TUNA-SPAGHETTI CASSEROLE (or Crab)

Serves: 4-6

"This tastes much fancier than just a tuna fish casserole!"

Easy   Prepare same day   Preparing: 30 min.
                                                   Baking: 1 hr.

1/2 lb. spaghetti
4 tbsp. butter
4 tbsp. flour
2 c. milk
1/2 lb. Cheddar cheese,
  grated
1 can condensed tomato soup
1 large can white tuna fish
1 onion, chopped fine
1 green pepper, chopped fine

Cook spaghetti. Make cream sauce by melting butter, adding flour until blended and then slowly adding milk, stirring continuously until blended and thick. Add grated cheese, stirring until melted and thoroughly blended. Add tomato soup to sauce mixture. In a 2 qt. casserole combine tuna, onion, green pepper and spaghetti. Add sauce and mix well. Bake at 350° for about l hr. or until bubbly. For a fancier casserole, use crab.

Mrs. Thomas G. Parris, Jr., Ridgewood

TUNA WITH FLAIR

Serves: 6-8

"This is an old stand-by with my own innovations!"

Easy   Freeze   Preparing: 20 min.
                                                   Baking: 40 min.

8 oz. pkg. noodles
2 cans tuna
1 can cream mushroom soup
salt to taste
1/3 soup can milk
1/3 soup can sherry or
  sauterne
1/4 tsp. Tabasco sauce
3/4 tsp. onion juice
1/2 tbsp. dried parsley
1/3 to 1/2 c. grated Cheddar
  cheese

Prepare noodles according to package directions. While noodles are cooking, break up tuna with a fork then, with the exception of the cheese, milk and wine, add all the other ingredients to the fish in recipe sequence. Add milk and wine separately. Stir fish mixture gently into noodles. Place in a greased, 3 qt. casserole. Top with grated cheese. Cover, bake 25 min., then remove the cover and bake 10 or 15 min. longer - until cheese is bubbly and golden.

Mrs. Ned W. Landis, Ridgewood

DEVILED TUNA

Serves: 4

"Rich, fattening, but Mmmmm!"

Easy   Do ahead   Preparing: 10 min.
                                                   Baking: 20 min.

4 tbsp. butter or margarine
4 tbsp. flour
1 c. milk
1/2 c. cream
2 tbsp. lemon juice
1/4 c. sherry
1 tsp. Worcestershire sauce
1/4 tsp. dry mustard
salt to taste
1 7-oz. can tuna
3 hard cooked eggs, chopped
4 thin slices lemon
paprika

Melt butter in saucepan. Stir in flour; add milk and cream. Cook until thick. Add lemon juice, sherry and seasonings. Stir in tuna and eggs. Turn into greased individual baking dishes. Top with lemon slices and dust with paprika. Bake at 375° for 20 min. This can be done the morning before serving. Serve with rice and a big salad.

Mrs. E. W. Many, Ramsey

TUNA CASSEROLE FOR A CROWD

Serves: 24

"A favorite with The Forum School children; equally great for grownups."

Easy   Freeze   Preparing: 20 min.
                                            Baking: 35 min.

3/4 c. chopped green pepper
3 c. sliced celery
2 c. chopped onion
1 stick butter
3 cans mushroom soup
1-1/2 c. milk
3 c. grated sharp cheese
24 oz. noodles, cooked
5 6-1/2 oz. cans tuna
1-1/2 c. mayonnaise
3/4 c. chopped pimento
1 c. slivered almonds, toasted
            or
buttered bread crumbs

Cook celery, pepper and onion in butter for
5 min. Blend soup and milk; add to skillet.
Heat and then add cheese. Stir until cheese
is melted. Combine cooked and drained noodles,
tuna, mayonnaise and pimento. Pour over
cheese sauce and mix. Put in two greased,
13x9 inch pans; sprinkle with almonds or bread
crumbs. Bake at 425° for 30-35 min. or until
hot and bubbly. This recipe is easily divided
for eight servings (use 2 cans of tuna).

Mrs. Arthur S. Whittemore, Jr., Ridgewood

RICE AND SHRIMP CEYLON (Chicken)

Serves: 6-8

"Chicken may be substituted or added to the shrimp in this recipe."

Average   Do ahead   Preparing: 20 min.
                                            Baking: 1 hr.

3 lbs. shelled shrimp or
   part scallops
2 c. uncooked rice
6 tbsp. oil
1 tsp. salt
1 onion, minced
1 c. water
2 chicken bouillon cubes
1 green pepper, cut up
1/4 tsp. garlic powder
optional - 1 tsp. curry powder
1/4 tsp. pepper
pinch cayenne
pinch saffron
1/2 lb. mushrooms
pimento

Saute uncooked rice until light brown in
3 tbsp. oil. Place in 3 qt. casserole. In
remaining oil saute onion, green pepper, mushroom; add to rice. Dissolve bouillon in cup
of hot water. Mix all ingredients except
shrimp and pimento. Then add shrimp last.
(Precook scallops a bit if used.) Garnish
with pimento. Bake at 350° for 1 hr. or
until rice is cooked.

To do ahead: Do not add shrimp, but cook
all other ingredients about 45 min. When
ready to serve add shrimp, a bit more water,
and heat about 20 min. until heated thoroughly.
This is a very flexible recipe and may be
changed around in many ways.

Mrs. Elias Schoen, Allendale

SCALLOPED OYSTERS

Serves: 4

Easy   Serve immediately   Preparing: 15 min.
                                            Baking: 30 min.

1 pt. oysters
1 c. cracker crumbs
   (I use Ritz)
1/2 c. melted butter
salt
pepper
4 tbsp. oyster liquid
2 tsp. milk

Stir butter into cracker crumbs. Put
thin layer into bottom of a buttered,
1-1/2 qt. baking dish. Cover with oysters
and sprinkle with salt and pepper. Add
2 tbsp. of oyster liquid and 1 tsp. milk.
Repeat these layers again and cover with
remaining crumbs. Bake at 450° for 30 min.

Mrs. Richard A. Grimley, Ridgewood

SHRIMPS DE JONGHE

Serves: 4

Average   Do ahead   Preparing: 15 min.
                                       Baking: 15 min.

24 large, uncooked shrimps
3/4 c. butter or margarine
1 large clove garlic,
  thoroughly crushed
2 tbsp. finely chopped onion
salt to taste
pepper to taste
1/4 c. dry sherry
2 tbsp. finely minced parsley
fine dry bread crumbs

Melt butter in heavy saucepan or skillet. Add onions and garlic; cook and stir over moderate heat until onions are transparent. Add shrimps which have been shucked and veined. Season with salt and pepper; cook and stir until opaque. Add sherry and parsley and transfer to four scallop shells or shallow, individual casseroles. Top with crumbs and pour excess butter from pan over the top. Bake in 350° oven for about 15 min. or until crumbs are golden in color.

Mrs. Morton Evans, Canton, Mass.

SHRIMP WITH WILD RICE

Serves: 4

Average   Do ahead   Preparing: 30 min.
                                       Cooking: 20 min.

1 lb. raw jumbo shrimp
2 tbsp. soft butter
1 tsp. minced parsley
1 sliver garlic, mashed
2 tbsp. dry sherry
      or
3 tbsp. warm cognac
1/4 tsp. Worcestershire sauce
1 tbsp. fine dry bread crumbs
6 slices bacon
1 c. wild rice
3 c. chicken broth

Peel shrimp, remove vein and make a deep cut to hold filling. Cream together butter, garlic, parsley, Worcestershire sauce, wine and bread crumbs. Wrap each shrimp in half a slice of bacon and broil until bacon is crisp. In the meantime, cook wild rice in chicken broth. Season well. Bed shrimp on wild rice on a heatproof platter and heat 2 or 3 min. in a 450° oven.

Mrs. Robert S. Cummings, Saddle River

EASY SHRIMP SCAMPI

Serves: 4-6

"A great electric frying pan recipe. Easy to do for unexpected guests."

Easy   No need to do ahead   Preparing: 15 min.
                                               Cooking: 20 min.

1/4 lb. butter
3 tbsp. minced parsley
1 small onion, chopped
1-1/2 lbs. frozen shrimp
generous sprinkling of:
  seasoned pepper
    (I use Lawry's)
  garlic salt
  onion salt
  M.S.G.
1 tsp. dill weed

Saute onion in 1/2 stick butter in frying pan until golden. Add parsley. Meanwhile, season shrimp with seasonings. Add to sauteed ingredients in frying pan. Add remaining 1/2 stick of butter as liquids begin to evaporate. Cook until lightly browned in covered pan, stirring occasionally. Cook approximately 20 min.; do not overcook or shrimp will become tough. Serve with rice, herb bread and salad.

Mrs. Vincent J. Nunno, Ridgewood

137

SHRIMP ELEGANTE

Serves: 8

"A great luncheon or supper dish."

Easy   Do ahead   Preparing: 15 min.

1/2 onion
1/2 stick butter
2-3 lbs. fresh or frozen
   shrimp
1/2 lb. mushrooms
1 tsp. salt
1/8 tsp. pepper
3 tbsp. chili sauce
1-2/3 c. water
1-1/3 c. instant rice
1 c. sour cream
1 tbsp. flour
1 tbsp. parsley
   or
1 tbsp. chives

Saute onion in butter. Add raw shrimp and mushrooms. Cook and stir until pink. Add salt, pepper and chili sauce to mix. Bring to a boil. Cook rice in water; drain. Combine sour cream and flour and add to cooked rice. Mix all together. Heat gently and sprinkle with chives or parsley.

Mrs. Jay B. Goerk, Ridgewood

SHRIMP CREOLE

Serves: 3

Easy   Do sauce ahead   Preparing: 15 min.
                                                  Cooking: 1 hr. + reheating

2 medium onions
2 green peppers
2 cans tomato soup
salt
pepper
1-1/2 lbs. shrimp, shelled
   (fresh or frozen)

Cut onions and peppers very small and brown in butter. Add undiluted tomato soup and simmer 1 hr. When reheating add cooked and cleaned shrimp. Season highly. Serve over rice or Chinese noodles with soy sauce.

Ed. Note: This can also be done with stewed tomatoes in place of tomato soup.

Mrs. William G. Tanner, Saddle River

SHRIMP AND MACARONI CASSEROLE

Serves: 4

"This is my own concoction - always a hit!"

Easy   Freeze   Preparing: 30 min.
                                          Baking: 20 min.

1 can frozen shrimp soup
3/4 c. milk
1 pkg. frozen shrimp
   (10 or 14 oz.)
1/2 lb. macaroni shells
1 tsp. minced onion
salt
pepper
paprika
3/4 c. flavored, dry bread
   crumbs
grated cheese
optional -
   1/4 c. sherry or white wine

Defrost soup; add milk and onion (and wine, if desired). Bring to a boil. Add frozen shrimp and cook 2 min. Pour over cooked macaroni in a 2 qt. casserole. Season well and sprinkle with grated cheese. Bake at 375° until bubbly, about 20 min. Freeze before baking, but even the leftovers can be frozen.

Mrs. Thomas E. McCullough, Ramsey

SHRIMP ISTANBUL

Serves: 4

Average   Do ahead

Preparing: 25 min.
Cooking: 15 min.

4 tbsp. butter
1-1/2 lbs. cooked shrimp
1/2 lb. mushrooms, sliced
4 tbsp. sherry
1/4 c. finely sliced green
  pepper
2 tbsp. tomato paste
1-1/3 c. light cream
1/2 c. sour cream
1/2 tsp. salt
1 tsp. cornstarch
2 large onions, sliced fine

Melt butter in a large skillet or electric frying pan. Toss shrimp in foaming butter for 2 min. Remove shrimp from skillet. Add more butter if necessary, then add mushrooms to skillet and cook for 5 min. Add the sherry and green pepper and cook for 5 min. longer. Place in a 2 qt. casserole and slowly stir in tomato paste, cream, sour cream and salt. Return the shrimp to the sauce and simmer for 15 min. Thicken the sauce slightly with cornstarch by dissolving first in a little cold milk. In a separate pan fry the onions and add to the shrimp mixture. Serve with Pilaf with Almonds on page 173.

Mrs. John J. Baughan, Ridgewood

ARTICHOKE-SHRIMP CASSEROLE (Adlai's Dish)   Serves: 4

"It is said that this was Adlai Stevenson's favorite casserole."

Average   Do ahead

Preparing: 30 min.
Baking: 20 min.

1 #2 can artichoke hearts
  (or 1 pkg. frozen)
3/4 lb. med. size shrimp,
  cooked (or 1 lb. fresh)
1/4 lb. fresh mushrooms
4 tbsp. butter
2 tbsp. flour
1-1/2 c. milk
1 tbsp. Worcestershire sauce
1/4 c. dry sherry
salt
pepper
1/4 c. grated Parmesan cheese
dash paprika
chopped parsley

Drain can of artichokes and arrange in buttered, flat baking dish. Spread the cooked shrimp over artichokes. Saute sliced mushrooms in 2 tbsp. butter for 6 min.; add to baking dish. Make a cream sauce of butter (1 tbsp.), flour and milk. Add Worcestershire sauce, sherry, salt and pepper to the cream sauce; pour over contents of baking dish. Sprinkle the top with Parmesan cheese; dust with paprika. Bake in 375° oven for 20 min. Cover dish with chopped parsley just before serving.

Mrs. Paul D. Douglass, Wyckoff

SHRIMP IN BEER

Serves: 4-6

"Fast, easy and so good!"

Easy   Part do ahead   Preparing: 15 min.
                  Cooking: 10 min.

2 lbs. raw shrimp
 (or frozen)
4 tbsp. butter
3 tbsp. minced onion
2 tbsp. flour
1-1/2 tsp. salt
1/8 tsp. Tabasco sauce
1 c. beer
1 bay leaf
2 tsp. minced parsley

Shell and wash shrimp; pat dry on paper toweling. Melt butter in a skillet; add shrimp and onion. Simmer about 2 min., stirring occasionally. Blend in flour, salt and Tabasco. Add beer and bay leaf. Bring to a boil. Reduce heat and simmer 5 min. Remove from heat; remove bay leaf. Sprinkle parsley over the shrimp. Serve as a hot hors d'oeuvr or as a main course over rice.

Mrs. Willard K. Thayer, Saddle River

SHRIMP CHINESE (Chicken or Tuna)

Serves: 8

Easy   Do ahead   Preparing: 20 min.
                  Baking: 40 min.

3 c. chopped celery
1 c. chopped onion
1/2 c. water
1 4-oz. can mushrooms
   or
1/2 lb. fresh mushrooms
3 lbs. raw or frozen shrimp,
 cut up
6 oz. cashews, chopped
1 4-oz. can pimentos, sliced
1 5-oz. can water chestnuts,
 cut up
2 cans mushroom soup
1 soup can water or sherry
salt
pepper
2 cans Chinese noodles

Cook celery and onion in 1/2 c. water until tender. If you use fresh mushrooms, saute them in 2 tbsp. butter. Cook shrimp. Mix all ingredients, except the noodles. Can be done ahead to this point. Line a 4 qt. casserole with 1 can of noodles. Add mixture. Cover with the other can of noodles. Bake at 350° for 30-40 min.

Ed. Note: This may also be made using approximately 3 cans of tuna or 2-3 cups cooked chicken, cubed, in place of the shrimp.

Mrs. Arthur H. Kiendl, Ridgewood

SHRIMP AND RICE CASSEROLE (Shrimp Harpin)   Serves: 6-8

"A good party dish that can't go wrong!"

Average   Do ahead   Preparing: 30 min.
                                       Baking: 55 min.

2-1/2 lbs. large shrimp,
  shelled (fresh or frozen)
1 tbsp. lemon juice
3 tbsp. salad oil
3/4 c. rice, uncooked
1/2 c. minced green pepper
1/4 c. minced onion
1 tsp. salt
1/8 tsp. pepper
1/8 tsp. mace
dash cayenne pepper
1 can tomato soup
1 c. heavy cream
1/2 c. sherry
3/4 c. slivered, blanched
  almonds

Cook shrimp in boiling, salted water for
5 min.; drain. Place in a 2 qt. casserole.
Sprinkle with lemon juice and salad oil.
Meanwhile, cook rice as label directs, drain
and refrigerate all. Heat oven to 350°.
Set aside 8 shrimp for garnish. Saute green
pepper and onion in butter for 5 min. Add
them, plus all other ingredients, to shrimp
in casserole and mix well. Bake, uncovered,
for 35 min. Then top with 8 shrimp and
almonds. Bake 20 min. longer or until mixture is bubbly and shrimp are lightly browned.

Mrs. William S. Hopewell, Ridgewood

SHRIMP CASSEROLE   Serves: 6

"If you have tardy guests, this is a recipe that can wait another hour."

Easy   Do ahead   Preparing: 15 min.
                                    Baking: 1-1/2 hrs.

2 lbs. raw or frozen shrimp
1/3 c. finely chopped onion
1 or 2 garlic cloves, minced
2 tbsp. butter
1 c. raw rice
1 large can tomatoes
2 c. canned beef consomme
small bay leaf
3 tbsp. chopped parsley
1/2 tsp. ground cloves
1/2 tsp. marjoram
1 tsp. chili powder
1 tbsp. salt
1/8 tsp. pepper

Brown onion and garlic in butter. Put all
ingredients in a deep 2 qt. casserole. Cover
tightly and bake at 350° for at least 1-1/2 hrs.
The seasonings are the trick and it's so easy
you really don't need to do it ahead. Serve
with green salad and crisp French or Italian
bread.

Mrs. Daniel M. Farrell, Ridgewood

SHRIMP AND CRABMEAT CASSEROLE

Serves: 6

"All ingredients can be kept on the shelf! Quick and tasty."

Easy   Do ahead   Preparing: 15 min.
                                                 Baking: 15 min.

1 can (6-1/2 oz.) crabmeat
1 can (4-1/2 oz.) shrimp
1 c. mayonnaise
1/2 c. chopped green pepper
1/4 c. chopped onion
1-1/2 c. finely chopped celery
1/2 tsp. Worcestershire sauce
2 c. crushed potato chips
paprika

Drain crabmeat, remove cartilage and flake. Combine all ingredients, except potato chips and paprika. Place in individual baking dishes or an ovenproof, flat baking dish. Top with crushed potato chips. Sprinkle with paprika. Bake at 400° for 15 min.

Mrs. D. E. Dilts, Ho-Ho-Kus

SHRIMP (CRAB OR LOBSTER) THERMIDOR

Serves: 4-5

"Looks elegant, but is quick and easy."

Easy   Do ahead   Preparing: 15 min.

1/4 c. chopped onion
2 tbsp. chopped green pepper
2 tbsp. butter or margarine
1 can frozen cream of potato
   soup
3/4 c. light cream
1/2 c. sharp cheese
2 tsp. lemon juice
2 c. cooked shrimp
   (split lengthwise)

Cook onion and pepper in butter. Add soup and cream; heat slowly, stirring constantly until blended. Bring just to a boil, add cheese and stir until melted. Add lemon juice and shrimp; heat through. Keep warm in top of double boiler until ready to serve, then transfer to chafing dish. Serve in puff pastry shells or over rice.

Mrs. Robert K. Upham, Ridgewood

QUICKIE SEAFOOD CASSEROLE

Serves: 4

"Serve with salad, rolls and sherbet for an easy, but elegant, meal."

Easy   No need to do ahead   Preparing: 15 min.
                                                 Baking: 45 min.

1 large box frozen macaroni
   and cheese
1 can frozen shrimp soup
1 can (7-1/2 oz.) crabmeat
optional - 1 tsp. chopped
   onion
paprika
parsley

Thaw macaroni and soup. Remove cartilage from crabmeat. Mix all ingredients together. Pour into a 1 qt. casserole and sprinkle paprika on top. Bake, uncovered, at 350° for about 45 min. Garnish with parsley.

Mrs. Lawrence W. McDaniel, Ridgewood

SEAFOOD SOUFFLE

Serves: 4-6

"Any seafood can be used in this - alone or in combination with others."

Average   Serve immediately   Preparing: 15 min.
                                                       Baking: 45 min.

1 4-1/2 oz. can shrimp
    and
1 7-3/4 oz. can lobster
    or
1 c. any fresh or canned
    cooked seafood
4 oz. can sliced mushrooms
1 tbsp. butter
3 tbsp. mayonnaise
1/4 c. butter
1/4 c. flour
1/2 tsp. salt
1/4 tsp. pepper
dash cayenne
1 c. milk
4 eggs, separated
1 c. grated sharp Cheddar
    cheese

Drain mushrooms and brown in butter. Mix with seafood and moisten with mayonnaise. Put in a 1-1/2 qt. greased souffle dish or casserole. Make white sauce by melting butter and blending in flour, salt, pepper and cayenne. Gradually add milk, stirring with whisk until it is thickened. Beat egg whites until stiff. Beat yolks until thick. Stir yolks into white sauce mixture then add cheese. Cool slightly and fold in egg whites. Pour over seafood mixture and set casserole in a pan of hot water. Bake at 325° for 45 min. Serve immediately.

Mrs. James T. Rogers, Ridgewood

BAKED SEAFOOD CASSEROLE

Serves: 6-8

Average   Do ahead   Preparing: 20 min.
                                                       Baking: 30 min.

1 large bag frozen shrimp
    (1-1/2 lbs.)
2 boxes frozen crabmeat
1 c. chopped celery
1 c. chopped green pepper
1 large onion, chopped
1 tsp. Worcestershire sauce
1 tsp. salt
pepper
1 can pimentos, sliced,
    plus juice
1 c. mayonnaise

Cook and clean shrimp. Mix everything together in a large bowl. Add mayonnaise, stir and place in a buttered, 2 qt. casserole (I use a flat one). Sprinkle with bread crumbs before placing in oven. Bake at 350° for 30 min.

Mrs. Paul J. Gilbert, Ridgewood

INSTANT NEWBURG

Serves: 2

"Easy as pie!"

Easy   No need to do ahead   Preparing: 5 min.
                                                       Cooking: 10 min.

1 can frozen shrimp soup
    (I use Campbell's)
3 oz. cream cheese
7 oz. frozen crabmeat
1 tbsp. sherry

Separate crab and remove any filaments. Combine ingredients in order listed. Heat in a double boiler and serve on rice.

Mrs. Charles J. Miller, Ramsey

SHRIMP AND CRABMEAT AU GRATIN

Serves: 4

"Excellent and very different."

Average   Do ahead

Preparing: 20 min.
Baking: 30 min.

1-1/2 lbs. shrimp, shelled
  and deveined
2 cans (7-1/2 oz.) king crab
  (1 lb. frozen)
1 pkg. frozen artichoke hearts
1/4 c. butter
1/2 lb. fresh mushrooms,
  sliced
1 clove garlic, crushed
2 tbsp. finely chopped
  shallots
1/4 c. flour
1/2 tsp. pepper
1 tbsp. snipped fresh dill
  (or dill seed)
3/4 c. milk
1/2 lb. sharp Cheddar cheese,
  grated
2/3 c. dry white wine
2 tbsp. seasoned corn flake
  crumbs
1/2 tbsp. butter

Cook shrimp in salted, boiling water for
3 min. Drain. Cook artichokes as label
directs. Drain. Preheat oven to 375°. Put
2 tbsp. hot butter in a skillet and saute
mushrooms 5 min. Put 2 more tbsp. butter in
saucepan; saute garlic and shallots 5 min.
Remove from heat and stir in flour, pepper
and dill; then stir in milk. Bring to a
boil. Stirring constantly, add half of
cheese; stir until melted. Stir in wine.
Drain crabmeat, remove cartilage, and flake.
In a 2 qt. casserole combine everything with
rest of cheese. Mix lightly. Sprinkle with
crumbs; dot with butter. Bake for 30 min.
at 375° until mixture bubbles and crumbs are
browned.

Mrs. John E. Button, Saddle River

IMPERIAL CRAB

Serves: 4

Easy   Do ahead

Preparing: 15 min.
Baking: 20 min.

1 lb. crabmeat, cleaned
2 tbsp. minced onion
1 tbsp. minced green pepper
1 tbsp. minced parsley
4 tbsp. butter
1 tsp. salt
pepper
4 tbsp. mayonnaise
2 egg yolks, beaten
buttered crumbs

Simmer vegetables in butter until soft.
Combine gently with other ingredients. Top
with bread crumbs. Bake at 450° for 20 min.
Can be prepared ahead and then just popped
into the oven.

Mrs. Carlton H. Butcher, Ridgewood

CRAB SUPREME

Serves: 6

"Refreshing with a jellied fruit salad."

Easy   Do ahead   Preparing: 15 min.

1 lb. crabmeat (fresh)
1 c. milk
1/2 lb. process cheese
  (I use Velveeta)
1/2 tsp. salt
3/4 tsp. paprika
1/4 tsp. curry powder

Scald milk. Melt cheese in hot milk. Add other ingredients. Heat thoroughly. May be kept hot in double boiler. Serve over rice.

Mrs. Robert E. Smith, Ho-Ho-Kus

CRABMEAT-EGG CASSEROLE

Serves: 4

"For busy girls who want a simple, but delicious, casserole."

Easy   Do ahead   Preparing: 15 min.
                                          Baking: 20 min.

2 cans (7-3/4 oz.) crabmeat,
  cleaned
1 c. fresh bread crumbs
  coarsely made or cubed
4 hard cooked eggs, diced
1 c. cream
1-1/2 c. mayonnaise
1 tbsp. parsley
1 tsp. minced onion
1/2 tsp. salt
pepper
1/2 c. toasted bread crumbs

Mix together all ingredients, except the toasted bread crumbs. Put in a 2 qt. casserole and top with toasted crumbs. Bake at 350° for 20 min. or until bubbly.

Mrs. Walter L. Fanning, Ridgewood

CRABMEAT CASSEROLE

Serves: 4

"It's a great luncheon or Sunday supper dish - if you like cheese!"

Easy   Do ahead   Preparing: 15 min.
                                          Baking: 15 min.

1 can (7-3/4 oz.) crabmeat
1 can mushroom soup
1 soup can milk
1/4 lb. Parmesan cheese,
  grated (1/2 large can)
2 tbsp. butter
2 tbsp. flour
2 tbsp. sherry
buttered crumbs

Melt butter, add flour and mix. Add soup and milk, cheese, sherry and crab (cleaned). Serve as a Newburg from a double boiler or place in a 1 qt. casserole, top with buttered crumbs and bake at 350° for 15 min.

Mrs. George M. Griffith, Franklin Lakes

CRABMEAT FONDUE

Serves: 4

"Guests will want seconds of this. Easily increased."

Easy   Do ahead   Preparing: 15 min.
                                                    Baking: 45 min.

3 c. buttered bread cubes
1 7-oz. can crabmeat
2 4-oz. cans mushrooms
1/4 c. diced green pepper
1 c. grated Cheddar cheese
2 eggs
1/4 tsp. dry mustard
1/2 tsp. salt
1-1/3 c. milk
paprika
1/4 c. sliced olives

Place half of bread crumbs in bottom of a greased, 8 inch square baking dish. Cover with crabmeat, mushrooms, green pepper and 1/2 c. cheese. Top with remaining bread and cheese. Combine eggs, mustard, salt and milk. Pour over bread. Sprinkle with paprika. Garnish with olives. Bake at 350° for 45 min. or until firm.

Mrs. Martin Doviak, Glen Rock

CRABMEAT LUNCHEON DISH

Serves: 4

Easy   Do ahead   Preparing: 20 min.
                                                    Baking: 1 hr.

1 large can crabmeat
   (7-3/4 oz.)
8 slices bread
American cheese slices
2 eggs
1-1/3 c. milk
little chopped onion

Butter a flat casserole well. Butter four slices of bread and cover each with a slice of cheese. Place one quarter of crabmeat on top of each serving and top with another piece of bread. Beat 2 eggs with the milk and add onion. Pour milk-egg mixture over bread. (Add a little chopped onion, if desired.) Bake at 350° for 1 hr.

Miss Gertrude Rowbatham, Canton, Mass.

HOT CRABMEAT SALAD

Serves: 6

Easy   Freeze   Preparing: 10 min.
                                                    Baking: 40 min.

1 can (7-3/4 oz.) crabmeat
1/2 lb. frozen shrimp
2 cans water chestnuts, sliced
1 c. finely chopped celery
1 c. mayonnaise

Drain crab, remove cartilage and flake. Mix all ingredients in any order. Place in a 2 qt. casserole and bake at 350° for 40 min.

Mrs. Samuel D. Koonce, Ridgewood

CRAB CUSTARD CASSEROLE

Serves: 4

"Wonderful for 'the girls.' Do the day before and just pop in oven."

Easy   Do ahead   Preparing: 5-10 min.
                                                    Refrigerating: overnight
                                                    Baking: 45 min.

1 can (7-3/4 oz.) crabmeat
1-1/2 c. grated sharp
  Cheddar cheese
4 slices bread (I use Arnold
  or Pepperidge Farm)
1 tsp. mustard
3 eggs, beaten
1/2 tsp. salt
1-1/2 c. milk

Butter bread on both sides and cut into cubes. Put first three ingredients into well greased casserole. Mix mustard, eggs, salt and milk; pour over crab combination in casserole. Cover and refrigerate all day or overnight. Bake at 350° for 45 min. Serve immediately.

Mrs. Robert S. McEwan, Ramsey

CRAB CROQUETTES

Yield: 12 small cakes

Average   Do ahead   Preparing: 30 min.
                                                    Chilling: 1 hr.
                                                    Frying: 5-10 min.

1 lb. crabmeat or 2 pkgs.
  frozen crab
  (I use Wakefield king crab)
1/2 med. onion, finely chopped
6-7 sprigs parsley, finely
  chopped
1 tbsp. vinegar
3 tbsp. butter
3 tbsp. flour
1/2 c. milk
1 egg, beaten
bread crumbs
fat for deep frying

Pick over crab, drain well and spread in a large pan. Sprinkle onion, parsley and vinegar over crab. Let stand while making cream sauce. Make a cream sauce with butter, flour and milk. Add sauce and egg to crab mixture and mix lightly. Chill. Form cakes and roll in crumbs. Chill. Fry in deep fat. Makes about 12 small cakes. Do not recommend freezing. Should be prepared well ahead of time, then deep fried at last moment.

Mrs. Warren D. Haggerty, Jr., Ridgewood

EASY FISH DELISH (Crab)

Serves: 8

Easy   Do ahead   Preparing: 25 min.
                                                    Cooking: 10 min.

1 lb. cooked crabmeat
  (fresh or frozen king crab)
1-1/2 lbs. fillet of haddock
1-1/2 tbsp. vinegar
1 bay leaf
water
1 tsp. salt
2 cans frozen shrimp soup
  (I use Campbell's)
1 tbsp. grated onion or
  garlic powder

Bring to boil enough water to cover haddock; add vinegar, salt and bay leaf with the fish and simmer for 7 min. only. Do not cook fast. Pour off liquid and bay leaf. Remove any skin there may be on fish. Add cooked crabmeat to the haddock. Add the soup. Serve on rice or in patty shells; or, mix with rice ahead and put in a casserole.

Mrs. Theodore R. Wolf, Ridgewood

147

TOMATO SAUCE (for Flounder Parmesan)   Serves: 4

"Marvelous on almost any baked or broiled fish."

Easy   Do ahead   Preparing: 10 min.
                                              Simmering: 20 min.

2 tbsp. butter   Melt butter and saute onion until golden
1 onion, thinly sliced   brown. Remove onion and add flour. Remove
2 tbsp. flour   from heat. Blend well and brown ever so
1-1/2 c. stewed tomatoes   slightly. Add tomatoes, onion, seasonings
salt   and heat to boiling. Simmer for 20 min.
pepper   Serve as topping on flounder fillets. This
dash sugar   sauce can be used on other baked or broiled
dash ginger   fish.
1 bay leaf

                            Mrs. George M. Griffith, Franklin Lakes

SEAFOOD SAUCE   Yield: 1/2 cup

"Great on shrimp or crabmeat."

Easy   Do ahead   Preparing: 5 min.

4 tbsp. catsup   Mix all ingredients and chill.
1 tbsp. horseradish
1 tbsp. lemon juice
1/2 tsp. shallots, chives
   or onion juice
salt
paprika
cayenne   *Mrs. John J. Baughan, Ridgewood*

Seafood Suggestions

Get your grill very hot before broiling fish - it will not stick if hot
    enough.

To eliminate the odor of boiling shrimp, add a few fresh celery leaves to
    the pot.

Vegetables Potatoes Rice and Pastas

FONDS D'ARTICHAUTS GRATINES   Serves: 4
(Artichoke Bottoms au Gratin)

"Marvelous with a roast or a tossed green salad."

Easy   Do ahead   Preparing: 15 min.
                                            Baking: 20 min.

1 14-oz. can French   Drain artichoke bottoms; place in buttered,
   artichoke bottoms   1 qt. casserole and set aside. In a heavy
1 tbsp. butter or margarine saucepan, melt butter. Stir in flour and mix
2 tbsp. flour   well. Gradually add milk, stirring constantly
1 c. milk   until smooth. Stir in salt, nutmeg, sugar and
1/4 tsp. salt   pepper. Remove from heat and add half the
1/4 tsp. nutmeg   grated cheese and the cream. Blend well. Pour
1/4 tsp. sugar   sauce over artichokes. Sprinkle with remaining
1/8 tsp. white pepper   cheese. Bake at 400° for 20 min. or until
1 c. grated Gruyere cheese   golden.
1 tbsp. light cream or milk

                             Mr. Edwin F. Bernhardt, Cheese Shop, Ridgewood

ASPARAGUS-ARTICHOKE CASSEROLE   Serves: 4-5

"Marvelous served warm as a side dish or great as a salad if chilled."

Easy   Do ahead   Preparing: 15 min.
                                            Baking: 30 min.

2 pkgs. frozen asparagus   Cook asparagus until nearly tender. Spread
1 jar marinated artichokes   in a shallow casserole or top-of-the-stove
1 bottle creamy Italian   serving dish. Slice artichokes in half.
   dressing   Place over asparagus and drizzle oil from the
1 jar pimentos   jar over both. Shake on a bit of salt.
salt   Smother with creamy Italian dressing. Cover
                             prettily with pimentos cut into thin strips.
                             If served as a salad, chill; if as a vegetable,
                             warm about 20 min. in a 300° oven. Do not
                             overheat.

                             Mrs. Charles G. Rodman, Ridgewood
ASPARAGUS SUPREME   Serves: 8

"This is a very elegant and pretty party vegetable. Always a hit."

Average   Do ahead   Preparing: 20 min.
                                            Baking: 30 min.

2 cans asparagus spears   Make a cream sauce by melting butter;
1 c. milk   adding flour until bubbling; then adding
3 tbsp. butter   milk slowly and cooking until thick, stir-
Tabasco sauce   ring constantly. Add cheese and all the
1 c. grated cheese   seasonings to the sauce and cook until
2 tbsp. flour   blended. In a greased 8x13 inch casserole,
1/4 tsp. salt   alternate layers of asparagus, sliced eggs,
3 hard cooked eggs   sauce and almonds to make two layers. Put
1/2 c. toasted almonds,   bread crumbs and butter on top and bake,
   chopped   uncovered, at 350° for 30 min.
buttered bread crumbs

                             Mrs. Bruce F. Banta, Ridgewood

ASPARAGUS-EGG-MUSHROOM CASSEROLE

Serves: 12

"Hearty enough for a luncheon with salad, or for dinner served with steak."

Average   Do ahead   Preparing: 20 min.
                                             Baking: 40 min.

4 pkgs. frozen asparagus
  (or fresh)
1-1/2 lbs. mushrooms
1 doz. hard cooked eggs,
  sliced
6 tbsp. butter
3 tbsp. flour
1-1/2 c. milk
1/4 c. cream
1/2 c. sherry
2 tsp. Worcestershire sauce
salt
pepper
paprika
1/2 c. corn flake crumbs
1/4 c. Parmesan cheese

Cook asparagus until barely tender. Saute mushrooms in a little butter. Make a cream sauce by melting the 6 tbsp. butter, adding flour and then the milk slowly; continue stirring until thick. Add cream, sherry, Worcestershire, salt, pepper and paprika. Alternate layers of asparagus, mushrooms and egg slices in a low, flat casserole which has been greased. Pour sauce over and top with corn flake crumbs and cheese. Bake at 350° for 30-40 min. or until bubbly. If you don't want to bother with making cream sauce, use a can of mushroom soup diluted with 1/2 c. milk and 1/2 c. sherry.

Mrs. Arthur H. Kiendl, Jr., Mt. Hermon, Mass.

GREEN BEAN CASSEROLE WITH WATER CHESTNUTS

Serves: 8-10

Easy   Do ahead   Preparing: 15 min.
                                             Baking: 35 min.

3 pkgs. frozen green beans,
  French style
1-1/2 c. water
1-1/2 tsp. salt
1 5-oz. can sliced water
  chestnuts, drained
1/2 lb. mushrooms
2 cans cream celery or
  mushroom soup
salt & pepper to taste
1/4 c. grated cheese
1 pkg. frozen onion rings

Cook beans in water and salt only until separated and thawed (4 min.). Drain. Layer beans, chestnuts and mushrooms in a greased, 3 qt. casserole. Mix cheese, soup and seasonings and pour over beans. Bake, covered, at 350° for 25 min. Do ahead to this point, if desired. Top with onion rings and bake, uncovered, an additional 10 min. or until crisp and brown.

Mrs. Robert C. Nienaber, Ridgewood

GREEN BEANS WITH TOMATOES

Serves: 6

Easy   No need to do ahead   Preparing: 5 min.
                                             Simmering: 30 min.

2 tbsp. olive oil
1-1/2 lbs. green beans - tips
  cut off and sliced in half,
  lengthwise
4 green onions, finely chopped
1/2 c. finely chopped parsley
1 c. canned tomatoes
salt & pepper to taste

Pour oil into the bottom of a heavy saucepan; add beans, onions, parsley, tomatoes, salt and pepper. Cover and simmer slowly for 20-30 min., or until beans are tender.

Mrs. Herbert Kuhl, Jr., Waldwick

GREEN BEAN CASSEROLE

Serves: 8

"Delicious 'party' dish served hot or cold."

Average   Do ahead   Preparing: 10 min.
                                    Cooking: 1 hr.

2 #303 cans whole green beans
bits of ham or bacon
1 large onion, sliced
1 c. mayonnaise
2 hard cooked eggs, chopped
1 heaping tbsp. horseradish
juice of 1 lemon
salt
pepper
garlic salt
celery salt
1 tsp. parsley flakes or
   1 tbsp. chopped, fresh
   parsley

Cook beans with meat and sliced onion for one hour. Blend mayonnaise and rest of ingredients and set aside. When beans are ready, drain and mix with mayonnaise mixture. Season to taste. Serve hot or cold.

Mrs. P. N. Becton, Tampico, Tamps., Mexico

SAVORY BEANS

Serves: 8

"Marvelous company beans."

Easy   Do ahead   Preparing: 10 min.
                                Cooking: 15 min.

1/4 c. oil
1 tbsp. chopped onion
3/4 c. chopped pepper
3 pkgs. cut green beans
1 tsp. salt
1 tsp. basil
1/2 to 3/4 c. Parmesan cheese

In a large saucepan saute onion and pepper in oil to the limp stage. Add frozen uncooked beans and break them up a bit with a fork. Add salt and basil. Put on low heat on top of the stove and cover. Do not add water. Cook until almost tender, then add one half of the cheese. When ready to serve add remaining cheese and stir around a little. Transfer to serving dish.

Mrs. John H. Cline, St. Thomas, Virgin Is.

FANCIED-UP STRING BEANS

Serves: 4-6

Easy   Do ahead   Preparing: 30 min.

1 lb. (or 2 boxes frozen)
   green beans, French cut
onion
2 tbsp. parsley
2 tbsp. butter
1 tbsp. flour
1/2 c. bean liquor
1 tsp. dill
1 tsp. sugar
1 tsp. vinegar
salt
pepper
1 c. sour cream

Cook green beans, drain and reserve liquor. Saute onion and parsley in butter. Work in flour and bean liquor. Cook until smooth. Add dill, sugar, vinegar, salt and pepper. Add beans. Stir in 1 c. sour cream. Excellent in large quantities for big parties. Do ahead, if desired, and refrigerate; reheat in oven.

Mrs. John E. Button, Saddle River

FANCY GREEN BEAN CASSEROLE

Serves: 12

"This is a delicious party casserole and well worth the effort."

Average   Freeze   Preparing: 20 min.
                   Baking: 45 min.

3 pkgs. frozen green beans,
 French style
1 5-oz. can water chestnuts
1 lb. fresh mushrooms, sliced
1 medium onion, sliced
1/2 c. butter
1/4 c. flour
2 c. milk
1 c. evaporated milk
3/4 lb. sharp Cheddar cheese
1/8 tsp. Tabasco sauce
2 tsp. soy sauce
1 tsp. salt
1/2 tsp. pepper
1 tsp. M.S.G.
1/2 to 3/4 c. sliced almonds

Cook beans until barely tender. Drain and slice water chestnuts. Saute mushrooms and onions in butter. Add flour and stir until smooth. Add milk and evaporated milk; stir. Transfer to double boiler and add grated cheese, Tabasco, soy sauce, salt, pepper and M.S.G. Stir constantly until cheese melts and mixes. Add water chestnuts. Add sauce to cooked, drained green beans. Put into two 1-1/2 qt. casseroles or one 3 qt. casserole. If serving six, freeze one casserole. Sprinkle with almonds. Bake at 350° for 30-45 min.

Mrs. R. T. Amos, Jr., High Point, N. C.

STRING BEANS ITALIENNE

Serves: 6

Easy   Do ahead   Preparing: 5 min.
                   Heating: 7 min.

2 1-lb. cans cut green beans
2 tbsp. salad oil
2 tbsp. wine vinegar
2 tsp. dry oregano
1 tsp. garlic salt
M.S.G.

Drain liquid from beans. Combine with other ingredients. Heat 5-7 min., stirring occasionally. Do not freeze.

Mrs. N. A. Boardman, Fair Lawn

HOT BEAN CASSEROLE

Serves: 12-14

"This must be made ahead. Men love it."

Easy   Freeze   Preparing: 15 min.
                   Baking: 30 min.

1 large onion
1 clove garlic
3 tbsp. bacon drippings
2 pkgs. frozen lima beans,
 cooked
1 can baked beans in
 tomato sauce
1 small can kidney beans
1/2 c. catsup
1/4 c. water
3 tbsp. vinegar
1 tbsp. brown sugar
1 tsp. dry mustard
1 tsp. salt
1/4 tsp. pepper
strips of bacon

Saute onion and garlic in bacon drippings. Add to beans and other ingredients. Put into a 2 qt. casserole with bacon on top. Bake at 300° for 30 min. Great with steak.

Mrs. Duncan H. Cameron, Saddle River

LIMA BEANS AND MUSHROOMS IN CREAM

Serves: 6

Easy   Do ahead

Preparing: 15 min.
Cooking: 40 min.

2 pkgs. frozen Fordhook
  lima beans
1/2 lb. fresh mushrooms
1/2 onion, grated
1/2 stick butter
1/2 pt. medium cream
salt
pepper

Cook beans according to directions. Saute onion in butter until limp. Add sliced mushrooms and saute 5 min. Add cream, salt and pepper. Combine with drained lima beans. Heat in double boiler for 30 min. or refrigerate in a covered casserole and warm in oven when serving.

Mrs. William T. Knight, III, Saddle River

LOUBIA

Serves: 10-12

"A savory Algerian bean dish."

Average   Do ahead

Soaking: overnight
Preparing: 30 min.
Cooking: 30 min.

1 c. Italian canellini*
  (white kidney beans)
4 cloves garlic, peeled
sprig parsley
2 tsp. salt
3 tbsp. olive oil
1 large tomato, quartered
1-1/2 tbsp. flour
salt
freshly ground black pepper
1 tbsp. cumin
3 cloves garlic, finely minced
2 tbsp. paprika

*Available in Italian
grocery stores.

Soak beans overnight in 4 c. water. Drain and add more water to cover. Add 2 garlic cloves, parsley and salt. Cover and cook until tender. Remove garlic and parsley. Heat oil and add tomato and remaining garlic cloves. Cook over high heat until slightly thickened. Sprinkle with flour, salt and pepper. Remove garlic. Stir the sauce well and add a little of the cooking liquid from the beans. Add this sauce to the beans and crush a few of the beans with back of a spoon. Add cumin and salt and pepper to taste. Add minced garlic and paprika.

Mrs. Lew Gotthainer, Montclair

HARVARD BEETS

Serves: 4

Easy   Do ahead

Preparing: 10 min.
Cooking: 35 min.

12 small beets
1/3 c. sugar
1-1/2 tbsp. flour
1/4 c. vinegar
8 whole cloves
1/4 c. water or beet juice
2 tbsp. oil
  (I use Wesson)

Cook beets and cut into cubes. Mix sugar and flour. Add vinegar, oil and water; boil for 5 min. Add beets and cloves and let stand over low heat for 30 min.

Mrs. William H. Rahe, II, Rye, N. Y.

BAKED BROCCOLI

Serves: 6-8

Easy   Do ahead   Preparing: 10 min.
                                         Baking: 30 min.

2 pkgs. frozen chopped
  broccoli
1/4 lb. process cheese
1/3 c. milk
2 tbsp. minced onion
1 c. mushroom soup
1/2 c. buttered bread crumbs

Cook broccoli and drain well. Melt cheese with milk in a double boiler. Add onion and mushroom soup. Mix well. Place broccoli in a 1-1/2 qt. casserole and pour sauce over it. Top with buttered bread crumbs. Bake at 325° for 30 min.

Mrs. R. L. Saunders, Jr., Ridgewood

CARROT CASSEROLE - No. 1

Serves: 8

"Easy to do, but takes a while to clean carrots. Excellent with lamb."

Easy   Freeze   Preparing: 20 min.
                                         Baking: 20 min.

2 lbs. carrots
2 tbsp. butter
small onion, grated
1/2 green pepper, chopped
salt
pepper
6-8 oz. sharp Cheddar cheese
bread crumbs
  (I use Pepperidge Farm)

Cut up and cook carrots. Mash with butter as you would mashed potatoes. Put into a greased 1-1/2 qt. casserole. Add grated onion and chopped green pepper, salt and pepper. Put grated cheese layer on top. Sprinkle with bread crumbs. Bake at 350° for 20 min.

Mrs. John E. Button, Saddle River

CARROT CASSEROLE - No. 2

Serves: 8-10

"People can't believe they are carrots! Pretty and good company fare."

Easy   Do ahead   Preparing: 25 min.
                                         Baking: 25 min.

12 carrots
1/2 c. butter
2 tbsp. dried onion
1/4 c. flour
1 tsp. salt
1/2 tsp. dry mustard
1/8 tsp. pepper
1/4 tsp. celery salt
2 c. milk
1/2 lb. sharp cheese slices
bread crumbs

Slice and cook carrots. Drain. Make a sauce with all remaining ingredients, except cheese and bread crumbs. In a 1 qt. casserole layer carrots with cheese slices, ending with a carrot layer. Pour sauce over top and sprinkle bread crumbs over all. Bake at 350° for 25 min.

Mrs. Edward E. Alley, III, Franklin Lakes

CARROT BALLS

Serves: 5-6

"Very good - even if you dislike carrots."

Easy | Freeze | Preparing: 20 min.
Baking: 30 min.

2 c. cooked carrots, sieved
1-1/2 c. soft bread crumbs
1 c. grated sharp cheese
1 egg white
salt
pepper
crushed corn flakes
parsley

Sieve the carrots and combine with crumbs and cheese. Season to taste. Beat egg white and fold in. Form into about 10 balls and roll in corn flake crumbs. Place on a baking sheet and bake at 375° for 30 min. or until brown. Garnish with parsley.

Mrs. Willard R. Harer, Glenside, Pa.

BAKED CELERY

Serves: 6

"Marvelous for the all-oven meal."

Easy | Do ahead | Preparing: 15 min.
Baking: 50 min.

1 lb. celery
1/3 c. sliced almonds
1/2 tsp. basil
1 tsp. salt
1 c. chicken bouillon

Trim celery and slice diagonally in thin slices. Add almonds, basil, salt and bouillon. Place in a 1-1/2 qt. casserole. Cover and bake at 350° for 50 min.

Mrs. Robert B. Ross, Ridgewood

SWISS CORN BAKE

Serves: 6

Easy | Do ahead | Preparing: 10 min.
Baking: 30 min.

3 c. fresh corn
6 oz. evaporated milk
1 egg, beaten
2 tbsp. finely chopped onion
1/2 tsp. salt
dash pepper
4 oz. Swiss cheese, shredded
1/2 c. soft bread crumbs
1 tbsp. butter, melted

Cook corn in 1 c. salted water for 3 min. Drain. Combine corn, milk, egg, onion, salt pepper and 3/4 c. cheese. Turn into a 10 x 6 inch baking dish. Toss crumbs with butter and remaining cheese and sprinkle on top. Bake at 350° for 30 min. (2 pkgs. frozen corn or 2 lbs. canned corn may be substituted.)

Mrs. David C. Beasley, Ridgewood

CORN SCALLOP

Serves: 8

Easy | Do ahead | Preparing: 5 min.
Baking: 30 min.

3-4 slices toast
3 c. creamed corn
1/2 green pepper, chopped
1/3 c. melted butter
1 egg, beaten slightly
1-1/2 c. milk
1/4 tsp. salt
1/4 tsp. paprika
dash pepper
1/4 tsp. celery salt

Put toast through a food chopper or cut very fine to make 2 c. Mix with remaining ingredients and place in a 1-1/2 qt. casserole. Bake at 325° for about 30 min. or until bubbly hot.

Mrs. Philip E. Sweeny, Ridgewood

WHITE CORN CASSEROLE

Serves: 8

"'Not-so-old' Southern treatment of corn."

Easy   Do ahead   Preparing: 15 min.
                                         Baking: 20 min.

2 pkgs. frozen shoe peg
  corn (white) lightly cooked
1 pt. sour cream
5 strips bacon
1 onion, minced

Cook bacon until crisp, drain on paper towel, then crumble. Saute minced onion in bacon drippings. Combine all ingredients in a 1-1/2 qt. casserole and toss together. Bake at 350° for 20 min. Do in morning for evening meal.

Mrs. Harland C. Essertier, Ridgewood

EGGPLANT CASSEROLE

Serves: 4-6

Average   Do ahead   Preparing: 30 min.
                                         Baking: 40 min.

1 eggplant
2 tbsp. butter
1 grated onion
1/4 c. bread crumbs
1 egg
1/4 lb. American cheese,
  grated
salt
pepper

Parboil eggplant until tender, but not soft. Remove skin and cut into small chunks. Mix with butter, onion, bread crumbs, beaten egg, cheese, pepper and salt. Put into a buttered, 1 qt. casserole. Bake at 350° for 40 min.

Mrs. Edwin M. Bate, Ridgewood

ST. PAULIN EGGPLANT AND TOMATOES

Serves: 6

Easy   No need to do ahead   Preparing: 15 min.
                                         Baking: 20 min.
                                         Broiling: 3-4 min.

6 slices unpeeled eggplant,
  1/2" thick
1 tsp. salt
1/8 tsp. ground black pepper
1/2 c. fine dry bread crumbs
1 egg, beaten
1 tbsp. milk
4 tbsp. shortening
1 lb. St. Paulin cheese*
3 med., fresh tomatoes
6 slices crisp bacon

*Available at The Cheese
Shop, Ridgewood

Rub both sides of eggplant slices with 1 tsp. salt mixed with 1/8 tsp. pepper. Dip into bread crumbs, then into egg which has been beaten with milk, and into crumbs again. Brown on both sides in shortening. Arrange in a baking pan and top each with 2 thin slices cheese. (To cut use a sharp knife and cut down through the cheese.) Wash tomatoes and cut in half crosswise. Place on a baking sheet and cook in a preheated 375° oven for about 20 min. Place one tomato half on each eggplant slice. Top with a thin slice of cheese. Broil 3-4 min. or until cheese melts. Serve with crisp bacon.

Mr. Edwin F. Bernhardt, Cheese Shop, Ridgewood

EGGPLANT LASAGNE

Serves: 6

"You don't have to be Italian to enjoy this."

Average   Do ahead

Preparing: 30 min.
Baking: 1 hr. 15 min.

2 med. eggplants
2 eggs
1/4 c. milk
1 c. flour
1/4 tsp. salt
4-6 tbsp. oil
2 lbs. ricotta cheese
1 large ball mozzarella
  cheese (or grated)
1 - 1-1/2 c. grated Romano
  cheese (or Parmesan)
1 qt. marinara spaghetti sauce
  (meat sauce)
  (I use Buitoni or my own)
2/3 c. water

Cut eggplant into 1/2 inch slices (do not soak or peel). Beat eggs and milk together. Mix flour and salt together. Place each mixture in a low pan. Dip eggplant slices into egg mixture, then into flour mixture. Saute in oil until golden brown; drain on paper toweling. Thin the spaghetti sauce with water and warm the sauce. Ladle some of the sauce onto the bottom of a 9x14 inch Pyrex baking pan. Make a layer of eggplant using a generous half of the total amount. Spread with all the ricotta cheese. Ladle half the remaining sauce over this and sprinkle freely with Romano cheese. Place a second layer of eggplant (use all) and top with remaining sauce. Again sprinkle with Romano cheese. Cover with foil and bake at 350° until bubbly, about 30 min. Uncover and bake 30 min. longer. Place sliced mozzarella cheese over all and bake about 10 min. more, until cheese is melted. Serve with green salad, crunchy bread and a good bottle of Chianti (the one with a black rooster on the label is excellent).

Mrs. Robert F. Hill, Wyckoff

EGGPLANT AU GRATIN

Serves: 8-10

"This is a southern recipe; delicious and different."

Easy   Do ahead

Preparing: 20 min.
Cooking: 45 min.

4 small eggplants
2 large onions
1 lb. sharp cheese
2 eggs
salt
pepper
cracker crumbs
butter

Peel and boil eggplants in salted water until soft; strain and mash. Fry sliced onions in butter. Beat eggs. Grate cheese; combine ingredients. Salt and pepper to taste. Place in a greased 1 qt. casserole and cover with crumbs. Dot with butter. Bake at 350° for 45 min. If you do not want a very strong cheese flavor, cut the cheese to 1/2 lb.

Mrs. Charles R. Moog, Ridgewood

PUFFY EGGPLANT CASSEROLE

Serves: 4-6

"Tastes a little like scalloped oysters; so puffy and very elegant."

Easy   Do ahead   Preparing: 15 min.
                                                   Baking: 30 min.

1/2 c. mushroom soup
1/3 c. mayonnaise
1 egg
little onion juice
1 large eggplant
3/4 c. cracker crumbs
1/3 stick butter, melted
1 c. sharp grated cheese
salt

Peel the eggplant and cook in boiling water (7-10 min.). Drain and season. Mix all ingredients and put some of the cracker crumbs in the mixture. Put into a 2 qt. casserole. Sprinkle remaining cracker crumbs on top and dot with butter. Bake at 350° for 30 min.

Mrs. William H. Rahe, II, Rye, N. Y.

MUSHROOMS MARCI

Serves: 3

"From deep in the heart of Texas."

Easy   Serve immediately   Preparing: 5 min.
                                                   Simmering: 15-20 min.

1/2 lb. fresh mushrooms
2 tbsp. butter
1 clove garlic, minced
1 small onion, finely chopped
1 tsp. parsley, finely chopped
1/2 c. canned tomatoes
salt
pepper

Saute mushrooms, onion and garlic in butter in a saucepan over medium heat for about 5 min. Season to taste. Add tomatoes. (Go light on the juice or you'll be simmering for years.) Add parsley and simmer, uncovered. Dish is ready when liquid has almost entirely evaporated. This will take longer than you expect.

Mrs. Donald B. Read, Ridgewood

MUSHROOMS

Serves: 12

"So easy and scrumptious!"

Easy   Do ahead   Preparing: 10 min.
                                                   Cooking: 10 min.

3 lbs. fresh mushrooms
2-3 shallots <u>and</u>
2 small white onions
        or
4-5 shallots
1/2 lb. butter
salt
pepper
1 to 1-1/2 c. dry white wine
  (Chablis)

Slice mushrooms. Saute onions and shallots, both chopped fine, in butter. Add mushrooms, salt and pepper. Cook until tender (6-10 min.). Add wine.

Mrs. John E. Button, Saddle River

NEW ORLEANS RAGOUT

Serves: 8

"Very good with ham, leg of lamb, or roast beef."

Easy   Do ahead   Preparing: 15 min.
                                               Baking: 20 min.

1 stick margarine, melted
1/2 c. flour, sifted
1-1/2 c. milk
1 c. grated cheese
1 can tomato sauce
  (I use Hunt's)
6-8 hard cooked eggs
1 c. tiny green peas
large can mushrooms or
  1/2 lb. fresh mushrooms
1 tbsp. Worcestershire sauce
salt
red pepper
black pepper
bread crumbs
butter

Melt margarine and slowly add flour over low heat. Very slowly add milk, stirring constantly to make a thick cream sauce. Add cheese until melted, then add tomato sauce. Cut the eggs into thick, round slices. Put all ingredients into a 2 qt. baking dish and scatter with bread crumbs. Dot with butter. Bake at 350° for 20 min. or until hot and brown.

Mrs. William H. Rahe, II, Rye, N. Y.

ONION CASSEROLE

Serves: 8

"Men adore it; tasty, attractive and a conversation piece."

Average   Do ahead   Preparing: 30 min.
                                               Baking: 40 min.

1 tbsp. butter
9-10 medium onions,
  sliced thin
4-5 slices buttered toast,
  cut into pieces
1/2 lb. American cheese,
  grated
1 egg
1 c. milk
1 tsp. salt
1/4 tsp. pepper
1 tsp. celery seed

Butter a flat, 2 qt. baking dish. Meanwhile, boil onions in water to cover until just tender. Drain. Line baking dish with toast, crust removed. Cover with layer of onions and layer of grated cheese. Repeat layer of toast, cover with layer of onions and layer of grated cheese. At this point casserole can be covered with plastic wrap and stored in refrigerator for the day. Beat egg slightly and add balance of ingredients; pour over contents. Bake at 375° for 40 min. Serve at once.

Mrs. Albert Winterhalder, Jr., Saddle River

PUMPKIN FRITTERS OR BERMUDA DELIGHT

Serves: 4

"Great as a dessert with powdered sugar and sherry - or with breakfast."

Easy   No need to do ahead   Preparing: 10 min.

3 c. cooked pumpkin
sugar to taste
evaporated milk
flour
1 whole nutmeg, grated
salt
2 tsp. baking powder

Put cooked pumpkin into bowl and mash. Add sugar to taste (about 1-2 tbsp.). Soften with a little evaporated milk and enough flour to make the consistency of pancakes. Add grated nutmeg, a little salt, and baking powder. Fry as you would griddle cakes.

Mrs. John P. Connelly, Jr., Upper Saddle River

SPINACH CASSEROLE

Serves: 4-6

"Almost like a souffle; so easy, yet great!"

Easy   Do ahead   Preparing: 10 min.
                                          Baking: 15 min.

1 pkg. frozen <u>chopped</u> spinach
3/4 c. mushroom soup
1 c. grated sharp cheese
1 tsp. sugar
1 tsp. salt
1 egg
buttered bread crumbs

Cook spinach with salt and sugar until tender. Drain. Beat egg well and add soup and cheese, then add drained spinach. Put into a buttered, 1 qt. casserole and cover with buttered bread crumbs. Bake at 325° for 15-20 min.

Mrs. Robert B. Ross, Ridgewood

SQUASH SOUFFLE

Serves: 8

Average   Do ahead   Preparing: 15 min.
                                          Cooking: 30 min.
                                          Baking: 20 min.

2 lbs. yellow summer squash
2 eggs
1/4 c. flour
1/4 c. butter
1-1/2 c. milk
1/4 lb. sharp cheese
1/2 tsp. onion juice
1 tsp. salt
1/4 tsp. pepper
little sugar
1/2 c. cracker crumbs
  (I use Ritz)
butter

Cook squash until tender; drain and mash into pulp. Add eggs which have been beaten. Make a cream sauce of the flour, butter and milk. Add cream sauce and grated cheese to squash. Add butter, a little sugar, salt and pepper. Cook in a double boiler for 1/2 hr. Put into a 2 qt. casserole. Top with buttered cracker crumbs. Bake at 375° until crumbs are brown (about 20 min.).

Mrs. William H. Rahe, II, Rye, N. Y.

SUMMER SQUASH CASSEROLE

Serves: 10

"Fresh idea from Pennsylvania Dutch country."

Average   Freeze   Preparing: 20 min.
                                 Baking: 45 min.

2 large onions
1 green pepper
3 summer squash
4 tbsp. butter
1/2 lb. extra sharp cheese
1 tsp. sugar
1/2 tsp. oregano
salt
pepper

Coarsely chop onions and pepper. Without peeling, quarter squash and remove seeds, then chop. Cook onions in 4 tbsp. butter until golden brown. Cook slowly. Add green pepper; cook 5 min. more. Place squash, onions and pepper in a buttered, 2-3 qt. casserole and mix well. Add sugar, oregano, salt and pepper; stir well. Top with grated cheese. Bake at 350° for 45 min.

Mrs. David P. Campbell, Ridgewood

BAKED TOMATOES

Serves: 4-6

"Especially nice in the summer when tomatoes are in season."

Easy   Do ahead   Preparing: 15 min.
                                Baking: 30 min.

4 tomatoes
1 tsp. seasoned salt
  (I use Lawry's)
1/4 tsp. black pepper
1/4 tsp. cayenne
1/2 tsp. brown or white sugar
1/4 tsp. fine herbs
  (I use Spice Island)
2 tbsp. chopped green onions
chopped green pepper, a bit
1 c. bread crumbs
  (I use Progresso Redi
  Flavored)
butter
1/4 c. grated sharp cheese
paprika

Peel and slice tomatoes into 1/2 inch slices. Place in a greased Pyrex flat baking dish. Season with salt, pepper, cayenne, sugar and herbs. Sprinkle with onions, green pepper and cover with bread crumbs. Dot with butter and sprinkle top with cheese. Dust with paprika. Bake at 375° for 15-30 min. Can be made in morning, covered with plastic wrap and baked when ready.

Mrs. Paul R. Davis, Saddle River

STUFFED BAKED TOMATOES

Serves: 4

Easy   Do ahead   Preparing: 10 min.
                                Baking: 30 min.

4 large tomatoes
1/4 green pepper
1 small stalk celery
4 small green onions
1/2 c. bread crumbs
1 tsp. salt
1 tbsp. grated Parmesan
  cheese

Cut the centers from tomatoes and chop the pulp that is removed. Cut pepper, celery and onions finely and add bread crumbs and salt to the pulp. Stuff tomatoes with this mixture. Place in a baking dish and sprinkle with cheese. Bake at 350° for 30 min. Each tomato may be wrapped in foil, if desired.

Mrs. Harry D. Adamy, Ridgewood

TOMATO PUDDING

Serves: 4

Mrs. Eisenhower, learning of our project, sent this to The Forum Quorum.

Easy   Do ahead   Preparing: 15 min.
                                            Baking: 30 min.

1 10-oz. can tomato puree
1/4 c. boiling water
1 c. light brown sugar
1/4 tsp. salt
1 c. white bread cubes
1/4 c. melted butter

Add boiling water to puree with salt and sugar and boil for 5 min. Cut bread into 1-inch cubes. Place bread cubes in a 1 qt. casserole and pour butter over bread cubes. Add tomato mixture and bake, covered, at 375° for 30 min.

Mrs. Dwight D. Eisenhower, Gettysburg, Pa.

CANDIED TOMATOES

Serves: 6

"A different way to serve a family favorite."

Easy   Do ahead   Preparing: 15 min.
                                            Baking: 25 min.

6-8 tomatoes
1 medium onion
1 stick butter
1/2 c. light brown sugar
3/4 tsp. salt
1-1/2 c. bread crumbs
2 tbsp. brown sugar

Peel and quarter tomatoes. Saute chopped onion in 1/2 stick of butter until golden; add brown sugar and salt. Stir until sugar is melted. Add remaining 1/2 stick of butter and bread crumbs; mix. Spoon over tomatoes in a flat, buttered baking dish. Sprinkle 2 tbsp. brown sugar over top. Bake, uncovered, at 375° for 20-25 min.

Mrs. Lambert J. Gross, Ridgewood

TOMATOES BABICHE

Serves: 6

"This makes a festive party recipe. Can be served in place of a salad."

Average   Do ahead   Preparing: 20 min.
                                            Chilling: 2 hrs.

6 medium, fresh tomatoes
seasoned salt
  (I use Lawry's)
seasoned pepper
  (I use Lawry's)
1 6-oz. jar marinated
  artichoke hearts, drained
3 3-1/2 oz. jars mushroom
  stems and pieces, drained
1/2 c. mayonnaise
1/3 c. sour cream
1 tsp. curry powder
1 tsp. lemon juice
1 tbsp. instant minced onion
paprika

Scoop out each tomato leaving 1/4 inch shell. Sprinkle generously with seasoned salt and pepper; fill with artichokes and mushrooms. Refrigerate. In a bowl combine mayonnaise, sour cream, curry, lemon juice and onion. Refrigerate. When ready to serve, top each tomato with some of the curry mixture. Place remainder of mixture in small bowl and set in center of large platter surrounded by filled tomatoes. Sprinkle tomatoes and bowl of curry mixture with paprika. I usually serve with a beef and wine casserole.

Mrs. Richard A. Grimley, Ridgewood

HERBED TOMATO BAKE

Serves: 4-6

"A simple dish, very well received with fish, meat or chicken."

Easy   Do ahead   Preparing: 15 min.
                                              Baking: 20 min.

1/4 c. butter or margarine
2 tbsp. brown sugar
3/4 tsp. salt
1-1/2 c. croutons
  (I use Kellogg's Croutettes)
1/4 c. finely chopped onion
  or instant onion flakes
2 tbsp. butter or margarine
4 c. peeled tomatoes
  (2 1-lb. cans)
1/4 c. brown sugar

Melt 1/4 c. butter and stir in 2 tbsp. brown sugar and salt. Add croutons, tossing lightly; set aside. Cook onions in 2 tbsp. butter until they are soft, not brown. (Use instant if you're pressed for time.) Divide tomatoes with a fork and combine with onions and 1/4 c. brown sugar in a 10x6 inch baking dish or casserole. Add crouton mixture and mix with tomatoes. Bake at 375° for 20 min. or until thoroughly heated. If dinner hour is flexible, bake longer at a lower heat.

Mrs. John W. Simmons, Franklin Lakes

WHIPPED TURNIP PUFF

Serves: 8

"Excellent Thanksgiving dish."

Easy   Part do ahead   Preparing: 10 min.
                                              Baking: 1 hr.

4 c. mashed cooked turnips
2 c. soft bread crumbs
1/2 c. melted butter
2 tbsp. sugar
2 tsp. salt
1/4 tsp. pepper
4 eggs, slightly beaten

Mix all ingredients together thoroughly. Spoon into a greased, 1-1/2 qt. casserole and brush the top with a little additional melted butter. Bake at 375° for one hour. Turnips may be prepared ahead, but do not freeze.

Mrs. John N. Zaccheo, Ramsey

ZUCCHINI

Serves: 4

"This is a recipe done by instinct."

Easy   No need to do ahead   Preparing: 10 min.
                                              Cooking: 15 min.

8 small zucchini squash
1/4 lb. butter
3 onions, sliced
salt
pepper
Parmesan cheese

Melt butter and fry onion slices until soft and golden. Add zucchini, which has been peeled and sliced, and fry with the onion. When squash is soft, shake lots of Parmesan cheese over all and let it blend with the zucchini. It's marvelous! Vary your ingredients to suit the size of your guest list.

Mrs. Charles R. Moog, Ridgewood

FRENCH FRIED ZUCCHINI

Serves: 4

"A different way to delicious squash."

Easy   Part do ahead   Preparing: 10 min.
                                                Sitting: 1 hr.
                                                Frying: 5 min.

3 med. zucchini squash
1 tbsp. salt
1 c. flour
3-4 c. salad oil

Cut zucchini into thin strips about 3 inches long and about 1/4 inch wide (like a French fried potato stick). Put into a large bowl and sprinkle generously with salt. Set aside for 1 hr. until all moisture is out of squash. Drain. Pour oil into a large skillet to 1 inch deep; heat oil. Put flour into a separate low pan and dredge zucchini strips in flour, doing so by the handful. Put squash into a strainer and shake loose flour from it. Dip squash into fat and fry about 5 min. - to a golden brown. Remove with a slotted spoon and place on paper toweling. Salt lightly. Keep warm in the oven until all is fried.

Mrs. Allan C. Morgan, Allendale

QUICK ZUCCHINI CASSEROLE

Serves: 6

"Marvelous with roast beef, and so simple to do."

Easy   Do ahead   Preparing: 5 min.
                                                Baking: 20 min.

2 cans Italian zucchini
  with tomatoes
1 tsp. oregano
1 tsp. basil
salt
pepper
1 clove garlic, crushed
1/2 c. Parmesan cheese

Stir all ingredients together and season as desired. Put into a 1-1/2 qt. casserole and top with Parmesan cheese. Bake at 325° for 20 min.

Mrs. John H. Cline, St. Thomas, Virgin Is.

EASY BROILED ZUCCHINI

Serves: 2-3

"Unless you have two broilers, don't try this for more than two or three people.

Easy   Serve immediately   Preparing: 5 min.
                                                Broiling: 10 min.

2 medium zucchini
1/2 c. Parmesan cheese
1/2 stick butter
salt
pepper

Preheat broiler. Slice zucchini into rounds about 1/8 inch thick. Place as close together as possible in a single layer on a cookie sheet that fits in your broiler. Place a small dob of butter on each round, sprinkle with cheese and season with salt and pepper. Broil to a light brown, but still crisp. Serve immediately

Mrs. F. Marsena Butts, Lincoln, Mass.

Vegetable Sauces

HOLLANDAISE SAUCE   Serves: 1

"A basic, reheatable hollandaise. Easily multiplied 1-1-1. Not too rich."

Easy   Do ahead   Preparing: 10 min.

1 tbsp. butter
1 egg yolk
1 tsp. lemon juice
salt
cayenne

Melt butter in a Pyrex bowl that is placed in a skillet containing hot, not boiling, water. Do not use a double boiler. Beat egg yolk in a saucer and add the lemon juice, salt and cayenne. Add this to the melted butter and stir until it thickens. Should it get too thick, add a little hot water from the skillet. This keeps indefinitely in the refrigerator. To reheat, just set the bowl in a little hot water and add a bit of the hot water to the sauce. Stir until smooth.

Mrs. Paul R. Davis, Saddle River

BLENDER HOLLANDAISE SAUCE   Serves: 4

"This won a prize for me from the Bergen Evening Record."

Easy   Do ahead   Preparing: 5 min.

1 stick margarine
3 egg yolks
salt
pepper
juice of 1/2 lemon
1/2 c. boiling water

Combine all but boiling water in the blender. Add water and blend until smooth. Put in top of double boiler and cook over hot, not boiling, water until thick. If you don't let the water boil, this NEVER FAILS. Can be made several days ahead.

Mrs. James R. Toombs, Ridgewood

MOCK HOLLANDAISE   Serves: 2

"This is a last-minute preparation and is practically fail-proof."

Very easy   Do not do ahead   Preparing: 5 min.
                                                    Cooking: 5-8 min.

1 egg yolk
1/2 tsp. salt
1/2 tsp. sugar
1/8 tsp. pepper
1-1/2 tsp. lemon juice
1/2 c. sour cream

Heat all ingredients, stirring constantly, for 5 to 8 min. until thickened. Do not overcook!

Mrs. Lambert J. Gross, Ridgewood

Vegetable Variations

Any vegetable, fresh or frozen, may be cooked in the oven. Place in a
covered dish, add salt, pepper and 2 tbsp. butter. Cook approximately
45 min. at 350°.

For a different flavor, cook vegetables in consomme rather than water.

* Almost any vegetable may be scalloped if you place 3 c. cooked vegetable in
layers with cheese sauce or cream sauce in a 1-1/2 qt. casserole. Top
with buttered bread crumbs, with cheese if desired, and bake in a hot
oven until bubbly, 10-15 min.

To spruce up a vegetable, add almonds, mushrooms, coconut, cream or cheese
sauce or mushroom soup.

Peas like minced mint leaves added to them; also, slivers of orange rind,
nutmeg, sherry and sliced sauteed mushrooms.

Add chestnuts or celery to Brussels sprouts or sprinkle with a little nutmeg.

Other nice additions to vegetables are:
Slivered, toasted almonds on peas, beans, limas, asparagus, cauliflower,
broccoli, etc.
Finely chopped hard cooked eggs on spinach, asparagus, or broccoli.
Crumbled crisp bacon on cabbage, spinach, carrots or broccoli.
Sliced olives on carrots, peas, beans, limas or cauliflower.
Diced pimento on peas, asparagus, cauliflower, beans or limas.

In place of butter on vegetables, try bread crumbs, fresh or packaged, sauteed
in butter until brown. Add a bit of lemon juice or grated cheese if
desired. Marvelous on cauliflower or broccoli.

To remove excess salt taste from foods while cooking, add 1 tsp. each of
vinegar and sugar.

To prevent eyes from watering when peeling onions, hold onion under running
water. Or, hold two matches, striking end out, in your teeth while
peeling.

To dice an onion easily and almost without tears, cut onion, unpeeled, in
half lengthwise. Peel. Lay flat side on a cutting board, then score
down almost to the root end. Score again parallel with the surface.
Then cut across the end for small chopped bits.

To peel tomatoes easily, place them in boiling water for a few seconds.

When a recipe says to seed tomato, remove the core, pierce inside of the
tomato several times with a sharp paring knife, squeeze the tomato
like a dish rag over a bowl - seeds and juice will come out.

Always add a little sugar when cooking tomatoes to bring out the flavor.

* Brush tomatoes with French dressing or sprinkle with cheese crumbs or
chopped scallions before broiling.

More Vegetable Variations

Try boiling carrots right in their skins - they pop off in a jiffy.

* Delicious, easy carrots are done in the oven by slicing 1 lb. of carrots and
    placing in a 1 qt. casserole. Sprinkle generously with chopped onions
    (or dried flakes), dried basil, salt and pepper. Dot with butter and
    add 1/2 c. water. Cover and bake 45 min. at 375° or at whatever temp-
    erature your other things are baking.

Use extra ears of corn by slicing off the kernels and heating in a little
    milk and butter.

When cooking beans or rice, add a bit of vinegar or lemon juice to keep
    your aluminum pot from turning dark.

A squirt of lemon or a bit of vinegar in the water in which you are cooking
    cauliflower will keep it white as long as you do not cook in aluminum.

Cut down the odor of cauliflower, cabbage, etc., when cooking by adding a
    little vinegar to the cooking water. A stalk of celery also helps.

* Place partially cooked frozen or fresh cauliflower in a casserole, pour a
    little milk over, sprinkle with cheese and nutmeg. Bake, covered, for
    15 min.

A piece of bread on top of cabbage will cut the odor.

If using fresh herbs, always double the quantity from dried herbs.

Always rub herbs, dried or fresh, briskly between the fingers to release the
    flavor oils.

To freeze garden herbs and enjoy them all winter:
    Select young sprays of parsley, mint or dill. Wash, then blanch in
    boiling water for 10 seconds. Chill in ice water for 1 min. Pat dry.
    Seal enough herb for one use in small freezer bag or foil. Clip all
    bags of same herb to a piece of cardboard, label and freeze. Use
    while frosty and snip into casserole, salad, soup, etc.

If hollandaise sauce should curdle, immediately beat in 1 to 2 tbsp. boiling
    water or put over hot water in a double boiler. Add sour cream by the
    teaspoonful until sauce is smooth - usually takes about 4 teaspoonfuls.

* For quick sour cream, put cream cheese into the blender and beat fine.

Use your blender to make fresh bread crumbs. Add small bits of cheese for
    topping vegetables or casseroles.

Potatoes

POTATO SURPRISE

Serves: 6

Easy   Freeze

Preparing: 20 min.
Baking: 20 min.

4 large baking potatoes
1/4 lb. butter or marg.
1/4 lb. Swiss cheese (bulk)
caraway seeds
3 onions
salt
white pepper
paprika

Parboil potatoes in salted water. Meanwhile saute onions in butter or margarine,
adding salt and dash of white pepper. Grease
bottom and sides of a 1-1/2 qt. baking dish.
Peel and then slice potatoes. Alternate
layers of potatoes and sauteed onions, sprinkling with caraway seeds. Dot each layer with
Swiss cheese. Sprinkle casserole lightly
with paprika. Bake at 350° until cheese has
melted, approximately 15-20 min. Serve at
once.

Mrs. David Rukin, Saddle River

COTTAGE POTATOES

Serves: 4-6

"Good with barbecue or any beef or lamb."

Easy   Do ahead

Preparing: 10 min.
Baking: 20 min.

2 c. hot mashed potatoes
   (fresh or instant)
1/2 tsp. dill weed
1 c. cottage cheese
2 tbsp. chopped chives
1 tbsp. butter

Add dill and cottage cheese to hot potatoes.
Put into a 1 qt. casserole. Sprinkle with
chives and dots of butter. Bake at 350° for
20 min.

Mrs. Franklin A. Dick, Princeton

POTATOES IN CREAM

Serves: 6-8

"Delicious and very easy."

Easy   Do ahead

Preparing: 20 min.
Marinating: overnight
Baking: 1 hr.

4 large potatoes (Idaho)
1 pt. coffee cream
1/2 c. grated cheese

Boil potatoes until fork will just go into potato, but do not overcook. Skin and let stand a few minutes to cool. Grate potatoes on a medium grater. Grease a 1-1/2 qt. casserole heavily. Put in potatoes, salting as you layer them. Cover with cream. Cover top with grated cheese. Put in refrigerator overnight. Two hours before serving remove from refrigerator for about 1 hr. Bake at 300° for about 1 hr.

Mrs. Michael O. Albl, Midland Park

SOUR CREAM POTATOES

Serves: 6-8

"Grandmother's recipe; distinctly different from the usual creamed potatoes."

Easy   Do ahead

Preparing: 10 min.
Cooking: 3-4 hrs.

6-8 large potatoes (Idaho)
2 pts. sour cream
salt
pepper
1 tbsp. butter

Peel and dice raw potatoes. Combine with sour cream in top of a double boiler. Rub a bit of butter on the inside of the double boiler to prevent the potatoes from crusting. Season to taste. Cook slowly for 3-4 hours. These will not get mushy. Don't let double boiler go dry. Stir occasionally.

Mrs. John H. Eide, Ridgewood

SCALLOPED POTATOES IN FOIL

Serves: 4

"This is great served with steak cooked on charcoal."

Easy   Do ahead

Preparing: 15 min.
Baking: 1-1/2 hrs.

4 potatoes (Idaho)
6 tbsp. butter
2/3 c. heavy cream
1 c. shredded Cheddar cheese
M.S.G.
paprika
salt
chopped parsley
foil

Cut a four-foot length of heavy foil and fold in half. In the forward half of foil place potatoes which have been pared and cut into strips as for French fries. Dot with butter. Use a heavy hand on the salt, M.S.G., paprika, and parsley. Sprinkle cheese over the top. Fold up the edges and pour the cream over all. Bring the other half of foil over and seal the edges by folding tightly several times. Bake at 350° for 1-1/2 hrs. Cut foil open and serve.

Mrs. John E. Merrihew, Saddle River

CREAMED POTATOES

Serves: 6

"Very good, easy party fare."

Easy   Do ahead

Preparing: 5 min.
Cooking: 1-1/2 - 2 hrs.
Baking: 1 hr.

6 large potatoes
1 pt. light cream
3 tbsp. butter
salt
pepper

Bake potatoes until done. Cool. Peel and cut into cubes. Put in top of a double boiler and cover with light cream. (May be less than 1 pt.) Add butter, salt and pepper. Cook 1-1/2 to 2 hrs.

Mrs. Tom C. Bingham, Ridgewood

SWEET POTATO AND APRICOT CASSEROLE

Serves: 8

"Wonderful at Thanksgiving."

Easy   Freeze

Preparing: 20 min.
Baking: 50 min.

2 lbs. cooked sweet potatoes
  (or 1 large can)
1 c. cooked dried apricots
1 c. brown sugar
1/4 c. butter, melted
1/4 c. liquid from apricots
1 tsp. grated orange rind
1/4 c. chopped walnuts

Cut sweet potatoes into thick slices and arrange in a layer in a 10x6 inch or 2 qt. casserole. Cover with a layer of apricots, sprinkle with some brown sugar and repeat layers. Combine butter, liquid, and orange rind and pour over layers. Bake, uncovered, at 375° for 45 min., basting a few times. Freeze at this point. When ready to serve, reheat and then top with nuts for 5 more minutes of baking.

Mrs. Frederick J. Kaiser, Jr., Ho-Ho-Kus

SWEET POTATO CASSEROLE

Serves: 6

"Delicious for Thanksgiving or Christmas dinner."

Easy   Do ahead

Preparing: 10 min.
Baking: 45 min.

8 average size sweet
  potatoes, cooked or
  1 can (1 lb. 8 oz.)
1 c. packed brown sugar
1/4 c. margarine
1/2 c. orange juice
  (fresh preferred)
1 tsp. orange rind
optional - 2 tbsp. honey

Mash together all ingredients. Add honey, if desired. Put into a buttered, 1-1/2 qt. casserole. Bake in 350° oven for 45 min.

Mrs. Theodore R. Wolf, Ridgewood

Rice

PILAF WITH ALMONDS

Serves: 6-8

"An easy oven-baked rice."

Average   Do ahead

Preparing: 15 min.
Baking: 30 min.

1 med. onion, chopped fine
1-1/2 c. uncooked rice
3 tbsp. butter
2-1/2 c. chicken stock
1/2 c. blanched shredded
  almonds

Brown onion and rice in a skillet in butter. Put in a 2 qt. baking dish and cover with chicken stock. Add the almonds and stir. Cover and bake at 375° for 30 min. or until rice is tender and liquid is absorbed.

Mrs. John J. Baughan, Ridgewood

WILD RICE CASSEROLE

Serves: 8

"Fit for royalty - the price, too!"

Average   Freeze

Preparing: 20 min.
Baking: 1 hr.

1/2 c. butter
2 small cans mushrooms
  sliced in buttersauce
1 onion, chopped
2 tbsp. chopped green
  pepper
1 clove garlic, minced
1 c. pecans, chopped
1 c. wild rice
3 c. chicken broth
salt
pepper

Heat butter; add mushrooms, onion, green pepper and garlic. Cook 5 min. Add pecans and cook 1 min. Wash rice well and drain. Mix with above mixture, add broth and season to taste. Turn into well greased 2 qt. casserole. Cover and bake at 350° for 1 hr. Holds well in warm oven or can be reheated. Delicious served with wined chicken and mushroom casserole.

Mrs. Charles E. Burton, Saddle River

QUICK WHITE AND WILD RICE CASSEROLE

Serves: 4-6

Easy   Do ahead

Preparing: 15 min.
Heating: 15 min.

1 box wild and white
  rice mix
1/2 to 1 c. mushroom soup
1/2 c. sour cream
slivered almonds
1/2 c. bread crumbs
butter

Cook rice as directed on package. Drain. Carefully rinse if soggy. Combine soup and sour cream in a bowl. Put rice in a shallow baking pan and combine with soup mixture. Brown almonds and bread crumbs in a little butter and sprinkle on rice. Heat at 350° for 15 min.

Mrs. Earl A. Wheaton, Jr., Ridgewood

GREEN RICE

Serves: 8

"Especially good with baked ham. Different and simple."

Easy   Do ahead

Preparing: 20 min.
Baking: 45 min.

3 c. cooked rice
1 c. milk
2 eggs, well beaten
1/4 c. butter
1/4 c. grated sharp cheese
1/2 tbsp. grated onion
1/3 c. chopped parsley
2/3 c. minced raw spinach
1 tsp. Worcestershire sauce
1-1/4 tsp. salt

To hot, fluffy rice, carefully stir in the remaining ingredients. Pour into a greased, 2 qt. casserole and bake at 325° for 45 min. Serve hot with meat, fish and vegetable. To do ahead, prepare and refrigerate until ready to bake.

Mrs. Edward E. Alley, III, Franklin Lakes

RISOTTO

Serves: 4

"Excellent served with many Italian dishes, especially veal and chicken."

Easy   Do ahead

Preparing: 10 min.
Cooking: 20 min.

1-1/2 c. regular rice
2-1/4 c. water
2 tbsp. butter
1 tsp. salt
1/2 c. Romano cheese
1/2 stick butter, melted

Melt 2 tbsp. butter in a large skillet with a cover. Saute rice until it is a light golden color. Add water and heat, stirring, until bubbly. Add lots of salt (about 1 tsp.). Cover and cook slowly about 20 min., until the rice is dry and fluffy. Add melted butter and cheese; toss. Serve with Veal in Caper Sauce on page 102.

Mrs. Robert F. Hill, Wyckoff

PINEAPPLE-NOODLE RING

Serves: 6

"This is a sweet dish and complements pot roast well."

Average   Do ahead   Preparing: 20-25 min.
                                                Baking: 40 min.

8 slices canned pineapple
1 qt. water
1 tsp. salt
2 c. dry medium-size noodles
2 eggs
1/4 c. melted shortening
  or oil
1/4 c. granulated sugar
cinnamon
1/4 c. chopped nuts
2 tsp. matzo meal or
  cracker crumbs
3/4 c. dark brown sugar
8 cherries

Drain pineapple slices and set aside. Bring water to boil, add salt. Boil noodles 10-12 min. Drain well. Beat eggs, shortening and sugar together until smooth. Stir in cinnamon and nuts. Combine with drained noodles. Stir in cracker crumbs as lightly as possible. Grease a 9 inch ring mold well. Scatter brown sugar in mold and press up side of pan with a fork. Place pineapple around sides of pan. Put a cherry in the center of each slice. Add noodle mixture as evenly as possible to the ring mold without pressing down too firmly. Bake at 375° for 40 min or until brown. Serve immediately.

Mrs. Joel J. Steiger, Paterson

NOODLE RING

Serves: 6-8

"Especially good, but must be served as soon as finished."

Easy   Do not freeze   Preparing: 20 min.
                                                Baking: 45 min.

2 c. cooked noodles
  (about 1-1/2 c. uncooked)
4 eggs, separated
1 large can unsweetened
  evaporated milk
3/4 c. grated cheese
salt
pepper

Beat egg yolks and add to cooked noodles, milk, cheese, salt and pepper. Beat egg whites and fold into above mixture. Bake 45 min. in oiled ring mold at 350°.

Mrs. Edward D. Doherty, Ridgewood

NOODLE-SOUR CREAM CASSEROLE

Serves: 6

"Perfect with Sweet Meatballs on page 77."

Easy   Freeze   Preparing: 15 min.
                                                  Baking: 45 min.

1 bag broad egg noodles   Boil noodles; add butter, sour cream,
  (I always use Pennsylvania   cottage cheese, cinnamon and brown sugar.
   Dutch brand)   Mix well. Sprinkle with sugar and cinnamon
1 pt. sour cream   and put into a 1-1/2 to 2 qt. casserole. Bake
1/4 c. brown sugar   at 350° for 45 min. Serve with Sweet Meat-
2 tbsp. cinnamon   balls and a green salad with a tart dressing.
1 c. cottage cheese
butter   *Mrs. James M. Shavick, Ridgewood*

NOODLE CASSEROLE

Serves: 8-10

"Goes with everything and is so-o-o tasty!"

Easy   Do ahead   Preparing: 15 min.
                                                  Baking: 45 min.

8 oz. fine noodles, cooked   Cook noodles. Mix 1 c. sour cream with
1 pt. sour cream   cottage cheese. Add salt to taste, onion
1 c. fine cottage cheese   and Worcestershire sauce. Mix this in with
salt   noodles and place in a 1-1/2 qt. casserole.
1 onion, finely chopped   Spread with remaining sour cream and sprinkle
1 tbsp. Worcestershire sauce   generously with Parmesan cheese. Bake at
Parmesan cheese, grated   350° for 45 min. Do not freeze. Excellent
                                served with Veal Marsala on page 101

                                Mrs. V. A. Walstrum, Ridgewood

FETTUCCINE

Serves: 4

"Quick to make, but must be served immediately."

Easy   Serve immediately   Preparing: 15 min.

10 oz. med. noodles   Cook noodles, strain and set aside. Melt
3 oz. butter (3/4 stick)   butter and add noodles. Add sour cream and
1/2 pt. sour cream   stir a minute over low flame. Add cream
1/2 pt. heavy cream   and cook slowly for 5 min. Add cheese, a
4 oz. Parmesan cheese, grated   sprinkling of nutmeg and 1 tbsp. chives.
  (fresh, if possible)   Continue stirring until cheese is melted.
2 tbsp. finely chopped chives   Serve in a tureen and sprinkle the remaining
nutmeg   chives on top.
salt
pepper   *Mrs. H. B. Millican, Jr., Saddle River*

MACARONI CASSEROLE

Serves: 4 as a main dish
6-8 as a side dish

"Marvelous served with almost any meat or alone as a supper dish."

Average   Freeze   Preparing: 30 min.
Baking: 30-40 min.

1/2 lb. macaroni
4 c. canned tomatoes
2 tsp. salt
1 tbsp. brown sugar
1 tsp. dried basil
dash of cayenne
3 tbsp. butter
1/2 lb. mushrooms (sliced or
  whole according to size)
1-1/2 c. finely chopped onions
1 c. coarsely grated Cheddar
  cheese

Cook and drain macaroni; place in a greased 2 qt. casserole. Season the tomatoes with salt, brown sugar, basil and cayenne; simmer 20 min. Saute the mushrooms in 1 tbsp. of butter. Saute the onions in 2 tbsp. of butter until golden. Combine the tomatoes, mushrooms and onions and pour over macaroni. Mix thoroughly. Sprinkle with 1 c. coarsely grated Cheddar cheese. Bake, uncovered, in a 350° oven for 30-40 min.

Mr. William W. W. Knight, Ridgewood

CHEESE GRITS

Serves: 6

"This very Southern dish is easy, delicious, digestible and cheap!"

Average   Do ahead   Preparing: 1 hr.
Baking: 1 hr.

1 c. grits
4 c. boiling water
1 stick butter
1-1/2 c. grated cheese
1 egg, separated
1 tbsp. salt
6 shakes Tabasco sauce
M.S.G.
pepper

Cook grits in boiling water for 30 min. (directions on box). Add butter, cheese, salt, M.S.G., Tabasco and egg yolk. Cool completely. Beat egg white until stiff and fold into cooled grits. Pour into a 2 qt. casserole and bake, uncovered, at 350° for 1 hr. Will be brown on top and puffy. Serve in place of rice or potatoes.

Mrs. Bruce F. Banta, Ridgewood

Potato, Rice and Pasta Particulars

* For pan roasted potatoes, parboil them 15 min., then put around roast and roast for 45 min.

  Place a bit of oil in the water when boiling potatoes - no ikky ring!

  Grease potatoes with oil or butter before baking for skins that won't be crusty or hard.

  Serve a dish of finely chopped chipped beef along with a dish of sour cream to make a delicious baked potato topping.

* For perfect baked potatoes, grease skin with salad oil and bake for 1 hour in a preheated 400° oven.

  When baking potatoes, place each in a hole of a muffin tin - no rolling around in the oven.

  For one baked potato, place in a metal pan with a water-tight cover and let cook on the top of the stove on the lowest heat.

  Leftover baked potatoes may be reheated if you dip them in hot water and re-bake in a 350° oven.

  For mashed potatoes, cut raw potatoes with your French fry cutter. Pieces cook evenly and quickly, reducing chance of lumping.

* Delicious sweet potato balls are easily made by mashing canned sweets with a little butter and rolling into balls or patties. Coat them with crushed corn flakes and heat in the oven until lightly browned.
  Sent by Mrs. George M. Griffith, Franklin Lakes

  To prevent pared sweet potatoes from discoloring, submerge them briefly in cold, salted water.

  To prevent gummy noodles, rice, spaghetti, etc., put 2 tsp. oil in the water before cooking.

  Macaroni doubles itself when cooked.

  Noodles increase by a third when cooked.

  As soon as spaghetti is done, run it under cold water to stop the cooking immediately.

  For white, fluffy rice, add 1 tsp. lemon juice to 1 qt. water.

  Leftover noodles, macaroni, rice and spaghetti may be frozen. To reheat, rinse first with cold water to remove excess starch. Drop into boiling water for 5 min., then drain.

Salads

SNAPPY TOMATO ASPIC

Serves: 6-8

"An excellent, spicy aspic."

Easy   Do ahead   Preparing: 25 min.
                                                  Chilling: 3-4 hrs.

3 c. tomato juice
1/2 tsp. sugar
1/2 tsp. ground cloves
1 tbsp. minced onion
1 tbsp. Italian seasoning
2 env. gelatin
1/2 c. water
1 tsp. lemon juice
2 tsp. Worcestershire sauce

Center: (if desired)
1 c. mayonnaise
1 can tiny shrimp
fresh, chopped chives

Mix tomato juice, sugar, cloves, onion and Italian seasoning in a large pot and simmer 15 min. Remove from heat and add, without straining, gelatin which has been soaked in cold water. Stir until gelatin dissolves and add lemon juice and Worcestershire. Stir briefly and pour into a wet, I qt. ring mold. Refrigerate until set. This is especially good if served with the center of ring filled with shrimp mixture. Mix all center ingredients together and chill. Fill center of ring when serving.

Mrs. William W. W. Knight, Ridgewood

TOMATO ASPIC

Serves: 10-12

"My mother's recipe which beats all other aspics I've ever had."

Easy   Do ahead   Preparing: 10 min.
                                                  Chilling: 3-4 hrs.

2-1/2 c. stewed tomatoes or
  tomato juice
2-3 bay leaves
1/4 c. diced celery
1/4 c. chopped onion
several peppercorns
6-8 whole cloves
1 tsp. thyme
1/4 tsp. cayenne
2 tbsp. gelatin
1/2 c. cold water

This is best made with whole tomatoes, but if you want to speed it up use juice. Cook all ingredients, except gelatin and cold water, until vegetables are soft. Strain and force tomatoes through a sieve. Soften gelatin in cold water and add to mixture. Pour into a wet, 1-1/2 qt. mold or individual molds. Serve on a nest of lettuce with homemade mayonnaise.

Mrs. Warren S. Malhiot, Ho-Ho-Kus

MOLDED TOMATO AND CREAM CHEESE SALAD

Serves: 6-8

"This always brings raves. The flavor is unusual, as well as pleasing."

Easy   Do ahead   Preparing: 15 min.
                                                  Chilling: 3 hrs.

2 envelopes gelatin
1/2 c. water
1 can tomato soup
3 3-oz. pkgs. cream cheese
1/2 c. chopped olives
1/2 c. chopped celery
1/2 c. chopped onions
1 c. mayonnaise

Soak gelatin in water. Heat soup to boiling and add gelatin. Pour over cheese in a bowl. Beat with a mixer or in the blender. Add vegetables and mayonnaise. Pour into a wet, I qt. mold. Serve with cottage cheese, sliced cucumbers and hard cooked eggs for garnish.

Mrs. Edward H. Page, Ridgewood

MOLDED CRAB SALAD

Serves: 8

"Wonderful with a cheese dish for luncheon."

Easy   Do ahead   Preparing: 15 min.
                                                    Chilling: 3-4 hrs.

1 pkg. lemon gelatin
1/2 c. boiling water
2 small cans crabmeat
1-1/2 c. mayonnaise
1 c. chopped celery
1 tsp. prepared mustard
1 small can pimentos
2 tbsp. minced onion

Dissolve gelatin in 1/2 c. boiling water and set aside until cool. Clean and remove membrane from crab. Cut up meat and mix all remaining ingredients into the cooled gelatin mixture. Pour into individual molds. Chill until set. A large mold may be used but, because of the crabmeat, the gelatin tends to break apart when serving.

Mrs. Harry D. Adamy, Ridgewood

TOMATO-CRAB ASPIC

Serves: 4-6

Easy   Do ahead   Preparing: 15 min.
                                                    Chilling: 3-4 hrs.

1 c. tomato juice
1 slice onion
1 bay leaf
1 stalk celery, quartered
1 tbsp. gelatin
1 tbsp. cold water
3/4 c. consomme or bouillon
1 tbsp. lemon juice
salt
pepper
4 stuffed olives, sliced
1 6-1/2 oz. can crab or
  shrimp

Heat tomato juice with onion, bay leaf and celery. Strain. Add gelatin which has been softened in water. Stir until dissolved. Add bouillon, lemon juice and seasonings. Cool until partially set. Add crab and olives. Pour into a 1 qt. mold. Chill until firm. Serve with mayonnaise mixed with a little horseradish and lemon.

Mrs. Richard C. Baxter, Ridgewood

CRAB MOUSSE

Serves: 4-6

"This is an original from my dear aunt who loved to cook."

Average   Do ahead   Preparing: 15 min.
                                                    Chilling: 3 hrs.

2 tbsp. gelatin
1/2 c. cold water
1 c. boiling water
1 c. mayonnaise
1 c. heavy cream, whipped
2 c. flaked crabmeat
2-1/2 tbsp. pimento
1/2 green pepper, minced
salt to taste
pepper to taste
6 stuffed olives
lettuce
tomato

Soften gelatin in cold water. Dissolve in boiling water. Cool, then add crabmeat, mayonnaise, whipped cream and other ingredients. Turn into a cold, wet, 1-1/2 qt. mold and chill until set. Garnish with sliced olives, pimento, lettuce and sections of tomato for color.

Mrs. William B. Widnall, Saddle River

SALMON MOUSSE WITH DILL SAUCE

Serves: 8-10

"Impressive addition to buffet table; also fine luncheon dish."

Easy   Do ahead   Preparing: 20 min.
                                                     Chilling: 3 hrs.

Mousse:
1 env. unflavored gelatin
1/4 c. cold water
1/2 c. boiling water
1/2 c. mayonnaise
1 tbsp. lemon juice
1 tbsp. grated onion
1/2 tsp. Tabasco sauce
1/2 tsp. paprika
1 tsp. salt
2 c. canned salmon, red
  (drained & finely chopped)
1 tbsp. chopped capers
1/2 c. heavy cream, whipped
optional - cottage cheese

Soften gelatin in cold water. Add boiling water; stir until gelatin is dissolved. Cool. Add mayonnaise, lemon juice, onion, Tabasco sauce, paprika and salt; mix well. Chill until consistency of unbeaten egg white. Add salmon and capers; beat well. Fold in whipped cream. Garnish bottom and sides of oiled, 2 qt. fish (or other) mold with sliced olives, hard cooked eggs and pimento, if you wish. Pour mousse carefully into mold. Cottage cheese may be added to fill mold, if desired. Chill until set. Unmold on serving platter; garnish with lemon slices, watercress or parsley. Serve with dill sauce.

Sauce:
1 egg
1 tsp. salt
pinch pepper & sugar
4 tsp. lemon juice
1 tsp. grated onion
2 tbsp. finely cut dill weed
1-1/2 c. sour cream

Dill sauce: Beat egg until fluffy; add other ingredients. Stir and chill.

Mrs. Joseph M. Turino, Saddle River

SEAFOOD RING

Serves: 6-8

Average   Do ahead   Preparing: 30 min.
                                                     Chilling: 3 hrs.

2 pkgs. gelatin
1 can tomato soup
1 can tomato puree
1 can consomme
1 can crabmeat
1 can shrimp
1 can tuna fish
1 can pimentos, chopped
1/2 c. chopped onions
1 c. chopped celery
1 green pepper, chopped
3 hard cooked eggs
3 cut tomatoes
chopped radishes
1 cucumber, cut in strips
1 lemon

Dissolve gelatin in heated soups. Add everything but seafood; cool. Line bottom of a 2 qt. mold with thin slices of lemon. When cool, fold in seafoods. Put in mold and chill.

Mrs. W. Claggett Martin, New York City

SHRIMP ASPIC SALAD

Serves: 8-12

"The shrimp provides an element of elegance."

Easy   Do ahead   Preparing: 15 min.
                                                    Chilling: 3-4 hrs.

2 c. tomato juice
2 large pkgs. lemon gelatin
10 large ice cubes
1/2 to 1 lb. cooked, cleaned
  shrimp
1 tsp. celery seed
1/2 tsp. salt
1 onion, chopped fine
chopped celery
1/2 cucumber, cut up
3 hard cooked eggs, sliced

Boil tomato juice, remove from stove and stir in gelatin until dissolved. Add ice cubes; stir until melted. Add remaining ingredients. (If desired, slice the shrimp horizontally to stretch it.) Pour into a 1-1/2 qt. mold. Chill until set. If desired, other things such as cut-up olives, bread-and-butter pickles, or leftover, cooked vegetables such as green beans can be used.

Mrs. Robert W. Peterson, Ramsey

SHRIMP MOUSSE

Serves: 4

"Absolutely marvelous! A good dip if you use only a half package of gelatin."

Average   Do ahead   Preparing: 15 min.
                                                    Chilling: 3-4 hrs.

1 pkg. gelatin
1/4 c. cold water
1 can tomato soup
8 oz. cream cheese
1/2 c. mayonnaise
2 stalks celery, chopped
1/2 c. grated onion
1/4 c. chopped green pepper
1-1/2 c. bite-size shrimp
salt
pepper
seasoned salt (I use
  McCormick's Season-All)
hot pepper sauce to taste

Dissolve gelatin in cold water. Heat soup and add to gelatin. Cool this mixture and add cheese. Beat with an electric beater. Add the remaining ingredients. Let set in a 2 qt. mold for several hours.

Mrs. Herman A. Poitras, Saddle River

CUCUMBER MOUSSE

Serves: 6-8

"Wonderful for a buffet supper."

Easy   Do ahead   Preparing: 15 min.
                                                    Setting: 30 min.
                                                    Chilling: 3-4 hrs.

scant 3/4 c. boiling water
1 small pkg. lime gelatin
1 c. grated cucumber
1 c. mayonnaise
2 tbsp. grated onion
1 c. sour cream
1/4 tsp. salt

Dissolve gelatin in boiling water. Pour into a 2 qt. mold and place in refrigerator until slightly thickened. When thickened, fold in remaining ingredients. Refrigerate until set.

Mrs. Jay W. Jackson, Ridgewood

184

ASPARAGUS MOLD

Serves: 6-8

"Slightly different."

Easy   Do ahead   Preparing: 10 min.
                                                Chilling: 3-4 hrs.

3/4 c. sugar
1/2 c. vinegar
1 c. water
2 tbsp. gelatin
1/2 tsp. salt
1 c. chopped celery
1/2 c. chopped pecans
2 pimentos, chopped
1 #2 can asparagus, chopped
juice of 1/2 lemon
2 tsp. grated onion
1/2 c. stuffed green olives,
   chopped

Dressing:
1/2 c. mayonnaise
1/2 c. sour cream

Boil together sugar, vinegar and water for at least 2 min. Dissolve gelatin in 1/2 c. cold water. Set 5 min. Add this to boiled vinegar mixture. Add remaining ingredients and mold in a 1-1/2 qt. mold until set. Serve with mixture of mayonnaise and sour cream.

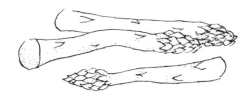

Mrs. John E. Button, Saddle River

MOLDED CANTALOUPE SALAD

Serves: 4-6

"Marvelous for a luncheon or brunch."

Easy   Do ahead   Preparing: 15 min.
                                                Chilling: 3-4 hrs.

1 pkg. unflavored gelatin
1/2 c. cold water
1/2 c. boiling water
1/3 c. sugar
1/8 tsp. salt
1/2 c. orange juice
1/3 c. lemon juice
2 c. small cantaloupe balls

Sprinkle gelatin over cold water in a mixing bowl to soften. Add boiling water; stir to dissolve gelatin. Add sugar, salt, orange and lemon juices. Stir to dissolve sugar. Chill until thick as unbeaten egg white. Fold in cantaloupe balls. Turn into a 2 qt. mold.

Mrs. Robert S. Van Riper, Ridgewood

BING CHERRY SALAD

Serves: 6

"A different and delicious molded salad."

Easy   Do ahead   Preparing: 15 min.
                                                Chilling: 3-4 hrs.

1 c. cherry juice
1/2 c. water
1 pkg. cherry gelatin
1/2 c. port wine
1 can pitted Bing cherries

Boil juice and water; add gelatin. Add wine, then cherries. Place in a wet, 1 qt. mold. Chill.

Mrs. Arthur J. Partrick, Ridgewood

SPICED APRICOT OR PEACH GELATIN SALAD

Serves: 8

Easy   Do ahead

Preparing: 20 min.
Chilling: 3-4 hrs.

3/4 c. canned apricot or
  peach juice
1/4 c. vinegar
1/2 c. sugar
12 whole cloves
2 sticks cinnamon
hot water or orange juice
1 pkg. orange gelatin
1 large can apricots or
  peaches

Mix together juice, vinegar, sugar, cloves and cinnamon; simmer for 10-15 min. Drain syrup from fruit and add to above mixture. Strain this and add enough hot water or orange juice to make a total of 2 cups liquid. Dissolv orange gelatin in this. Chill slightly and add canned apricots or peaches. Place in a wet, 1 qt. mold. Let set.

Mrs. Jack E. Ross, Ridgewood

PINEAPPLE-CUCUMBER MOLD

Serves: 8-10

"A wonderful, cool luncheon dish."

Average   Do ahead

Preparing: 20 min.
Chilling: 6 hrs.

1 c. crushed pineapple
1 pkg. lemon gelatin
1/2 tsp. salt
1/2 c. finely grated carrots
1 env. unflavored gelatin
1/4 c. cold water
1 c. mayonnaise
1/2 c. light cream or
  sour cream
1/2 tsp. salt
1 tbsp. grated onion
1/2 c. finely chopped celery
1/2 c. grated cucumber,
  drained

Pineapple Layer: Drain pineapple. Add enough water to syrup to make 1-3/4 c. liquid. Heat to boiling and dissolve gelatin in it. Chill until slightly thickened. Add salt, carrots and crushed pineapple. Turn into a 1-1/2 qt. ring or fancy mold. Chill until firm.

Cucumber Layer: Soften gelatin in cold water. Dissolve over hot water. Combine remaining ingredients. Add gelatin and blend. If desired tint a pale green with food coloring. Pour over pineapple layer. Chill until firm. Unmold and garnish with salad greens.

Mrs. Albert F. Lilley, Allendale

STRAWBERRY GELATIN SALAD

Serves: 6

Easy   Do ahead

Preparing: 20 min.
Chilling: 3-4 hrs.

1 pkg. strawberry or
  cherry gelatin
1 c. boiling water
1 pkg. frozen, sliced
  strawberries
1 small can crushed pineapple
1 mashed banana
1/2 pt. sour cream

Dissolve gelatin in boiling water. Add unthawed strawberries, pineapple and banana. Put half of mixture into a 1-1/2 qt. mold and jell until set. Spread with sour cream. Add remaining gelatin mixture. Chill.

Mrs. Michael O. Albl, Midland Park

LIME AND COTTAGE CHEESE SALAD

Serves: 6

"Wonderful addition to a buffet supper."

Easy   Do ahead   Preparing: 10 min.
                                                    Chilling: 3-4 hrs.

1 pkg. lime gelatin
2 c. cottage cheese
1 small can crushed pineapple
1 c. mayonnaise
juice of 1 lemon
3/4 c. boiling water

Put gelatin into boiling water. Mix well. Add mayonnaise and lemon juice. Beat with a rotary beater. Fold in cottage cheese and pineapple. Pour into a wet, 1 qt. mold. Refrigerate for several hours before serving.

Mrs. Thomas P. Ford, New York City

CRANBERRY SALAD

Serves: 10-12

"A special treat with poultry."

Average   Do ahead   Preparing: 30 min.
                                                    Chilling: 3 hrs.

1 small can diced pineapple
  (1 cup)
hot water
4 c. cranberries (1 qt.)
2 c. sugar
3 tbsp. gelatin
1/2 c. cold water
pinch salt
1 c. white nutmeats
  (almonds, etc.)
1 c. seeded grapes

Add hot water to the juice from the pineapple until you have 3-1/2 c. Cook cranberries in this until they pop open (about 5 min.). Add sugar while berries are cooking. Dissolve gelatin in cold water. Add to berries as soon as removed from heat. Let set until cool and beginning to set. Add salt, nuts, pineapple and grapes. Pour into a 2 qt. or larger mold. Let set in refrigerator. Serve with whipped cream or any dressing you desire.

Mrs. Gilbert R. Rogers, Ridgewood

FIVE-CUP SALAD

Serves: 8-10

"Rich, but tasty, and so simple to make."

Easy   Do ahead   Preparing: 10 min.

1 c. mandarin oranges
1 c. miniature marshmallows
1 c. cocoanut
1 c. crushed pineapple
1 c. sour cream

Combine all ingredients and mix well. Serve on a lettuce bed.

Mrs. Joseph Kresky, Rutherford

CHEESE-ORANGE SALAD

Serves: as you like

"A whole lunch, if you want a light meal."

Easy   No need to do ahead   Preparing: 5 min.

Holland Edam or Gouda cheese
mandarin orange sections
watercress
red onions
Italian dressing

Arrange wedges of cheese and chilled oranges on a bed of crisp watercress. Garnish with thin red onion rings. Serve with Italian dressing.

Mr. Edwin F. Bernhardt, Cheese Shop, Ridgewood

CURRIED CHICKEN SALAD

Serves: 12

"A different, exotic chicken salad."

Easy   Do ahead

Preparing: 15 min.
Chilling: several hours

2 qts. cooked chicken, cubed
1 #2 can water chestnuts,
   drained and sliced
2 lbs. seedless grapes,
   halved
2-3 c. celery, sliced
2-1/2 c. almonds, sliced
3 c. mayonnaise
1 tbsp. curry powder
2 tbsp. soy sauce
2 tbsp. lemon juice

Combine chicken, water chestnuts, grapes, celery and 1-1/2 c. almonds. Mix all remaining ingredients, add to chicken and toss well. Chill several hours. Serve on lettuce bed. Top with remaining almonds.

Mrs. Robert G. Rogers, Pelham, N. Y.

CHICKEN SALAD

Serves: 8

"A rich, different chicken salad."

Easy   Do ahead   Preparing: 30 min.

3 c. diced chicken
1/2 c. mayonnaise
1/2 c. whipped cream
1 c. pineapple bits
1/2 c. slivered almonds

Whip cream and fold into mayonnaise. Mix this with the chicken and pineapple, tossing lightly. Serve on crisp lettuce topped with warm almonds which have been lightly toasted in the oven.

Mrs. Allen D. Patterson, Saddle River

MONTEREY SALAD

Serves: 8

"A delight at picnics and outdoor barbecues, as well as on your dinner menu."

Easy   No need to do ahead   Preparing: 10 min.

2 6-oz. jars marinated
   artichoke hearts
   (I use Cara Mia brand)
1 head iceberg lettuce
1 head romaine
2 green onions
2 tomatoes
2 tbsp. garlic-flavored
   wine vinegar
salt
pepper
optional - 1 hard cooked egg

Drain artichokes and reserve the oil. Break lettuce into bite-size bits and mix with chopped onions and most of the artichokes in a large salad bowl. Add vinegar, salt and pepper to the oil saved from the artichokes to make a dressing. Pour on dressing and toss lightly. Top with tomato wedges, remaining artichoke hearts and egg slices, if desired. Garnish with romaine.

Mrs. Frank Sanclementi, Jr., Haskell, N. J.

COLESLAW

Serves: 6

Average   Do ahead   Preparing: 30 min.

1/2 c. mayonnaise
1 tsp. salt
pepper
1 tsp. celery seed
2 tbsp. lemon juice
1 tsp. sugar
1/2 tsp. prepared mustard
1 tsp. minced onion or
  scallions
4 c. finely shredded cabbage
M.S.G.

Mix all ingredients together. Do not freeze. Serve with hot or cold meats or fish.

Mrs. N. A. Boardman, Fair Lawn

SWEET SLAW

Serves: 4-6

"Easily made for any size crowd."

Easy   Do ahead   Preparing: 15 min.
                                    Marinating: overnight

1 pkg. pre-cut slaw mixture
1 small can pineapple bits
1 small box seedless raisins
1/2 c. mayonnaise

Thin mayonnaise to the consistency of heavy cream by adding pineapple juice. Mix together drained pineapple, raisins and mayonnaise. Cover and marinate overnight in the refrigerator. When ready to serve, add slaw mix and toss. Serve on lettuce or "just so."

For 24: Multiply all ingredients except the mayonnaise. Begin with 2 cups and thin with juice. Sauce should lightly coat slaw.

Mrs. William T. Knight, III, Saddle River

CABBAGE SALAD

Serves: 10

"Best if made ahead. Stays crisp for days."

Easy   Do ahead   Preparing: 10 min.
                                    Chilling: 1 hr.

1 med. head cabbage
2-3 large onions, sliced thin
7/8 c. sugar
1 c. vinegar
3/4 c. oil
2 tsp. sugar
1 tsp. salt
1 tsp. dry mustard
1 tsp. celery seed

Alternate layers of sliced cabbage and onion and cover with 7/8 c. sugar. Make dressing by boiling remaining ingredients. While still hot, pour over cabbage. Cover. Chill.

Mrs. Earle E. Bogardus, Ramsey

GUACAMOLE SALAD

Serves: 16

"A typical southern California recipe. A meal in itself."

Easy   Do ahead   Preparing: 30 min.

2 heads iceberg lettuce
6 tomatoes
3 cans white tuna
4 cans black olives, sliced
1 c. green onions, sliced
  (stems and all)

Dressing:
1-1/2 c. mashed avocado
1-1/2 c. sour cream
1/2 c. salad oil
1 tbsp. lemon juice
1 tsp. Tabasco sauce
1-1/2 tsp. garlic salt
1-1/2 tsp. chili powder

1 bowl grated Cheddar cheese
1 bowl corn chips

Break lettuce as for tossed salad. Cut tomatoes into eighths or bite-size pieces. Break up tuna. Mix all ingredients together like a tossed salad in bowl for buffet service or served on plates for luncheon.

Dressing: Mix all ingredients together.

To serve: Prepare for buffet table to follow salad or to pass at luncheon table –
    1 bowl Guacamole dressing
    1 bowl grated Cheddar cheese
    1 bowl corn chips – broken up, but not
      crushed (Med. bag is sufficient)
Have guests help themselves to salad. Sprinkle generously with cheese, add a dollop of dressing and sprinkle with corn chips.

Mrs. Stephen M. Opremcak, Jr., Franklin Lakes

NIGHT-BEFORE SALAD

Serves: 8

"A marvelous salad made with a new twist."

Easy   Do ahead   Preparing: 15 min.
                                          Chilling: 1-2 hrs.
                                          Refrigerating: overnight

3 carrots
1/2 c. sugar
head of lettuce
bunch of celery
chopped green onions
1 pt. mayonnaise
6 strips bacon

Pare and cut carrots into slivers. Cover with water, add sugar and chill for 1-2 hrs. Pour off water and sugar and put carrot slivers on bottom of a large salad bowl. Add a layer of lettuce that has been broken into small pieces. Add a layer of chopped celery and lastly a thin layer of chopped green onions. Cover this entirely with all the mayonnaise. Do not stir. Cover tightly with plastic wrap and refrigerate overnight. Before serving fry the bacon crisp and drain. Sprinkle bacon over top of salad when it is served. Ask your guests to dig deep!

Mrs. James W. Allred, Ridgewood

PINEAPPLE AND BEAN SALAD

Serves: 10-16

"Good with any meat and chicken. A fine picnic salad."

Easy   Do ahead   Preparing: 30 min.
                                                    Chilling: 3 hrs.

1 14-oz. can pineapple chunks
1 1-lb. can red kidney beans
1 pkg. frozen lima beans
1 pkg. frozen cut green beans
1 green pepper, chopped
1 c. sliced celery

Dressing:
pineapple liquid (above)
1 tbsp. cornstarch
1/4 c. wine vinegar
1 tbsp. dry mustard
1/2 tsp. pepper
1/2 tsp. dill
2 tsp. sugar
1 tsp. seasoned salt
1/4 c. olive oil

Drain pineapple and reserve liquid. Place with drained kidney beans in a large bowl. Parboil other beans until barely tender and add to bowl with pepper and celery. Cover and chill several hours.

Dressing: Blend 1/2 c. pineapple liquid with cornstarch, vinegar, mustard, pepper, dill, sugar and salt in a small saucepan. Cook and stir over moderate heat until thickened (about 5 min.). Remove from heat and beat in olive oil. Cover and chill. When ready to serve, add to salad and mix.

Mrs. John L. Dwyer, Franklin Lakes

BEAN SALAD

Serves: 8

"Men love this. Great for buffets, indoors or out."

Easy   Do ahead   Preparing: 20 min.
                                                    Marinating: 24 hrs.

15-oz. can wax beans
15-oz. can red kidney beans
15-oz. can chick peas
1 box frozen green beans,
  cooked
1 med. onion, chopped
1 green pepper, chopped

Dressing:
1/2 c. sugar
2/3 c. wine vinegar
1/2 c. oil
1 tsp. salt
1 tsp. pepper
1/2 tsp. Worcestershire sauce
chopped parsley

Drain beans and peas and mix together in a large bowl with onion and pepper. Mix all dressing ingredients together and pour over bean mixture. Let marinate in refrigerator for at least 24 hrs., stirring a few times. Serve with a large slotted spoon.

Mrs. David I. Meriney, Saddle River

SARA SALAD

Serves: 8

"This salad makes its own dressing."

Easy   Do ahead   Preparing: 15 min.
Chilling: 2 hrs.

1 head lettuce
1 head escarole
1 head romaine
4 heads endive
1-1/2 c. peas, cooked
6 tbsp. mayonnaise
1 med. onion, sliced
1 c. julienne Swiss cheese
6 slices bacon, cooked
3 tsp. sugar
salt
pepper

Wash and dry greens. Place 1/3 of mixed greens in a bowl. Dot with 2 tbsp. mayonnaise and 1/3 of onion slices. Sprinkle with 1 tsp. sugar and dash of salt and pepper, 1/3 of the peas and 1/3 of the cheese. Repeat for three layers. Do not toss. Cover and chill at least two hours. Crumble the bacon. Just before serving top with bacon and toss.

Mrs. Ralph F. Barry, Jr., Saddle River

HUNGARIAN CUCUMBER SALAD

Serves: 6

"Delicious extra vegetable for dinners or picnics; also a refreshing salad."

Average   Do ahead   Preparing: 20 min.
Chilling: 2 hrs.

4 large or 6 med. cucumbers
salt
pepper
1 med. onion, chopped fine
1/2 c. heavy cream
and
lemon juice
or
sour cream, if desired

Slice cucumbers very thin. Salt heavily and let stand in a large bowl for a few hours or refrigerate overnight. Pour off all liquid, pressing out all possible juice from the cucumbers. Add onion, cream and a few tbsps. lemon juice. (If using sour cream, do not use lemon juice.) Pepper to taste. Toss well. Removing the juice makes this very digestible even to those who claim not to be able to eat cucumbers.

Mrs. Arthur J. Werger, Ramsey

GREEK TOMATO SALAD

Serves: 6

"The longer this stands at room temperature the better."

Easy   Do ahead   Preparing: 15 min.
Marinating: 4 hrs.

3 large, ripe tomatoes
12 ripe olives, pitted
3/4 c. Feta cheese*
3 tbsp. wine vinegar
1/2 c. olive oil
1/2 tsp. oregano
1/2 tsp. thyme
salt to taste
freshly ground pepper to taste
optional - 1 clove garlic

Cut tomatoes to bite size. (A basket of small ones may also be used.) Cut olives in half. Crumble the cheese coarsely or cube. Rub bowl with garlic; add tomatoes, olives and cheese. Sprinkle with vinegar and olive oil. Add seasonings and toss. Marinate for at least 4 hrs. If longer, store in refrigerator until 1-2 hrs. before serving. Serve at room temperature. Great with pork or lamb.

*Available in gourmet cheese shops.

*Mrs. Constantine G. Vasiliadis
Harrington Park*

HERRING SALAD

Serves: 20-24

"Traditionally served in Germany on New Year's Day. Delicious!"

Average   Do ahead   Preparing: 30 min.
                                        Marinating: 24 hrs.

1-lb. jar herring fillets (in
  sour cream or wine sauce)
1 c. cold, cooked veal
  (or chicken)
2 hard cooked eggs
1-1/2 c. pickled beets
1/2 c. onions
1/2 c. dill pickles
1-1/2 c. potatoes, boiled
  in their skins
1 c. diced apples
2 tbsp. capers
1/2 c. mayonnaise
1 tsp. prepared mustard
1 tbsp. lemon juice or
  vinegar

Cut all ingredients into 1/4 inch cubes; add capers. Mix together mayonnaise, mustard and lemon juice. Pour over other ingredients and mix well. Let stand in a cool place overnight. Serve on a bed of lettuce.

Mrs. B. M. Brown, Ridgewood

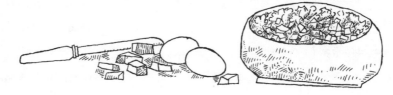

TABBOULEH (Lebanese)

Serves: 6

"This salad should be served in a bed of lettuce. Good with a fish course."

Average   Do ahead   Preparing: 20 min.
                                        Setting: 15 min.

1 c. cracked wheat*
4 bunches parsley
2 tomatoes
1 onion
4 tbsp. lemon juice
1 tsp. salt
1/2 c. oil
1 tsp. dried mint
1 head lettuce

*Cracked wheat is called
Burgul or Bulgar and can be
obtained at any Greek or
Armenian store. Olympia Food
of All Nations in Riverdale
carries this.

Wash cracked wheat and set aside for 1 hr. to soak. Remove parsley leaves from stems and discard stems. Wash and chop parsley leaves, tomatoes, and onion. Add to soaked, cracked wheat. Add all other ingredients and mix well. Let stand about 15 min. before serving so that juices can be absorbed by cracked wheat.

Mrs. Maurice F. Deraney, Ridgewood

Salad Dressings

SWEET FRUIT DRESSING
Yield: 1-1/2 cups

"Marvelous on all summer fruits; i.e., peaches, melons, citrus, avocado."

Easy   Do ahead   Preparing: 10 min.

1/2 c. sugar
1 tsp. salt
1 tsp. dry mustard
1 tsp. paprika
1 tbsp. grated red onion
1 c. salad oil
1/4 c. vinegar
1 tbsp. poppy seed

Mix dry ingredients, except poppy seed, and add onion. Add oil, a small amount at a time, alternating with vinegar and finishing with vinegar. Beat with rotary beater. Add poppy seed.

Mrs. William H. Rahe, II, Rye, N. Y.

FRENCH DRESSING
Yield: 1-1/2 pints

"Especially good on tossed salad."

Easy   Do ahead   Preparing: 5 min.

1 can tomato soup
1 c. salad oil
  (I use Mazola)
2/3 c. vinegar
1/2 c. sugar
2 tsp. salt
1/4 tsp. paprika
1 tsp. dry mustard
1/2 tsp. onion salt
1/2 tsp. celery salt

Beat all ingredients together. Store in the refrigerator.

Mrs. Martin Hoeksema, Ridgewood

CHATTERBOX FRENCH DRESSING
Yield: 1-1/2 cups

"This is very popular at the Chatterbox Club in Rochester, New York."

Easy   Do ahead   Preparing: 5 min.

6 tbsp. sugar
1 tsp. salt
1 tsp. celery salt
1 tsp. dry mustard
1 tbsp. catsup
1 tbsp. onion juice or
  grated onion
3 tbsp. vinegar
1 c. oil
juice of 1/2 lemon

Put everything into a bowl and beat with an egg beater until well blended. Strain into a jar. Cover and refrigerate.

Mrs. Robert Y. Murray, Ridgewood

BLENDER ROQUEFORT DRESSING

Yield: 1-1/2 cups

Easy   Do ahead   Preparing: 5 min.

2/3 c. salad or olive oil
3 tbsp. lemon juice
1 clove garlic
1 tbsp. Worcestershire sauce
1 c. (1/4 lb.) crumbled
  Roquefort cheese

Place all ingredients in order given into blender. Blend about 1 minute.

Mrs. Warren D. Haggerty, Jr., Ridgewood

ROQUEFORT DRESSING - No. 1

Yield: 1 pint

Easy   Do ahead   Preparing: 10 min.

1 pt. mayonnaise
  (I use Hellmann's)
3 tbsp. hot water
1 tsp. onion, fresh or
  instant
few drops of lemon juice
4 oz. Roquefort cheese

Mix mayonnaise and hot water, lemon and onion well. Add enough softened cheese to make as thick as you wish. This will keep in the refrigerator indefinitely.

Mrs. William W. Bowyer, Franklin Lakes

ROQUEFORT DRESSING - No. 2

Yield: 1-1/4 pints

Easy   Do ahead   Preparing: 5 min.

1 c. mayonnaise
1 c. sour cream
1 tsp. garlic salt
1 tsp. celery salt
2 tbsp. lemon juice or
  vinegar
1 3-oz. wedge Roquefort,
  crumbled

Combine ingredients and refrigerate in a glass jar.

Mrs. Kenneth S. Talbot, Ridgewood

GREEN GODDESS SALAD DRESSING

Yield: 2 cups

"A true West Coast dressing for tossed salad."

Easy   Do ahead   Preparing: 10 min.
                                          Chilling: 4 hrs.

1 3/4-oz. can anchovy fillets
1 clove garlic
1 small onion
1 c. mayonnaise
2/3 c. heavy cream
1/4 c. white wine tarragon
  vinegar
2 tbsp. lemon juice
1/2 c. minced parsley
1/4 tsp. coarsely ground
  black pepper
salt

Put all ingredients into the blender and blend thoroughly. (Or, chop fine and blend with electric mixer.) Let stand in refrigerator at least 4 hrs. to chill dressing and blend flavors. Serve over greens or, for a heartier luncheon, add chicken, crabmeat or shrimp. Dressing stores well for several days in the refrigerator.

Mrs. Theodore S. Jadick, Franklin Lakes

THOUSAND ISLAND DRESSING   Yield: 3 cups

"Perfect on hearts of lettuce or any tossed green salad."

Easy   Do ahead   Preparing: 5 min.

1 c. mayonnaise
1/2 c. chili sauce
3 hard cooked eggs, minced
1/3 c. green pickle relish
1/3 c. finely chopped green
  pepper
1/3 c. finely chopped celery
1 small onion, minced

Mix all ingredients and chill. Serve over
any green tossed salad or hearts of lettuce.

Mrs. Corbett U. Allen, Jr., Ramsey

HOMEMADE MAYONNAISE   Yield: 1 quart

"Especially good on molded salads; as a mock hollandaise, delicious!"

Tricky, not hard   Do ahead   Preparing: 30 min.

2 egg yolks
1 qt. salad oil
  (I use Wesson)
juice of 1 lemon, strained
1 tbsp. salt
6 shakes Tabasco sauce
1 tsp. vinegar
paprika

Chill oil and beaters in freezer while
squeezing lemon, separating eggs, etc. Put
yolks into a bowl and beat 10 min. until very
light and foamy. Add cold oil a drop at a
time, beating constantly until you have used
about 1-1/2 c. and the mixture becomes thick.
Don't interrupt this step, even to answer the
phone, until this is thickened. When thick,
add lemon juice a little at a time, alternating with remaining oil, until you have used
all the oil and lemon juice. Add salt,
Tabasco, vinegar, paprika and beat well.
Season more, if desired, and beat again. This
is much easier to do the second time around.

Mrs. Bruce F. Banta, Ridgewood

MAYONNAISE   Yield: 1 pint

"Delicious, easy, and often saves a trip to the store."

Easy   Do ahead   Preparing: 15 min.

1 whole egg
1 tsp. sugar
1 tsp. dry mustard
1 tsp. salt
dash pepper
dash paprika
1-1/2 c. Wesson-type oil
2 tbsp. vinegar

Beat egg. Add seasonings. Add half the
oil, a tbsp. at a time, while beating. The
second half can be dumped in all at once.
Add vinegar last. Store in refrigerator.

Mrs. William W. Hall, Ridgewood

Salad Secrets

Put paper towels under washed salad greens, cover with another and refrigerate
for an hour or more. Moisture is all taken up.

To freshen wilted salad greens, douse them quickly in hot water, then in ice
water to which a little vinegar has been added.

To core lettuce easily, smack it hard, stem down, on the counter top. The
core will twist right out. When storing lettuce, wrap in a turkish
towel - it will not turn brown.

Watercress, parsley and mint will keep well if washed and drained and then
placed in air-tight jars in the refrigerator.

Put celery tops into your tossed lettuce salad. They add a nice flavor.

Parsley can easily be dried by placing on a cookie sheet and leaving it in
the oven with only the pilot light on for a few days. When dry, store
in covered jars.

Freeze parsley by wrapping tightly in foil after washing and drying. When
needed, this can be grated and replaced in the freezer.

To liquify gelatin, pour gelatin powder over a small amount of cold liquid in
a heat-proof dish. Set the dish in a pan of hot water until gelatin is
liquid, then add it to room temperature, not cold, ingredients.

When using pineapple in a gelatin salad, add a bit of sugar to help it jell
well. Pineapple does not generally jell very well.

* A nice dressing for a gelatin salad is made by reserving a bit of the gelatin
mixture. Before serving, melt to unjell. Then have mixture get to the
thick stage by placing in an ice bath (set inside a bowl of ice cubes).
When syrupy, whip with a rotary beater until frothy. Serve over the
gelatin mold - it will match your salad. *Sent by Mrs. Robert B. Ross.*

A molded salad is easier to remove if you grease the mold with salad oil
before filling it.

To unmold a congealed salad: Run a spatula around the edge of the mold to
loosen it. Invert over the serving platter and shake gently to release.
If necessary, place a hot, damp dish cloth over mold. Shake again to
release. *Sent by Mrs. Paul R. Davis, Saddle River*

Some salads may be frozen - those with cream cheese, cottage cheese or whipped
cream as a base do best. Those with a lot of mayonnaise tend to
separate if frozen. These are best if served before they are completely
thawed.

Use a No. 2 or No. 2-1/2 can for frozen salad mold. After freezing, allow to
stand a few minutes. Cut bottom out of can, push salad out and slice
and serve.

* A good hearty salad is made be adding 4 quartered tomatoes and half a thinly
sliced red onion to a large can of kidney beans, drained. Add 1/2 bottle
of French dressing (Miracle French is especially good) and marinate in
the refrigerator overnight.

More Salad Secrets

* For a great extra salad or cold vegetable, marinate whole, fresh, cooked green
  beans in a mixture of 1/2 c. wine vinegar, 2 tbsp. salad oil, 1 tbsp.
  sugar, 1 tsp. salt, and a dash of pepper to which you add a few fresh
  scallions or half a chopped onion. Marinate 1 hr. or more, tossing
  occasionally. Drain before serving.

* Easy shrimp salads:
    1. Fold through the shrimp salad 2 small cans of pineapple chunks and
       3 drops of lemon juice.

    2. Add 4 tsp. lemon juice to mayonnaise mixture and top a salad with
       honey-dew or muskmelon balls. *Sent by Mrs. Robert A. Don, Ridgewood*

* For a marvelously easy chicken salad for six, mix 2-1/2 c. diced cooked
  chicken with 1 c. chopped celery, 1 c. sweet white grapes halved and
  1/2 c. salted almonds. Toss with mayonnaise (I use Hellmann's) to
  moisten and season with salt and pepper. Chill and serve.
  Sent by Mrs. Jack E. Ross, Ridgewood

* Sliced red onions with orange slices make a delicious salad when served on a
  bed of watercress with French dressing.

  Pretty onion rings for salads can be made by slicing into pickled beets and
  letting them soak the juices.

  Fresh tarragon leaves are great served on tomato slices with a tart French
  dressing.

* A sprinkling of toasted sesame seeds adds a little something to a tossed salad.
  Especially nice with slivers of Romano cheese added.

  Walnuts toasted in a bit of butter with garlic salt added are delicious in a
  tossed salad.

* For easy garlic croutons for your salad, cut bread into 1/2 inch cubes and
  cook in 1/2 c. hot salad oil. Stir until lightly browned. Drain.
  Sprinkle with half an envelope of Garlic Salad Dressing Mix (Good
  Seasons is excellent).

  Use kitchen scissors to cut grapes in half; remove seeds with another snip.

* For fluffy fruit salad dressing, a cup of "softish" vanilla ice cream with
  3 tbsp. of mayonnaise beaten in is marvelous.

* Clear French dressing is made by mixing and shaking 3 tbsp. sugar, 1 tsp. salt,
  5 tbsp. white vinegar, 1/2 c. oil, 1/4 tsp. paprika and onion salt, and
  1/8 tsp. pepper. *Sent by Mrs. George M. Griffith, Franklin Lakes*

* Add juice of half a lemon to 1 c. sour cream or yogurt and salt and pepper to
  taste for a nice salad dressing. Catsup can also be added.

  You can thicken French dressing if just before serving you remove it from the
  refrigerator and drop an ice cube into it. Stir thoroughly.

* The proper proportion for perfect vinegar and oil dressing is 1 part wine
  vinegar to 2 parts olive oil.

Soups

CANTALOUPE SOUP (Cold)

Serves: 6

"The blender at its best."

Easy   Do ahead   Preparing: 10 min.
                                                    Chilling: 2 hrs.

1 large, ripe cantaloupe
1/2 tsp. cinnamon
2 tbsp. lime juice
fresh mint sprigs
2 c. orange juice

Remove seeds from melon and cube the pulp. Place pulp and cinnamon in the electric blender and puree. Combine orange and lime juices and stir into the puree. Chill and serve in chilled soup bowls. Garnish with mint sprigs.

Mrs. Robert D. B. Carlisle, Montclair

SOUP SENEGALESE

Serves: 6

"Easy, but elegant as a perfect first course on a hot summer night."

Average   Do ahead   Preparing: 20 min.
                                                    Chilling: 3 hrs.

5 c. chicken broth
4 egg yolks
2 c. heavy cream
2 tsp. curry powder
dash cayenne
pepper lemon juice
2 tsp. salt
1 c. chicken breast,
   finely chopped
parsley

Heat chicken broth in top of a double boiler to the scalding point. Mix together egg yolks, cream, curry, dash of cayenne and a little lemon juice. Stir a little of the hot broth into the egg yolks and then pour the mixture into the hot broth. Cook, stirring constantly until it thickens slightly. Remove from the heat and let it cool. Season with salt and pepper and chill until very cold. When ready to serve, stir in chicken. Serve in chilled soup cups with chopped parsley.

Mrs. Earl A. Wheaton, Jr., Ridgewood

DUCHESS SOUP

Serves: 8

"A wonderful cold soup (which can be served hot as well)."

Easy   Do ahead   Preparing: 15 min.
                                                    Simmering: 30 min.
                                                    Chilling: 2 hrs.

1/2 c. butter
1/4 c. flour
1 tsp. salt
pepper
4 chicken bouillon cubes
4 c. hot water
2 slices onion
2 c. heavy cream
1/2 c. grated Cheddar cheese
2 hard cooked eggs, sieved
croutons

Melt butter and blend in flour, salt and pepper. Dissolve bouillon cubes in hot water; gradually stir in flour mixture. Cook, stirring constantly, until slightly thick. Add onion and cream and simmer for 30 min., stirring occasionally. Remove onion. Chill. Just before serving stir in cheese and egg. Top with croutons.

Mrs. Richard C. Baxter, Ridgewood

VICHYSSOISE

Serves: 8-10

Average   Do ahead

Preparing: 20 min.
Cooking: 30 min.
Chilling: 2 hrs.

4 to 5 leeks
2 tbsp. butter
6 potatoes
4 c. chicken broth
1 stalk celery, minced
parsley
1 pt. cream
1 tsp. chopped chives
dash Worcestershire sauce

Cut white part of leeks into thin slices. Saute in butter for 10 min. Add potatoes which have been cooked and mashed, broth, and celery. Cover and simmer for 30 min. Strain. Add cream, salt, pepper, Worcestershire and chives. Chill and serve cold. Garnish with parsley.

Mrs. Peter H. Zecher, Ho-Ho-Kus

BLENDER VICHYSSOISE

Serves: 4-6

"A true, but very easy, vichyssoise."

Easy   Do ahead

Preparing: 5 min.
Chilling: 4 hrs.

2 cans frozen potato soup
  (I use Campbell's)
2 cans milk
chives
freshly ground black pepper

Mix soup and milk together in a saucepan and bring to a rolling bubble, stirring constantly. Let cool. Put into the blender and blend until smooth. Place in a metal bowl and chill at least 4 hrs. Serve with chopped chives and freshly ground black pepper.

Mrs. Robert F. Hill, Wyckoff

GIN SOUP

Serves: 4-6

"How to score before the game begins. Don't taste too often or you may end up on the kitchen floor."

Average   Do ahead

Preparing: 15 min.
Simmering: 15 min.

2 c. clam juice
2 c. chicken broth
1 pt. heavy cream
1 tbsp. chopped dill
  or dill seed
2 tbsp. chopped chives
2 tbsp. minced parsley
onion salt
celery salt
2-3 tbsp. cornstarch
2/3 c. gin

Mix all ingredients, except cornstarch and gin, and bring to a boil (stir constantly or do in a double boiler). Remove 2 c. liquid and blend into cornstarch to form a thick paste. Pour paste-like mixture back into the rest of soup, stirring constantly. Add gin and bring to a boil again. Let soup simmer for a few minutes. Taste and add seasonings as desired. Pour into a thermos and you're off to a game. This can also be served chilled - a lot like vichyssoise with a lively kick.

Mrs. John W. Foster, Jr., Montvale

GARDEN TOMATO SOUP

Serves: 6-10

"A refreshing luncheon dish or start-off for a dinner."

Easy   Do ahead   Preparing: 15 min.
                                                Simmering: 15 min.
                                                Chilling: several hours

4 large tomatoes
1 c. chicken broth
4 scallions, snipped
1 large cucumber, thinly
  sliced
1/2 c. diced green pepper
1 c. vegetable juice
  (I use V-8)
juice of 1 lemon
2 tsp. granulated sugar
1 tbsp. seasoned salt
1/4 tsp. seasoned pepper

Skin tomatoes and cut into chunks. In a large, covered saucepan, simmer scallions with cucumber slices, peppers and tomatoes in chicken broth for 5 min. Add vegetable juice, lemon juice, sugar, salt and pepper. Simmer, covered, 10 min. Transfer to a large, covered bowl. Chill. Serve after letting set for several hours. Be sure to do ahead.

Mrs. Morton Evans, Canton, Mass.

GAZPACHO ANDALUZ

Serves: 4

"Traditional, cold Spanish soup; delightful on a hot summer day."

Easy   Do ahead   Preparing: 15 min.
                                                Chilling: 24 hrs.

1 clove garlic
1 med. onion
4-5 sprigs parsley
2 tbsp. vinegar
3 tbsp. olive oil
1/4 tsp. paprika
1 c. consomme
5 very large tomatoes,
  peeled
salt
pepper

Liquify garlic and onion in blender. Add other ingredients and blend until smooth. Season with salt and pepper. Chill in refrigerator at least 24 hrs. Serve in chilled soup plates. Pass garnishes in separate bowls to be sprinkled onto soup at the table.

Garnish:
chopped cucumber
chopped tomatoes
chopped green pepper
diced white bread

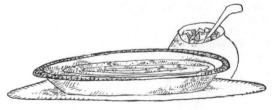

Mrs. J. C. Alford, Saddle River

ASPARAGUS-CRAB SOUP

Serves: 6-8

"Easy and great for luncheons."

Easy   Do ahead   Preparing: 10 min.

1 can mushroom or
  cream celery soup
1 can asparagus soup,
  undiluted
1/2 c. cream or whole milk
12-14 oz. fresh or frozen
  crabmeat
1/2 c. sherry

Mix together soups and milk and heat. Clean crab and add to heated soup. Add sherry and heat through.

Mrs. William H. Rahe, II, Rye, N. Y.

GREEN SPLIT PEA SOUP

Serves: 6-8

Easy   Do ahead   Preparing: 5 min.
Cooking: 2-1/2 hrs.

1 lb. split peas
1 ham bone
2 qts. boiling water
1 carrot, quartered
1 celery stalk, quartered
1 med. onion, diced
pinch ground clove
salt
pepper

Rinse and sort peas; drain. Rinse ham bone; add bone and onion to boiling water. Add peas and other vegetables. Boil moderately fast for 2-1/2 hrs. More water may be added during cooking if necessary. Stir occasionally to prevent sticking. Remove ham bone; rub through sieve. Serve hot with diced ham bits as garnish.

Mrs. A. Steffee Smith, Ridgewood

BEEF SOUP

Serves: 4

"I always prepare this in the morning and reheat it for dinner."

Easy   Do ahead   Preparing: 20 min.
Simmering: 3 hrs.

1-1/2 lbs. beef cubes
1 tsp. salt
1/2 tsp. pepper
2 bay leaves
4-5 carrots
pinch oregano
1 #2 can Italian tomatoes
1 tsp. Worcestershire sauce
1 bouillon cube
1/2 c. chopped onions
1 c. chopped celery
optional -
  1 c. chopped cabbage

Cover meat with cold water and put into a covered 4-qt. pan. Add salt, pepper and bay leaves and let come to the bubbly stage. Turn heat low, add celery, carrots and onions (cabbage if desired) and simmer at least 2-1/2 hrs. until meat is tender. Add tomatoes, Worcestershire and bouillon cube. Simmer 1/2 hr. more. Remove bay leaves. Serve.

Mrs. Herbert Kuhl, Jr., Waldwick

COUNTRY CHEESE SOUP

Serves: 8

"Good luncheon dish for the gals. Serve with hot rolls and salad."

Average   Do ahead   Preparing: 15 min.

3/4 c. butter
6 tbsp. flour
3 c. milk
1 c. light cream
1 tsp. salt
2 c. grated American cheese
1/2 c. chopped celery
1/2 c. chopped green pepper
1/2 c. chopped onion
1/2 c. chopped carrots
1 pt. clear chicken broth

Melt 1/2 c. butter and slowly add flour. Mix well, stirring constantly. Add milk, cream and salt slowly to make a rich sauce. Add cheese and stir until melted. Saute celery, pepper, onion and carrot in 1/4 c. butter to the crunchy stage. Add chicken broth and then combine with the cheese sauce. Heat over low heat.

Mrs. Richard A. Church, Ridgewood

LENTIL SOUP

Serves: 6

Easy   Do ahead   Preparing: 30 min.
                                              Cooking: 30 min.

1 lb. lentils
2-1/2 qts. water
6 oz. bacon, diced
1-1/2 c. onions, chopped
1/2 c. bacon fat
  (or other shortening)
3/4 c. flour
1 large bay leaf

In a stainless steel pot cook lentils in water with bay leaf until soft. Fry onions and bacon in bacon fat. When onions begin to dry up, add flour and brown it to a dark coffee color. Add onion-flour mixture to lentils. Add salt and pepper to taste and bring to a boil. Remove bay leaf. Serve.

Mrs. William W. Schmitz, Ho-Ho-Kus

SEAFOOD SOUP

Serves: 4-6

"The quick way to a truly elegant soup."

Easy   Do ahead   Preparing: 10 min.

1 pkg. king crab in wine sauce
  (I use Stouffer's)
1 can frozen cream of shrimp
  soup
1 can minced clams, drained
1/2 pt. half-and-half cream
1 tsp. curry powder
1 tbsp. catsup for color
2-3 tbsp. sherry

Put crab, soup and clams into a double boiler and heat until melted. Add half-and-half cream and curry powder which has been dissolved in a bit more cream. Add catsup for color and sherry to taste.

Mrs. Arthur Espy, II, Ho-Ho-Kus

DUTCH SKATERS' SOUP

Serves: 6-8

"Almost incredibly good!"

Easy   Do ahead   Preparing: 10 min.
                                              Cooking: 15 min.

1/4 c. butter
2 c. light cream
1/2 tsp. salt
1/2 tsp. Worcestershire sauce
2 c. finely grated Holland
  Gouda Cheese
1/4 c. flour
2 c. milk
dash pepper
2 drops Tabasco sauce
paprika for garnish

Melt butter in saucepan. Add flour and stir until well blended. Gradually add cream and milk, mixing well. Cook over low heat until soup base is thickened. Remove from heat and add salt, pepper, Worcestershire and Tabasco. Place cheese in a blender. Gradually add hot mixture to cheese, running blender until soup is smooth. Reheat over very low heat, stirring frequently, until piping hot. Serve in soup cups garnished with a dash of paprika. If not served immediately, reheat in a double boiler and blend again in blender.

Mr. Edwin F. Bernhardt, Cheese Shop, Ridgewood

KIDNEY BEAN-SAUSAGE CHOWDER

Serves: 6

"Good before a football game; very popular with men; so hearty!"

Easy   Freeze   Preparing: 10 min.
                                                  Cooking: 1-1/2 hrs.

1 lb. bulk sausage
2 cans kidney beans
1 can tomatoes (1 lb. 3 oz.)
1 qt. water
1 onion, chopped
1/2 green pepper, chopped
1 bay leaf
1/2 tsp. seasoned salt
1/2 tsp. garlic salt
1/2 tsp. thyme
1 c. diced potatoes

Cook sausage until brown, breaking up. Pour off fat. Combine all ingredients except potatoes and green pepper. Simmer 1 hr. Freeze at this point, if desired. Add potatoes and green pepper. Cook 20 min. more. Remove bay leaf before serving. Tastes best done a day or two ahead.

Mrs. Arthur H. Kiendl, Jr., Mt. Hermon, Mass.

OLD FASHIONED CORN CHOWDER

Serves: 6-8

"A meal in itself; wonderful for a cold winter's day."

Average, but easy   Do ahead   Preparing: 15 min.
                                                  Cooking: 15 min.

1-1/2" cube salt pork
1 onion
4 potatoes
2 c. water
1 med. can cream-style corn
4 c. milk
salt
pepper
butter

In a large, deep pan fry salt pork which has been cut into small cubes. Add sliced onion and cook slowly for about 5 min., stirring constantly. Add potatoes which have been cut in small cubes. Then add water to the fat. Cook until potatoes are tender. Add corn and scalded milk. Heat. Add seasonings and butter. Serve.

Mrs. John M. Burnham, Hingham, Mass.

NEW ENGLAND CLAM CHOWDER

Serves: 4-6

"A true chowder for a cool winter or summer night."

Average   Freeze   Preparing: 30 min.
                                                  Simmering: 10 min.

1 large onion
5 slices bacon
2 c. diced potatoes
2 doz. large clams, ground
  (big quahogs [hard shelled])
1 qt. milk
1 tsp. M.S.G.
1/4 tsp. pepper
1 tbsp. flour
1/4 c. milk

Fry diced onion and bacon together until golden. Add diced potatoes and cover with water. Boil until potatoes are done. Grind clams and add the clams and broth to potato mixture. Pour in 1 qt. milk. Add M.S.G. and pepper. Heat to a simmer only. Mix 1/4 c. milk and flour and add to clam mixture. Simmer 10 min. Do not boil. Chowder is now ready to serve with pilot crackers.

Mrs. Frederic H. Butts, II, Wellesley, Mass.

NEW ENGLAND FISH CHOWDER

Serves: 6

"I always make double this recipe and freeze some."

Average   Freeze   Preparing: 30 min.
                                            Simmering: 35 min.

2 lbs. haddock   Cook haddock slowly in 2 c. water about
2 oz. salt pork, diced   15 min. Drain and measure broth. Add water
2 onions, sliced   to make 3 c. broth. Remove bones and skin from
4 large potatoes, diced   fish (unless you use the frozen fillets as I
1 c. chopped celery   do) and flake coarsely. Cook fish, potatoes,
1 bay leaf   celery, bay leaf, salt, pepper and 3 c. broth.
2 tsp. salt   Cover and simmer gently 30 min. (Freeze at
pepper   this point, if desired.) Add milk and butter
1 qt. milk   before serving and simmer 5 min. Sprinkle with
2 tbsp. butter   pork pieces which have been sauteed crisp and
                          drained.

Mrs. Lawrence E. Loeffler, Oakland

LOBSTER STEW

Serves: 4

"A real down-East recipe. How my mouth waters when I think of this."

Easy   Do ahead   Preparing: 15 min.
                                            Setting: 5-6 hrs.

1 cooked lobster (1-1/2 to   Remove lobster meat from the shell and
  2 lbs.) or leftover meat cut into 3/4" cubes. Melt butter in large
3 tbsp. butter   heavy pan and add lobster. Cook slowly for
1 qt. milk   5 min., stirring constantly. Add milk very
salt   slowly, always stirring. Heat slowly, but
pepper   do not boil. Season to taste. Let it set
onion salt   for 5-6 hrs. then when ready to serve reheat.
optional - 1/4 c. sherry Do not boil. A bit of sherry may be added,
                          if desired. Be sure to do ahead.

Mrs. John M. Burnham, Hingham, Mass.

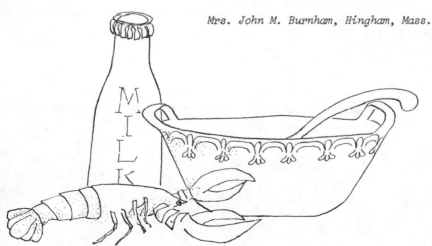

207

Soup Specialties

Some delicious soup accessories:
    Salami slices, thinly sliced, to tomato, pea or celery soups
    Chopped bacon in celery, bean or tomato soups
    Croutons in any soup
    Grated cheese on all chowders and onion soup
    Thinly sliced olive rings on jellied consomme
    Thin lemon slices on consomme and clam chowder
    Toasted almonds on most cream soups
    Frankfurter slices browned in fat in pea, bean, tomato, asparagus or
        celery soups
    Banana slices sauteed in butter on top of chicken soup
    Popped corn in tomato, pea or corn soups (children love this)
    Chopped walnuts, pecans or toasted almonds in cream of chicken or
        celery soup
    Chopped raw celery, green pepper or onion tops in any soup

In place of croutons, try bite-size cereals toasted in a bit of butter.

To desalt that over-salted soup, slice raw potato into it and allow to boil
for a short time. Remove potato.

To remove grease from soup, place a leaf of lettuce on the hot soup. Remove
before serving.

Use a bouillon cube for extra flavor when adding water to canned or homemade
soup.

Add a package of dehydrated chicken soup to chicken stock to make it more
flavorful.

Sweets

SOUFFLE AU GRAND MARNIER

Serves: 6

Average   Part do ahead   Preparing: 15 min.
                                         Baking: 40 min.

3 tbsp. butter
3 tbsp. flour
1 c. milk
pinch of salt
1/4 c. sugar
4 eggs, separated
3 oz. Grand Marnier

Melt butter and slowly stir in flour. Add milk a little bit at a time. Stir constantly to make a thick cream sauce. Add sugar and cool. This may be done ahead. Beat in egg yolks, one at a time. Add Grand Marnier. Beat egg whites until stiff and gently fold into other mixture. Pour into a buttered 1-1/2 qt. souffle dish and bake in a preheated oven at 350° for 30-40 min.

Mrs. Albert C. Cluzel, Paterson

ROULAGE LEONTINE

Serves: 6-8

"Probably my most cherished recipe as it was requested by 'Gourmet.'"

Average   Freeze   Preparing: 20 min.
                                 Chilling: 1 hr.
                                 Baking: 25 min.

5 eggs, separated
1 c. sugar
3 tbsp. water
6 oz. German sweet chocolate
  (I use Baker's)
1 c. whipping cream
cocoa

Separate eggs and beat yolks with 3/4 c. sugar. Melt chocolate with water. Cool slightly and mix into yolks. Beat whites with remaining 1/4 c. sugar and fold into the chocolate mixture. Butter a large jelly-roll pan (approximately 11x17 inches) and line it with wax paper and butter the paper. Spread the mixture evenly on the paper and bake at 300° for 15 min. and then at 350° for 10 min. Remove and immediately cover with a damp dish towel. Allow to chill thoroughly. Remove towel and sprinkle heavily with cocoa. Turn over onto another sheet of wax paper. Remove top piece of paper and spread with whipped cream which has been sweetened a bit. Roll up like a jelly roll using the bottom paper as a guide. Cracks can be mended with your fingers. Et voila! Be sure and freeze if kept more than one day.

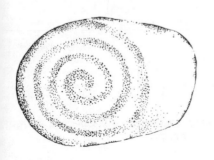

Mrs. Norman Liedtke, Montreal, Canada

GATEAU VIENNE

Serves: 12

"A very elegant, rich dessert. Will your friends be impressed!"

Complicated
  Worth it

Freeze part

Preparing: 20 min.
Baking: 12 min.
Assembling: 20 min.
Chilling: 1 hr.

Pastry:
4 eggs, separated
1/2 c. sugar
4 sq. semisweet chocolate
1-1/2 tbsp. strong coffee
3/4 tsp. vanilla
sugar

Chocolate-Almond Paste:
2 egg whites
1/4 c. sugar
1 tsp. vanilla
1/2 tsp. almond extract
1/4 c. ground almonds
  (use blender or grate finely)
2 sq. semisweet chocolate

Almond Cream:
1/2 c. heavy cream
1-1/2 tsp. sugar
1/4 c. lightly toasted
  almonds, ground
confectioners' sugar

chocolate curls (made with
  parer)

Pastry: Beat egg whites with pinch of salt until they hold soft peaks. Add sugar a tbsp. at a time, beating well after each addition. Beat yolks with a fork. Stir in semisweet chocolate which has been melted, coffee and vanilla. Fold one fourth of egg whites into mixture. Fold chocolate mixture into remaining egg whites very gently. Spread evenly on a 15x10 inch jelly-roll pan lined with wax paper. Bake at 375° for 12 min. or until top is firm. Cool in pan on a rack. Turn pastry out of pan onto wax paper which has been sprinkled with sugar. Carefully peel off pan paper. Slice into five 3x10 inch slices. Even edges carefully with a sharp knife. This can be frozen at this point.

Chocolate-Almond Paste: Beat egg whites to hold soft peaks. Carefully add sugar and beat until whites are stiff. Fold in vanilla, almond extract, ground almonds and melted chocolate.

Almond Cream: Whip cream with sugar. Fold in almonds.

Assembling: Put one strip of pastry on a serving platter and spread with half the Chocolate-Almond Paste. Top with second cake strip. Spread with half the Almond Cream. Top with third cake and spread with remaining Almond Cream. Top with fourth cake strip and spread with remaining Chocolate-Almond Paste. Top with last cake strip. Sprinkle with grated chocolate on sides of cake if desired. Sprinkle top with sifted confectioners' sugar and chocolate curls. Chill 1 hr. or more. Cut into thin crosswise slices to serve.

Mrs. Arthur S. Whittemore, Jr., Ridgewood

PEACH DELIGHT

Serves: 4

"The easiest of desserts!"

Easy

No need to do ahead

Preparing: 10 min.

4 large peach halves,
  fresh or canned
1/2 c. heavy cream, whipped
1/2 c. peanut brittle,
  crushed

Top each half of a peach with whipped cream. Sprinkle peanut brittle on top.

Mrs. Harry F. Jones, III, Westfield

STUFFED PEACHES

Serves: 8

"This is an old Italian recipe."

Easy   Freeze   Preparing: 30 min.
                                                  Baking: 40 min.

8 large peaches
16 ladyfingers
16 almond macaroons
1/4 c. sugar
1 egg
1 tsp. almond extract
1/3 c. milk
2 tbsp. butter
whipped cream for garnish

Split peaches and remove pits. Remove and reserve about 1/3 of pulp, leaving 2/3 attached to the skin of peach, making a shell. Place in a greased baking pan, cut side up. Chop remaining pulp and place in a mixing bowl. Crumble ladyfingers and 12 macaroons. Add sugar and egg which has been beaten, then the almond extract and enough milk to make a medium-soft stuffing. Mix well and fill peach shells. Crush remaining macaroons and sprinkle on top. Dot with butter and bake in a 350° oven for about 40 min. or until lightly browned. Serve with a rosette of whipped cream on top of each.

Mrs. B. D. Forster, Ridgewood

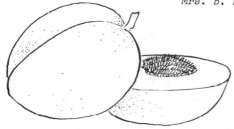

APPLE PUDDING (Apple Crunch)

Serves: 6

"A yummy, apple-y, crunchy dessert that is sure to please."

Easy   Do ahead   Preparing: 20 min.
                                                  Baking: 1 to 1-1/2 hrs.

4-5 c. sliced apples
1 tsp. cinnamon
1 stick butter
1/2 c. water
1 c. sugar
3/4 c. flour
vanilla ice cream or
  whipped cream

Place apples in a buttered 1-1/2 qt. casserole and pour over water and cinnamon which have been mixed. Mix together sugar, flour, butter (sliced thin) and spread over the top. Bake at 350° for 1 to 1-1/2 hrs. Serve with whipped cream or vanilla ice cream. Serve warm or cold.

Ed. Note: A nice variation of this can be obtained by using brown sugar, melted butter and corn flake crumbs in place of the sugar and flour. Bake at 350° about 30 min.

Mrs. John C. Ramsey, Franklin Lakes

APPLE OR PEACH PUDDING CAKE

Serves: 6-8

Easy   Do ahead

Preparing: 20 min.
Baking: 30 min.

6 apples or peaches
1 c. sugar
1/4 tsp. cinnamon
2 eggs, slightly beaten
1/2 c. flour
2 tsp. baking powder
1 tsp. vanilla
pinch of salt
butter
whipped cream

Set oven at 350°. Butter an 8 or 9 inch square baking dish. Slice and pare apples or peaches and add 1/2 c. sugar and cinnamon. Make a batter of the remaining 1/2 c. sugar, flour, baking powder, vanilla, salt and eggs. Place fruit in the baking dish. Pour batter over the fruit. Dot with small pieces of butter. Bake at 350° about 30 min. or until brown and crusty on top. Serve warm or cool with whipped cream.

Mrs. Edward C. Kaiser, Ridgewood

TOPSY TURVY PUDDING

Serves: 10-12

Easy   Do ahead

Preparing: 20 min.
Baking: 35-40 min.

2 c. flour
2/3 c. sugar
2 tsp. baking powder
1/2 tsp. salt
3/4 c. milk
1/2 c. chopped nuts
1 c. dates, cut up
3/4 c. water
3/4 c. orange juice
2/3 c. brown sugar
3 tbsp. butter
whipped cream or
   ice cream

Mix together flour, sugar, baking powder and salt. Add milk, nuts and dates and put in a greased 8 inch square pan. Mix water, orange juice, brown sugar and butter and cook slowly until sugar is melted. Pour brown sugar mixture over the first mixture. Do not stir. Bake at 325° for 35-40 min. Serve with whipped cream or ice cream, if desired.

Mrs. Martin Hoeksema, Ridgewood

OZARK PUDDING

Serves: 4

"A quick and easy everyday dessert."

Easy   Do ahead

Preparing: 10 min.
Baking: 30 min.

1 egg
3/4 c. sugar
2 tbsp. flour
1-1/4 tsp. baking powder
1/4 tsp. salt
1 tsp. vanilla
1/2 c. nutmeats
1/2 c. chopped apples

Beat egg. Add sugar gradually. Beat until smooth. Add flour, baking powder, and salt. Mix well. Add flavoring, nuts and apples. Turn into a greased, 8x8 inch pan and bake at 350° for 30 min.

Mrs. Harry F. Jones, III, Westfield

DATE PUDDING

Serves: 8-10

"A marvelous dessert - hot or cold."

Easy   Do ahead   Preparing: 20 min.
                                                     Baking: 45 min.

1 c. sugar
1 c. flour
1/4 tsp. salt
2 tsp. baking powder
1 c. chopped nuts
1 c. chopped dates
1/2 c. milk
1 c. brown sugar
2 c. boiling water
1 tbsp. butter
whipped cream or
  ice cream

Sift sugar, flour, salt and baking powder together. Add the nuts and dates. Mix in milk. Pour evenly in an 8 inch square pan. In a saucepan, mix together brown sugar, water and butter. Bring to a boil. Pour this mixture over the cake mixture. Bake at 350° for 45 min. Leave in baking dish until ready to serve. When serving turn piece over so the "goo" is on the top. Serve with whipped cream or ice cream on top.

Mrs. Melvin R. Campbell, Ridgewood

FROSTY MANDARIN DESSERT

Serves: 8

"From a bride! Easy, cool, good and cheap."

Easy   Do ahead   Preparing: 15 min.
                                                     Chilling: 2 hrs.

2 3-oz. pkgs. orange gelatin
2 c. boiling water
1 can mandarin oranges
1 pt. orange sherbet

Dissolve gelatin in boiling water. Drain oranges; reserve juice and add water to make one cup. Add to gelatin. Chill until slightly thickened. Fold in sherbet and oranges. Pour into a 1-1/2 qt. mold or individual serving dishes. Chill until firm.

Mrs. William R. Tunkey, Gainesville, Fla.

ORANGE MERINGUE DESSERT

Serves: 4-6

"A great way to use leftover egg whites."

Average   Do ahead   Preparing: 30 min.
                                                     Baking: 30 min.
                                                     Cooling: 1 hr.

1 pkg. ladyfingers
1-1/2 c. orange juice
1 pkg. vanilla pudding mix
1/2 c. heavy cream
1 tsp. grated orange rind
2 egg whites
1/4 c. sugar

Cover the bottom of an ovenproof 9x13 inch casserole with ladyfingers. Sprinkle with 1/2 c. orange juice. Empty pudding mix into a saucepan and gradually stir in remaining orange juice. Cook over medium heat until thick and smooth. Blend in cream and 1/2 tsp. orange rind. Pour over ladyfingers. Beat egg whites until foamy and add sugar gradually, beating until whites are stiff and glossy. Fold in remaining 1/2 tsp. rind. Spoon meringue over pudding and bake at 300° about 30 min. until puffy and golden. Serve at room temperature.

Mrs. John W. Foster, Jr., Montvale

LEMON PUDDING

Serves: 5

"It's an old one but everyone still loves it."

Average   Do ahead   Preparing: 15 min.
                                   Baking: 45 min.
                                   Setting: 3 hrs.

1 c. sugar
4 tbsp. flour
2 tbsp. butter
1/8 tsp. salt
5 tbsp. lemon juice
grated rind of 1 lemon
1-1/2 c. milk
3 eggs, separated

Add milk to beaten egg yolks. In a large bowl cream sugar, flour and butter. Add rest of ingredients, except the egg whites. Beat whites stiff and fold into mixture. Pour into a buttered, 1-1/2 qt. casserole. Set casserole in pan of hot water in oven that has been pre-heated to 350°. Bake 45 min., uncovered. It will be slightly brown on top. There will be cake on top and pudding on the bottom. Each serving should include a little of each. Make this the morning it is to be served. Serve at room temperature.

Mrs. David I. Meriney, Saddle River

PINEAPPLE UPSIDE-DOWN CAKE

Serves: 8-10

"This is a never-fail."

Easy   Do ahead   Preparing: 15 min.
                                Baking: 45 min.

1/4 c. butter
1 c. light brown sugar
maraschino cherries
1 #2 can crushed pineapple
1-1/2 c. white sugar
3 eggs, separated
8 tbsp. pineapple juice

1/4 tsp. vanilla
1-1/2 c. cake flour
1 tsp. baking powder

Using a large black iron skillet or a 9 inch cake pan, melt butter and add light brown sugar. Spread evenly over the bottom and place a cherry so that each slice of cake will have a cherry in the center when sliced. Drain pineapple and reserve the juice. Place pine-apple on top of cherries. Make a batter by mixing egg yolks, sugar, pineapple juice and vanilla. Sift cake flour and baking powder together and add to egg mixture. Beat whites until stiff, but not dry, and gently fold into the other ingredients. Gently pour over the pineapple in the skillet. Bake at 350° for 45 min. or until cake is done. Turn out onto plate immediately. Serve right away if desired.

Mrs. Leonard R. Hines, Ridgewood

216

PINEAPPLE ELITE

Serves: 12

"Extremely rich! Tricky to spread but not difficult."

Average   Do ahead   Preparing: 30 min.
                               Chilling: 24 hrs.

2 c. butter
3 c. confectioners' sugar
4 eggs
1 lb. vanilla wafers
2 1-lb. cans crushed pineapple
1 pt. heavy cream
1 c. pecans, halved

Cream butter, sugar and eggs together. Grind the vanilla wafers and whip the cream. Drain the pineapple. Line a large flat pan (approximately 13x13 inches or equivalent) with wax paper and sprinkle half the vanilla wafer crumbs over the bottom. Spread with butter-sugar mixture, then the drained pineapple. Top with a layer of whipped cream. Scatter the pecan halves over the top and cover with the rest of the vanilla wafer crumbs. Refrigerate for 24 hrs. Cut into squares to serve.

Mrs. Robert R. Gulick, Ramsey

EASTBROOK CHERRY CRUNCH

Serves: 8-9

"A neighborhood favorite; quick, easy and delicious."

Easy   Do ahead   Preparing: 10 min.
                            Baking: 45 min.

1 can cherry pie filling
   (1 lb. 6 oz.) or other
   filling
1/2 pkg. yellow cake mix
1/4 lb. butter or margarine,
   melted
optional - whipped cream or
            ice cream

Put pie filling into an 8 or 9 inch square pan. Spread dry cake mix over it and sprinkle with melted butter. Bake at 400°, uncovered, until very brown and crusty, 30-45 min. This is best if served warm, but good any time. Serve with whipped cream or ice cream, if desired.

Mrs. D. F. Hazen, Ridgewood

FRUIT COCKTAIL TORTE

Serves: 8-12

"You'd never guess the ingredients in this. Rich and delicious!"

Easy   Do ahead   Preparing: 10 min.
                            Baking: 40 min.

1 egg
1 1-lb. can fruit cocktail
1 c. flour
1 c. sugar
1/2 tsp. salt
1 tsp. soda
1 c. brown sugar
1 c. chopped nuts
whipped cream for garnishing

Beat egg in a bowl. Add fruit cocktail with juice. Sift flour, sugar, salt and soda together and add to fruit mixture. Stir until completely blended. Pour into a greased, 9x12 inch pan. Sprinkle with brown sugar, then nuts. Bake at 350° for 40 min. or until toothpick comes out clean. Serve at room temperature with whipped cream. Best done the day before.

Mrs. Richard R. Ryen, Oradell

STRAWBERRY TORTE

Serves: 8

"Always creates a sensation! Looks yummy! It is!"

Average   Do ahead

Preparing: 30 min.
Baking: 1-1/2 plus 1 hr.
Chilling: 6 hrs.

6 egg whites (cold)
2 c. sugar
1-1/2 tsp. white vinegar
1 pt. heavy cream
1 tsp. vanilla
1 pkg. gelatin
2 tbsp. warm water
2 pts. strawberries

Beat egg whites until foamy. Add sugar and vinegar alternately <u>very slowly</u>. When stiff, pour into a 9 inch spring form pan which has been heavily greased. Coat sides and bottom of pan to form a shell of the meringue. Bake at 275° for I hr. without peeking. Open the oven after the hour is up and leave for another 1-1/2 hrs. with the heat off. Cool completely. Soften gelatin in warm water for a few minutes and when completely cool, whip the cream, add gelatin mixture, vanilla and a little sugar if desired. Take out about 8 big strawberries for decoration and slice the rest. Fold sliced strawberries into the whipped cream. Skim off the hard top of the center of the meringue. Fill shell with the strawberry mixture. Crumble the extra meringue on top and decorate with whole strawberries. Chill at least 6 hrs. Wow!

Mrs. Henry J. Studley, Saddle River

ELEGANT STRAWBERRIES

Serves: 4-6

"A perfect dessert for a ladies' luncheon during the strawberry season."

Easy   Do ahead

Preparing: 10 min.
Cooking: 5 min.
Chilling: 1 hr.

1 qt. fresh strawberries

Sauce:
1/4 c. raspberry jam
2 tbsp. sugar
1/4 c. water
1 tbsp. kirsch
1/4 c. slivered almonds

Combine jam, sugar and water in a small saucepan and simmer for about 2 min. Add kirsch and chill. Pour over individual dishes of washed and hulled berries. Sprinkle with almonds. Sauce stores well in the refrigerator.

Mrs. Richard W. Poor, Ridgewood

DESSERT BERRIES WITH ZABAGLIONE SAUCE

Serves: 6

"Lovely to look at and delicious!"

Easy   Do ahead

Preparing: 15 min.

1 pt. strawberries
1 pt. blueberries
1 pt. raspberries

Sauce:
6 egg yolks
6 tbsp. sugar
2/3 c. Marsala wine

Wash and chill berries.

Sauce: Beat egg yolks, gradually adding sugar and wine. Cook over boiling water, whipping with a wire whisk until the sauce foams up and begins to thicken. Serve warm over chilled berries.

Mrs. John B. Cave, Summit

FROSTED GRAPES

Serves: 4

"Very simple and very good."

Easy   Do ahead   Preparing: 10 min.
                                                    Chilling: 24 hrs.

1 lb. seedless grapes   Wash grapes and remove stems. Place in a
1/3 c. honey   serving bowl. Mix honey, brandy and lemon
2 tbsp. good brandy or cognac   juice together and pour over grapes. Mix
2 tbsp. lemon juice   well and place in refrigerator overnight.
1 pt. sour cream   Stir occasionally during the evening and the
                           next day. When ready to serve, place in
                           dessert dishes and top each portion with
                           1/2 c. of sour cream.

Mrs. Herman Van Nouhuys, Ho-Ho-Kus

APRICOT SOUFFLE WITH CUSTARD SAUCE

Serves: 4-6

"A great dessert! The custard sauce may be served with other desserts."

Average   Do ahead   Preparing: 30 min.
                                                    Baking: 30 min.
                                                    Cooling: 1 hr.

Souffle: Souffle: Cook apricots in water until soft.
11 oz. dried apricots   Mash. Add sugar and cook until sugar dissolves.
1 heaping c. sugar   Add lemon juice. Measure 1-1/2 c. of this
4 egg whites   mixture for use. The rest is discarded if any
1 tbsp. lemon juice   extra remains. Beat egg whites until very stiff.
1-1/2 c. water   Cut and fold in 1-1/2 c. apricot mixture. Bake
                           in a china or glass 2 qt. dish (or individual
Sauce: dishes) which has been set in a pan of hot water.
4 egg yolks   Bake at 300° for 30 min. Turn off oven and set
2-1/2 tbsp. sugar   oven door slightly ajar. Cool souffle in oven.
pinch salt   Serve with Custard Sauce.
1-1/2 c. scalded milk
1/4 tsp. vanilla   Custard Sauce: Beat the egg yolks slightly.
1/4 tsp. almond extract   Add sugar and salt. Slowly pour scalded milk
                           into the egg yolk mixture. Cook in a double
                           boiler until thickened, stirring constantly.
                           Strain and cool. Add vanilla and almond
                           extract.

Mrs. Stanley A. Winters, Allendale

CANTABERRY

Serves: 2

"An easy, good summer dessert."

Easy   Do ahead   Preparing: 10 min.
                                                    Chilling: 1 hr.

1 cantaloupe melon   Halve melon and remove seeds. Cut ends off
1/4 c. kirsch   melon halves so they will sit flat. Combine
2 tbsp. confectioners' sugar   remaining ingredients. Fill center of melon
1/2 tsp. lime juice   and chill for one hour before serving.
1 pt. blueberries

Mrs. Helen Lucas, Radburn

CANTALOUPE SUPREME

Serves: 4

"This is a marvelous summer dessert. So elegant!"

Complicated   Do ahead   Preparing: 30 min.

2 cantaloupes
1-1/2 pts. strawberries
1 pt. vanilla ice cream
2 egg whites
1/2 c. sugar
dash Kirschswasser

Cut bottoms off melons so they sit easily on a cookie sheet. Cut in half and remove seeds. Use a grapefruit knife and loosen fruit from rind. Cut fruit into fairly small pieces and put back in the rind. Cut strawberries in half and add just enough sugar to sweeten. Add these to the melons. Put a dash of Kirschwasser over all. Make a meringue from egg whites. Beat eggs stiff and add rest of sugar slowly. Turn on broiler and put rack on the second rung. Put one scoop of ice cream on each melon and cover well with meringue. Put in oven just long enough to brown lightly. Even if it melts it tastes elegant. This can be fixed ahead, all but the meringue, and even this can be done in the afternoon and refrigerated separately, coating after filling with ice cream just before serving.

Mrs. Robert R. Deutsch, Mahwah

CANTALOUPE-LIME DESSERT or SALAD

Serves: 4

"Colorful, cool and easy to prepare."

Easy   Do ahead   Preparing: 20 min.
                                 Chilling: 2 hrs.

1 pkg. lime gelatin
1 cantaloupe

For Dessert:
Whipping Cream

For Salad:
8 oz. cream cheese

Cut off end of melon and remove seeds. Peel. Make lime gelatin according to directions. When gelatin begins to thicken, spoon into cantaloupe. Cover with foil or plastic wrap so that refrigerator odors will not be mixed. Stand in a small bowl in refrigerator until set.

As Dessert: Serve plain or garnish with whipped cream after slicing into individual servings.

As Salad: Coat whole cantaloupe with softened cream cheese. Re-cool and slice. Serve on lettuce bed.

Mrs. Robert K. Schell, Ridgewood

WATERMELON FREEZE

Serves: 20

"Perfect for a small summer reception or a child's birthday party."

Takes time   Freeze   Preparing: 30-45 min.
  Not difficult   Chilling: 2 hrs.

1 medium watermelon
1/4 c. sugar
2 tbsp. lemon juice
mint leaves

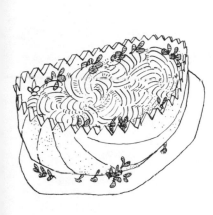

Cut watermelon in half lengthwise. Carefully remove all pink meat to within 1 inch of the rind. Save the shell, refrigerating for later use. Remove seeds from watermelon and break meat into small chunks. In the blender or large mixer bowl, place about 3 c. of watermelon chunks. Add sugar and lemon juice. Beat until mixture looks like applesauce. Repeat until all the watermelon is used. Spoon watermelon mixture into ice cube trays or small loaf cake tins and place in the freezer until mixture is frozen to within 1 inch of the edge of the trays (about 1 hr.) Turn 2 or 3 trays of mixture into a chilled bowl and quickly beat with beater until smooth but not melted. Return mixture to trays and refreeze, this time until firm. The mixture will resemble sherbet. With a sharp knife cut zig-zag along the top of one shell for decorative serving. About 45 min to 1 hr. before serving remove watermelon mixture and let stand at room temperature. Place prepared shell on tray or large platter. Heap serving spoonfuls of mixture into the shell. Garnish with mint leaves. Keeps indefinitely in the freezer.

Mrs. Gilbert R. Rogers, Ridgewood

RASPBERRY RHAPSODY

Serves: 8-10

"Very rich! Portions will vary with the guests' capacities!"

Average   Freeze   Preparing: 20 min.
                                  Freezing: 24 hrs.

1 pt. heavy cream
1-1/2 c. confectioners' sugar
6 tsp. sherry
1/4 c. maraschino cherries,
  chopped
1/2 c. chopped pecans
1 qt. raspberry sherbet

Sauce:
2 boxes frozen raspberries
1/2 c. sugar
4 tbsp. water
4 tsp. lemon juice
6 tbsp. sherry

Whip cream, adding sifted sugar, sherry, chopped cherries and pecans. Pour half this mixture into a 9 inch square pan. Spread 1 qt. sherbet over mixture. Add the remaining half of mixture. Freeze for 24 hrs.

Sauce: Add all the ingredients, except the sherry, in a pan and boil for 5 min. Add sherry and boil just long enough to remove the alcohol. Remove the frozen cream mixture from the freezer about 15 min. before serving. Have sauce at room temperature, and pour it over each square-cut portion.

Mrs. Robert R. Gulick, Ramsey

LEMON CURD

Serves: 6-8

"Fabulously good, elegant but easy dessert. An old New England recipe."

Easy   Part do ahead   Preparing: 20 min.

1-1/2 c. sugar
1/4 lb. butter or marg.
3 lemons (1/2 c. juice)
grated rind of 3 lemons
6 eggs, slightly beaten
1/2 pt. heavy cream
6-8 patty shells

Put sugar, butter, lemon juice and rind in top of a double boiler and melt. Beat eggs very slightly and add to mixture in double boiler, stirring until thick, about 5 min. Cool. This will thicken as it cools. This can be done ahead 2-3 days to this point and kept refrigerated. Upon serving, whip cream stiff and fold into an equal amount of the lemon mixture. Stir gently until smooth. Serve over patty shells. (Frozen ones are good.)

Mrs. George M. Griffith, Franklin Lakes

FROZEN PEACH TORTE

Serves: 6-8

"Delicious and quick."

Easy   Freeze   Preparing: 20 min.
                                         Freezing: 4 hrs.

2 c. mashed peaches
1 c. sugar
1 tbsp. lemon juice
1 c. heavy cream, whipped
1 c. coarse macaroon crumbs

Add sugar and lemon juice to the mashed peaches. Fold in the whipped cream. Place 1/2 c. of crumbs in the bottom of a 1 qt. refrigerator tray and pour in the mixture. Top with remaining crumbs and freeze until firm, 4 to 6 hrs. Cut into wedges, squares or slices and serve.

Mrs. William W. Bowyer, Franklin Lakes

SALZBURGER NOCKERLN

Serves: 2

"A favorite Austrian recipe, easily multiplied."

Easy   Serve immediately   Preparing: 20 min.
                                                    Baking: 25 min.

4 eggs, separated
4 tbsp. sugar
4 tbsp. flour
1 tbsp. butter
2 tbsp. milk
confectioners' sugar
vanilla bean stick

To increase this, allow 2 eggs per person and multiply accordingly. Separate eggs and mix yolks with sugar and flour. Beat egg whites until stiff and fold into yolk mixture. Heat oven to 350°. Melt butter and heat milk in a 9 inch cake pan. Pour mixture into it and place in a hot oven. Bake until raised and until toothpick comes out clean (about 15-25 min.). Serve hot, spooning it onto serving plates. Sprinkle with confectioners' sugar which has been flavored with vanilla bean.

Mrs. Fritz Godart, Ridgewood

SACHER TORTE

Serves: 8

"A rich, delicious Austrian cake."

Average   Do ahead   Preparing: 30 min.
Baking: 1 hr.

3/4 c. softened butter
3/4 c. sugar
6 eggs, separated
6 oz. chocolate (bitter
  or semisweet)
3/4 c. less 2 tbsp. flour
2 tsp. baking powder
apricot jam

Mix butter and sugar. Add yolks and melted chocolate. Sift flour and baking powder together and add to above. Beat egg whites until stiff. Fold lightly into other mixture. Place in a greased and floured 9 inch cake pan. Start oven at 250° and when cake has risen, increase temperature to 325°. Bake until toothpick comes out almost clean. (About 1 hr.) Do not overbake. Turn cake out on a rack after letting it stand for 10 min. Let it finish cooling. Spread top with apricot jam and pour icing over cake. Spread icing quickly to coat top and sides. This is best done the day before. Can be served with whipped cream.

CHOCOLATE ICING for Sacher Torte

Easy   Do Ahead   Preparing: 10 min.

1/2 c. sugar
1/3 c. water
3-1/2 oz. semisweet chocolate

Simmer sugar and water in a saucepan until sugar is dissolved (2 min.). Remove from heat. Add chocolate and stir until it is melted and mixture is smooth. Bring to a boil while stirring. Remove from heat and stir until it starts to thicken. Pour over cake.

Mrs. Fritz Godart, Ridgewood

CHEESE TORTE

Serves: 8-10

Average   Freeze   Preparing: 30 min.
Baking: 25 min.
Chilling: 24 hrs.

12 double graham crackers
1/4 c. butter
1/4 c. sugar
dash cinnamon
12 oz. cream cheese
1/2 c. sugar
1/4 tsp. vanilla
2 eggs, separated
1 pt. sour cream
1/4 tsp vanilla
5 tbsp. sugar

Mix graham cracker crumbs with melted butter, sugar and cinnamon. Line a 9 or 10 inch spring form pan with mixture, saving some for the top. Combine cream cheese with 1/2 c. sugar, add 1/4 tsp. vanilla and 2 egg yolks. Beat egg whites until stiff and fold into cream cheese mixture. Pour into form and bake at 375° for 20 min. Cool for 20 min. Beat sour cream and add 1/4 tsp. vanilla and 5 tbsp. sugar. Pour slowly over top of cake. Bake at 475° for 5 min. Chill thoroughly for at least 24 hrs.

Mrs. J. Harris Fleming, Ridgewood

CHEESECAKE - No. 1

Serves: 12

"I've never been able to tell if this keeps 10 days; it's devoured by then."

Average   Freeze

Preparing: 30 min.
Baking: 1 hr. + 2 hrs.
Chilling: 6 hrs.

1 lb. cottage cheese, creamed
1 lb. cream cheese
1-1/2 c. sugar
4 eggs
juice of 1/2 lemon, strained
1 tbsp. vanilla
3 tbsp. flour
3 tbsp. cornstarch
1/4 c. melted butter
1 pt. sour cream

Cream cheeses in a large bowl and gradually add sugar, continually beating. Beat eggs until light and add to cheeses, beating until smooth. Stir in lemon juice, vanilla, flour and cornstarch. Add melted butter. Mix until smooth. Blend in sour cream and beat well. Pour into a well greased, 10 inch spring pan and bake at 325° for 1 hr. Turn off oven and allow cake to remain in oven for 2 hrs. longer. Do not open the oven door for the entire 3 hrs. Let cool about 6 hrs. before taking sides off spring pan. Keep refrigerated until served. This will keep 10 days unfrozen.

Mrs. Louis Schoenleber, Saddle River

CHEESECAKE - No. 2

Serves: 16

"Everyone asks for this recipe. Stolen from an Atlantic City hotel!"

Average   Freeze

Preparing: 25 min.
Baking: 1 hr.
Cooling: overnight

16 zwieback, crumbled
1/4 c. sugar
1/8 tsp. cinnamon
1/4 c. melted butter

Filling:
6 eggs
2-1/4 c. sugar
1/4 c. flour plus 2 tbsp.
1 tsp. salt
juice of 1 lemon
1 tsp. vanilla
3 lbs. cream cheese
  (6 8-oz. pkgs.)
1-1/2 c. light cream
confectioners' sugar
optional -
  1 can cherry pie filling
  cornstarch
  red food coloring

Mix first four ingredients together and pack on bottom of a 10 inch angel food pan with removable bottom. In one bowl beat eggs with mixer for at least 5 min., adding sugar slowly. Add flour, salt, lemon and vanilla. In a second bowl, beat cream cheese with mixer, adding cream until smooth. Add contents of first bowl to second bowl and beat! beat! beat! Pour over zwieback mixture and bake in a 325° oven for 1 hr. Open oven door and leave in oven until cool. (Or leave overnight until cool.) Refrigerate at least 8 hrs. before serving. Sprinkle confectioners' sugar on top or make sour cherry topping following the directions on the can and adding red coloring and more cornstarch to make it thick.

Mrs. James R. Toombs, Ridgewood

CHEESECAKE - No. 3   Serves: 12

"Rich, creamy and delicious! Always gets raves."

Average   Freeze   Preparing: 30 min.
                                             Baking: 1 hr. 10 min.

1 pkg. zwieback
2 tbsp. butter, softened
2 tbsp. sugar
1/2 c. sugar
2 tbsp. flour
1/4 tsp. salt
1 lb. cream cheese
1 tsp. vanilla
4 eggs
1 c. cream

Topping:
2 c. sour cream
3 tbsp. sugar
1 tsp. vanilla

Crush zwieback and mix well with soft butter and sugar. Press into a 9 inch spring form pan and up the sides. Mix the sugar, flour and salt. Soften the cream cheese with a wooden spoon. Add the dry ingredients and cream together. Separate the eggs. Add vanilla and the unbeaten egg yolks and beat. Stir in the cream and fold in stiffly beaten egg whites. Pour this mixture on top of the crumbs. Bake at 350° for 1 hr. Let cake cool. When cool spread the topping made by mixing all ingredients, over the top of the cake and bake again for 10 min. at 500°. This may be made one day ahead and refrigerated.

Mrs. George A. Banino, Saddle River

PEANUT BRITTLE CAKE (Topping)

"Sensational!"

Easy   Do ahead   Preparing: 10 min.

1 angel food cake
1/4 lb. peanut brittle
1 pt. heavy cream, whipped

Whip cream until stiff. Add enough peanut brittle to whipped cream so it is nice and crunchy. Serve on angel food.

Mrs. Theodore R. Wolf, Ridgewood

COLD CHOCOLATE SOUFFLE   Serves: 6-8

"A very rich, mousse-like dessert."

Easy   Do ahead   Preparing: 20 min.
                                            Chilling: overnight

1 pkg. gelatin
1/2 c. cold water
1/2 c. boiling water
5 sq. baking chocolate
5 eggs, separated
1 c. sugar
1 tsp. vanilla
1 c. milk

Topping:
1 c. heavy cream
1/2 tsp. sugar
1 tsp. vanilla

Stir gelatin in 1/2 c. cold water and let stand for 5 min. Dissolve by adding boiling water. Place chocolate and 1 c. milk in a double boiler. Stir and mix until melted. Let cool slightly. Beat egg yolks with 1 c. sugar until smooth and creamy. Add to the chocolate mixture and mix well. Add gelatin mixture and vanilla. Cool thoroughly. Beat egg whites stiff and fold into the cooled chocolate mixture. Pour into a 1 qt. bowl or individual sherbet glasses. Chill. Whip the cream with sugar and vanilla and top souffle just before serving. Make this the day before serving.

Mrs. Howard W. Arnold, Ridgewood

CHOCOLATE VELVET

Serves: 4

"This recipe originally came from the Pastene Wine makers."

Easy   Do ahead   Preparing: 20 min.
                                            Chilling: 4 hrs.

3/4 c. semisweet chocolate
  bits
1/4 c. mellow (cream) sherry
  (I use Pastene)
dash of salt
4 eggs, separated
whipped cream for garnishing

Melt chocolate bits in top of a double boiler over hot, not boiling, water. Remove from heat and stir in sherry and salt. Add unbeaten egg yolks one at a time, beating well after each addition. Beat the whites until stiff but not dry. Fold into chocolate mixture. Stir gently until smooth and well blended. Pour into 4 sherbet glasses and refrigerate at least 4 hrs. Serve with dots of whipped cream.

Mrs. George W. Warch, Ho-Ho-Kus

CHEATER CHOCOLATE-RUM MOUSSE

Serves: 6-8

"No one will ever guess how easy this is."

Easy   Do ahead   Preparing: 5 min.
                                            Chilling: 3 hrs.

1 pkg. chocolate Whip'n Chill
1/2 c. cold milk
2 tbsp. dark rum
1/2 c. heavy cream
whipped cream for garnishing

Follow step #1 on the Whip'n Chill box. Then in a measuring cup put 2 tbsp. rum (or more if desired), adding heavy cream to make 1/2 cup. Follow step #2 on the box. Put in small wine glasses or stem glasses and chill. Top with a dab of whipped cream before serving. This should be made ahead but taken from the refrigerator an hour before serving. Serve using demitasse spoons with the small wine glasses.

Mrs. James D. Patton, Saddle River

TOFFEE CAKE

Serves: 10-12

"This won first prize in a contest conducted by a Boston newspaper."

Easy   Do ahead   Preparing: 20 min.
                                            Refrigerating: overnight
                                            Chilling: 2 hrs.

1 angel food cake
1 pt. whipping cream
4 tbsp. cocoa
1 c. confectioners' sugar
6 Heath bars, crushed

Cut angel cake twice, making three layers. Spread the following mixture between layers, on sides and top. Let whipping cream stand in beating bowl in refrigerator overnight with cocoa and confectioners' sugar added. Next day whip and add Heath bars which have been crushed (between wax paper works well). Fill and frost cake. Chill in refrigerator before serving.

Mrs. Charles L. Van Inwagen, Ridgewood

EGG-LESS CHOCOLATE PUDDING

Serves: 6-8

"Quick and nourishing - calories present!"

Average   Do ahead   Preparing: 20 min.
                                                 Chilling: 1 hr.

3 c. milk
2 sq. chocolate or
   3 tbsp. cocoa
1/2 c. sugar (more if desired)
3 tbsp. cornstarch
1/2 tsp. vanilla

Using a double boiler, place 2-1/2 c. of milk in top and add chocolate. When melted add sugar. Then dissolve cornstarch in remaining 1/2 c. of milk. Put together with hot mixture and cook about 10 min., stirring. Just before removing from heat, add vanilla. Mix thoroughly and pour into individual dessert glasses or sherbet glasses. This may also be used as a pie filling.

Mrs. William R. Stott, Ridgewood

HEATH BAR DESSERT

Serves: 12

"The easiest of make-ahead desserts - simply scrumptious and gooey rich!"

Easy   Do ahead   Preparing: 20 min.
                                                 Chilling: 6 hrs.

12 Heath Bars
   (or Nestle's Crunch)
2 pkgs. ladyfingers
1 pt. heavy cream, whipped

Finely crunch or crush candy bars. This is easily done by chilling first and rolling with a rolling pin. Place bars between two layers of wax paper. You can also use a blender doing 3-4 bars at a time. When crushed, fold into the whipped cream. Place a layer of ladyfingers in a 9x13 inch pan. Spread a layer of candy cream mixture, a layer of ladyfingers and another layer of candy-cream. Refrigerate at least 6 hrs. before serving.

Mrs. Raymond J. Simone, Glen Rock

CHARLOTTE RUSSE

Serves: 12

"A longtime family recipe."

Average   Do ahead   Preparing: 30 min.
                                                 Chilling: 4 hrs.

2 env. unflavored gelatin
1/2 c. cold water
2 c. milk
6 eggs, separated
1 c. sugar
1 tsp. vanilla
1-1/2 doz. ladyfingers
2 c. heavy cream, whipped

Soften gelatin in water. Scald milk in top of a double boiler. Beat egg yolks and sugar until well blended. Stir into milk. Cook over boiling water, stirring constantly until mixture coats a spoon. Remove from heat and add gelatin. Stir until dissolved. Add vanilla. Cool thoroughly. Meanwhile line sides of a 10x4 inch tube pan with ladyfingers. When custard is cool, beat egg whites until stiff. Fold in custard. Fold in whipped cream. Turn into pan. Chill until set.

Mrs. Samuel D. Koonce, Ridgewood

BROWNIE WHIPPED CREAM DESSERT

Serves: 8-10

"An elegant, rich dessert that is very simple to make."

Easy   Freeze

Preparing: 15 min.
Baking: 20 min.
Chilling: 1 hr.

1 pkg. brownie mix or
  your favorite recipe
3/4 pt. heavy cream, whipped
confectioners' sugar
1 tsp. vanilla
optional -
  1 c. finely chopped nuts

Make brownies (with nuts if desired) and spread evenly in a 13x9 inch greased pan. Bake until just done (about 20 min.). Be sure they are still moist. Cool brownies. Sweeten whipped cream with confectioners' sugar and add vanilla. Slice brownie sheet into five 2-1/2 inch slices. Put together with whipped cream stacking so brownies stand on edge, not flat. Coat entire cake with remaining whipped cream. Chill at least 1 hr. or freeze. Slice thin to serve.

Mrs. Earl A. Samson, Jr., Ridgewood

SHERRY ICEBOX CAKE

Serves: 12

"A wonderful party dessert; quite rich."

Easy   Do ahead

Preparing: 30 min.
Chilling: overnight

1 large angel food cake
4 eggs, separated
1 c. sugar
2/3 c. sherry
1 env. gelatin
1/3 c. milk
1 pt. whipping cream

Beat egg yolks, place in a double boiler and add 1/2 c. sugar and sherry. Cook, stirring constantly until thick. Soak gelatin in milk until soft. Add to yolk mixture. Cool. Beat egg whites until stiff and add 1/2 c. sugar slowly. Whip 1 c. of cream and fold into egg whites. Fold both mixtures together. Break angel food into bite-size pieces. Using a large tube pan, alternate layers of cake bits and sauce. Let stand in the refrigerator overnight. When ready to serve, remove from pan and frost with 1 c. of cream, whipped.

Mrs. William T. Knight, III, Saddle River

POT DE CRÈME

Serves: 4

"So simple! So chocolaty! So rich tasting! So dietary!"

Easy   Do ahead

Preparing: 15 min.
Chilling: 1 hr.

2 oz. unsweetened chocolate
3 eggs, separated
1/2 c. sugar
optional - whipped cream

Melt chocolate and cool. Beat egg whites stiff until they hold a peak. Beat yolks and sugar together until lemon color. Add chocolate; beat until smooth. Fold in egg whites and put into sherbet glasses or demitasse cups and chill in refrigerator 1 hr. or longer. Can be served with a dab of whipped cream on top.

Mrs. Gilbert R. Rogers, Ridgewood

INDIVIDUAL ICEBOX CAKES

Yield: 18 cakes

"Excellent for a crowd. Very rich. Small servings are satisfying."

Average | Do ahead | Preparing: 30 min.
Chilling: 4 hrs.

3 4-oz. pkgs. German chocolate
  (I use Baker's)
3 tbsp. water
1 tsp. vanilla
1/8 tsp. salt
1/8 tsp. cream of tartar
4 eggs
18 ladyfingers
cream de Cacao, rum or brandy
1/2 pt. heavy cream, whipped
paper muffin cups

Melt 8 oz. chocolate in 3 tbsp. water with salt. Cool to lukewarm. Place paper muffin cups in muffin pans, using about 18. Split ladyfingers, cut in half, and line cups. Drizzle liqueur on them, using enough to be sure flavor will penetrate. Separate eggs, beating yolks one by one with chocolate. Add vanilla. Beat egg whites until foamy. Add cream of tartar and beat until stiff but not dry. Fold into chocolate mixture. Fill muffin tins and refrigerate. Before serving top with whipped cream and sprinkle with shaved chocolate from the third bar. May be made 24 hrs. ahead. Add whipped cream when serving.

Mrs. David F. Cook, Passaic

EASY CHOCOLATE ICEBOX CAKE

Serves: 4-5

Easy | Freeze | Preparing: 15 min.
Chilling: 12 hrs.

1 pkg. German sweet chocolate
  (I use Baker's)
1-1/2 tbsp. water
1 egg yolk, unbeaten
1 tbsp. confectioners' sugar
1/2 c. heavy cream, whipped
1 egg white, stiffly beaten
9 double lady fingers
whipped cream for garnishing

Melt chocolate in double boiler. Add water and blend. Remove from heat and add egg yolk and beat vigorously with an egg beater until smooth. Add sugar and mix well. Fold in whipped cream, then fold in beaten egg white. Line the bottom and sides of an 8x4 inch loaf pan with wax paper. Separate lady fingers and arrange on bottom and sides of pan. Pour in chocolate mixture. Arrange remaining lady fingers on top. Chill 12 to 24 hrs. In refrigerator. Unmold, slice and serve with additional whipped cream.

Mrs. Jack E. Ross, Ridgewood

COFFEE MARSHMALLOW SOUFFLE

Serves: 6

"This is best made the morning or day before serving."

Easy | Do ahead | Preparing: 15 min.
Chilling: 3 hrs.

28 marshmallows
1 c. hot strong coffee
1 c. heavy cream, whipped
1/2 tsp. vanilla
pinch salt

Cut marshmallows in small pieces or quarters with wet scissors and dissolve in hot coffee. When cool add stiffly whipped cream. Add vanilla and salt. Pour into sherbet glasses and chill. This will not freeze.

Mrs. Craig deV. Simpson, Ridgewood

COFFEE SOUFFLE

Serves: 6-8

Easy   Do ahead   Preparing: 15 min.
                                        Chilling: 3-4 hrs.

1-1/2 c. coffee infusion   Mix coffee infusion with milk and one half
  (strong liquid coffee)   of the sugar which has had gelatin added to
  (I do not use instant)   it. Heat this in the top of a double boiler.
1/2 c. milk   Add remaining sugar, salt and egg yolks which
3/4 c. sugar   have been beaten slightly. Cook until mix-
1 tbsp. gelatin   ture thickens. Remove from heat. Beat egg
1/4 tsp. salt   whites stiffly; fold into coffee mixture along
3 eggs, separated   with the vanilla. Pour into a mold or pretty
1/2 tsp. vanilla   serving bowl and chill. Serve with cream.

Mrs. Philip E. Sweeny, Ridgewood

LEMON SOUFFLE

Serves: 6

"A delicious, light dessert; especially good after a big dinner."

Average   Do ahead   Preparing: 30 min.
                                        Chilling: 3 hrs.

1 env. gelatin   Sprinkle gelatin over water to soften. Put
1/4 c. cold water   lemon juice, egg yolks, 1/2 c. sugar and salt
1/2 c. lemon juice   in the top of a double boiler. Cook, stirring
4 eggs, separated   constantly, until thick and custardy. Remove
1 c. sugar   from heat. Stir in gelatin and 1 tsp. lemon
1/2 tsp. salt   rind. Cool. Beat egg whites until they form
2 tsp. grated lemon rind   soft peaks. Add remaining sugar and beat
1 c. heavy cream, whipped   until stiff. Beat cream until it holds its
                                shape. Mix all together lightly and pour
                                into a 2 qt. souffle dish or bowl. Sprinkle
                                with more lemon rind and chill.

Mrs. William J. F. Dailey, Jr., Ridgewood

BRANDY COFFEE JELLY

Serves: 4

"A delicate, easy dessert for coffee lovers."

Easy   Do ahead   Preparing: 5 min.
                                        Chilling: 2 hrs.

1 pkg. gelatin   Mix gelatin and sugar. Add to hot coffee a
1/4 c. sugar   when dissolved and cooled a bit, add brandy.
1-3/4 c. strong hot coffee   Pour into a 2 c. mold or individual molds or
1/4 c. brandy   sherbet glasses. Chill until set. Serve wit
whipped cream   whipped cream.

Mrs. Frederick J. Kaiser, Jr., Ho-Ho-Kus

RICE DELIGHT

Serves: 6-8

Average   Part do ahead   Preparing: 30 min.
Chilling: 1 hr.

2 c. hot cooked rice
  (2/3 c. uncooked)
2 c. miniature marshmallows
1/2 c. crushed pineapple
  or fruit cocktail
1/4 c. maraschino cherries
optional -
  1/4 c. chopped pecans
1/2 pt. heavy cream

Cook rice until tender. Drain and rinse in hot water. Measure 2 cups. Add marshmallows and let stand 10 min. or until marshmallows melt. Mix and cool thoroughly. Add rest of ingredients except cream. Whip cream and fold in just before serving. Place in a serving bowl or individual sherbet or dessert dishes.

Mrs. Joseph Kresky, Rutherford

CREAM PUFFS

Serves: 6

"Much easier than one would think."

Easy   Do ahead   Preparing: 15 min.
Baking: 40 min.

1/2 c. milk
1/4 c. butter
1/2 c. sifted flour
1/8 tsp. salt
2 eggs

Heat milk and add butter and flour. Bring to a boil while stirring. Add salt. Cook and stir batter until mixture forms a ball or pulls away from the pan. Remove from heat and add eggs, beating in one at a time. Divide mixture into 6 large puffs on a greased cookie sheet. Bake at 400° for 30 min., then at 350° for 10 min. Let cool on cookie sheet. Cut for filling when cool. Fill with custard filling and frost with chocolate icing.

CUSTARD FILLING for Cream Puffs

Yield: 6 puffs

"This is a good filling for many dessert uses."

Easy   Do ahead   Preparing: 15 min.

1-1/2 c. milk
1-1/2 tbsp. cornstarch
1/4 tsp. salt
5 tbsp. sugar
2 egg yolks
vanilla

Heat milk and add cornstarch, salt and sugar. Mix. Beat egg yolks and add to mixture. Cook over low heat until thick, stirring constantly. Cool and add vanilla to taste. Add to cooled puffs. The filling MUST be kept refrigerated after filling puffs.

CHOCOLATE ICING for Cream Puffs

Yield: 6 puffs

"A delicious icing for almost any cake."

Easy   Do ahead   Preparing: 10 min.

2 oz. unsweetened chocolate
3 tbsp. butter
1/4 c. water
1 tsp. vanilla
2 c. confectioners' sugar

Melt chocolate and butter and water. Stir. Cool and add vanilla. Mix in confectioners' sugar, beating until smooth. Frost puffs.

Mrs. William D. Gallinger, Franklin Lakes

231

Dessert Sauces

CHOCOLATE SAUCE

Yield: 2 cups

"This is the one thing my children will always remember about my cooking!"

Easy   Do ahead   Preparing: 10 min.

1-1/2 c. sugar
1 tbsp. flour
3 tbsp. cocoa
1 tbsp. butter
1/2 c. hot water
3/4 c. evaporated milk
1 tsp. vanilla
pinch of salt

Mix and cook the sugar, flour, cocoa, butter and hot water. Cook these ingredients to the custard stage, about 5 min., at a slow boil. Add the milk, vanilla and salt and let it cook a few min. longer. Sauce will be fairly thick. May be served hot or cold. Serve over ice cream. May be topped with Coffee Crunch Topping below.

Mrs. David G. Bragg, Ridgewood

COFFEE CRUNCH TOPPING (or CANDY)

Yield: 2 cups

"Tricky, but delicious over chocolate sauce on ice cream!"

Average   Do ahead   Preparing: 30 min.

1-1/2 c. sugar
1/4 c. coffee
1/4 c. white corn syrup
3 tsp. sifted baking soda

Put sugar, coffee and corn syrup in a heavy saucepan 5 inches deep. Stir and combine these ingredients, then bring them to a boil. Cook to the hard crack stage (310° on a candy thermometer). Remove this from the heat and immediately add the soda. Stir until mixture thickens and pulls away from the sides of the pan. Don't destroy foam by excessive beating. Immediately pour foamy mass into an ungreased shallow square pan. Do not spread or stir. Let stand without moving until cold. Knock out of pan and crush between wax paper to form coarse crumbs. Can be stored for months in a coffee can in the refrigerator. This should not be made on a humid day.

Mrs. David G. Bragg, Ridgewood

SHERRY SAUCE

Serves: 4-6

Easy   Do ahead   Preparing: 5 min.

1-1/3 c. butter (scant)
1-1/2 c. water
1 tbsp. corn starch
1 c. sugar
3 tbsp. sherry

Mix all ingredients well in a double boiler. Heat and keep warm until time to use. Serve over ice cream, cake, plum pudding, date cake, etc. This stores very well in refrigerator.

Mrs. Theodore R. Wolf, Ridgewood

BUTTERSCOTCH SAUCE

Yield: 3 cups

"A spoonful is so much better than candy!"

Easy   Do ahead   Preparing: 15 min.

3/4 c. brown sugar, packed
1 c. clear corn syrup
1/4 c. butter
1 c. heavy cream
  (light for a thinner sauce)

Boil sugar, syrup and butter for 5 min. Stir until sugar is dissolved. Add cream and bring to a brisk boil. This thickens as it stands. Serve over angel food or French vanilla ice cream. Stores well.

Mrs. Paul S. Hensel, Ridgewood

BROWN SUGAR-BRANDY SAUCE

Yield: 1 cup

"Marvelous on fruits such as peaches, Bing cherries, or on ice cream."

Easy   Do ahead   Preparing: 5 min.
                                                  Simmering: 10 min.

1/2 c. brown sugar
1/2 c. water
pinch salt
1/2 tsp. cornstarch
2 oz. cognac or dark rum

Mix brown sugar, water and salt. Bring to a boil and simmer 3-4 min. Mix cornstarch with 2 tbsp. water and add to mixture. Cook until it thickens. Remove from heat and add liquor to taste. Serve over fruit or ice cream topped with sliced almonds.

Mrs. Hamilton B. Bowman, Duxbury, Mass.

POLYNESIAN SAUCE

Serves: 4

Easy   Do ahead   Preparing: 5 min.
                                                    Warming: 10 min.

1/4 c. pineapple preserves
1/4 c. apricot preserves
1/3 c. rum

Mix all ingredients together and warm - DO NOT COOK. Serve flambe. The secret to having the sauce flaming is to be sure and <u>warm</u> before setting a match to it. Delicious served over fruit, cake or vanilla ice cream. For a special treat, top the ice cream with sliced bananas, pineapple and flaked coconut.

Mrs. Kenneth S. Talbot, Ridgewood

Dessert Dividends

When melting baking chocolate, place it on a piece of aluminum foil in its own wrapper and put into the oven while it is preheating or into the top of a double boiler - the chocolate will be ready when you need it.

Always add a little salt to recipes containing chocolate - it brings out the flavor.

If a recipe calls for brown sugar, use light brown unless otherwise specified

To soften hardened brown sugar, place a crisp lettuce leaf or a slice of fresh bread in the container. Or, place package in a 250° oven for 10 min., then roll out the lumps with a rolling pin or press them out with a spoon or fingers. When heated, the sugar must be used immediately

Heavy cream doubles in volume when whipped - 1/2 c. of whipping cream will make 1 c. of whipped cream.

A pinch of salt added to heavy cream will make it whip faster.

Slip a piece of wax paper over the mixing bowl when whipping cream. Have the beaters poke up through a hole in the center - no splatters.

Freeze dollops of whipped cream on a cookie sheet. When frozen transfer carefully to a box for storage. Nice for garnishing.

* Sprinkle strawberries with sugar and pour a bit of brandy or orange juice over them. Chill for several hours. Before serving, pour pink champagne over the strawberries and garnish with mint.

If custard curdles, pour it through a sieve.

* Fill the center of honeydew melon halves with lime sherbet for a delicious dessert.

* Honeydew is marvelous filled with strawberries and fresh pineapple with a sauce of beaten vanilla ice cream and brandy poured over.

Serve crystallized ginger or powdered ginger with any melon.

Some wonderful, different toppings for ice cream are: brandied mincemeat; green creme de menthe; coffee grounds over coffee ice cream; maple syrup

Nice garnishes for puddings, cakes, pies, etc.:
Chocolate shavings made by using a parer on semisweet or cooking chocolate squares.
Frosted grapes made by dipping grapes into slightly beaten egg whites and coating with granulated sugar. Allow to dry on wax paper.
Melt semisweet chocolate and paint onto the backs of small leaves. Refrigerate. When cool peel off leaf. You will have a chocolate leaf.
Toast almonds, finely chopped or slivered, in hot skillet or on a cookie sheet in a slow oven. Be sure to keep almonds stirred for an even medium brown.

Pretty mint garnish for berries can be done by brushing them with egg white and dipping into fine granulated sugar.

Cakes

KENTUCKY GLAZED ORANGE CAKE

Serves: 10-12

"Gets better with age. May be kept a week without freezing."

Average   Freeze   Preparing: 30 min.
Baking: 1 hr.

1 c. butter
2 c. sugar
3/4 c. fresh orange juice
3 c. sifted flour
3 tsp. baking powder
1/4 tsp. salt
grated rind of 1 orange
5 eggs (room temperature)

Cream butter until fluffy. Beat in sugar until light. Beat in 1 egg at a time. Sift dry ingredients together and add to creamed mixture alternating with orange juice. Add grated rind. Pour into a greased and floured tube pan and bake at 350° for 1 hr. or until tester comes out clean. Remove from oven to rack.

Glaze:
1 c. melted butter
2/3 c. sugar
1/3 c. bourbon whiskey

Glaze: While cake is cooking make glaze by heating butter and sugar until sugar is dissolved. Add bourbon. Leave cake in pan and pour glaze over hot cake. Leave in pan until thoroughly cooled. Freeze or serve.

Mrs. William W. Welch, Jr., Ridgewood

ORANGE KISS-ME CAKE

Serves: 12-16

"Delicious to serve as a dessert or coffee cake."

Easy   Freeze   Preparing: 10 min.
Baking: 45 min.

6 oz. orange juice concentrate
2 c. flour
1 c. sugar
1 tsp. baking soda
1 tsp. salt
1/2 c. shortening
1/2 c. milk
2 eggs
1 c. raisins
1/3 c. chopped walnuts

Thaw orange juice. Grease and flour bottom of a 13x9 inch pan. Combine 1/2 c. orange juice concentrate with remaining ingredients in a large mixing bowl. Blend at lowest speed on a mixer for 30 sec. Beat 3 min. at med. speed. Pour into pan and bake at 350° for 40-45 min. Drizzle remaining orange concentrate over warm cake. Sprinkle with topping.

Topping:
1/3 c. sugar
1/4 c. chopped walnuts
1 tsp. cinnamon

Topping: Combine all ingredients in a small bowl. Sprinkle over cake.

Mrs. Calvin E. Ramsey, Ramsey

LEMON CAKE

Serves: 12

"A treat for lemon fans and a snap to make!"

Easy   Freeze   Preparing: 15 min.
                                                   Baking: 35 min.

1 pkg. lemon cake mix
  (I use Betty Crocker
  Lemon Velvet)
3 oz. pkg. lemon gelatin
4 eggs
3/4 c. cold water
3/4 c. salad oil
2 c. confectioners' sugar
juice of 2 lemons

Mix cold water and gelatin. Add slightly beaten eggs. Add cake mix, then add oil and mix. Pour into a 9x13 inch pan which has been greased and floured. Bake at 350° for 35 min. or until it stops sizzling. While still warm make holes all over the cake about 2 inches apart being sure to go all the way to the bottom. (A meat thermometer is a good tool.) Mix lemon juice and confectioners' sugar; drizzle over cake, being sure to cover completely and to get it into all the holes. Best served warm.

Mrs. Kenneth S. Talbot, Ridgewood

BARBER'S CAKE

Serves: 8

"I know of two youngsters who can finish this off in half an hour."

Easy   Freeze   Preparing: 10 min.
                                                   Baking: 50 min.

1 yellow cake mix
1 pkg. instant vanilla pudding
4 eggs
3/4 c. oil
3/4 c. water
1 tsp. vanilla
confectioners' sugar

Mix all ingredients in a large bowl. Beat three min. with electric beater or 400 strokes by hand. Place in an ungreased angel food pan. Bake at 350° for 45-50 min. in a gas oven or at 325° for 40-45 min. in an electric oven. When cool sprinkle confectioners' sugar with a shaker over the top of cake.

Mrs. Samuel A. Hird, Jr., Ridgewood

LEMON-RUM CAKE WITH CITRUS GLAZE

Serves: 10

"This has an elegant taste that's perfect for guests after a hearty meal."

Average   Freeze   Preparing: 15 min.
                                                   Baking: 1 hr

1 pkg. lemon cake mix
  (I use Duncan Hines Lemon
  Supreme)
4 eggs
1/2 c. + 2 tbsp. butter
1 c. milk
rind of 1 lemon, grated
1 to 2 jiggers rum

Glaze:
1-1/4 c. confectioners' sugar
rind of 1/2 lemon, grated
rind of 1 orange, grated
2 tbsp. fresh orange juice
1 tsp. fresh lemon juice

Combine eggs, soft butter, milk and lemon rind; beat until foamy. Add cake mix and beat slowly to combine ingredients. Add rum. Pour into a greased tube pan and bake at 350° for 1 hr. Cool on a cake rack.

Glaze: Sift confectioners' sugar and combine with other ingredients. Spread over top and side of cake. Let stand to set before serving.

Mrs. Thomas E. Dater, Ramsey

SUSAN'S DELUXE ANGEL FOOD (Orange Angel Food)   Serves: 8-10

"High, light and moist."

Average   Freeze   Preparing: 30 min.
                                                     Baking: 35 min.

1-2/3 c. egg whites
  (about 12 medium eggs)
1 c. + 2 tbsp. cake flour,
  sifted
1-3/4 c. granulated sugar,
  sifted
1/2 tsp. salt
1-1/2 tsp. cream of tartar
1 tsp. vanilla
3/4 tsp. almond extract

Set egg whites out about 1 hr. ahead. Pre-heat oven to 375° and sift flour with 3/4 c. sugar five times. In a large mixer bowl, beat whites and salt at high speed until foamy. Add cream of tartar. Beat until whites are stiff and stand in peaks (about 2-1/2 min.). While beating, rapidly sprinkle in 1 c. sugar. Beat only until sugar is blended (about 1 min.). Using a rubber spatula, scrape bowl toward beaters, then up and over. Add extracts. Turn mixer to low speed. Sprinkle in sifted flour evenly and quickly, beating just to blend (about 1-1/2 min.). Gently scrape bowl toward beaters, then up and over, using folding motion. Gently push batter into an ungreased 10 inch tube pan. With spatula, cut complete square through batter without removing spatula. Bake 35 min. or until done. Immediately invert pan. Leave until cool, then remove from pan.

To make Orange Angel Food: Add 3 tbsp. grated orange rind to sifted flour and sugar. Toss with a fork. Substitute 1 tsp. orange extract for vanilla and almond extracts.

Mrs. John P. Ingham, Allendale

BEST POUND CAKE   Serves: 10-12

Average   Freeze   Preparing: 15 min.
                                                     Baking: 1 hr.

1 c. butter
1-2/3 c. sugar
5 eggs
2 c. flour
1/4 tsp. baking powder
pinch of salt
1 tsp. vanilla
1-1/2 tsp. lemon extract

Soften butter and add sugar. Cream thoroughly. Add flour and unbeaten eggs, one at a time, alternating flour and eggs and ending with flour. Add flavorings and place in a greased and floured 9 inch tube pan. Bake at 350° for 1 hr. or until toothpick comes out clean.

Mrs. Robert E. Taylor, Ridgewood

COCONUT POUND CAKE

Serves: 18-20

"This is a special of most men."

Easy   Freeze

Preparing: 15 min.
Baking: 1 - 1-1/2 hrs.

1 lb. butter
2 c. sugar
2 c. flour
6 eggs
7 oz. angel flake coconut
1 tsp. vanilla

Glaze:
1 c. sugar
1/2 c. water
1 tsp. coconut flavoring
  (or almond if coconut is
  not available)

Cream butter and sugar. Add 1 c. flour and mix well. Add eggs, one at a time, mixing in well. Mix remaining cup of flour with coconut and add to cake mixture. Then mix in vanilla. Place in a 9 inch tube pan. Bake at 350° for 1 hr. to 1 hr. 15 min. or until cake begins to pull away from sides of pan. Turn from pan and glaze while hot.

Glaze: While cake is baking, combine glaze ingredients and simmer for 10 min. Brush onto wrong side of warm cake. Let cake cool. Best served 24 hours after baking.

Mrs. Robert S. Aman, Ho-Ho-Kus

NORWEGIAN POUND CAKE

Serves: 12-16

"Everyone enjoys its light but moist texture. The perfect gift."

Easy   Freeze

Preparing: 25 min.
Baking: 1 hr. 20 min.

2-1/4 c. sugar
6 eggs
3/4 lb butter
3/4 c. milk
3 c. sifted self-rising flour
  (I use Presto)
1 tsp. vanilla
1/2 tsp. almond flavoring

Put all ingredients into a mixing bowl and beat for 20 min. at medium speed. Grease and flour a large tube pan. Bake at 350° for 1 hr. 20 min. Turn out immediately on a cake rack and cover with a cloth to cool. Be sure to bake the full time; cake will have raw streaks if not properly baked. Frost with Norwegian Chocolate Icing. Frost only the top and let dribbles run down the sides. Frost cake turned upside down or, if desired, dust top of cake with confectioners' sugar.

NORWEGIAN CHOCOLATE ICING

Yield: for 1 cake

Easy   Freeze

Preparing: 5 min.

8 oz. chocolate bits
  (or imported bittersweet
  chocolate)
2 eggs
1/4 lb. butter
drop of almond extract

Melt chocolate over hot water. Beat eggs with butter and mix with cooled chocolate. Add almond flavoring. Frost pound cake.

Mrs. Graham B. Conklin, Ridgewood

GERMAN CHOCOLATE POUND CAKE

Serves: 15-20

"Almost better after freezing. The man of the house will love this."

Easy   Freeze   Preparing: 15 min.
                                  Baking: 1-1/2 hrs. plus

1 bar German sweet chocolate
  (I use Baker's)
2 c. sugar
1 c. butter
4 eggs
3 tsp. vanilla
1 c. buttermilk or sour milk
3 c. sifted flour
1/2 tsp soda
1 tsp. salt

Cream butter and sugar. Add eggs, one at a time, and beat well. Melt chocolate and add to butter-egg mixture. Then add vanilla and buttermilk. Sift flour, soda and salt together and add to the first mixture. Grease a 10 inch tube pan well and pour cake mixture into it. Bake at 300° for 1-1/2 hrs. When done, leave in the pan and cover, air tight, with plastic wrap or foil until cool. Remove from pan.

Mrs. Edwin H. Johnson, Jr., Ridgewood

FUNNY CAKE

Serves: 4-6

"A Pennsylvania Dutch coffee cake or dessert."

Average   Freeze   Preparing: 20 min.
                                  Baking: 30 min.

Sauce:
1 c. water
6 tbsp. sugar
3 tbsp. cocoa
1 tsp. vanilla

Batter:
1 c. flour
1/2 c. sugar
2 eggs
1/2 c. milk
2 tsp. baking powder
2 tbsp. butter

8" unbaked pie shell

Sauce: Bring the water, sugar, cocoa and vanilla to a boil. Let cook until the sauce thickens - a few minutes. Let it stand.

Batter: Mix all ingredients for batter together. Blend until they are smooth.

Assembling: Place the chocolate sauce in pie shell. Spread the cake batter on top of the sauce, starting along the edge of the pie shell first. Bake at 350° for 30 min. - no longer as the sauce on the bottom should be slightly soft.

Mrs. Walter J. Minton, Saddle River

WACKY CAKE

Serves: 8-10

"This is a rich, dark chocolate cake - such fun to make!"

Easy   Freeze   Preparing: 5 min.
                                  Baking: 35 min.

1-1/2 c. flour
1 c. sugar
3 rounded tbsp. cocoa
1 tsp. soda
1/2 tsp. salt
5 tbsp. melted shortening
  or oil
1 tbsp. vinegar
1 tsp. vanilla
1 c. cold water

Put a sifter in an ungreased 8 inch square pan. Into the sifter put dry ingredients and sift into the pan. Make three wells in dry mixture. In largest well put shortening or oil, in the next put vinegar and in the third put vanilla. Pour water over all. Mix thoroughly with a fork and bake at 350° for 30-35 min.

Mrs. Robert C. Mackenzie, Jr., Ridgewood

DEVIL'S FOOD

Yield: 9-inch layer cake

"In our family it's 'Make any kind of cake as long as it's your Devil's Food.'"

Average   Freeze

Preparing: 15 min.
Baking: 35 min.

2-1/2 c. sifted cake flour
  (I use Swan's Down)
1-3/4 c. sugar
1-3/4 tsp. soda
1 tsp. salt
2/3 c. butter
1-1/3 c. milk
1 tsp. vanilla
2 eggs, unbeaten
3 sq. unsweetened chocolate

Preheat oven to 350°. Measure flour after sifting and add sugar, soda and salt. Sift twice. Have butter at room temperature and stir to soften. Sift in dry ingredients and add 1 c. milk and vanilla. Beat 2 min. at medium speed on the electric mixer. Add eggs and melted chocolate, then rest of milk. Beat 2 more min. Line bottoms of two 9 inch layer pans with paper. Pour in batter evenly between the two pans and bake for 35 min. (Three 8 inch pans may be used and cake baked for 30 min.) Cool on racks. Frost with Mocha Frosting.

MOCHA FROSTING

Yield: 2 layer cake

Easy   Freeze

Preparing: 10 min.

6 tbsp. cocoa
6 tbsp. hot coffee
6 tbsp. butter
1 tsp. vanilla
3 c. confectioners' sugar

Combine cocoa and coffee. Add softened butter and vanilla. Beat until smooth. Gradually add sugar until spreading consistency.

Mrs. Thomas H. Boyd, Clifton

SOUR CREAM VELVET CAKE

Serves: 12

"Takes a bit longer than a mix, but well worth it!"

Average   Freeze

Preparing: 20 min.
Baking: 40 min.

3 oz. baking chocolate
1 c. boiling water
1-1/4 tsp. baking soda
1/2 c. butter or margarine
1-1/2 tsp. vanilla
1 tsp. red food coloring
2 c. sugar
3 eggs, separated
2-1/2 c. sifted cake flour
1/2 tsp. salt
1 c. sour cream

Melt chocolate and combine with water. Cool slightly and add soda. Cream butter or margarine until soft and add vanilla. Add 1-1/2 c. sugar gradually, beating well after each addition. Add egg yolks; beat well. Sift flour with salt. Add flour mixture alternately with sour cream, beating until smooth. Add chocolate mixture and food coloring. Blend thoroughly. Beat egg whites until soft peaks form. Gradually add remaining 1/2 c. sugar and beat until egg whites form stiff peaks. Fold into first mixture. Pour into three 8 inch greased cake pans. Bake at 350° for 35-40 min. Fill layers with chocolate-nut frosting (I use a mix) and frost with any seven-minute white icing.

Mrs. Richard D. Major, Allendale

240

CHOCOLATE CHIP CAKE

Serves: 10-16

"Stays moist a long time, and not difficult."

Average | Freeze | Preparing: 15 min.
Baking: 40 min.

1 regular size pkg. dates
1-1/4 c. boiling water
1 c. sugar
3/4 c. shortening or
　1-1/2 sticks margarine
1 tbsp. cocoa
2 eggs
2 c. flour, sifted
1 tsp. soda
1/2 tsp. salt
1 tsp. vanilla

Topping:
1/2 c. nutmeats
7 oz. pkg. chocolate chips

Pour boiling water over cut-up dates. Let cool. In a bowl, cream the sugar and shortening, then add eggs and dates. Add the dry ingredients and mix well. Lastly add the vanilla. Pour into a greased 9x13 inch pan and spread with topping. No frosting is needed. Bake at 350° for 35 to 40 min. This may be made a day or two ahead or frozen.

Mrs. Martin Hoeksema, Ridgewood

WEARY WILLY CAKE

Serves: 6

"A small, light chocolate cake from my Grandmother's recipe."

Easy | Freeze | Preparing: 10 min.
Baking: 30 min.

1 c. flour
1 c. sugar
1 tsp. baking powder
pinch salt
1 sq. baking chocolate
1 heaping tbsp. butter
1 egg
milk (about 3/4 c.)

Sift dry ingredients together. Melt chocolate with butter in a measuring cup. Add egg to chocolate in cup and then enough milk to make one cup. Add to dry ingredients and beat hard. Pour into a loaf pan (approximately 9x5 inch). Bake at 350° for 25-30 min. or until tester comes out clean. Frost with Browned Butter Frosting.

BROWNED BUTTER FROSTING

Yield: 2 layers

Easy | Freeze | Preparing:

1/3 c. butter
1/8 tsp. salt
3 c. confectioners' sugar
1/4 c. milk or cream
1-1/2 tsp. vanilla

Sift sugar. In a heavy skillet brown the butter. Slowly add sugar and salt right in the skillet and stir fast and well. Alternate milk and sugar, adding vanilla, until you get the spreading consistency you desire. Work fast and stir hard. Frost while warm. Make half this for the Weary Willy Cake.

Mrs. Arthur S. Whittemore, Jr., Ridgewood

MOCHA CAKE

Serves: 18-20

"A super cake, worth all the effort."

Average   Freeze   Preparing: 25 min.
                                         Baking: 30 min.

2-1/2 c. sugar
1 c. butter
5 eggs, separated
1 c. buttermilk
3 c. flour
5 tbsp. very strong coffee
4 tsp. cocoa
1 tsp. soda
pinch salt
2 tsp. vanilla

Cream together butter and sugar. Sift together dry ingredients. Beat egg yolks and add to butter-sugar mixture. Add dry ingredients alternately with milk. Stir in coffee (instant may be used) and vanilla. Beat egg whites until stiff but not dry. Fold into cake mixture. Pour into three greased and floured 9 inch cake pans and bake at 375° for 30 min. Frost with Mocha Frosting.

MOCHA FROSTING

Yield: 3 layer cake

Easy   Best not frozen   Preparing: 10 min.

1 c. butter
2 egg yolks
4 tsp. cocoa
5-6 tbsp. strong coffee
1-1/2 tbsp. vanilla
2 boxes confectioners' sugar

Sift sugar. Cream butter and add 1-1/2 c. sugar and cocoa. Add egg yolks and coffee (instant may be used). Add vanilla and beat until fluffy. Add more sugar until correct spreading consistency is reached.

Mrs. Arthur Espy, III, Ho-Ho-Kus

MYSTERY MOCHA CAKE

Serves: 8

"A favorite pudding-cake plain, with ice cream or whipped cream."

Easy   Freeze   Preparing: 15 min.
                                         Baking: 40 min.

3/4 c. sugar
1 c. flour
2 tsp. baking powder
1/8 tsp. salt
1 sq. baking chocolate
2 tbsp. margarine
1/2 c. milk
1 tsp. vanilla

Mix sugar, flour, baking powder and salt in a 9 inch square pan. Add melted chocolate and margarine. Blend well. Combine milk and vanilla and add to mixture.

Topping: Combine sugars and cocoa; sprinkle over the batter. Pour cold coffee over this. Do not stir. Bake at 350° for 40 min.

Topping:
1/2 c. brown sugar
1/2 c. white sugar
4 tbsp. cocoa
1 c. cold double strength
   coffee (instant can be used)   *Mrs. James O. McLain, Metuchen*

WASHINGTON CREAM PIE

Serves: 12

" This is the specialty of our house. Balances the angel food I make."

Average   Do ahead   Preparing: 30 min.
Baking: 25 min.

6 egg yolks
1 c. sugar
1/2 c. boiling water
1-1/2 c. cake flour
2 tsp. baking powder
1/4 tsp. salt
1 tsp. grated orange rind

Filling:
2 c. milk
1/4 c. sugar
3 tbsp. cornstarch
2 whole eggs or
  4 egg yolks
2 tbsp. butter
1/4 tsp. salt
2 tbsp. lemon juice or
1 tsp. flavoring
  (half orange, half vanilla)

Beat egg yolks until thick and lemon-colored. Add sugar gradually and continue beating. Add the boiling water and mix well. Add flour which has been sifted with baking powder and salt. Beat until smooth. Add the orange rind and pour into two greased and floured layer cake pans. Bake at 325° for 25 min. or until it begins to shrink from pans. Cool on a rack. Split each layer into two layers with a knife and spread with filling making two pie-cakes of two thin layers each. Top with sweetened whipped cream. Drape with fruit in its own syrup.

Filling: Beat eggs. Add the blended sugar and cornstarch. Then add the milk which has been scalded. Cook 15 min. over hot water, stirring occasionally. Add the butter, salt and flavoring. Cool before spreading. Half the filling may be stored in the refrigerator and used later on the second cake.

Mrs. John P. Ingham, Allendale

ZWIEDACK CAKE

Serves: 10-12

"A delicious, complete dessert. This was my grandmother's recipe."

Average   Freeze   Preparing: 20 min.
Baking: 35 min.

5 eggs, separated
1 c. sugar
1 tsp. cinnamon
1 tsp. allspice
pinch salt
1 c. walnuts, chopped
1 tsp. baking powder
1/2 pkg. zwieback
1/2 pt. cream, whipped

Mix sugar and egg yolks. Add spices and salt; mix well. Add nuts which have been finely ground (a blender is great for this). Beat egg whites stiff and fold into yolk mixture. Use one layer from the zwieback package, saving three pieces for later use. Place the zwieback in a plastic bag and roll fine with a rolling pin. Mix these crumbs with the baking powder and then add to the first mixture. Place in two layer cake pans and bake at 350° for 30-35 min. When cool put a layer of whipped cream in the middle and on the top of the cake. Sprinkle the last three zwieback pieces, finely ground, on the top of the cake.

Mrs. Adrian B. Van Riper, Ridgewood

CARROT CAKE

Serves: 10

"Tasty enough for party fare in spite of the odd combination."

Average   Freeze   Preparing: 15 min.
                                          Baking: 45 min.

1-1/2 c. oil
  (I use Wesson)
2 c. sugar
4 eggs
2 c. flour
2 tsp. soda
1 tsp. salt
3 tsp. cinnamon
2 tsp. vanilla
3 c. grated carrots

Combine sugar and oil and add eggs. Sift flour, soda, salt and cinnamon together. Add to sugar mixture and beat well. Add vanilla and grated carrots. Bake in three 8 inch layer cake pans which have been well greased. Bake at 325° for 45 min. When cool ice with Cream Cheese Icing.

CREAM CHEESE ICING

Yield: 3 layers

Easy   Freeze   Preparing: 10 min.

1 stick margarine
8 oz. cream cheese
1 pkg. confectioners' sugar
2 tsp. vanilla

Soften margarine and cream cheese and beat together. Add confectioners' sugar and vanilla until spreading consistency. Frost cake.

Mrs. Owen Calderwood, Ridgewood

CRAZY CUP CAKES

Yield: 1 doz.

"Couldn't be easier. Great for picnics, children's parties, etc."

Easy   Freeze   Preparing: 10 min.
                                          Baking: 30 min.

1 c. sugar
1 egg
1/2 c. milk
1/2 c. cocoa
1/2 c. shortening
1-1/2 c. cake flour
1/2 tsp. salt
1 tsp. baking powder
1/2 tsp. soda
1/2 c. boiling water
1 tsp. vanilla

Sift salt with cake flour. Put all ingredients into a bowl and beat for 3 min. Bake in muffin pans which have been greased or lined with paper cups. Bake at 325° for 30 min. Ice with Confectioners' Sugar Icing.

CONFECTIONERS' SUGAR ICING

Yield: 1 doz. cup cakes

Easy   Freeze   Preparing: 5 min.

2 c. confectioners' sugar
dash salt
1 tsp. vanilla
a little cream

Sift sugar with salt. Add vanilla and beat in enough cream to make a good spreading consistency.

Mrs. Harry N. Ives, Ridgewood

PETITS FOURS

Yield: 4 doz.

"The easy way to impress your friends at luncheon or tea. Takes time."

Easy   Freeze   Preparing: 1 hr.

2 pound cakes
  (homemade or purchased)

Icing:
2 lbs. confectioners' sugar
1/4 c. butter or margarine,
  melted
1 c. light cream
1 tsp. almond or vanilla
  flavoring
vegetable coloring
sprinkles, coconut, candied
  cherries, chopped nuts,
  etc., for decorating

Cut cakes into desired shapes - small rectangles, diamonds, etc.

Icing: Place all ingredients in the top of a double boiler over hot water. Stir until smooth. Divide into smaller groups and color each as desired.

To ice: Spear each piece of cake and dip into icing. Remove from icing and twirl so icing covers evenly. Place on wax paper to dry and decorate as desired with sprinkles, etc.

Mrs. John H. Cline, St. Thomas, Virgin Is.

FRESH APPLE CAKE

Serves: 10-12

"An easy cake that stays moist for a long while."

Easy   Do ahead   Preparing: 15 min.
                                Baking: 1 hr. 15 min.

2 c. flour
2 c. white sugar
2 tsp. baking soda
1 tsp. cinnamon
1/2 tsp. nutmeg
1/2 tsp. salt
4 c. diced raw apples, peeled
1/2 c. chopped walnuts
1/2 c. butter, melted
2 eggs
confectioners' sugar

Preheat oven to 325° and grease a pan approximately 13x9x2 inches. In a large bowl sift flour, sugar, soda, cinnamon, nutmeg and salt together. Add apples, nuts, butter and slightly beaten eggs. This will be a thick mixture. Mix it all well. Bake 1 hr. to 1 hr. 15 min. (until cake springs back at the touch). Cool slightly and sprinkle with confectioners' sugar, if desired. Serve warm or cold with whipped cream or ice cream.

Mrs. Martin Hoeksema, Ridgewood

APPLESAUCE CAKE

Serves: 8

Average   Freeze   Preparing: 20 min.
                                Baking: 40 min.

1 c. applesauce
7/8 c. brown sugar
1/2 c. melted shortening
  or salad oil
1-3/4 c. flour
1 tsp. baking soda
1/2 tsp. salt
1 tsp. cinnamon
1 tsp. ginger
1/2 tsp. cloves
1/2 c. raisins
1/2 c. chopped nuts

Mix thoroughly the applesauce, sugar and melted shortening. Sift into a large bowl the flour, soda, salt, cinnamon, ginger and cloves. Add the raisins and nuts. Add the applesauce mixture to the flour mixture and blend well. Spoon into a greased and floured 9 inch square pan. Bake at 350° about 40 min. Serve with whipped cream, or frost.

Mrs. Charles M. Carlsson, Ridgewood

PEOPLES CHURCH BAZAAR FRUIT CAKE

Yield: 2-4 cakes

"This will keep for two months if well wrapped. Marvelous for gift giving."

Easy   Do ahead   Preparing: 30 min.
                                                      Baking: 1-3/4 hrs.

1 pkg. mincemeat
  (I use None Such)
1 c. nutmeats
1 c. raisins
1 c. candied fruits in jar
1 c. sugar
1/4 c. melted butter
1/4 c. brandy
2 eggs, separated
1 tsp. soda
2 c. sifted flour
1 tbsp. boiling water

Prepare mincemeat as directed. Mix together mincemeat, nuts, raisins, fruits,
sugar, butter, brandy and egg yolks. Mix
well. Add soda, flour and boiling water.
Beat egg whites and fold in. Bake in coffee
cans lined with wax paper and filled about
2/3 full or in two loaf pans approximately
4 x 8 inches. Bake at 300° for 1-3/4 hrs.
When cool, wrap in aluminum foil or colored
cellophane and tie with ribbon

Mrs. Richard C. Baxter, Ridgewood

PECAN LOAF

Yield: 1 large or
       2 small cakes

"The perfect fruit cake! A wonderful gift at holiday time."

Average   Freeze   Preparing: 30 min.
                                                      Baking: 1 hr. 45 min.

1 c. flour
1 c. sugar
4 eggs, slightly beaten
3/4 tsp. salt
2-1/2 tsp. baking powder
1 tsp. vanilla
4 c. whole pecans (1 lb.)
1-3/4 c. dates (3/4 lb.)
3/4 c. candied cherries
3/4 c. candied pineapple
brandy
  or
orange juice

Sift flour, sugar, salt and baking powder
together. Beat eggs slightly and add vanilla.
Put nuts, dates, and coarsely chopped cherries
and pineapple in a large bowl. Add sifted
flour to fruit and mix well. Add beaten egg
and vanilla and mix until eggs take in all the
flour. Pack firmly in a 3-lb. loaf pan or 2
smaller pans. Bake at 275° for 1 hr. 45 min.
for large pan or 1 hr. 15 min. in smaller pans.
When cool, wrap in an orange juice or brandy
soaked cloth then in foil. Store in refrigerator. Slice and serve. This will keep for
several weeks.

Mrs. Melvin R. Campbell, Ridgewood

GAIL'S ICING

Yield: 1 cake

"Almost as easy as boxed icing - to which you will never return."

Easy   Freeze   Preparing: 5 min.

2 tbsp. butter
1 egg
1 box confectioners' sugar
2 sq. chocolate, melted

Beat together butter and whole egg. Add
sugar until it is nice to spread. Add melted
chocolate.

Mrs. Albert F. Lilley, Allendale

Cake Cues

To mix cake easily, put all dry ingredients into a bowl and mix thoroughly with a whisk. This takes the place of sifting.

When mixing any cake, shortening should be soft so that when beaten with the sugar the mixture will be the consistency of whipped cream. If soda is used in the recipe, it should be added at this point, as should the vanilla and spices for the best flavoring.

Keep a large kitchen salt shaker full of flour - great for dusting cake pans.

Wax paper line loaf cake pans - you can then lift out cake when done without cracking.

Keep butter and margarine wrappers in your refrigerator and use for greasing pans.

To test a cake for doneness, insert a toothpick into the center; if it comes out clean the cake is done.

To keep cakes fresh, put an apple cut in half into the storage container.

If you cool baked goods in their pan they become a little tough and will not absorb as much liquid. Always do this with jelly rolls and trifles.

Freeze cakes after baking.

To determine whether baking powder is still active, mix 1 teaspoonful with 1/2 c. hot water; use only if it bubbles enthusiastically.

* For children's birthdays, bake cupcakes in flat-bottom ice cream cones, then frost them.

To frost cupcakes quickly, dip the top of each cupcake into soft icing, twirl slightly and quickly turn right side up.

When frosting a layer cake, place two strips of wax paper about 5 inches wide on the plate to cover it. Place cake on top of this. Frost cake. When done pull out the wax paper and your plate will be clean - no frosting drips to clean up.

When cooked icing doesn't thicken, beat it in strong sunlight or near an open oven door or in a double boiler over boiling water.

Dust a little flour or cornstarch on your cake before icing it - this way the icing won't run off.

A pinch of salt added to the sugar in icings will prevent graining.

* Use leftover egg whites, beaten stiff, with a small glass of <u>tart</u> jelly for cake icing.

Use a nutmeg grater to remove burnt edges from a cake.

KEY LIME PIE

Serves: 6

"So refreshing. Easy to make and marvelous for summer entertaining."

Easy   Do ahead

Preparing: 15 min.
Chilling: 6 hrs.

9" graham cracker pie shell
3 eggs
1/3 c. <u>fresh</u> lime juice
1 can <u>condensed</u> milk

Separate eggs. Beat whites until dry.
Beat yolks until creamy, add lime juice
and beat well. Add condensed milk and
beat again. Fold in egg whites and pour
into graham cracker pie shell.   Refrigerate
at least 6 hrs. before serving.

Mrs. William W. Dulles, Ridgewood

GRAHAM CRACKER PIE SHELL

Yield: 9" pie

Easy   Freeze

Preparing: 5 min.

1-1/2 c. graham cracker crumbs
  (approximately 15 crackers)
1 stick butter or margarine
3 tbsp. sugar
dash cinnamon

Melt butter and mix with graham cracker
crumbs (put crackers between wax paper and
crush with rolling pin), sugar and cinnamon.
Pack into a 9 inch pie pan.

Mrs. John E. Button, Saddle River

COLD LEMON PIE

Serves: 8

"My sons' favorite dessert."

Easy   Do ahead

Preparing: 15 min.
Chilling: overnight

2 cans <u>condensed</u> milk
3 lemons
15 graham crackers
1/3 c. melted butter
1/2 pt. cream, whipped

Grate lemon rind into a large bowl, then
squeeze the juice. Add condensed milk. Whip
with an electric beater. Roll graham crackers
into even crumbs and mix with melted butter
right in a 10 inch pie plate. Spread as
pastry. Add lemon mixture and top with
whipped cream. Store in refrigerator overnight. (That is if you're possessed of
sufficient will power!)

Mrs. Theodore R. Wolf, Ridgewood

GREAT GRANDMOTHER'S LEMON MERINGUE PIE

Serves: 6

Easy   Do not freeze

Preparing: 20 min.
Baking: 30 min.
Cooling: 2 hrs.

juice of 1 lemon
rind of 1 lemon, grated
1 teacupful boiling water
1 teacupful sugar
3 tbsp. cold water
butter the size of a walnut
   (1 tbsp.)
yolks of 2 eggs
2 rounded tbsp. cornstarch
whites of 2 eggs
1/8 tsp. cream of tartar
4 tbsp. confectioners' sugar
9" cooked pie shell

Whisk egg yolks in top of double boiler.
Add lemon juice, rind, cornstarch and cold
water and blend well. Add sugar, boiling
water and butter and put over heat, stirring
until thick. Cover and cool. Beat egg
whites until stiff. Add cream of tartar and
confectioners' sugar. Beat in well. Pour
lemon mixture into cooked pie shell and cover
with meringue mixture. Bake at 225° until
brown, about 20-30 min. Cool on rack away
from drafts.

Mrs. John J. Baughan, Ridgewood

MULBERRY PLANTATION LEMON CREAM MERINGUE PIE

Serves: 8

"Calorie watchers come back for seconds when I serve this southern dessert."

Moderately difficult   Do ahead

Preparing: 30 min. plus
Baking: 40 min.
Chilling: at least 8 hrs.

4 egg whites at room temp.
1 tbsp. cold water
1/2 tsp. cream of tartar
1 c. sugar
4 egg yolks
1/2 c. sugar
2 tsp. grated lemon rind
3 tbsp. lemon juice
2 c. heavy cream
1 tbsp. sugar

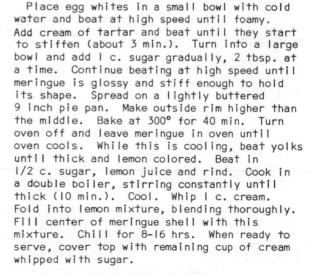

Place egg whites in a small bowl with cold
water and beat at high speed until foamy.
Add cream of tartar and beat until they start
to stiffen (about 3 min.). Turn into a large
bowl and add 1 c. sugar gradually, 2 tbsp. at
a time. Continue beating at high speed until
meringue is glossy and stiff enough to hold
its shape. Spread on a lightly buttered
9 inch pie pan. Make outside rim higher than
the middle. Bake at 300° for 40 min. Turn
oven off and leave meringue in oven until
oven cools. While this is cooling, beat yolks
until thick and lemon colored. Beat in
1/2 c. sugar, lemon juice and rind. Cook in
a double boiler, stirring constantly until
thick (10 min.). Cool. Whip 1 c. cream.
Fold into lemon mixture, blending thoroughly.
Fill center of meringue shell with this
mixture. Chill for 8-16 hrs. When ready to
serve, cover top with remaining cup of cream
whipped with sugar.

Mrs. Graham B. Conklin, Ridgewood

STRAWBERRY PIE

Serves: 6-8

Easy   Do ahead

Preparing: 15 min.
Chilling: 3 hrs.

1 cooked 9" pie shell
1 c. crushed strawberries
1 c. granulated sugar
1 tbsp. cornstarch
1 pt. fresh strawberries
1/2 c. heavy cream, whipped

Fill pie shell with fresh whole strawberries. Boil crushed strawberries, sugar and cornstarch together until transparent. Pour this syrup over the strawberries in pie shell. Chill. Top with whipped cream when serving.

Mrs. Peter H. Zecher, Ho-Ho-Kus

STRAWBERRY CHIFFON PIE

Serves: 8

"Oh, la la!"

Average   Do ahead

Preparing: 20 min.
Chilling: 4 hrs.

10 oz. pkg. frozen straw-
  berries, thawed
3 oz. pkg. strawberry gelatin
3/4 c. boiling water
2 tbsp. lemon juice
1/2 c. heavy cream, whipped
dash salt
2 egg whites
1/4 c. sugar
9" baked pie shell
whipped cream for garnish

Drain strawberries, reserving juice. Add water to juice to make 2/3 c. Dissolve gelatin in boiling water; add lemon juice and strawberry syrup. Chill until partially set. Beat mixture until soft peaks form. Fold in strawberries and whipped cream. Add salt to egg whites and beat until stiff peaks form. Fold egg whites into strawberry mixture. Pour into cool pie shell (have high edges as this filling is generous). Chill until set. Trim with whipped cream and a few berries.

Mrs. Edward E. Alley, III, Franklin Lakes

AMBROSIA PEACH PIE

Serves: 6-8

Easy   Do ahead

Preparing: 15 min.
Chilling: 1 hr.

Crust:
2 c. shredded coconut
1/3 c. melted butter or marg.

Filling:
3 large peaches, sliced
  or canned peaches, drained
1 pkg. instant coconut pudding
1 c. milk
1/2 c. heavy cream, whipped
sugar

Crust: Combine coconut and melted butter and press into a 9 inch pie pan to form a pie shell. Refrigerate 1 hr.

Filling: Fill crust with peach slices. Make coconut pudding with 1 c. milk and fold in sweetened whipped cream. Cover peaches. Chill.

Mrs. Charles R. Yennie, Allendale

COUNTRY APPLE PIE (Blueberry, too)

Serves: 6-8

"Great as either an apple or blueberry pie."

Average   Freeze

Preparing: 15 min.
Baking: 1 hr.

5 c. sliced apples
3/4 c. sugar
4 tbsp. flour
1/4 tsp. salt
1/2 tsp. cinnamon
1 c. heavy cream
1 tbsp. sugar
1/4 tsp. cinnamon
9" uncooked pie shell

Line uncooked pie shell with thinly sliced apples. Mix together sugar, flour, salt, cinnamon and cream and pour over apples. Sprinkle 1 tbsp. sugar and 1/4 tsp. cinnamon mixed together over the top of pie. Bake at 400° for 50-60 min.

With Blueberries: Use 4 c. berries and 2/3 c. sugar with all other ingredients the same. Bake at 400° for 35-45 min.

Mrs. Louis C. Clelland, Jr., Saddle River

APPLE PIE TOPPING

Yield: 1 pie top

"A different way to make a good pie even more delicious."

Easy   Do ahead

Preparing: 5 min.
Baking: 5 min.
Cooling: 1 hr.

1 hot apple pie (2 crust)
4 tbsp. butter
1/2 c. brown sugar, packed
2 tbsp. cream
1/2 c. chopped pecans

Melt butter in a small saucepan. Stir in brown sugar and cream. Heat slowly to boiling. Remove from heat and stir in pecans. Spread over the top of hot pie. Bake at 400° for 5 min. or until topping bubbles and crust is glazed. Cool about 1 hr. before serving.

Mrs. Richard C. Baxter, Ridgewood

BANANA CREAM PIE

Serves: 6

"A child's delight - something she can do by herself."

Easy   Do ahead

Preparing: 10 min.
Chilling: 1 hr.

9" baked pie shell
1 or 2 bananas
1 pkg. instant pudding
  (banana cream or vanilla)
1-1/2 to 2 c. milk
  (use pudding directions)
whipped cream

Prepare instant pudding according to package directions. Layer banana slices and pudding in pie shell, ending with pudding. Cool at least 1 hr. in refrigerator. Just before serving, garnish with whipped cream.

Mrs. Richard D. Major, Allendale

BLUEBERRY CREAM PIE

Serves: 6

"Easy and so fattening!"

Easy   Do ahead   Preparing: 10 min.
                                                    Chilling: 3 hrs.

1 can condensed milk (14 oz.)
1 box frozen blueberries or
  1 pt. fresh blueberries
1/4 c. lemon juice
9" pie shell, baked

Combine lemon juice and condensed milk; stir until thick. Stir in berries and pour into a baked pie shell. Chill.

Mrs. Edward E. Alley, III, Franklin Lakes

BLUEBERRY PIE

Serves: 6

"A great old-fashioned pie."

Easy   Freeze   Preparing: 30 min.
                                                    Baking: 45 min.

pastry for 9" two-crust pie
2 c. fresh blueberries
3/4 c. sugar
1/2 c. coarse dried bread
  crumbs
1 tbsp. lemon juice
dash salt
1/4 tsp. nutmeg
2 tbsp. butter

Line a 9 inch pie pan with the bottom crust. Mix remaining ingredients and pour into pie. Dot with butter. Cover with top pie crust. Dampen edges and crimp well. Bake at 400° for 45 min.

Mrs. Bessie Mae Coleman, Ridgewood

PUMPKIN PIE

Serves: 6

"A wonderful dessert for Thanksgiving or anytime in the fall."

Easy   Do ahead   Preparing: 10 min.
                                                    Baking: 50 min.

1-1/2 c. canned pumpkin
  (I use Libby's)
1-1/2 c. evaporated milk
3/4 c. sugar
1 tsp. ginger
1/2 to 2 tsp. cinnamon
  (depending on your taste)
1/2 tsp. salt
2 eggs, well beaten
9" unbaked pie shell

Mix all ingredients together and pour into unbaked pie shell. Vary cinnamon according to your personal taste. Bake at 375° for about 50 min. or until a silver knife inserted in the center comes out clean. Do not overbake.

Mrs. L. R. Hines, Ridgewood

CHEESECAKE PIE

Serves: 6-8

"Melts in your mouth!"

Average   Freeze

Preparing: 15 min.
Baking: 30 min.
Chilling: 2 hrs.

9" graham cracker pie shell
  (see page 248)

Filling:
4 eggs
1/2 c. sugar
1 tsp. vanilla
4 3-oz pkgs. cream cheese

Topping:
1 c. sour cream
4 tbsp. sugar
1 tsp. vanilla

Filling: Beat eggs until lemon colored, add sugar and beat well. Add vanilla and cream cheese. Beat until smooth and creamy and pour into pie shell. Bake at 375° for 20 min. or until set like custard. Remove from oven and cool 10 min.

Topping: Mix sour cream, sugar and vanilla. Spread over pie and return to oven and bake at 400° for 8 min. Chill before serving.

Mrs. John E. Button, Saddle River

CRACKER PIE

Serves: 4-6

"So different from what you would expect from the ingredients."

Easy   Freeze

Preparing: 15 min.
Baking: 30 min.

12 single saltines
1 c. white sugar
1/2 tsp. baking powder
1/2 to 3/4 c. chopped nuts
3 egg whites, beaten stiff
2 tbsp. butter

Put the butter in a 9 inch pie pan and place in a 350° oven to melt. Mix together crumbled saltines, sugar, nuts and baking powder. Fold egg whites into the mixture. Bake at 350° for 25-30 min. Cool. Serve alone or with ice cream, whipped cream or custard sauce.

Mrs. John D. Dorsey, Ridgewood

SHOO-FLY PIE

Serves: 6

"Typical Pennsylvania Dutch dish served for breakfast or dessert."

Average   Freeze

Preparing: 20 min.
Baking: 25 min.

3/4 c. sifted flour
1/2 c. light brown sugar
1/8 tsp. nutmeg
1/8 tsp ground cloves
1/2 tsp. cinnamon
1/4 tsp. salt
2 tbsp. butter
1 egg yolk, well beaten
1/3 c. light molasses
1-1/2 tsp. baking soda
2/3 c. boiling water
8" unbaked pie shell

Sift the first six ingredients together. Cut in butter or shortening with 2 knives or pastry blender until mixture resembles cornmeal. Combine egg yolk, molasses and baking powder that have been dissolved in boiling water. Place alternating layers of flour mixture and liquid mixture in the pie shell having flour mixture as a base and top. Bake at 450° for 10 min., then at 350° for 15 min. or until set.

Mrs. Ralph B. Metzger, Ridgewood

PECAN PIE

Serves: 6

"A marvelous, easy, true pecan pie."

Easy   Freeze   Preparing: 10 min.
Baking: 40 min.

1/2 c. sugar
1/2 c. brown sugar
1/4 c. butter, melted
1/2 c. corn syrup
3 eggs, well beaten
1 c. pecan halves
9" unbaked pie shell

Combine sugars, melted butter and syrup. Add beaten eggs and pecans. Pour into pie shell. Bake at 375° for 40 min.

Mrs. William W. W. Knight, Ridgewood

REAL SOUTHERN PECAN PIE

Serves: 6

"Deadly rich, but oh! so great. A light pie with delicious flavor."

Easy   Freeze   Preparing: 15 min.
Baking: 50 min.
Setting: 3 hrs.

2 eggs, well beaten
1 c. white sugar
1 c. white corn syrup
1/8 lb. butter, melted
1/4 tsp. salt
1 c. pecan meats, chopped
a few pecan halves
9" uncooked pie shell
vanilla ice cream

Preheat oven to 400°. Mix eggs with sugar, syrup, butter, salt and chopped pecans. Pour into pie shell and decorate with pecan halves. Bake at 400° for 15 min. Reduce heat to 350° and bake for 35 min. more. Serve with vanilla ice cream after letting pie stand at room temperature for a few hours.

Mrs. William L. Bradford, Wyckoff

PECAN CHESS PIE

Serves: 6

"Exactly as my mother made it."

Easy   Do ahead   Preparing: 10 min.
Baking: 45 min.

a generous half stick butter
1 c. brown sugar
2 eggs
1/4 tsp. salt
9" uncooked pie shell
1 c. pecan halves

Put butter in a saucepan with sugar and salt and melt over low heat, stirring all the while. Remove from heat; add well beaten eggs. Beat mixture well. Put in uncooked pie shell. Bake at 325° for about 45 min. or until done. Cover with pecan halves before serving. Cut and serve while warm.

Mrs. H. R. Chace, New York City

254

CHESS PIE

Serves: 6-8

"This is very southern and very delicious. Rich and always a hit."

Easy   Freeze   Preparing: 5 min.
                                           Baking: 40 min.

9" unbaked pie shell
1 c. light brown sugar
1/2 c. sugar
1 rounded tsp. flour
1 stick butter, melted
2 eggs
1/2 egg shell milk (2 tbsp.)
1 tsp. vanilla
whipped cream

Mix together dry ingredients and add to melted butter. Mix with a fork. Add eggs, milk and vanilla and whip with a fork. Pour into pie shell. Bake at 325° for about 40 min. Allow to cool. Top with whipped cream when serving.

Mrs. James D. Patton, Saddle River

CHOCOLATE PIE

Serves: 10

"If you have chocolate lovers in your family, be sure to make two!"

Easy   Freeze   Preparing: 10 min.
                                           Chilling: 4 hrs.

2/3 c. butter or margarine
1 c. confectioners' sugar
3 eggs, well beaten
2 sq. unsweetened chocolate
1/3 c. semisweet chocolate bits
9" graham cracker pie shell
1 c. heavy cream, whipped

Cream butter and sugar together. Beat until light. Blend in eggs and beat well. Add both chocolates which have been melted together and beat until smooth and even-colored. Pour into chilled graham pie shell. Chill 3-4 hrs. or overnight. Just before serving, decorate with whipped cream and shavings of unsweetened chocolate. Pure calories, but oh! so good.

Mrs. Philip M. Johnson, Ridgewood

CHOCOLATE ANGEL PIE

Serves: 6-8

"I have this dessert often and it is always a big hit."

Easy   Do ahead   Preparing: 30 min.
                                           Baking: 50 min.
                                       Chilling: 2 hrs.

2 egg whites
1/8 tsp. cream of tartar
1/8 tsp. salt
1/2 c. sifted granulated sugar
1/2 c. finely chopped walnuts
1/2 tsp. vanilla

Filling:
4 oz. German sweet chocolate
   (I use Baker's)
3 tbsp. water
1 c. heavy cream, whipped
1 tsp. vanilla

Beat egg whites with cream of tartar and salt until foamy. Add sugar slowly and beat until stiff peaks form. Fold in nuts and vanilla. Spread in a greased 8 inch pie pan. Build up sides 1/2 inch above pan. Bake at 300° for 50 min. Cool.

Filling: Melt chocolate and water over low heat, stirring constantly. Cool until it is thick. Add vanilla and fold in whipped cream. Pile into shell. Chill at least 2 hrs. before serving.

Mrs. Paul A. Vermylen, Hillsdale, N.J.

CHOCOLATE VELVET CREAM PIE

Serves: 10-12

"Elegant! I always have one in the freezer."

Easy   Freeze

Preparing: 20 min.
Baking: 10 min.
Chilling: 3 hrs.

Crust:
1 box chocolate wafers
1/3 c. margarine

Filling:
8 oz. cream cheese
1/2 c. sugar
1 tsp. vanilla
2 egg yolks
6 oz. semisweet chocolate
2 egg whites
1 c. heavy cream, whipped
3/4 c. pecans, chopped

Crust: Crush chocolate wafers finely to make 1-1/2 c. of crumbs. Combine with melted margarine and press onto bottom of a 9 inch spring pan. Bake at 325° for 10 min.

Filling: Soften the cream cheese and add 1/4 c. sugar and vanilla mixing until well blended. Stir in beaten egg yolks and chocolate which has been melted. Beat egg whites until soft peaks form. Gradually beat in 1/4 c. sugar. Fold into chocolate mixture. Fold whipped cream and pecans into the mixture. Pour over the crumbs. Freeze.

Mrs. Michael O. Albl, Midland Park

CHOCOLATE WHIPPED CREAM PIE

Serves: 8

" A simple, delicious pie not unlike a Grasshopper Pie."

Easy   Freeze

Preparing: 15 min.
Chilling: 4 hrs.

17 thin chocolate wafers
1/4 c. melted butter or marg.
16 large marshmallows
1/3 c. hot milk
1 pt. whipping cream

Crush chocolate wafers and mix with butter. Press into a 9 inch pie pan, saving some for the topping. Melt the marshmallows in milk over a low flame, stirring constantly. Cool. Fold in whipped cream and pour the filling into the pie shell. Chill several hours before serving. Sprinkle remaining chocolate crumbs on top of pie.

Mrs. Robert K. Upham, Ridgewood

FRENCH SILK CHOCOLATE PIE

Serves: 6

"This is a rich, but truly French pastry."

Easy   Do not freeze

Preparing: 15 min.
Chilling: 2 hrs.

8" baked pie shell
1/2 c. butter
3/4 c. sugar
2 oz. unsweetened chocolate,
  melted
1 tsp. vanilla
2 eggs
heavy cream, whipped
walnuts
  or
chocolate shavings

Cream butter. Gradually add sugar in mixer. Blend in melted chocolate when it is fairly cool. Add vanilla. Add eggs, one at a time, beating 5 min. at medium speed after each egg. Turn into cooled, baked pie shell. Chill at least 2 hrs. before serving. Cover with whipped cream and either chopped walnuts or chocolate shavings before serving.

Mrs. James R. Toombs, Ridgewood

GRASSHOPPER PIE

Serves: 8

Easy   Freeze

Preparing: 15 min.
Freezing: 3 hrs.

16 cream-filled chocolate
  cookies (I use Hydrox)
4 tbsp. butter, melted

Crush cookies and add to melted butter. Mold into the bottom of a buttered 9 inch pie plate and freeze to set.

Filling:
24 marshmallows
2/3 c. milk
2 oz. green creme de menthe
1 oz. white creme de cocoa
1 c. heavy cream, whipped

Filling: Melt marshmallows in milk in a double boiler. When melted, remove from heat and cool. When cold, add liqueurs. Fold in whipped cream. Place in crust that is well set and sprinkle with a few cookie crumbs on top. Freeze until ready to serve.

Miss Gertrude Rowbatham, Canton, Mass.

FUDGE SUNDAE PIE

Serves: 10-12

"Can be made months ahead. Oh, so rich!"

Easy   Freeze

Preparing: 20 min.
Freeze: 2 hrs.

1 pkg. vanilla wafers
6-oz. chocolate bits
1 c. evaporated milk
1/4 tsp. salt
1 c. miniature marshmallows
1 pt. vanilla ice cream
1/2 c. chopped nutmeats

Line a deep 9 inch pie pan or round cake pan with vanilla wafers (bottom and sides). Place chocolate bits, milk and salt in a heavy pan and melt over low heat, stirring constantly until all bits melt. Add marshmallows and allow these to melt. Take off heat and cool. Spoon vanilla ice cream over cookies in pan and add one half the chocolate mixture which has been cooled. Add another layer of ice cream and then a layer of chocolate mixture. Sprinkle with nutmeats. Put in freezer. Stores well.

Mrs. Martin Hoeksema, Ridgewood

ICE CREAM PIE

Serves: 8

"Very easy and liked by all. Can't fail!"

Easy   Freeze

Preparing: 20 min.
Freezing: 2 hrs.

3 tbsp. butter
6 oz. chocolate bits
2 c. Rice Krispies
1 qt. ice cream
  (chocolate chip mint or
   strawberry)
a few strawberries (if desired)

Melt butter and chocolate bits over hot water. Add Rice Krispies and mix well. Line an 8 inch pie shell with mixture and place in refrigerator to set. Fill with ice cream and freeze until needed. Remove from freezer 10 to 15 min. before serving. Top with chocolate shavings if using chocolate chip mint ice cream. Use sliced strawberries if using strawberry ice cream.

Mrs. Adrian B. Van Riper, Ridgewood

Pie Productions

Excellent readymade pie crusts - regular, chocolate and graham cracker - are available in most grocery stores. The mixes are also very good.

Roll pie crust in wax paper. Turn upside down over pie plate; roll off wax paper.

Put another pie plate on top of crust when baking pie shell so that it does not bubble up.

When making a baked, single crust, prick well with a fork so it does not bubble up.

To prevent a deep-dish pie from bubbling over, turn a custard cup upside down in the center of the dish. Pour the fruit in; top with the crust. Cup also lifts the pastry so it won't get soggy.

Two-crust pies should be frozen with no vents. They can be cut as soon as the pie thaws as it is baking.

Try adding a little cheese to the crust of an apple pie.

* A nice pie shell is made by mixing 1-1/2 c. gingersnap crumbs with 6 tbsp. butter and a bit of confectioners' sugar. Chill 1 hour before serving. Also try hydrox cookies (18 cookies plus 4 tbsp. butter) or vanilla wafers for an interesting variation.

Pies will be brown and glossy if brushed with milk before baking.

Never use all butter in pastries - it will be tough.

To measure shortening, fill cup with water less the amount desired. Add shortening. Pour out water.

Too much moisture in pastry dough will make it tough and the pie will steam instead of bake.

Custard-base pies (pumpkin, too) may be made ahead and frozen unbaked. A frozen 8" pie will bake in 1 hr. at 400°.

Always remove refrigerator pies from the refrigerator 20 min. before serving to remove the chill from the crust.

To prevent fresh pared apples from discoloring, submerge them about 1 min. in cold water with a little lemon juice added to it.

* For perfect non-weeping meringue on your pie, use 3 egg whites, 1/4 tsp. cream of tartar, 3 tbsp. sugar and 1/2 tsp. vanilla. Beat eggs at room temperature with cream of tartar until foamy. Gradually add sugar until stiff and glossy. Put meringue on pie and seal all edges. Cool away from drafts after cooking about 8-10 min. at 400°. If you want an extra high meringue, add 1/2 tsp. baking powder along with the cream of tartar.

Cookies and Squares

SWEDISH BUTTER COOKIES

Yield: 12 doz.

"Be sure you have a lot of time; it is easy, but makes a huge amount."

Easy   Freeze   Preparing: 10 min.
Baking: 12 min. per batch

1 lb. butter
1/2 lb. lard
pinch salt
1/2 pkg. confectioners' sugar
4-5 c. flour

Mix all ingredients together and add enough flour to bind dough together so it handles well and can be made into small balls without sticking to the hands. Form small balls and place on ungreased cookie sheet. Bake at 375° for 10-12 min. These will keep well for weeks in a cookie jar or tin. Decorate with colored sprinkles, if desired.

Mrs. Robert C. Nienaber, Ridgewood

SHORTBREAD COOKIES

Yield: 3 doz.

"Makes a wonderful Christmas cookie, especially when decorated."

Easy   Freeze   Preparing: 15 min.
Baking: 15 min.

4 hard cooked egg yolks
1/2 lb. butter
1/2 c. sugar
2-1/2 c. flour

Cream the yolks and butter, adding sugar slowly. Cream well. Add flour and work with hand until the dough is shining and ready to roll. Flour board lightly and roll dough out 1/8-inch thick using only part of the dough at a time. Cut out with cookie cutters or small juice glass. Put on a greased cookie sheet and bake at 325° for 15 min. or until lightly browned. Cool on rack. These will keep well for two weeks if stored in a tightly covered tin.

Mrs. L. P. Schultz, Allendale

NO-BAKE COOKIES

Yield: 3-4 doz.

"Children's special. Peanut butter and cocoa, almost a candy."

Easy   Freeze   Preparing: 10 min.

2 c. sugar
4 tbsp. cocoa
1/2 c. milk
1/2 c. margarine
1/2 c. peanut butter
1 tsp. vanilla
2-1/2 c. quick oats

In a large saucepan bring the sugar, cocoa, milk and margarine to a boil. Cook for 1-1/2 min. Add the peanut butter and vanilla. Mix well. Pour this mixture over the quick oats. Drop by teaspoonfuls onto wax paper. If you desire a flat cookie, pat it down while warm. Store in a cool place.

Mrs. Martin Hoeksema, Ridgewood

CHINESE COOKIE CONFECTIONS

Yield: 3 doz.

"These can be served as a candy or as a cookie- Delicious!"

Very Easy   Freeze   Preparing: 15 min.
                                                 Chilling: 30 min.

12 oz. butterscotch bits
2 c. chow mein noodles
1 c. dry roasted peanuts
  (without skins)

Melt bits over hot, not boiling, water. Remove from heat and stir in noodles and nuts. Drop by teaspoonfuls onto a cookie sheet covered with wax paper. Refrigerate until set. Store in a tightly covered tin in the refrigerator. Will keep several weeks without freezing; or will freeze.
These may also be made with a mixture of half chocolate and half butterscotch bits for a different flavor.

Mrs. Jack A. James, Ridgewood

OATMEAL CRISP COOKIES

Yield: 6 doz.

"A truly great cookie."

Easy   Freeze   Preparing: 10 min.
                                                  Chilling: 1 hr.
                                                  Baking: 12-15 min.

1 c. butter or margarine
2 tbsp. water
2 tbsp. maple pancake syrup
1 c. flour
1 c. sugar
1/2 tsp. soda
1 tsp. baking powder
2-1/2 c. quick oatmeal
  (not instant)
1/2 c. sugar for rolling

Melt shortening with water. Add syrup. Sift dry ingredients together and add oatmeal to dry ingredients, mixing very thoroughly. Combine butter mixture with the dry ingredients and chill. Form into 1 inch balls and roll in sugar. Place on an ungreased cookie sheet and flatten slightly. Bake at 350° for 12-15 min. Remove from sheet immediately and cool on a rack.

Mrs. James W. Allred, Ridgewood

TORTE COOKIES

Yield: 2 doz.

"Great for 'CARE' packages - pack easily for mailing and arrive well."

Easy   Freeze   Preparing: 20 min.
                                                  Baking: 30 min.

1 c. brown sugar
6 tbsp. flour
1/2 c. melted butter
1/2 tsp. salt
2 eggs
1 tsp. baking powder
1 tsp. vanilla
1 c. dates, cut up
1/2 c. chopped nuts

Mix all ingredients in the order given and spread in a greased 8x12 inch Pyrex pan. Bake at 350° for 30 min.

Mrs. Samuel D. Koonce, Ridgewood

DREAMS

Yield: 5 doz.

"Here's the stuff that dreams are made of! Nice at Christmas."

Easy   Freeze   Preparing: 30 min.
                                                  Baking: 30 min.

1 c. sweet butter
3/4 c. sugar
2 tsp. vanilla
1 tsp. baking powder
2 c. flour
35 blanched almonds
  (split in half)

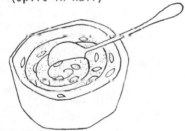

Brown butter slightly in a heavy pan and pour into a bowl. Cool in refrigerator. Split almonds by blanching them in boiling water for a few minutes. They will then split easily with a sharp knife. Add sugar to butter and stir until fluffy. Add vanilla then flour and baking powder which have been sifted together. Work dough until smooth. Roll into small marble-sized balls. Place on a buttered baking sheet. Insert an almond half upright in each cookie so that only the point of the almond sticks out. Bake at 250° until golden, about 30 min. These cookies will hold their ball-like shape. Improve even more with storing.

Mrs. Fred W. Vinroot, Ridgewood

NUT PUFFS

Yield: 3 doz.

"Almost a candy. Especially nice at Christmastime."

Easy   Do ahead   Preparing: 15 min.
                                                  Baking: 30 min.

1 c. pecans, finely chopped
  (or other nuts)
1/2 c. butter
2 tbsp. sugar
1 tsp. vanilla
1 c. flour
confectioners' sugar

Cream butter and sugar with vanilla. Add flour and mix well. Stir in nuts. Form into marble-sized balls and place on a cookie sheet. Bake at 325° for 30 min. As soon as removed from the oven roll in confectioners' sugar. This will form almost a glaze.

Mrs. Ernest R. L. Zellweger, Saddle River

COOKIES WITH BAKED-ON FROSTING

Yield: 4-5 doz.

"These come out of the oven all iced."

Easy   Do ahead   Preparing: 15 min.
                                                    Baking: 20 min.

1/2 c. shortening
  (I use Crisco)
1 c. sugar
2 eggs, well beaten
1/2 tsp. vanilla
1/2 tsp. salt
1-1/2 c. flour
1 tsp. baking powder

Frosting:
1 egg white, beaten stiff
1 c. brown sugar
1/2 tsp. vanilla
1/2 - 3/4 c. chopped nuts

Cream shortening and sugar together. Add eggs, vanilla and salt. Sift flour with baking powder and add to other mixture. Spread 1/4 inch thick on a greased cookie sheet with sides (approximately 15 x 10 inches).

Frosting: Fold brown sugar into stiffly beaten egg white and add vanilla. Spread evenly on the uncooked batter. Sprinkle with chopped nuts. Bake at 325° for 20 min. Cut into small squares while warm.

Mrs. Philip E. Sweeny, Ridgewood

CHOCOLATE TOP OATMEAL SQUARES

Yield: 4 doz.

"A rich, easy, brownie-like goodie."

Easy   Freeze   Preparing: 15 min.
                                                    Baking: 20 min.

1 c. butter
1/2 c. light brown sugar
1/2 c. granulated sugar
2 egg yolks
1 c. sifted flour
1 c. rolled oats
6 oz. milk chocolate bar
2 tbsp. butter
1/2 c. chopped nuts

Cream butter and sugar thoroughly. Beat in egg yolks. Add flour and rolled oats and mix well. Spread in a well greased and floured 13x9 inch pan (or two 8 inch square pans) and bake at 350° for 20 min. only. No longer. Cool 10 min. Melt chocolate bar with butter and spread over cooled cookie layer. Sprinkle with nuts. Cut in 1-1/2 inch squares.

Mrs. Henry B. Douglas, Saddle River

FLAKY CRESCENTS

Yield: 4-6 doz.

"Marvelous with coffee or tea."

Easy   Freeze part   Preparing: 20 min.
                                                    Chilling: overnight
                                                    Baking: 25 min.

1/2 lb. cream cheese
1/2 lb. butter
2 tsp. sugar
2 c. flour
confectioners' sugar

Fillings:
sugar and cinnamon
coconut
nuts
raisins

Cream butter and cheese. Add sugar and flour and mix well. Form into three balls and refrigerate overnight. Next day roll each ball on a floured board to about 1/8 inch thick. Cut into triangles about 2-3 inches per side. Fill with one of the fillings and roll in a cornucopia shape. Bake on a cookie sheet at 350° for 20-25 min. After baking sprinkle with confectioners' sugar.

Mrs. Charles Chotiner, Fair Lawn

MERINGUE COOKIES

Yield: 2-1/2 doz.

"Quick and easy as long as you don't have to use your oven for 6 hours."

Easy   Do ahead   Preparing: 10 min.
Baking: 6 hrs.

2 egg whites
3/4 c. sugar
6 oz. chocolate bits

Preheat oven to 350°. Beat egg whites stiff. Beat in sugar very slowly. Fold in chocolate bits. Drop by teaspoonfuls onto a cookie sheet covered with wax paper. Place in oven. Shut oven door and immediately turn off oven heat. Don't open the door. Leave overnight or at least 6 hrs.

Mrs. Ian B. MacCallum, Ridgewood

WALNUT SPICE KISSES

Yield: 2 doz.

"Spicy, easy, and delectable."

Easy   Do ahead   Preparing: 15 min.
Baking: 35 min.

2 egg whites
1/2 c. sugar
2 tsp. cinnamon
1/4 tsp. nutmeg
1/4 tsp. cloves, ground
1 c. finely ground walnuts
2 dashes salt

Beat egg whites with salt until stiff. Gradually add sugar which has been mixed with spices. Fold in nuts. Arrange by teaspoonfuls on a well greased cookie sheet. Bake at 250° for 35-40 min. Keep in a tight container.

Mrs. Willard R. Harer, Glenside, Pa.

CHRISTMAS HOLLY COOKIES

Yield: 3 doz.

"Christmas could not really come in our house without these!"

Average   Freeze   Preparing: 15 min.
Baking: 20 min.
Decorating: 30 min.

1/2 c. prepared shortening
1 c. brown sugar
1 egg, well beaten
1/2 c. milk
1/2 tsp. soda
1/4 tsp. salt
2 sq. chocolate
1 c. chopped nuts
1 tsp vanilla
1-3/4 c. flour

Icing:
boiling water
confectioners' sugar
green food coloring
cinnamon drops

Cream shortening and sugar. Add egg and beat mixture until creamy. Sift flour, soda and salt together. Add alternately with milk. Add melted chocolate, nuts and vanilla. Drop by heaping teaspoonfuls onto greased cookie sheet. Bake at 350° for 15-20 min. Cool well before decorating.

Decorating: Combine a little boiling water with confectioners' sugar to make an icing of spreading consistency. Tint green with food coloring. Place small quantity of icing on each cookie and spread to form a holly leaf using the tip of a toothpick. Add cinnamon drops for berries. These can be eaten all year round, undecorated.

Mrs. Carey J. Chamberlin, Jr., Royal Oak, Mich.

263

SAND TARTS

"The kind grandma used to make."

Easy   Freeze

Preparing: 15 min.
Chilling: 1 hr.
Baking: 15 min.

2/3 c. shortening
  (I use Crisco)
1-1/4 c. sugar
2 eggs
3 c. flour
1-1/2 tsp. salt
2 tsp. baking powder
1 tsp. vanilla

Cream shortening, sugar and eggs together.
Add vanilla. Mix and sift flour, salt and
baking powder. Add flour mixture to egg-
sugar mixture. Chill. Roll thin on floured
board and cut into shapes with cookie cutters.
Brush with egg white and sprinkle with sugar,
then dust with cinnamon and decorate each
with an almond in the center. Bake at 325°
for 12-15 min.

Topping:
1 egg white, beaten frothy
cinnamon
5-6 doz. almonds, blanched

Mrs. Bessie Mae Coleman, Ridgewood

WALNUT DREAMS

Yield: 2-3 doz.

"A favorite of everyone; so easy to make."

Easy   Do ahead

Preparing: 15 min.
Baking: 20 min.

1/2 c. butter or shortening
1/4 c. confectioners' sugar
1 c. cake flour
2 eggs, beaten
1-1/2 c. brown sugar
2 tbsp. flour
1/2 tsp. baking powder
1 c. walnuts, chopped
1/2 c. coconut

Mix together butter, confectioners' sugar
and cake flour. Spread in an 11x15 inch
pan. Mix the remaining ingredients and
spread over the first layer. Bake at 300°
for 20 min. Cut in squares while still warm.

Mrs. Louise Emery, Wayne

LEMON BARS

Serves: 10-12

"A tasty luncheon dessert and equally delicious for tea."

Average   Do ahead

Preparing: 30 min.
Baking: 45 min.

Bottom Layer:
1 c. flour
1/4 c. confectioners' sugar
1/4 c. butter, melted

Bottom Layer: Mix flour and sugar. Add
butter. Blend well and press flat and even
in an 8x8 inch pan. Bake at 350° for 20 min.
While this is baking mix the Top Layer.

Top Layer:
1 c. sugar
2 tbsp. flour
1/2 tsp. baking powder
2 eggs, beaten
3 generous tbsp. lemon juice
confectioners' sugar

Top Layer: Mix sugar, flour and baking
powder. Add beaten eggs and mix well. Add
lemon juice and mix again. Pour over crust.
Bake at 350° for 25 min. Cool a little and
cut while warm. Dust with confectioners'
sugar.

Mrs. B. F. Martin, Grosse Pointe, Mich.

CHOCOLATE REFRESHERS

Yield: 5 doz.

"Moist, rich bar cookies - and mixed right in the saucepan."

Easy   Freeze   Preparing: 20 min.
Baking: 30 min.

1-1/4 c. sifted flour
3/4 tsp. soda
1/2 tsp. salt
1-1/4 c. dates, cut (8 oz.)
3/4 c. brown sugar, packed
1/2 c. water
1/2 c. butter
6 oz. chocolate bits
2 eggs, unbeaten
1/2 c. orange juice
1/2 c. milk
1 c. walnuts, chopped

Sift flour, soda and salt together. Combine in a large saucepan the dates, brown sugar, water and butter. Cook over low heat, stirring constantly, until dates soften. Remove from heat and immediately stir in chocolate bits and unbeaten eggs. Stir well. Add dry ingredients, alternately with milk and orange juice and blend. Stir in nuts. Spread on a 15x10 inch jelly roll pan. Bake at 350° for 25-30 min. Cool and frost with Orange Glaze. Cut into 2-1/2x1 inch bars.

ORANGE GLAZE

Yield: 5 doz bars.

Easy   Freeze   Preparing: 10 min.

1-1/2 c. confectioners' sugar
2 tbsp. soft butter
1 tbsp. grated orange rind
 or lemon rind
1/2 tsp. lemon extract
 or orange extract
2 to 3 tbsp. cream
optional -
 nutmeats, cherries, fruits,
 etc.

Combine sifted sugar with butter, rind and extract. Blend in cream, a tbsp at a time until you have a good spreading consistency. Spread on Chocolate Refreshers and decorate if desired with nutmeats, candied cherries, or bits of candied fruits.

Mrs. Joseph Sage, Ramsey

TOFFEE SQUARES

Yield: 3 dozen

"Our favorite Christmas cookie."

Easy   Freeze   Preparing: 10 min.
Baking: 20 min.

1 c. butter
1 c. light brown sugar
1 egg yolk
2 c. flour
1 tsp. vanilla
3 oz. semisweet chocolate bits
1 c. finely chopped nuts

Cream butter and sugar and add egg yolk. Add flour and vanilla and mix well. Spread on a 16x11 inch sheet with sides and bake at 350° for 15-20 min. While this is baking, melt chocolate bits. Spread melted chocolate on dough while it is still hot. Sprinkle with chopped nuts. Cool slightly and cut into 2 inch squares.

Mrs. Jay B. Goerk, Ridgewood

ALMOND BARS

Yield: 2 dozen

"Delicious. Worth the time they take."

Average   Freeze   Preparing: 15 min.
                                            Cooking: 35 min.

1 c. flour
1/2 c. butter
1/4 c. confectioners' or
   brown sugar
raspberry jam

Topping:
1/2 c. butter
2/3 c. white sugar
2 eggs, well beaten
2/3 c. rice flour*
1/2 tsp. almond extract
pinch salt

Almond Icing:
1-1/2 c. confectioners' sugar
1 tsp. almond extract
1/4 c. butter
a bit of milk

*Rice flour is available at
diet stores. (Co-Op in
Ridgewood)

Mix flour, butter and sugar; pat into
bottom of 9x9 inch pan. Bake at 350° for
10 min. Remove from oven and spread with
a thin layer of raspberry jam.

Topping: Mix all topping ingredients
together, spread gently over jam layer and
bake at 375° for 25 min. until light brown.
When cool, ice with icing.

Icing: Mix together sugar, extract and
butter. Add enough milk to make it spread
easily.

Mrs. Edward W. Many, Ramsey

TWENTY-MINUTE BROWNIES

Yield: 3 doz.

"Frosted warm, right out of the oven - so quick and easy!"

Easy   Freeze   Preparing: 10 min.
                                          Baking: 20 min.

2 c. flour
2 c. sugar
1/2 tsp. salt
1 stick margarine
1 c. water
1/4 c. cocoa
1/2 c. shortening
   (I use Crisco)
1/2 c. buttermilk or sour milk*
1 tsp. baking soda
1 tsp. vanilla
2 eggs

Frosting:
1 stick margarine
1/4 c. cocoa
1/3 c. buttermilk or sour milk
1 box confectioners' sugar
optional - coconut
            chopped nuts

Sift and set aside flour, sugar and salt.
Boil together the margarine, water, cocoa and
shortening. Pour the boiled chocolate mixture
over the flour mixture and mix well. Add
buttermilk, eggs, baking soda and vanilla.
Mix well and pour into a greased and floured
11x16 inch pan (or two 9x9 inch pans). Bake
at 400° for 20 min. While brownies are
baking, boil margarine, cocoa and buttermilk.
Add sifted confectioners' sugar and frost
immediately out of the oven. If desired add
coconut or nuts to the frosting.

*To sour milk: Add 1-1/2 tbsp. vinegar or
lemon juice to 1 c. lukewarm milk. Let set
a minute or two.

Mrs. Carl Stuehrk, Leawood, Kansas

BROWNIES

Yield: 2 doz.

"A tasty way to get fat!"

Easy   Freeze

Preparing: 15 min.
Cooking: 25 or 40 min.

1/2 lb. butter
4 oz. unsweetened chocolate
4 eggs
2 c. sugar
1 c. flour
1 tsp. vanilla
pinch cinnamon
1/2 tsp. salt
optional -
  1 c. chopped nutmeats
  or raisins

In top of a deep double boiler put butter and chocolate. Melt and blend together. Turn off heat and add sugar (use only 1-1/2 c. if you want a little more chocolaty brownies). When slightly cooled, add eggs and beat well. Add scant cup of unsifted flour and beat well. Add a bit of cinnamon and real vanilla and salt. Mix well. Add chopped nuts or some raisins, if desired. Turn into a greased 9x12 inch pan. For soft-type brownies bake at 325° for 40 min.; for chewy ones, bake at 350° for 25 min.

Mrs. Richard W. Deane, Ridgewood

BLOND BROWNIES

Yield: 1 doz.

"So easy and a favorite with everyone!"

Easy   Freeze

Preparing: 20 min.
Baking: 30 min.

2 c. flour
1 tsp. baking powder
1/2 tsp. soda
1 tsp. salt
1/2 c. chopped nuts
2/3 c. butter or marg.
2 c. brown sugar, packed
2 eggs, slightly beaten
2 tsp. vanilla
6 oz. chocolate bits

Mix flour, baking powder, soda, salt and nuts together well and set aside. Melt butter in a saucepan and remove from heat. Add brown sugar to butter and cool this mixture slightly. Add eggs and vanilla to sugar mixture and then add all of this to the flour mixture, a small amount at a time. Spread in a well greased 9 inch square pan and sprinkle with chocolate bits. Bake at 325° for 25-30 min.

Mrs. Robert C. Burnet, Glen Ridge

BUTTERSCOTCH BROWNIES

Yield: 3 doz.

"Luscious. So chewy!"

Easy   Freeze

Preparing: 15 min.
Baking: 30 min.

1/4 lb. butter
2 c. light brown sugar, packed
2 eggs
1-1/2 c. sifted flour
2 tsp. baking powder
1 tsp. vanilla
1 c. chopped nuts

Melt butter over low heat in a heavy saucepan. Add brown sugar and bring to a boil. Cool for 5 to 10 min. so eggs will not cook when added (no longer or it will harden). Add eggs, one at a time, beating well after each addition. Add flour sifted with baking powder. Add vanilla and nuts. Mix well. Place in a well greased 13x9 inch pan and bake at 350° for 30 min. Do not overbake. Serve with vanilla ice cream or alone.

Mrs. Leonard R. Hines, Ridgewood

DREAM BARS
Yield: 2 doz.

"Especially good over the holidays!"

Easy   Store well   Preparing: 15 min.
                                                      Baking: 30 min. total

1/2 c. dark brown sugar
1 c. flour
1/2 c. melted butter
1 c. dark brown sugar
1 c. chopped pecans
2 eggs
1/4 tsp. salt
1/2 tsp. baking powder

Mix 1/2 c. brown sugar, flour and melted butter together and pat into a greased and floured 9x6 inch pan. Bake at 350° for 15 min. Remove from oven. Beat eggs and add remaining ingredients, mixing well. Spread over the first part and bake at 350° for 15 min. more. Cut into 1x2 inch bars when cool. These will keep in a covered tin almost indefinitely.

Mrs. H. B. Millican, Jr., Saddle River

TOFFEE-NUT BARS
Yield: 2-1/2 doz.

"A chewy bar cookie that's even better the day after it's made."

Easy   Freeze   Preparing: 15 min.
                                                      Baking: 35 min.

Bottom Layer:
1/2 c. butter or marg.
1/2 c. brown sugar
1 c. sifted flour

Topping:
2 eggs
1 c. brown sugar
1 tsp. vanilla
2 tbsp. flour
1 tsp. baking powder
1/2 tsp salt
1 c. moist shredded coconut
1 c. sliced almonds (3/4 oz.)

Bottom Layer: Cream butter and sugar together. Stir in flour. Press and flatten with hand to cover bottom of an ungreased 13x9 inch pan. Bake at 350° for 10 min.

Topping: Beat eggs well. Add sugar gradually. Stir in vanilla. Sift together the dry ingredients. Add to sugar and egg mixture. Mix coconut and nuts and add to mixture. Spread over bottom layer. Return to oven and bake at 350° for 25 min. or until topping is golden brown. Cool and cut into bars.

Mrs. Gerald F. Corcoran, Ramsey

BRANDY BALLS

Yield: 4-1/2 dozen

Easy   Do ahead   Preparing: 30 min.

2 pkgs. vanilla wafers,
   crushed
1/4 c. brandy
1/4 c. rum
1/2 c. strained honey
1 lb. ground walnuts
confectioners' sugar

Mix first five ingredients thoroughly. Form into small balls; use a level tbsp. for each ball. Roll in sugar. Store in stone jar, tightly covered. Will keep as long as six weeks.

Mrs. J. C. Bamford, Wayne

BOURBON BALLS

Yield: 2-3 dozen

"Marvelous Christmas goodie. Great with egg nog."

Ease   Freeze   Preparing: 20 min.

1 c. graham cracker crumbs
1 c. chopped pecans
2 tbsp. cocoa
1 c. confectioners' sugar
1-1/2 tbsp. white corn syrup
1/4 c. bourbon
more confectioners' sugar

Mix the first six ingredients and form into balls about the diameter of a quarter. Roll in confectioners' sugar. Freeze on a cookie sheet.

Mrs. John B. Cave, Summit

SHERRY FUDGE

Yield: 1-1/2 lbs.

"This is a smooth, rich fudge; never grainy. Always brings raves."

Easy   Freeze   Preparing: 30 min.

1 6-oz. pkg. semisweet
   chocolate bits
2 tbsp. butter
1/4 c. sherry (more, if
   sugar is hard to handle)
1 egg yolk, unbeaten
1 lb. confectioners' sugar
1 c. nutmeats, broken
optional - 1 tsp. vanilla

Melt chocolate and butter in sherry over hot, not boiling, water. Add egg yolk to sifted sugar. Add chocolate mixture to sugar and mix thoroughly. It is at this point that more sherry may need to be added. Try one tsp. first. Add nuts. Spread in 8x8 inch buttered pan or dish and after cutting into squares put into refrigerator.

Mrs. Eric H. Berg, Ridgewood

269

PEANUT BUTTER FUDGE (or Peanut Butter Cream)

Yield: 2 doz. pieces
3 cups sauce

"Children love to make (and eat) this treat."

Easy   Do ahead

Preparing: 30 min.
Chilling: 2 hrs.

2 c. sugar
1/8 tsp. salt
3/4 c. milk or cream
2 tbsp. light corn syrup
4 tbsp. peanut butter
1 tsp. vanilla

Cook sugar, salt, milk and corn syrup to 230° using candy thermometer. Cool for about 20 min. to lukewarm. Add peanut butter and vanilla. Beat until creamy. Pour into lightly buttered 8x8 inch pan. Refrigerate for about 2 hrs. and cut into squares.

To make cream: Add peanut butter and vanilla as soon as other ingredients are removed from stove. Great on ice cream.

Mr. W. Wilder Knight, II, Ridgewood

MAMIE'S MILLION DOLLAR FUDGE

Yield: 2 lbs.

Easy   Do ahead

Preparing: 15 min.
Standing: 2 hrs.

4-1/2 c. sugar
pinch salt
2 tbsp. butter
1 tall can evaporated milk
12 oz. semisweet chocolate bits
12 oz. German sweet chocolate
1 pt. marshmallow cream (2 jars)
2 c. nutmeats

Blend first four ingredients; heat and boil 6 min. Meanwhile, combine last four ingredients in bowl. Pour boiling syrup over chocolate, marshmallow cream and nutmeats; beat until chocolate is melted. Pour into 8x8 inch baking pan and let stand a few hours before cutting. Store in tin box.

Mrs. Albert F. Lilley, Allendale

UNCOOKED PEANUT BUTTER CANDY

Yield: about 1 lb.

"A wonderful candy for children as it has no sugar - only honey."

Easy   Stores well   Preparing: 10 min.

1/2 c. non-hydrogenated peanut butter*
1/2 c. natural honey
1 c. powdered milk

Mix peanut butter and honey together. Stir in 3/4 to 1 c. milk powder. Turn onto buttered wax paper and press to thickness of 3/4 inch. Cut into cubes.

Variations: Add 1/2 c. nutmeats (any kind). Or, add 1/2 to 1 c. coconut and 1 tsp. vanilla, make into balls and roll in coconut, confectioners' sugar or crushed nuts. Use as a stuffing for prunes, dates, figs, etc., or press between halves of dried apricots, peaches, nuts, etc. Make into rolls, chill and cut into slices. This candy should always be kept in the refrigerator.

*Available from a health food store

Mr. Stephen Cline, Franklin Lakes

VANILLA CARAMELS

Yield: 10 dozen

"Marvelous!"

Easy   Do ahead   Preparing: 5 min.
                                                 Cooking: 1 hr.

1 c. sugar
1 c. light corn syrup
1/4 c. butter
1/8 tsp. salt
1 c. light cream
1 tsp. vanilla

Combine all ingredients except vanilla. Place over low heat and bring slowly to the boiling point, stirring frequently. Cook slowly (to avoid curdling) to 250° on a candy thermometer or until firm ball forms in cold water. Remove from heat and add vanilla. Pour into a greased 9x9 inch pan and cool. Cut into 1/2 inch cubes and wrap individually.

Mrs. Thomas M. Brown, Nashville, Tenn.

SESAME CANDY (Benne Candy)

Yield: 2 dozen

Easy   Do ahead   Preparing: 30 min.

1 lb. brown sugar
1 tbsp. butter
1/2 c. milk
1 tbsp. vinegar
1-1/2 c. sesame seeds*
1 tsp. vanilla

Toast seeds in 350° oven until light tan. Watch carefully; they burn quickly. Boil together first four ingredients. When beginning to thread, remove from stove and beat in seeds and vanilla until creamy. Drop 1 tsp. at a time on greased pan and let cool.

*Available at spice counter

Mrs. William T. Knight, III, Saddle River

TOASTED ALMOND CRUNCH

Yield: 1 lb.

"The yummiest of yummy candies!"

Complicated, but   Stores well   Cooking: 30 min.
  not difficult

1 c. butter or margarine
1 c. sugar
3 tbsp. water
1 tbsp. light corn syrup
3/4 c. toasted slivered
  almonds
3 sq. semisweet chocolate

Melt butter in medium-size heavy saucepan. Stir in sugar and heat very slowly, stirring constantly, just until the sugar dissolves. Remove from heat. Slowly stir in water and corn syrup. Heat, stirring constantly until boiling. Cook over medium heat, stirring often and wiping sugar crystals from side of pan with a moistened pastry brush until candy reaches 300° on a candy thermometer (hard, but not brittle, stage). Remove from heat at once. Stir in 1/2 c. of almonds. Pour into buttered 9 inch square pan. Cool. Melt chocolate over warm water. Spread evenly over candy and sprinkle with 1/4 c. almonds. Break into bite-size pieces. Store in tightly covered tin in refrigerator. Will keep 3 to 4 weeks.

*Mrs. Albert J. Morrison
Maichingen, W. Germany*

CRUNCHY ENGLISH TOFFEE

Yield: 2 lbs.

"A snap to make and delicious!"

Easy   Freeze

Cooking: about 30 min.
Refrigerating: 30 min.

1 lb. butter or margarine
1-1/4 c. sugar
2 c. sliced almonds
   (2 3/4 oz. pkgs.)
2 4-oz. bars milk chocolate
1 c. walnut bits

Melt butter in large pan. Add sugar and cook over high heat, stirring constantly with a wooden spoon until mixture is thick and caramel color. Add almonds and stir together. Pour into large flat pan (such as a jelly-roll pan or one about 15x9 inches) and smooth out instantly. Break one chocolate bar into small pieces and distribute over the top, smoothing chocolate evenly as it melts. Sprinkle with half the walnut bits and press lightly with the palm of the hand. Place in refrigerator to cool until chocolate is firm. Lift entire piece and turn. Melt remaining chocolate over hot water and spread evenly over candy. Sprinkle with remaining walnut bits; press. Refrigerate. When chocolate is hard, break candy into irregular pieces. Try to eat just one piece!

Mrs. Gerald F. Corcoran, Ramsey

PRALINES

Yield: 2 dozen

"How to add calories in one easy bite!"

Average   Do ahead

Preparing: 30 min.

2 c. sugar
3/4 c. milk
pinch soda
pinch salt
kitchen spoon of sugar
1/3 stick butter
2 c. pecans
1 tsp. vanilla

Mix sugar and milk in large pot. In small iron skillet put one heaping kitchen spoon of sugar and caramelize (let brown while stirring). While this is on stove, put milk and sugar mixture on stove and when it begins to boil add a pinch of soda. When it bubbles up and boils again, add caramelized sugar. Cook about 7 min. When at soft-ball stage, add vanilla, butter and pecans. Remove from heat and beat. When mixture starts hardening around the edges, drop by spoonfuls onto wax paper with newspaper underneath. Place a pecan half in center of each. Let cool.

Mrs. Richard D. Jones, Mercer Island, Wash.

PEANUT BRITTLE

Yield: 1 lb.

Easy   Do ahead   Preparing: 20 min.

2 c. sugar
1 tbsp. butter
1 c. salted cocktail peanuts
 (not dry roasted; either
 Spanish or regular)

Grease generously a large shallow pan or cookie sheet. Sprinkle nuts evenly on pan. Set aside. Melt sugar in heavy iron skillet, stirring constantly. Remove from heat when all lumps disappear and sugar is a light, golden brown. Add butter and stir to dissolve. Pour over nuts on pan. As edges cool, begin pulling from sides to make sheet as thin as possible. Break into pieces.

Mrs. William T. Knight, III, Saddle River

NO-BAKE BARS

Yield: 3 dozen

"Guaranteed to put on weight!"

Easy   Do ahead   Preparing: 10 min.
                 Chilling: 1 hr.

1/2 c. sugar
1/2 c. light corn syrup
3/4 c. peanut butter
1/2 tsp. vanilla
3 c. Special K cereal
2 c. semisweet chocolate bits

Mix sugar and corn syrup; bring to a boil. Remove from heat and add peanut butter, vanilla and cereal. Spread on a greased jelly-roll pan (cookie sheet with sides) and pat out evenly with hands. Melt chocolate and spread over the top. Refrigerate. Break into bite-size pieces.

Mrs. Thomas M. Brown, Nashville, Tenn.

CINNAMON NUTS

Yield: 1 lb.

Easy   Do ahead   Preparing: 10 min.
                 Baking: 30 min.

2 c. shelled almonds and
 pecans
1 unbeaten egg white
1/2 c. sugar
2 tbsp. cinnamon

Mix nuts and egg white thoroughly. Mix cinnamon and sugar. Add to nuts. The egg white will absorb it all. Spread on an ungreased cookie sheet. Bake at 300° for 30 min. Cool and break into pieces.

Mrs. Thomas M. Brown, Nashville, Tenn.

Cookie and Candy Can-Do's

Use powdered sugar in place of flour when rolling cookies. The cookies will be a little sweeter but won't get tough.

When baking cookies and they stick to the cookie sheet, quickly run the sheet over a top burner or return to the oven for a few minutes.

When using baking paper (as in jelly rolls or on cookie sheets), do not butter the pan or the paper.

* An easy tea cake is made by slicing day-old bread into strips 3/4 by 2 inches. Spread all sides with condensed milk and cover with coconut. Toast in the oven at 325° until lightly brown.
  Sent by Mrs. Theodore R. Wolf, Ridgewood

For an attractive top to dropped cookies, press each cookie down with a fork dipped in confectioners' sugar. For a waffle effect, press a second time in the opposite direction.

For <u>very thin</u> rolled cookies, roll directly on the bottom of a greased and floured cookie sheet. Cut the dough into shapes and remove surplus dough between them.

Allow very thin cookies to cool for a minute or two before removing them from the pan. If they become too hard, reheat them quickly.

For gay seasonal cookies, make dough of any sugar cookie recipe. Roll and cut a few at a time, then decorate with paint made as follows. Blend an egg yolk with 1/4 tsp. water, divide into several custard cups, add a different food coloring to each cup to make bright colors. Paint designs directly on cookies using your imagination with small paint brushes. Add a few drops of water if coloring thickens. Do not let cookies get brown. Have fun!

Candy is best not made in hot, moist weather. It becomes sticky and sugary.

Cook candy in a very large pot. To prevent candy from boiling over, butter the inside edge to a depth of 2 inches.

Cover the pan for the first 3 min. of boiling to prevent crystals from forming.

Do not beat candies until they are cool - almost cold - for a creamy texture.

When making hard candies, gently remove from heat and allow to set for a minute or two before pouring from pan.

If candy should sugar, add a bit of water and bring to a boil again.

Etcetera

CHILE RELLENOS (Mexican Dinner)

Serves: 15

Average   Do ahead

Preparing: 30 min.
Cooking: 15 min.

10 cans whole green chiles*
  (I use Ashley's)
1/2 lb. sharp cheese, slivered
10 eggs
1/2 c. flour
oil

Separate eggs. Beat whites until stiff. Add flour to yolks and beat. Fold whites into yolk mixture. Stuff chiles with the cheese.

Dip in the egg batter. Put 1/4 inch oil in frying pan and fry chiles. Serve with tomato sauce. This can be made the day before and reheated in the oven while frying the tacos.

Sauce:
1 large can tomatoes
1 onion, chopped
1 small piece chile

Sauce: Simmer tomatoes with onions and a small piece of chile. Remove the chile before serving. Or, use a canned Mexican sauce. Serve this with quacamole (mashed avocados), tacos and refritos.

Refritos:
2 cans refried beans
onion, chopped
cheese, grated

Refritos: Heat beans with melted cheese, sprinkle with onions.

Tacos:
use canned

In the summer this is nice with a large honeydew, peeled and cut up in small pieces. Serve lots of beer.

*Available at food specialty shops such as Bloomingdale's, etc.

Mrs. William Spinrad, East Paterson

DIFFERENT LUNCHBOX SANDWICHES

Apple slices between thin slices of bread spread with deviled ham.

Liverwurst combined with celery and mayonnaise.

Hard cooked eggs and pickled beets, both finely chopped, with salt, pepper and mayonnaise.

India relish mixed with cottage cheese and salt and spread on rye bread.

Date and nut bread spread with cream cheese.

Apple butter sandwiches sprinkled with zippy grated cheese.

Baked beans mashed and mixed with pickle relish and a bit of mayonnaise on brown bread.

Quince jelly and minced ham on rye bread.

Peanut butter combined with canned applesauce and chopped celery on brown bread.

Mrs. William L. Bradford, Wyckoff

GENTLEMAN'S TIDBITS

Serves: 4

"A wonderfully different hot sandwich."

Easy   Do ahead   Preparing: 5 min.
Browning: 5 min.

4 slices boiled ham
8 slices thin white bread
butter
5 oz. Port-Salut cheese
3 tbsp. butter
3 tbsp. salad oil

Butter the bread. Cut cheese into 8 strips. On 4 slices of bread place a strip of cheese, a slice of ham and another strip of cheese. Cover with the other bread slices. Heat butter and oil in skillet on low heat. Brown on both sides. Serve piping hot.

Mr. Edwin F. Bernhardt, Cheese Shop, Ridgewood

ROLLED CHICKEN SANDWICHES

Yield: 3 dozen

Easy   Do ahead   Preparing: 15 min.
Chilling: 3 hrs.
Broiling: 3 min.

36 to 40 thin slices very
  fresh white bread,
  crusts removed
3 3-oz. pkgs. cream cheese
2 c. firmly packed, finely
  ground cooked chicken
1/2 c. finely ground celery
1/4 c. chopped parsley
1/2 c. dry white wine
1 tsp. grated onion
1 tsp. Worcestershire sauce
salt
softened butter

Have cheese at room temperature. Add chicken, celery and parsley and blend well. Gradually beat in wine, onion, Worcestershire and salt. Roll bread with rolling pin, spread with softened butter, then chicken mixture. Roll up, cover and chill.

For toasted sandwiches: Omit softened butter. Chill, then just before serving brush outside with melted butter and toast under broiler. Can be prepared and refrigerated day before.

Mrs. Richard C. Baxter, Ridgewood

HAWAIIAN SANDWICH

Serves: 4

"A good luncheon dish most women enjoy."

Easy   Do ahead   Preparing: 20 min.
Baking: 5 min.
Broiling: 2 min.

6 slices white sandwich
  bread, lightly toasted
1/2 c. Thousand Island
  dressing
1 small can crushed pineapple,
  drained
6 slices turkey roll
6 slices ham
6 slices Cheddar cheese

Set out baking sheet. Preheat oven to 350°. Place bread slices on baking sheet. Spread with Thousand Island dressing, then pineapple. Top with ham and turkey slices. Bake 5 min. Remove from oven. Place cheese slices on bread and place in broiler until cheese melts. Cut in half diagonally - 3 halves per serving. Garnish.

Mrs. Walter F. Anderson, Upper Saddle River

DAY-AFTER-THANKSGIVING SANDWICH

Serves: 4

Easy   No need to do ahead   Preparing: 5 min.
                                            Broiling: 5 min.

4 slices bread
1 c. chopped turkey or
  5-oz. can
1/2 c. grated American
  cheese
2 tbsp. mayonnaise or
  salad dressing
2 tbsp. pickle relish
2 tbsp. finely chopped
  onion
2 tbsp. finely chopped
  celery
1/4 tsp. salt
pepper to taste

Toast bread on one side. Combine remaining ingredients and spread on untoasted side of bread. Broil about 4 inches from heat 3-5 min. or until bubbly and brown. Serve hot.

Mrs. Richard C. Baxter, Ridgewood

CHEESE DREAMS

Serves: 4

"This is a favorite with men."

Easy   Part do ahead   Preparing: 10 min.
                                      Broiling: 10 min.

4 slices white bread
  (or whole wheat)
4 slices process cheese
  (I use Velveeta)
4 thick tomato slices
12 whole slices bacon
seasoned salt
dash pepper
dash basil
1 tsp. mayonnaise

Cover bread with mayonnaise. Cover with a medium thick slice of cheese. Cover all the bread. Cover with slices of tomatoes. Season well. Spread bacon slices over tomato, allowing them to spread on to the broiler rack. Put in preheated broiler. Watch. When bacon is done on one side turn and watch again. Serve at once. All but broiling can be done ahead.

Miss Jean Gillmor, Ridgewood

BOLOGNA AND CHEESWICH (Hot)

Serves: 6

"Great 'Sunday night supper' fare."

Easy   Do ahead   Preparing: 15 min.
                                 Chilling: 1 hr.
                                 Baking: 25 min.

1 lb. bulk bologna
3/4 lb. bulk Swiss cheese
1 tbsp. India relish
1 tbsp. chopped onion
1/4 c. mustard
1/3 c. mayonnaise
6 frankfurter rolls

Coarse grind bologna, cheese, relish and onion together. Add mustard and mayonnaise. Butter the rolls and fill with mixture. Wrap individually in foil and refrigerate for 1 hr. Bake, still wrapped, at 325° for 25 min.

Mrs. Reginald F. Wardley, Ridgewood

MENNONITE WHOLE STRAWBERRY JAM

Yield: 2 qts.

Easy   Do ahead

Preparing: 20 min.
Setting: overnight

1 qt. fresh firm strawberries
1 qt. sugar
1 tbsp. cold water

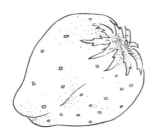

Wash and drain fruit for a short time. Place berries and sugar in a large kettle. Add cold water. Place over very slow heat until the sugar is melted. Turn heat up higher and when fruit begins to boil check the clock and boil well for exactly 10 min. Remove from heat. Skim and pour into shallow platters where fruit will not be more than 1 inch deep. Leave overnight. In the morning each berry will be lying in a delicious thick syrup. Bottle in cold, sterilized jars.

Mrs. John J. Baughan, Ridgewood

EASY SPICED PEACHES

Serves: 6-8

Easy   Do ahead

Preparing: 15 min.
Chilling: 24 hrs.

2 large cans yellow
  cling peach halves
1/2 c. vinegar
2 3" sticks cinnamon
1/4 tsp. whole allspice
1/4 c. sugar
1 tsp. whole cloves

Dressing:
3 tbsp. mayonnaise
dash milk or cream
1 tsp. orange marmalade

Drain syrup from peaches. Combine syrup with vinegar, sugar and spices. Boil 5 min. Add peach halves and simmer 5 min. Cool in covered container and put in refrigerator at least 24 hrs. Serve on watercress with the following orange-mayonnaise dressing.

Dressing: Mix together mayonnaise, milk and marmalade and serve over peaches.

Mrs. Charles R. Moog, Ridgewood

PEACHES (Relish)

Serves: 8-12

"These are a nice change from spiced apples."

Easy   Do ahead

Preparing: 10 min.
Chilling: overnight

3 cans freestone peaches
2 lemons, whole
2 c. confectioners' sugar

Drain peaches well. Place in a glass pan, hollow side up. Grind 2 whole lemons and mix with confectioners' sugar. Fill peach hollows with the mixture. Chill overnight or longer.

Mrs. B. F. Martin, Grosse Pointe, Mich.

HOT FRUIT COMPOTE

Serves: 6-8

"Adds an elegant touch to chicken. Children and grown-ups think its yummy!"

Easy   Do ahead   Preparing: 10 min.

1/4 lb. butter
1 c. brown sugar
1 tsp. curry powder
1 med. can pears
1 med. can peaches
1 med. can pineapple

Melt butter, add sugar and curry, and stir over medium heat until mushy. Drain fruit and slice. Add to the above mixture and serve warm. Can be made in advance, refrigerated and warmed slowly on top of the stove.

Mrs. William C. Bartlett, Sr., Ridgewood

ORIENTAL FRUIT COMPOTE

Serves: 6

"Easy to make and always a hit with our guests."

Easy   Do ahead   Preparing: 15 min.
                                                     Cooking: 1 hr.

1 large can pear halves
1 large can peach halves
1 med. can pineapple chunks
1 large can mandarin oranges
  (or 2 small cans)

Sauce:
3/4 c. brown sugar
1/2 c. butter, melted
1-1/2 tbsp. cornstarch
1 tsp. curry (or more)

Drain fruit well and arrange in an 8x12 inch baking dish.

Sauce: Blend all ingredients and pour over fruit. Bake about 1 hr. at 325°. Marvelous with almost any meat.

Mrs. Farrand Williamson, Ho-Ho-Kus

GRAPE CONSERVE

Yield: 8 jelly glasses
        (1/3 pint size)

"Delicious with cold meat, especially lamb."

Easy   Do ahead   Preparing: 30 min.
                                                     Cooking: 1 hr.

4 lbs. grapes (purple)
4 c. sugar
2 c. light corn syrup
3/4 c. orange juice
1/4 c. lemon juice
2 c. broken walnuts
1/4 tsp. salt

Wash grapes, remove skins, and cook pulp until soft. Sieve to remove seeds. Add skins; stir in sugar, corn syrup, orange juice and lemon juice. Boil rapidly for 50 to 60 min. Add walnuts and salt. Pour into hot, sterilized jars; paraffin at once. Cool; cover.

Mrs. George M. Griffith, Franklin Lakes

GREEN TOMATO RELISH

Yield: 3 pints

Easy   Do ahead

Preparing: 15 min.
Cooking: 30 min.

2 qts. chopped green
  tomatoes
2 green peppers, chopped
2 c. chopped onions
1 pt. pickling vinegar
1/4 c. salt
3 c. sugar
1 box pickling spices

Put pickling spices into a small bag. Mix all ingredients and put, with the spice bag, into a 6 qt. Dutch oven. Bring to boiling point. Simmer for 30 min., stirring occasionally. Remove spice bag. Put into jars while hot. Jars need not be sterilized, but should be washed in the dishwasher just before filling.

Mrs. William W. W. Knight, Ridgewood

CORN RELISH

Yield: 4 pints

Average   Do ahead

Preparing: 30 min.
Cooking: 40 min.

10 ears of corn
1-1/2 c. chopped celery
3 c. chopped cabbage
2 c. chopped onion
1 chopped green pepper
1 qt. pickling vinegar
1 c. sugar
1/2 c. flour
1/4 c. salt
1/4 tsp. dry mustard
1/8 tsp. cayenne
1/4 tsp. turmeric

Cut corn from cob. Mix dry ingredients with vinegar. Put everything into a 6 qt. Dutch oven and bring to the boiling point. Simmer for 40 min., stirring frequently to prevent sticking. Put into mason jars or old peanut butter jars while hot. Jars need not be sterilized, but should be washed in the dishwasher just before filling.

Mrs. William W. W. Knight, Ridgewood

TOMATO CONSERVE

Yield: 6 pints

Easy   Do ahead

Preparing: 30 min.
Cooking: about 3 hrs.

8 lbs. tomatoes
  (fresh or canned)
5 lbs. sugar
2 lemons
1-1/2 tsp. powdered ginger
  and/or
4 sticks cinnamon
1 lb. walnuts, broken

Cut tomatoes into pieces. Slice lemons thin and discard seeds. Cook slowly all ingredients, except the nuts, until fairly thick. Drain off water if you wish to speed up the cooking. Stir occasionally. Add nuts and cook 10 min. longer. Fill hot, sterilized jars to within 1/2 inch of top. Let stand until cool, then stir, seal and store. Refrigerate after opening.

Mrs. A. S. Whittemore, Brookfield Center, Conn.

ENGLISH CHUTNEY

Yield: 4 pints

Easy   Do ahead   Preparing: 30 min.
                                            Simmering: 1 hr.

3 green peppers, seeded   Put peppers, onion, apples and raisins
1 med. size onion   through food chopper; place in large sauce-
13 tart apples, pared   pan and add remaining ingredients. Simmer
1-1/2 c. seeded raisins   about 1 hr. or until quite thick. Turn into
1 tbsp. salt   sterilized, hot jars and seal at once.
3 c. vinegar
1-1/2 c. sugar
1-1/2 tbsp. ground ginger
1-1/2 c. tart grape jelly
3/4 c. lemon juice
1 tbsp. grated lemon rind   *Mrs. George M. Griffith, Franklin Lakes*

CHUNKS (Cucumber Pickles)

Yield: 6-8 pints

"A crisp cucumber pickle."

Average   Do ahead   Preparing: 15 min.
                                            Marinating: 2 hrs.
                                            Assembling: 15 min.

10 cucumbers, cut into chunks   Combine cucumber chunks, onion slices and
6 onions, sliced   salt and let stand for 2 hrs. Drain. Com-
1/2 c. salt   bine remaining ingredients and bring to a
2 c. vinegar   boil. Place cucumber and onion mixture in
2 c. water   hot, sterilized jars. Pour boiling liquid
1 tbsp. celery seed   over to fill. Seal.
1 tbsp. mustard seed
1-1/2 c. sugar
1 tsp. ginger
1 tsp. turmeric   *Mrs. Joseph Sage, Ramsey*

CHICKADEE PUDDING

"This is for the BIRDS! They love it."

Easy   Freeze   Preparing: 15 min.

ground suet   Mix all ingredients, except bacon fat, in
flour   whatever proportions you happen to have on
sugar   hand. Melt plenty of fat and, while hot,
corn meal   pour over the mixture, stirring well. Pour
old cake, bread, doughnuts   into disposable aluminum pie plates. Freeze.
wild bird seed   Cut as needed for happy birdies.
peanut butter
ground apples
kitchen seeds
  (apple, squash, etc.)
nuts
raisins
bacon fat   *Mrs. A. L. Van Wart, Ridgewood*

Miscellaneous Etceteras

When a recipe calls for a greased casserole, spread a piece of bread with butter and grease the casserole. Use it cut up in the casserole or as topping.

If you want to bake your casserole ahead, bake all the required time except the last 20 min. Cool and store casserole in the refrigerator, covered. Allow 10 min. extra baking time for re-warming, plus the last 20 min. required.

Crushed potato chips make an excellent topping for many casseroles.

When using ovenglass baking pans, always lower the temperature by 25°.

Keep shelled nuts in the refrigerator - they keep indefinitely.

Warm shelled nuts before chopping - it brings out the natural nut oils.

To make nutmeats come out whole, soak whole nuts in salted water over-night before cracking.

Cut dates up fine with wet scissors after measuring.

Put leftover bread crusts and heels in your blender for always-handy bread crumbs. Store in a covered jar after drying out.

Heat lemons before extracting juice for twice as much juice.

You may use canned mandarin oranges whenever a recipe calls for fresh. Drain the mandarins and marinate in fresh orange juice for at least an hour.

Prepared orange and lemon rind found on the spice shelves of grocery stores are excellent.

If you place oranges in a hot oven before you peel them, no white fiber will be left on the orange.

To scald milk without scorching, rinse pan in hot water before using.

Light or excessive heat causes deterioration in vanilla. Always keep the bottle in the box in which it comes.

If honey turns sugary, stand the jar in a pan of hot water until it liquifies again.

Corn syrup or honey may be substituted for one half the amount of sugar called for as long as the liquid in the recipe is decreased by one fourth the amount.

To measure molasses, grease the cup in which it is to be measured.

More Miscellaneous Etceteras

Curry powder and chili powder should always be added in a recipe when you are browning, not into the sauce directly. Browning it will remove the bitter taste.

White pepper is stronger than black pepper. It is ground from ripe pepper. Use about half as much as black.

For crushed garlic, put it between two layers of wax paper and hit it with a hammer - nothing to clean.

Leftover pimentos can be kept if you put them in a small jar and cover with vinegar. Refrigerate.

* To make a quick white sauce in the blender, add 1 c. scalded milk and 2 slices fresh white bread to the blender. Blend until smooth. Flavor with 1/2 c. cheese or 1 tbsp. sherry, if desired.
    Sent by Mrs. Edith Koen, Arlington, Va.

* For delicious sandwiches, cut off bread crusts and spread with mustard and butter. Fill with ham and Swiss cheese or chicken and Swiss cheese; chill the sandwiches. When ready to serve, beat 3 eggs with 1/2 c. cream or evaporated milk and dip sandwiches. Fry in butter or deep fat.

If you burn a pan, fill it with water, add 2 tbsp. baking soda and boil. Repeat if necessary.

Ice pans will not stick in the refrigerator if you place wax paper underneath.

To clean copper or brass, make a thin paste of salt and vinegar. Clean article, then rinse and dry.

To remove lacquer from new copper molds before you use them, let them soak for a couple of minutes in boiling water to which 3 tbsp. of baking soda are added.

For storing wraps, wax paper, plastic bags, etc., on your shelf, use a cardboard soft drink carton. A box fits into each pocket. Turn either on its side or store upright.

To increase or decrease any recipe, use the new number of servings as the numerator and the number of servings provided by the recipe as the denominator. For example, if a recipe calls for 6 servings and you would like to make 8 servings, it would be figured as follows:
$$3/4 \text{ c.} \quad -- \quad 3/4 \times 8/6 \ (4/3) = 12/12 = 1 \text{ c.}$$

Freezing Fortunes

Line casseroles with heavy foil, freeze food in it, then remove from container, wrap and store in freezer. When ready to use, peel off foil, place in original casserole and heat.

Always wrap anything to be frozen as air tight as you can. Get all the air bubbles out of package. This can be done by partially submerging plastic bag in water and sealing close to article.

Cool cooked food quickly and completely for freezing.

Carefully seal packages and label with date. Use oldest ones first.

When juicing a lemon or orange needed in a recipe, don't throw away the rind. Peel it with a paring knife (no white membrane) and run it through a Mouli-type grater. Store in plastic containers in the freezer and you will always have freshly grated rind on hand.

To freeze berries, only use firm, ripe berries. Wash thoroughly in cold water and place in freezing containers. Then pour in syrup. Handle them quickly. Make syrup by stirring 1-2/3 c. sugar into 2 c. boiling water. Stir until sugar is dissolved. Use more sugar if a sweeter taste is desired. Berries may also be sweetened by tossing washed fruit lightly with about 1/2 to 1/3 c. sugar per quart. Package and freeze at once; do not wait until you have them all packaged, but freeze a few packages at a time.

Berries may also be frozen whole by placing on a cookie sheet in the freezer. When frozen, store in plastic bags. These will be quite watery when removed from freezer so should be used in sauces, etc. Do not completely defrost before use.

Melons may be easily frozen by cutting into melon balls or small cubes. Place in containers and cover with syrup. Add 1 to 2 tsp. ascorbic-citric acid powder for each quart of syrup used. Or, use fresh orange juice, pineapple juice or ginger ale for a different flavor in place of the syrup. Crumple a piece of cellophane on top of the fruit before sealing and freezing. Do not defrost; place in the refrigerator and serve still frosty. Great for winter salads or fruit cocktails.

To freeze fresh vegetables, select mature fresh vegetables. Wash thoroughly and blanch by placing in boiling water and bringing again to a boil. Boil asparagus, green beans, limas, cauliflower and spinach 2 min. Boil broccoli 3 min.; peas 1 min.; corn on the cob 8 min.; and cut corn 2-1/2 min. Submerge vegetables immediately in cold water for 4 to 5 min. Drain and package immediately for freezing.

Do not freeze salad greens, radishes, tomatoes, celery, cabbage, cucumbers or onions.

Fresh peppers, green or red, and chives are easily frozen by slicing or chopping and storing in plastic bags. When ready to use in casseroles, etc., just take out the number of rings and cut up frozen. Marvelous to have all winter when peppers are expensive or when you only need a small amount.

Frying Facts

To extinguish a fat fire, throw handfuls of salt on the base of the fire.

Be sure all utensils are completely dry when cooking with fat. Any water on things will cause splattering.

To prevent fat from splashing while cooking, sprinkle salt in the frying pan before adding meat, etc.

To clear bacon fat for further use, pour while warm, not hot, into a can containing cold water. Burned portion will drop to the bottom. Clean fat can be skimmed off.

Frying oil can be reused several times if you add a quartered, unpeeled potato to it and heat for a few minutes. Fish is the only taste that may not be completely removed. Strain through cheesecloth.

Add 1 tbsp. oil to butter when frying. It will keep the butter from burning.

Never put too many pieces in a frying pan when frying. You will steam instead of browning.

When deep frying, be sure fat is at least 4 inches deep. Allow 2 to 3 inches between fat and top of pan to prevent bubbling over.

Have food to be fried in deep fat at room temperature before cooking. If it has been chilled, remove from the refrigerator 1 hour before frying.

To flour food easily for frying, such as chicken or fish, place flour and seasonings in a plastic bag, add a few pieces of food at a time and shake hard. Food will be evenly floured. Good also for flouring stew meat to be browned.

For perfect breaded foods that are to be fried, roll food in crumbs, then dip into egg mixture and roll a second time in crumbs. Use one hand for breading, the other hand for dipping - your hands will not get sticky. Bread foods at least 1/2 hour before frying.

If fried food should be served hot, place cooked food on a baking pan covered with paper toweling and place in a 300° oven while frying remaining food. Bring fat back to desired temperature before cooking the second batch of food. Skim off any loose food particles to prevent smoking.

Index

Items followed by a star (*) appear in Hints Sections.
The recipes themselves are starred as well.

APPETIZERS AND HORS D'OEUVRES

BEVERAGES

BREADS, COFFEE CAKES & PANCAKES

Pancakes, Waffles

CANDIES

CASSEROLES
(Main Dishes)

Beef:

Poultry:

CHEESE DISHES

CONDIMENTS, ETC.

DESSERTS

MISCELLANEOUS

PASTAS

POTATOES

POULTRY

Casseroles: *See Casserole Section*

RICE

SALADS

Molded:

Other Salads:

Salad Dressings and Accompaniments:

SAUCES AND ACCOMPANIMENTS
(For Main Dishes and Vegetables)

SANDWICHES

SEAFOODS

Casseroles: *See Casserole Section*

Seafood Sauces and Accompaniments:

SOUPS

Chowders:

Stews: *See Meats and Poultry*

VEGETABLES

Casseroles:

VOLUME COOKING
(For 12 or Over)

FORUM FEASTS
Box 43
Waldwick, N. J. 07463

Send me ...... copies of your book at $10.00 per copy, which includes postage and handling.

Please make checks payable to "The Forum School Cookbook Fund."

Name ....

Street ....

City .... State .... Zip Code ....

All profit contributed to The Forum School
NEW JERSEY RESIDENTS MUST ADD TAX
CANADIAN RESIDENTS USE POSTAL MONEY ORDERS
Prices subject to change without notice.

FORUM FEASTS
Box 43
Waldwick, N. J. 07463

Send me ...... copies of your book at $10.00 per copy, which includes postage and handling.

Please make checks payable to "The Forum School Cookbook Fund."

Name ....

Street ....

City .... State .... Zip Code ....

All profit contributed to The Forum School
NEW JERSEY RESIDENTS MUST ADD TAX
CANADIAN RESIDENTS USE POSTAL MONEY ORDERS
Prices subject to change without notice.

FORUM FEASTS
Box 43
Waldwick, N. J. 07463

Send me ...... copies of your book at $10.00 per copy, which includes postage and handling.

Please make checks payable to "The Forum School Cookbook Fund."

Name ....

Street ....

City .... State .... Zip Code ....

All profit contributed to The Forum School
NEW JERSEY RESIDENTS MUST ADD TAX
CANADIAN RESIDENTS USE POSTAL MONEY ORDERS
Prices subject to change without notice.

FORUM FEASTS
Box 43
Waldwick, N. J. 07463

Send me ...... copies of your book at $10.00 per copy, which includes postage and handling.
Please make checks payable to "The Forum School Cookbook Fund."

Name ....

Street ....

City .... State .... Zip Code ....

All profit contributed to The Forum School
NEW JERSEY RESIDENTS MUST ADD TAX
CANADIAN RESIDENTS USE POSTAL MONEY ORDERS
Prices subject to change without notice.

FORUM FEASTS
Box 43
Waldwick, N. J. 07463

Send me ...... copies of your book at $10.00 per copy, which includes postage and handling.
Please make checks payable to "The Forum School Cookbook Fund."

Name ....

Street ....

City .... State .... Zip Code ....

All profit contributed to The Forum School
NEW JERSEY RESIDENTS MUST ADD TAX
CANADIAN RESIDENTS USE POSTAL MONEY ORDERS
Prices subject to change without notice.

FORUM FEASTS
Box 43
Waldwick, N. J. 07463

Send me ...... copies of your book at $10.00 per copy, which includes postage and handling.
Please make checks payable to "The Forum School Cookbook Fund."

Name ....

Street ....

City .... State .... Zip Code ....

All profit contributed to The Forum School
NEW JERSEY RESIDENTS MUST ADD TAX
CANADIAN RESIDENTS USE POSTAL MONEY ORDERS
Prices subject to change without notice.